Asian Worldviews

Asian Worldviews

Religions, Philosophies, Political Theories

Rein Raud

Registered Offices
John Wiley & Sons, Inc., 111 River Street, Hoboken, NJ 07030, USA
John Wiley & Sons Ltd, The Atrium, Southern Gate, Chichester, West Sussex, PO19 8SQ, UK

Editorial Office
111 River Street, Hoboken, NJ 07030, USA

For details of our global editorial offices, customer services, and more information about Wiley products visit us at www.wiley.com.

Wiley also publishes its books in a variety of electronic formats and by print-on-demand. Some content that appears in standard print versions of this book may not be available in other formats.

Library of Congress Cataloging-in-Publication Data

Names: Raud, Rein, author.
Title: Asian worldviews : religions, philosophies, political theories /
    Rein Raud, Professor of Asian and Cultural Studies, Tallinn University,
    Estonia.
Description: Hoboken, NJ : Wiley-Blackwell, 2021. | Includes index.
Identifiers: LCCN 2020023699 (print) | LCCN 2020023700 (ebook) | ISBN
    9781119165972 (paperback) | ISBN 9781119165989 (adobe pdf) | ISBN
    9781119166009 (epub)
Subjects: LCSH: Asia–Intellectual life.
Classification: LCC DS12 .R35 2021 (print) | LCC DS12 (ebook) | DDC
    950–dc23
LC record available at https://lccn.loc.gov/2020023699
LC ebook record available at https://lccn.loc.gov/2020023700

Cover Design: Wiley
Cover Image: © Rosita Raud

Set in 9.5/12.5pt STIXTwoText by SPi Global, Pondicherry, India
Printed and bound by CPI Group (UK) Ltd, Croydon, CR0 4YY

10 9 8 7 6 5 4 3 2 1

Contents

Preface

The aim of this book is to acquaint its reader with the rich thought traditions of Asia (India, China, Japan, Korea, Tibet, and South East Asia), which have mutually influenced each other throughout history and consequently share large parts of their intellectual heritage. It can serve both as an introductory textbook for the future specialist and as a source of background knowledge for those whose primary interest lies outside Asian studies, be it religious studies, Western philosophy, political science or anything else. No previous knowledge of the history or cultures of this region is presupposed, entanglement in specific debates is avoided and names and terms have been kept to the minimum. If you think that an educated person anywhere in the world should know who are St Augustine, Luther, and Mother Theresa or Aristotle, Kant, and Wittgenstein or Machiavelli, Rousseau, and Marx, or what is the meaning of 'cardinal sin', *cogito*, and 'separation of powers', the names and terms printed bold in this book are those you should be familiar with from a range of Asian points of view. I have done my best to keep the scope of the book equally balanced throughout and to maintain a more or less similar level of coverage in all areas. The book thus addresses all teachings, schools, and individuals that have usually been included in the range of such introductory intellectual histories. However, the reader will notice that some authors and ideas not always present in similar overviews, such as feminist theorists, have been given more space here than has been customary up to now.

   The worldviews described in this book influence the choices and actions of the people who currently make up about one half of the world's population. This alone is reason enough to be interested in Asia, but there is more. Having been economically handicapped for over a century by Western domination and inefficient, if not directly harmful domestic politics, Asian countries have now emerged to form the world's most quickly developing region, one that can no longer be excluded from global decision-making. Culturally, geographically and politically, Asia is perhaps more diverse than any other part of the world. Dominated by two ancient, multilayered, and rich civilizations, India and China, this region is the home of some of the world's oldest and worthiest literary and philosophical cultures, theatrical traditions, and aesthetic systems. So undoubtedly at least some knowledge of Asian worldviews is necessary for anyone with an interest in the world beyond one's own home ground, were it for cultural history or current political and economic affairs.

Of course, traditional opposition pairs such as 'east–west' always rely on simplifications. Norway differs from Portugal and Texas from Scotland perhaps more significantly than Singapore from Vancouver. Moreover, for the purposes of this book the 'West' includes also a large portion of what most Westerners consider to be in the East, namely the Islamic world. This may seem strange, because religious wars throughout centuries and recent political conflicts as well as European colonial presence in the 'Orient' have shaped the image of Muslims for most Westerners as the Other, whose cultural and social habits are incompatible with 'Western values'. However, historically and etymologically, Islam is most certainly a part of 'Western' culture, sharing both in the traditions of Greek antiquity – which it actually preserved for Europe during the times when the West was militantly fundamentalist – and the Judaic legacy of monotheism. Muslims themselves have always felt a unity with other 'people of the Book', that is, those whose religion is based on the foundations of the Old Testament, and Islamic thought has exercised a decisive influence on Western intellectual history through the work of such thinkers as, for example, Ibn Rushd (Averroes) or Ibn Sina (Avicenna). Thus, even though Islam is prominently present also in Asia, it is treated there as a Western import that has taken on local colour, but nonetheless has its roots elsewhere – not unlike Christianity or Marxism. The reader who would like to be better informed about the teachings of Islam will find a few suggestions in the section of further reading recommendations at the back of this book.

As a result, the term 'Asia' does not refer in this book to the entire geographical range that includes also the Middle East, the majority of the territory of Russia and the former Soviet republics of central Asia, but only to those parts of Asia that are usually addressed in publications dedicated to 'Asian religions', 'Asian philosophies', and 'Asian politics', namely south, east and southeast Asian countries as well as Tibet. More attention has been dedicated to the two most ancient civilizations of Asia, India and China, as well as to Japan as the first successful modernizing country to have emerged from outside the traditional West. Smaller subchapters have been dedicated to Korea, Tibet, Indic South East Asia and Vietnam, not because their intellectual contributions would be less valuable, but largely due to the fact that these regions have, for historical reasons, had less impact on the global processes and the interest in their intellectual history has been mostly academic up to the present.

There are quite a few good introductions to the religions, philosophies and political ideologies of each of the countries and regions that this book deals with, but most of the time these different types of convictions and beliefs are kept separate. However, as soon as we leave the Western cultural environment, the division of worldviews into 'religions', 'philosophies', and 'political theories' starts to obscure more than it reveals. Philosophy and religion have been in a complicated relationship in the West, almost since their moment of separation, when Socrates was accused of disrespect for the gods, yet many Western philosophers, too, have been devoutly religious and have made significant efforts to bring their beliefs and their reasoning into harmony. Religions can seldom manage without a certain metaphysical grounding, and we often see them prompting rulers how to conduct their affairs properly. Political ideologies are always grounded in theories of justice and ideas about the course of history, which are related to both the religious and the philosophical convictions of their proponents. It therefore makes sense, especially when stepping on unfamiliar ground, to highlight these connections rather than the divisions, and to treat worldviews as holistic, even if they occasionally seem incoherent to us – they seldom do to the people whose lives they guide.

But we might want to go even further than that and question at the outset the very validity of the concepts 'religion', 'philosophy', and 'ideology' as such for a broader perspective. Most Westerners associate religion on a non-analytical level with belief in a god, or gods, which is grounded in a certain doctrine, one normally fixed in scriptures and upheld by an institution of spiritual professionals. Religions are also exclusive and make strong claims on the identity of the individuals who profess them, often causing distrust or even open hatred between religiously defined communities. Philosophy, in turn, is a kind of rational and conceptual inquiry into the first principles of how the world is, how we are in it, and how we should reason about things, while political theories and ideologies are sets of principles on which their proponents consider the build-up of society and its governing should be based – these principles can also be implicit and presented to the community as a sort of natural order, which nonetheless does not affect their ideological character.

All of these commonsensical assumptions are challenged to a certain degree by Asian worldviews. In fact, what is known as an Indian or Chinese religion and philosophy may not correspond to these tentative definitions at all. Quite a few so-called religions, such as early Buddhism or Confucianism, do not speak about any supernatural agency, others, such as Shintō, do not have doctrines or scriptures. Their institutions, like the huge Buddhist monasteries of pre-Islamic India, may appear more similar to what we call universities than to what look like monasteries from our point of view. And people can often identify with several religions at the same time in many regions of the area. Strangely enough, the term 'religion' is often forced on such worldviews that lack some, if not most of the characteristics many Westerners consider to be core properties of religion – such as the belief in a transcendent agency – while the label of 'philosophy' is being denied to sophisticated conceptual constructions because they lack some particular element that the critic considers crucial, even though there are Western thinkers, who are legitimately called philosophers and lack that same element as well.

The entanglement of different intellectual pursuits is also one of the reasons why the book is organized according to a historical principle rather than treating worldviews such as Buddhism or Confucianism one by one. Asian worldviews are more often than not lacking in the type of jealousy that characterizes Western religions, and ideas, motifs, and practices migrate relatively freely over their borders. Thus, for example, the Japanese Shintō took shape as a kind of an institution only when the Dao creed had entered Japan from China, and the Dao creed itself had been inspired to do the same by Buddhism, which had been imported to China from India. A treatment by tradition might perhaps encourage us to emphasize the borders between them, while progressing along the historical timeline makes it easier to trace borrowings and influences and to understand how and why the worldviews developed in the way they did.

Another related problem that often occurs in literature is the separation of classical heritages from the ideas of the present. Excellent books on traditional thought seldom venture to see it reflected in modern ideas, and brilliant analyses of new views often summarize their classical origins in succinct introductions and then proceed to treat the thinkers of the last 150 years exclusively in the context of Western discourses. These have undeniably played a decisive role in the development of present-day Asian societies and their worldviews, but the ways how all these Western discourses have been received, interpreted, and modified can hardly be understood without a sufficient knowledge of past thought systems. It could be said that many people in contemporary Asia operate with parallel conceptual structures in which traditional ideas and Western notions are used side by side. A treatment of Asian ways of thought as simply local and possibly imperfect versions of universal patterns best exemplified by Western cultures is not only racist and imperialist, it is also quite wrong. Asian ideas have been in dialogue with Western thought in the past and should be doing so also in the future, and mutual understanding between structurally different cultures should start with an open approach to the other. This book is for those who would like to take the first step on this way and I can only hope that it will inspire its readers to pursue their study of Asian worldviews forward to higher levels of competence.

The transcription of Indian names and terms is given in a simplified spelling, thus Shankara instead of Śaṅkara and Vishishtādvaita instead of Viśiṣṭādvaita, given that the nuances of pronunciation indicated by these diacritics are largely ignored also by advanced readers of Indian texts. Unlike in many texts that use a simplified spelling, the distinction between short and long vowels is maintained and the reader is encouraged to make note of it. Chinese terms and names have been written in the pinyin transcription unless used in a different form by the persons in question, Japanese terms and names are given in the modified Hepburn transcription, Korean names are given in the Revised Romanization system, with the exception of widespread family names such as Kim and Pak/Park. Vietnamese names appear in the quoc ngu Latin script without the diacritics, Tibetan names in phonetic approximations regularly used in literature.

Unless indicated otherwise, all translations of quoted source texts are my own.

Acknowledgements

First of all, many thanks go to all of the students who have participated in my classes on the topics of this book – and in particular those who have asked questions – in the Free University of Berlin, Tallinn University, University of Helsinki, and University of Tōkyō.

Many heartfelt thanks are also due to Douglas Berger, Matthew Kapstein, Viktoria Lysenko, Margus Ott, Jin Y. Park, and Geir Sigurdsson for reading and commenting on parts of the manuscript. There would have been so many errors and misreadings without you.

I hope colleagues will forgive me that instead of quoting them by name, I refer to their (as well as my own) views as 'recent scholarship' throughout this book which, meant as it is for novices in the discipline, is in any case already over-crowded with names and terms. But let those to whom my work is most directly indebted be listed here (in alphabetical order): Roger Ames, Stephen C. Angle, Christopher Bartley, Douglas Berger, John Berthrong, Richard Bowring, Bidyut Chakrabarty, Anne Cheng, Chung-ying Cheng, Julia Ching, George Chryssides, Edward Chung, Philip Clart, Fred Clothey, Arthur Cotterell, Paul Dundas, Gavin Flood, Jeaneane Fowler, James D. Frankel, Edmund S. Fung, Yiu-ming Fung, Jonardon Ganeri, Jay Garfield, Richard Gombrich, Angus Graham, Chad Hansen, Chang Hao, Peter Harvey, Richard Hayes, James Heisig, Barbara Hendrischke, Radhika Herzberger, Tze-ki Hon, Yong Huang, Tao Jiang, Matthew Kapstein, Thomas Kasulis, Halla Kim, Nick Knight, Gereon Kopf, Karyn Lai, Whalen Lai, Jae-Cheon Lim, Liu Feng, JeeLoo Liu, Donald S. Lopez Jr., David Loy, Dan Lusthaus, Vera Mackie, John Makeham, Linnart Mäll, Arvind-Pal Singh Mandair, John Maraldo, Daigan and Alicia Matsunaga, John McRae, Maurice Meisner, Bo Mou, Charles A. Muller, Randall L. Nadeau, Jan Nattier, Nguyen Van Huyen, Steve Odin, Rosalind O'Hanlon, Patrick Olivelle, Gail Omvedt, Charles Orzech, Margus Ott, Rajendra Kumar Pandey, Jin Y. Park, Graham Parkes, Lauren Pfister, Red Pine, John Powers, Gil Raz, Young-chan Ro, Isabelle Robinet, Henry Rosemont Jr., Li-Hsiang Lisa Rosenlee, Stuart R. Schram, Anna Seidel, Mark

Siderits, Edward Slingerland, Paul Swanson, Sor-hoon Tan, George J. Tanabe Jr., Ithamar Theodor, Hoyt C. Tillman, Justin Tiwald, Bryan van Norden, Rudolf Wagner, Xinzhong Yao, Carl Young, Michiko Yusa, and Brook A. Ziporyn. Thank you.

This has been a work of many years and has benefited from various grants. Two field trips were financed by a research grant of the University of Helsinki, a grant of the Nordic Institute of Asian Studies enabled me to stay at the École Française d'Extrême-Orient in Paris and use its library. Several stays as a visiting scholar at the University of Cambridge have greatly contributed to the work, and a DAAD scholarship enabled me to carry out parts of it at the Free University of Berlin. The final part of the research for this book was funded by the Estonian Research Council (ETAG) research grant PUT1365.

1

India

Introductory remarks. India is home to one of the oldest continuous civilizations on Earth and simultaneously to a degree of cultural variativity with which few other regions can compare. It is also the birthplace of many inventions and discoveries that have influenced the development of science, philosophy, linguistics, literature, art, architecture, theatre, and religion far beyond its borders. Indian religions have attracted a large following in many Asian countries and Buddhism, in particular, around the whole world. Today, the Republic of India, with a population over 1.3 billion people, is the world's biggest democracy. At present, India has the world's seventh biggest economy, but only ranks third in purchasing power parity. It is projected to bypass the United States in the next decades and rank second only to China on this scale. Besides, when we speak of the 'Indian subcontinent', we do not think only of India as a country, but also of quite a few neighbouring states that have a common cultural history with it and, for some of these, experts project similarly spectacular growth. What takes place in these societies, however, is difficult to understand without a knowledge of the background concepts that inform all spheres of thinking in Indian and related cultures, from the most general views of how the universe is organized to particular processes of decision-making and political preferences.

All of this should be enough to promote interest in Indian thought. Nonetheless, it would be just as worth studying even if India would not have such a growing role in the world of the present. Some Hindu and Buddhist philosophical systems belong to the most profound achievements of human thought. Indian views on language, logic, psychological processes as well as ontological problems have historically influenced Western thought and are able to contribute to philosophical debates also in the present. Many twentieth century landmarks of Western philosophy bear similarities to the positions of Indian thinkers, which put these advances into a much broader perspective. The developments of science, the move from a Newtonian space populated primarily by solid, self-identical objects

Asian Worldviews: Religions, Philosophies, Political Theories, First Edition. Rein Raud.
© 2021 John Wiley & Sons Ltd. Published 2021 by John Wiley & Sons Ltd.

to relativity and quantum physics, have lent even more actuality to Indian thought, which historically has developed many categories and conceptualizations that are often better equipped to speak of such phenomena than the language of traditional Western metaphysics.

Periods of cultural history. The highly advanced Harappan civilization, which dominated the north-western part of the Indian subcontinent for the better part of the second millennium BCE, has unfortunately left us only with very short inscriptions, up to now undeciphered. Thus, the documented history of India begins with the advent of the Aryans, a mixed company of nomadic tribes who shared an Indo-European language, which later evolved into Sanskrit. Starting with the arrival of the Aryans, we can divide the historical development of Indian thought into six distinct periods. First, there is the Vedic period (c. 1500–600 BCE), which has received its name after the Vedas, initially orally transmitted Aryan scripture, which allegedly forms the basis of the Hindu worldview to this day. During that time, a worldview usually called **Brahmanism** was developed out of the Indo-European shared corpus of beliefs, possibly influenced by a substratum derived from the Harappan civilization, and reflecting the adaptation to local circumstances that the Aryan society went through during that time. One of these was the emergence of the **caste** system, which placed the priests at the top of the social ladder. A theory of divinely sanctioned kingship helped them to maintain this position even though they did not directly hold any political power after states began to consolidate.

The Vedic period is followed by the period of reform movements (c. 600–200 BCE), sometimes also called the period of 'second urbanization'. During this time, social processes, notably the transformation of a large number of small-scale settlements into republican states collectively governed by the warrior estate, led to religious innovation, which opposed the simultaneous opposite development of strict social divisions within the Brahmanist tradition. The questioning of the Brahmanist worldview by such reform movements, primarily the Jains and the Buddhists, also triggered a sophisticated response on the traditionalist side that started the development of new practices and religious trends that gradually formed what we now call **Hinduism**.

It is also during this time that the first contacts of the Indian civilization with other cultures were established. The eastern outposts of the Iranian empire of the Achaemenids served to open up both trade and the movement of ideas. Towards the end of the period of reform movements, India was briefly invaded by Alexander the Great (327–325 BCE), which inaugurated a dialogue between Greek and Indian thought, with ideas moving in both directions. Even though Alexander retreated quite soon, Hellenic states continued to exist for some time in the Indian north-west and, a few centuries afterwards, Greek and Roman traders started a commercial maritime traffic to the extent that trade stations were established in the south of India.

Soon after Alexander, India was united into a short-lived empire by the Maurya dynasty (c. 322–180 BCE), which inaugurated the period of classical Indian culture (c. 200 BCE–1200 CE), during which kingdoms were the norm of government, even though only one of them, the empire of the Guptas (c. 240–590 CE), gained control of most of the subcontinent for a longer period of time. The culture of the classical period is characterized by a highly sophisticated urban lifestyle, a tremendous amount of literature in a variety of genres as well as theatre, music, and science. During that time Buddhism and Hinduism existed side by side in India and influenced each other, and both of them also spread to neighbouring countries. The Hindu religion became dominant in both continental and maritime South East Asia, while Buddhism spread to the south and south-east, on the one hand, and to the north and north-east (China and Tibet), on the other.

But this was not to last. The start of a new era was predicted by waves of immigration of Parsis (Persians), the followers of the ancient Iranian religion of Zoroastrianism, fleeing from Muslims who were taking over their country. The period of Islamic conquests (c. 1200–1800) led the Indian subcontinent to be dominated by Muslim rulers, dynasties of various origins replacing each other until the Mughals finally established themselves as the rulers of the country. The Muslims introduced Islam to India, but the greatest rulers of the Mughal empire, such as Akbar (1542–1605), were tolerant leaders interested in interfaith dialogue rather than the subjugation of all other religions. This led to attempts at the synthesis of Muslim beliefs with the Hindu heritage – from one such effort, the creed of the Sikhs emerged – and fierce struggles for domination. Buddhism, however, having already lost much of its royal patronage before the Muslim invasion, now suffered a final blow from which it never fully recovered in India.

The discovery of the sea route around Africa to India by Vasco da Gama (1498) soon led to an era of colonial wars, during which the Portuguese, the Dutch, and the British vied for control of the Indian subcontinent. The British finally emerged victorious over their competitors as well as the Mughal empire and its descendant states. Modern Indian thought (approximately from 1850 onwards), started to emerge already under the British colonial regime and provided the discourses for a cultural and political independence movement. Contemporary Indian thought, from after the end of the colonial rule and the partition of the subcontinent (1947), presents us with multiple efforts at synthesis of concepts inherited from the past and imported from the West, and this dialogue is still ongoing. However, this has also been the period when various nationalist and fundamentalist ideologies have tried to gain control of the public space.

Linguistic diversity. It should be noted that cultural and linguistic diversity has been one of the characteristic features of the Indian subcontinent for many centuries, and attempts to create discourses for living together have constantly competed with conservative strivings to separate different ethnic and religious groups from each other. The Aryan tribes that invaded India spoke Indo-European dialects that were related to English and many other European languages, while many indigenous people (possibly including the creators of the Harappan civilization) spoke Dravidian dialects, the forefathers of modern Tamil, Telugu, and other languages.

The classical Indian civilization was based on the single, shared, and strictly normed literary language of Sanskrit. However, Sanskrit was a learned skill for all its users, who spoke a variety of Indo-European and Dravidian languages as their mother tongues – a situation quite similar to medieval Europe, where Latin was used for official and scholarly purposes, while local vernacular languages were used in daily communication. After Sanskrit lost its position due to the Islamic conquest, new Indian languages (Hindi, Urdu, Bengali, Punjabi, Marathi, and so on) have gradually developed into full-fledged vehicles of cultural self-expression and modern Dravidian languages have similarly been able to establish themselves. This has created a cultural and linguistic diversity comparable perhaps only to Europe, which also functions as a political and supranational entity with a shared cultural base.

Practice. Before moving on to the discussion of the views expressed in Indian thought systems, it should be pointed out that none of these were conceived for mere intellectual beauty or out of the need to learn the truth for its own sake. They were meant to elucidate and give a conceptually sound foundation to the various methods to achieve, or at least proceed towards, a fulfilment of one's purpose in life. For most of these systems, this goal was synonymous with 'liberation' or 'emancipation' from the circle of rebirths. Knowledge about the architecture of the universe and its internal dynamism was only necessary in order to understand why and how the practice one had undertaken would lead to this goal. Not all forms of practice needed such a justification – for some, the intellectualism of the Hindu philosophical systems might even appear as a hindrance rather than help in their religious advancement. However, for most Hindus, practice pervades their life in any case: to be alive is tantamount to engendering new karma, and being careful about it is not necessarily a distinct activity or sphere of life, but just a commonsensical attitude to things like, for example, being mindful of what one eats or drinks or remembering to have one's documents in order before a journey. Ritualist practice is thus also a way to maximize the positive karma-producing potential of one's position in the world. Just as medieval Europeans, Indians did not have a distinct word for *religion*, which was just another natural aspect of their life.

All in all, there are three distinct directions of practice that most Indian worldviews could take: ritualist, ascetic, or devotionalist. All three can be traced back to the scriptures. *Ritualist* practice derives from the assumption that transcendent agency responds to ritualist action and can therefore be manipulated by priests who are, through the scriptures, privy to secret knowledge of how this is done. By performing certain lower-level rituals laypeople may similarly assure themselves of a certain degree of goodwill of the gods and contribute to the upholding of the cosmic order. This is in accordance with the view that the logical order of the universe is manifested in the social hierarchy. Therefore the kind of involvement in ritual practice expected from people with different social standing and in different stages of life varies accordingly.

Ascetic practices are grounded in the belief that by controlling the body one can increase and manipulate the energy of life and put it to unexpected uses. In particular, the epics abound with stories how ascetics, by accumulating spiritual power, can perform supernatural acts. On a more realistic level, asceticism of varying degrees has been advocated by some Hindu and Jain traditions as a method for calming the emotions and clearing the mind to such a level that one can perceive the truth and attain liberation. Ascetic practices are normally combined with psychotechnical exercises, including various forms of meditation, which are meant to emancipate the mind from the confines of daily routines and to control its activity. The historical Buddha has warned against ascetic practices as an excess and advocated a 'middle path' between extreme approaches to the body, but also advocates meditation as the way to spiritual progress. This is in accordance with the Buddhist rejection of all attachments: when someone starts to engage in ascetic mortification of the flesh, it may quickly turn into a sport practised for its own sake to commit increasingly further feats of corporal austerity. However, such an attitude is not conducive to mental liberation at all.

The last variety of practice is *devotionalism*, which is an attitude first met in some Vedic hymns that credit a particular deity with maximum power and positive attributes that can just as well be attributed to some other deity in some other hymn. Constantly ongoing activities of worship and veneration, dedicated to particular deities, have later become the main form of practice of some sectarian movements that have gathered a strong following. In particular, the *bhakti* movement, which arose in south India in the seventh century, has been influential in supporting the split of Hinduism into branches of devotees of different gods, primarily Vishnu and Shiva. The word *bhakti* means 'devotion, love, attachment', but a primarily spiritual one, even if sex and erotic connotations often also have a significant role in Hindu beliefs.

The Brahmanist Worldview

Background. The worldview that developed from the beliefs of the Indo-Aryan tribes who moved into India between 1500 and 1300 BCE is designated by two terms, Brahmanism and Hinduism. Hinduism normally refers to the newer (including present) forms of it, because the term 'Hindu' started to gain general currency only after the Muslim invasion as a term for people who were not Muslims. However, their forms of worship started to evolve already during the classical period. Sometimes the term 'Hindu' is also used for the much earlier forms of this religion, especially in popular literature.

During the Vedic period, Indian society went through a series of changes. Initially, it was a fairly egalitarian association of householders, who were responsible for both the economic well-being of their dependents and the performance of necessary rituals, that is, sacrifices to the gods. Soon enough, the society evolved into a much more strictly organized hierarchical system, with an institutionalized division of labour. This fostered the appearance of small states and the development of urban culture. Dealing with the divine became a profession and the knowledge associated with it a closely guarded form of cultural capital, which was used by the priests to guarantee themselves the leading position in the social system.

Eventually, the political system started to change and the privileged status of the priests came to be questioned by new religious movements that did not recognize their authority. These reform movements, two of which (the Jain religion and Buddhism) have survived to this day, forced Brahmanism to reinterpret some of its own basic tenets and started a philosophical dialogue which provided Indian thought with a broadly accepted conceptual foundation for centuries to come.

Vedic scripture. The word *veda* means 'knowledge'. Technically, the term refers to four groups of texts, each of which is headed by a collection (*samhita*) of hymns and formulas used during the sacrifice ritual. However, the titles of these collections all contain the word 'veda', so quite often the term is used to refer to these alone, without the other texts in the group. Collectively, the Vedic scriptures are also called *shruti*, 'what is heard', because they were initially transmitted in oral form, and opposed to authored treatises as well as the epic poems that describe, in wildly mythicized form, the history of ancient Aryan India. Older sources credit the vedas to ancient sages, who have given shape to this authorless wisdom, but in some texts we find them also attributed to the creator-god Brahmā. The orthodox tradition considers the Vedas to be uncreated eternal truth.

The oldest and most important samhita is called ***Rigveda***. It is divided into 10 books and contains the hymns and invocations (1017 in number) used for summoning gods to participate in the ritual. Other collections contain formulas to be used during the ritual and after the ritual, checking its efficacy. There is a great deal of overlap between the five collections. While the *Rigveda* has been partially (and sometimes also in full) translated into several Western languages, including English, and is widely studied by scholars of comparative religion and mythology as well as philosophy, most of the others are of interest mainly for specialists in early India.

The secondary texts in each group are divided into three further categories and present early comments on Vedic knowledge. Of these, the last category of the ***upanishads*** is the most important. This group of texts originates from the very end of the Vedic age and the period of reform movements, reflecting the changes towards a more philosophically grounded worldview that Brahmanism was undergoing at the time.

---

veda ('knowledge') the scriptural tradition of Brahmanism/Hinduism, collections of ancient, initially orally transmitted hymns and comments to them

---

Vedic gods. Most Vedic hymns are dedicated to a particular deity, although there are some that evoke them collectively or tell the story of creation. The gods of the Vedas are called *devas* and *asuras*. While deva remained the standard designation of a divine being, asuras were later described as demons. The early Vedic texts still talk about them in a positive key and sometimes even the same deity can be categorized in both groups. The difference, however, must have been developing from earlier on, as it had been one of the causes to split the Aryan tribes into Indians and Iranians – for Iranians, it was the asuras who were the good deities and devas were considered evil.

Many of these deities are originally of shared Indo-European stock, with possibly a few additions from the Harappan civilization. Thus, for example, we find in some hymns of the *Rigveda* invocations to Dyaus pitar (Father Heaven), who is recognizably the same figure as the Greek Zeus pater or the Roman Jupiter. In the Vedas, Dyaus pitar is usually mentioned together with Prithivi, or Mother Earth. In contrast, we know almost nothing about the Harappan gods. There is a figure, depicted on many seals, sitting in a lotus posture with horned headgear and an erect penis, has sometimes been identified as a predecessor of the god Shiva, even though Shiva (bearing the name Rudra) only plays a minor part in the Vedas. Most of the Vedic gods are male, but there are a few goddesses as well.

Characteristically, many Vedic deities are personalized natural phenomena, so Agni (Fire, important for his central role in rituals), Vāyu (Wind), Sūrya (Sun), Vāk (Speech), and Soma (a certain hallucinogenic drug) are glorified by names that are the usual Sanskrit words referring to these things. Similarly, the river Sarasvati also appears as a deity.

The greatest of all Vedic gods, however, is **Indra**, whose name has no other meaning. He is depicted as a warrior, and the most important story about him is the slaying of the dragon or serpent Vritra, the personification of drought. Later on, Indra becomes the god of thunder and the smashing weapon he uses is transformed into a thunderbolt. He is also often depicted consuming large amounts of the hallucinogenic soma, which gives him power to combat his enemies. One of his companions is Vishnu, who later eclipses him as one of the central figures of the pantheon.

The Vedic gods can be grouped into categories, but they are not organized into a clearly hierarchical system, where one of them would have the power to command others. Hymns dedicated to each of them mostly extol the virtues of that particular god as the supreme figure, and they often credit their addressee with the creation of the universe, while another hymn may ascribe that feat to some other deity.

> He has a form corresponding to every form; this form of his is for display.
>   Indra keeps going about in many forms through his magical powers, for ten hundred fallow bays are yoked for him.
> (Rigveda VI 47: 18, trans. S. Jamison and J. Brereton)

Similarly, to Greek gods, Vedic gods, especially Indra, can adopt different shapes. This eventually led to the appearance of another well-known characteristic feature of Indian deities: they have certain more stable forms in which they can appear among the humans of the Earth and perform certain tasks. These forms came to be called *avatars*. The word means 'descent', that is, the descent from heavens of a deity to assume an earthly shape. The word does not yet appear in Vedic texts, although the idea is already there, but it is met in some Brahmanist texts written during the period of reform movements. The concept is most often associated with the god Vishnu, but some others are known to engage in such appearances as well.

---

avatar   the form a deity takes to appear and act on Earth

Towards the end of the Vedic period, we see a new figure appearing on the scene who soon displaces Indra as the greatest god. This is Brahmā, more powerful than any other deity, the creator of the universe, before whom all other deities are just as powerless as humans. The appearance of Brahmā signalizes the transition from a mythological pantheon to a philosophically conceptualized view of divinity, as elaborated in the last layer of Vedic texts, the *upanishads*, where **Brahmā**, a personalized creator god (a masculine noun) gradually approaches *Brahman* (a neuter noun signifying 'foundation'), the absolute, ubiquitous world-spirit.

Upanishads. The *upanishads* are only loosely associated with the samhitas and even though they claim to uphold their authority, they present a worldview that is already quite different from what can be deduced from earlier Vedic scriptures. They present a philosophical response – or an array of related responses – to the changes in the society and the challenges to the Brahmanist worldview posed by the reform movements.

A later tradition identifies the *upanishads* as the final and deepest teaching that a knowledgeable person has to grasp in life. During the first centuries of the common era, the followers of the Brahmanist tradition started to divide the ideal human life into four stages (student, householder, forest ascetic, recluse), but some scholars think that such a division was already being invented at the time when the principal *upanishads* were written. In any case, it conveniently corresponds to the fourfold division of Vedic scripture and credits the *upanishads* with the ultimate wisdom of the sage. The precise original meaning of the word *upanishad* is unclear, and the classical explanation of it as 'secret teachings', meant only for the most advanced followers, is unfounded. Recent scholarship has suggested that the word indicates a 'juxtaposition', that is, a doctrine establishing an equivalence between the external and the internal, or the macrocosm and the microcosm.

There are altogether more than 200 *upanishads* of varying length and importance. The more important ones have been composed during the eighth to fourth centuries BCE. The two best-known texts of this category are the *Brihadāranyaka* and the *Chāndogya upanishads*, which both date from before the advent of Buddhism and thus represent the internal development of Brahmanist thought.

Concepts and doctrines. As any student of Asian worldviews quickly discovers, the very terms Indian thought uses to speak about the world differ considerably from the vocabulary Westerners usually take for granted. However, even though there is considerable variation between Indian worldviews as well, most of them share a common conceptual vocabulary that has been developed by and inherited from Brahmanism and is thus shared also by those religions and philosophical schools that have challenged it and do not recognize the authority of the Vedas.

In Greece, one of the foundational moments of philosophy was the trial of Socrates, accused of disrespect for gods. The early impulses inspiring the Brahmanist philosophical tradition, however, stem from the opposing need to uphold the worldview expounded in the scriptures. That said, the concept of divinity in Indian and Greek thought is quite different, even though both systems are polytheist. While Greek gods are organized in a hierarchy, on the one hand, and myths report their (very human) struggles, on the other hand, Indian gods form a curious polycentric system of various layers. The scriptures contain several conflicting accounts of creation and texts dedicated to particular gods often place their particular object of veneration above all others. Perhaps this could be interpreted as excessive politeness – after all, the goal of the hymns was to incline the gods to grant what was asked of them during rituals of sacrifice. This resulted in an interesting view: knowledgeable humans started to see themselves on par with the gods they were addressing, because their activities were able to manipulate them. Professionals well-versed in techniques of interaction with the divine did not think they were at the mercy of their gods any longer. On the contrary, it was them who controlled the rituals on which the gods were dependent. The knowledge of the general order which the gods also had to obey became the real target of learning. This supported the emergence of a strictly hierarchical society in which the priests, or Brāhmans, were at the top, the warriors-rulers (*kshatriya*) ranked second, the self-employed (*vaishya*, or agriculturalists, merchants, and owners of handicraft businesses) ranked third, and hired labour (*shūdra*) ranked fourth. The upper three castes were called 'twice-born', because their male members had to go through an initiation ritual that qualified them for instruction in some scriptural wisdom, while hired labour was not supposed to do that. At the bottom of this society were the casteless, or untouchables, contact with whom was considered polluting. These included many indigenous ethnic groups as well as such professions that were not considered pure enough by the dominant culture. A legitimation of this division is to be found in one of the scriptural hymns, which describes the emergence of the universe from the symbolically sacrificed body of a primary Man.

When they apportioned the Man, into how many parts did they arrange him? What was his mouth? What his two arms? What are said to be his two thighs, his two feet?

The brahmin was his mouth. The ruler was made his two arms. As to his thighs – that is what the freeman was. From his two feet the servant was born.

The moon was born from his mind. From his eye the sun was born. From his mouth Indra and Agni, from his breath Vāyu was born.

From his navel was the midspace. From his head the heaven developed. From his two feet the earth, and the directions from his ear. Thus they arranged the worlds.

(*Rigveda* X 90: 11–14, trans. S. Jamison and J. Brereton)

This view came to have a strong bearing on the concept of social and cosmic order, and consequently on the morality based on it. In particular, it inspired the theory that the actions of all persons had to correspond to their station in life and not to universal rules. Soon enough this view found its way into political and legal treatises and was later elaborated further by Hindu (particularly Mīmānsā) thinkers. Combined with the emergent doctrine of reincarnation, this produced a workable ethical system, according to which the task of individual people was thus not to perform well on a universal scale, but to live out their particular destinies. These were dependent on the circumstances of their birth, which, in turn, were not random, but determined by their previous actions. The idea of reincarnation is not yet articulated in early Vedic texts, but appears in later layers and emerges as orthodoxy in the *upanishads*.

---

karma   the consequences of one's actions which influence one's destiny in future existences

samsāra   the cycle of rebirths, the conditions of which are determined by one's karma and liberation from which is considered to be the target of one's earthly striving

---

The mechanics of reincarnation theory is very simple: each action an individual performs creates a trace, karma, which influences that individual's future. No actions (apart from breathing and involuntary bodily movements) are ethically neutral, all of them are either in accordance with the individual's duty or not. Those that correspond to one's duty contribute to the future good of that individual, those that are not will have negative consequences. After an individual dies, their core self (*ātman*) moves to another body. Thus all individuals transmigrate through a cycle of rebirths (*samsāra*), through different bodies and different spheres of existence, depending on how well they have performed their duties in each life. However, even though everyone can ensure themselves comfortable future lives by behaving properly, this in itself is not what life should be about.

Brahman   all-pervasive world soul, the absolute, a philosophical derivate of an omnipotent and ubiquitous divinity

ātman   the core individual self, which survives after the death of the person and transmigrates to another body; it is the form in which the absolute is present in each individual

---

The major contribution of the *upanishads* to the Brahmanic worldview is the idea that the absolute world-soul, *Brahman*, is essentially identical to the core self of a person, or *ātman*. The goal of religious practice is to attain a deep-level knowledge of this, which makes it possible that the self of the individual is released after death and can dissolve itself in the *Brahman*, instead of transmigrating to another body. This is the idea of liberation, which becomes one of the central topics also for the reform movements. Even though the Jains and the Buddhists have their own terms for some of these concepts and they may disagree about the details of how the mechanics work, the idea that individuals should liberate themselves from an otherwise uninterrupted circle of rebirths by proper behaviour and practice remains the same.

> 'Put this chunk of salt in a container of water and come back tomorrow'. The son did as he was told, and the father said to him: 'The chunk of salt you put in the water last evening – bring it here'. He groped for it but could not find it, as it had dissolved completely.
>
> 'Now, take a sip from this corner', said the father. 'How does it taste?' 'Salty'.
>
> 'Take a sip from the center. – How does it taste?' 'Salty'.
>
> 'Take a sip from that corner. – How does it taste?' 'Salty'.
>
> 'Throw it out and come back later'. He did as he was told and found that the salt was always there. The father told him: 'You, of course, did not see it there, son; yet it was always right there. The finest essence here – that constitutes the self of this whole world; that is the truth; that is the self (*ātman*). And that's how you are, Shvetaketu'.
>
> (*Chāndogya Upanishad*, 6.13, trans. Patrick Olivelle)

Language. Even before the rise of properly philosophical thinking, we can observe the development of critical views on language, as the only vehicle that can articulate such ideas. In India, we find language in a prominent role already in the sacred Vedic texts. The *Rigveda* contains a hymn (X 125) dedicated to the goddess Vāk, the impersonation of speech, which credits her, in the usual Vedic manner, with the most supreme powers including omnipresence and involvement in everything that happens. This view is taken even further in later texts, where language is called the endless source of what all gods consist, the primary truth, the mother of knowledge, and the navel of immortality. Occasionally language is in rivalry with thought and their relation to each other is not made quite clear. Finally, in the *Brihadāranyaka Upanishad*, *Brahman* itself, the absolute world-soul, is equated with speech (4.1.2).

Given the multilayered and multicentral nature of the early Indian worldview, we cannot, of course, draw very broad conclusions from these extracts. In some other narratives of creation and order maintenance, language is much less central, if mentioned at all. Nonetheless, even occasional attributing of such colossal powers to language is not accidental. The emergence of the caste system with the priests, or Brāhmans, at its head had to be justified by their extraordinary capacity to manipulate the world order. The privileged knowledge that the scriptures contained, in particular the technology of sacrifices, made the divine creatures dependent on the priests who could control them by their actions. This knowledge was embodied in linguistic form, and particularly the sacred formulas called *mantra* (more often than not senseless syllables, even though full of esoteric meaning explained to the followers), which had to be appropriately pronounced at certain stages of the ritual.

> [Language speaks:] I am ruler, assembler of goods, observer foremost among those deserving the sacrifice.
>   Me have the gods distributed in many places – so that I have many stations and cause many things to enter me.
>   Through me he eats food – whoever sees, whoever breathes, whoever hears what is spoken.
>   Without thinking about it, they live on me. Listen, o you who are listened to: it's a trustworthy thing I tell you.
>   Just I myself say this, savored by gods and men:
>   'Whom I love, just him I make formidable, him a formulator, him a seer, him of good wisdom'.
>   (*Rigveda* X 125: 3–5, trans. S. Jamison and J. Brereton)

Sacred knowledge. The possession of this knowledge was almost equivalent to mastery over the universe. This is most likely the origin of the belief in the magic powers of words, also written texts, shared everywhere in Asia where currents of Indian thought (such as Buddhism) have reached. It was believed that studying texts, reciting them (in the Brahmanist tradition) and copying them (in Buddhism) created significant karmic merit. The Buddhist *Diamond Sūtra*, for example, asserts plainly that understanding and explaining no more than four lines of it creates more merit than filling ten thousand galaxies with treasures to be distributed to the poor. But even understanding is not really necessary. In the Jain tradition, for example, certain texts have been so sacred and important that even the priests were not supposed to touch them, until those manuscripts had to be rescued from decay. And in Japan we find a priest covering the body of a blind musician with phrases from *sūtras* when he is sought after by ghosts who want to listen to his performance, so that only the ears, difficult to write on, remain unprotected – and are therefore ripped off by disappointed ghosts. Such powerful words or phrases encapsulating the sacred were called **mantras**.

The same kind of power continued to be attributed to mantras also during later times, when the political centre of the Indian society shifted to the warrior class, but held on to this body of higher knowledge. But gradually their rationale changed: little by little some mantras acquired the status of psychotechnical devices, with the help of which the Hindu or Buddhist ascetic could manipulate his or her (some, albeit very few of the ascetics were women) own consciousness. It was believed that the sounds affect the mind directly and may produce mental states necessary for reaching higher understanding. These practices are still alive today, among the Hindu in India as well as esoteric Buddhist traditions which have survived in Japan and Tibet.

Attention to form. Whatever the cosmogonic role of language may have been, its function as the carrier of sacred knowledge in the Vedic tradition and, accordingly, its crucial importance for the successful implementation of rituals, was beyond any doubt. This is why a distinction was made at a very early stage between texts belonging to the sacred 'heard' and the humanly produced 'remembered' texts – the former had to be memorized exactly in their correct phonetic form, while, for the latter, only the semantics mattered and they could be paraphrased or even translated into spoken languages, which gradually started to diverge from the Vedic norm. As a result, various procedures of linguistic analysis were undertaken by the priests in order to preserve the integrity of the most holy texts. The early Indian linguists noticed quite soon that certain regularities govern the behaviour of sounds that share other traits and devised a fairly sophisticated classification of sounds as a result, something that has not only become the foundation of all domestic Indian scripts, but has also influenced the composition of other writing systems from Tibet to southeast Asian islands and even Japan. But certain analytical procedures even predated the invention of Indian scripts: it was necessary to break the texts down into single words in order to best preserve their form and content. The structure of their language made this undertaking quite complicated: it is customary in Sanskrit to fuse the last sounds of preceding words with the first sounds of the following ones so that long compounds result within which single individual meaning-carrying units – words and grammatical indices – are not always easy to identify. Moreover, the relations between the singular units of such compounds can be very different, they can form new words (with up to 30 elements joined into one semantic whole), but they can also be sentences in which syntactically connected words similarly melt into each other (as, for example, in the English expression 'killjoy').

Language as a system. A radical leap in the Indian debate on the nature of language took place with the grammar of **Pāṇini** (around 400 BCE). Among other things, he devised a tentative classification of such compounds which made it easier for a reader to establish the relations between single meaning-carrying units in a long word, or sentence, or a fusion of both. But what is perhaps most innovative about his work is the ingenious metalanguage he created to formulate rules that cover grammatical material. For example, he inserted markers into the phonetically arranged systemic sequence of Indian sounds in order to define borders of sound groups by them – from vowel 'a' up to the mark 'K', that is, a group consisting of a, i, u, ṛ, and ḷ, would be denoted as 'aK', an artificial term that could then be treated as an independent word and accept, for example, case endings. (A group consisting of only u, ṛ, and ḷ would correspondingly be 'uK'.) Thus Pāṇini could very efficiently code the rules of regular sound alterations as short formulas that were easy to remember and decode. Similarly, he developed formulas for categories of morphemes, such as case and tense endings, and as a result achieved a complete and flawless system of rules that could describe the entire system of Sanskrit.

Even more important than this practical toolbox, however, was the methodological separation of the language under scrutiny from the language used to describe it. The former contained everything normal people would say or write, the latter was a code for the initiated that enabled them to formulate rules, systematic principles quite unknown to most users of the language themselves, to which any single sentence they pronounced nonetheless had to conform. For Pāṇini, Sanskrit was most probably still quite close to the language that he himself grew up with. For most later grammarians, it was an acquired cultural language, which they learned already together with Pāṇini's metalevel view of it. Thus his accomplishment also linked the notion of a perfect order not to language as such, but to a distinct form of it, the classical Sanskrit.

This understanding of language as a system of rules that generates specific individual utterances was remarkably advanced for those early times and subsequently served as a foundation for rather sophisticated discussion about other issues in linguistic philosophy, such as the theory of meaning. A need for a good theory of meaning was again dictated by priestly concerns. For example, early texts had specified with precision the materials and ways of producing necessary implements for conducting rituals in the proper way, but migration to new places of settlement had made some of these materials, such as particular plants, unavailable. How, then, were the priests to preserve the integrity of their sacred knowledge? The answer was a linguistic theory that explained how names had been given to particular objects, and how the efficient sacred essences of these objects could be preserved even though the objects themselves would be replaced.

Theory of universals. Thus, for example, one of the central concerns of later authors was the principle by which words were connected to the objects that they denoted, and the systematicity of such links. According to earlier grammarians, these links are a permanent part of reality and grounded in qualities that objects have in their essential selfsameness – a sheep is a sheep because of its 'sheepness'. Similarly, the sentence 'the sky is blue' refers to a 'sky-is-blue-ness' that characterizes reality at that moment, a little like 'the snow is white', in Tarski's view, is true if and only if the snow is white. Approximately eight centuries later, however, this theory was superseded by that of **Bhartrihari** (c. fifth century CE), who developed the observations of other earlier grammarians into a claim that meaning is not sustained by qualities of things, but universals. The distinction may seem like hair-splitting, but is actually substantial. For example, both aspirin and paracetamol can help against headache. But there is a difference between drugs sold under various commercial labels that contain paracetamol and those that are based on aspirin, because quite a few people are allergic to paracetamol, while aspirin would not be a problem for them. So it is possible that two things share the same universal as two concoctions based on the same ingredient, while sharing a quality such as curing a headache would not necessarily require that. This makes it possible to put the priestly concerns on a more substantial footing. For example, if the texts specify that a white goat has to be sacrificed and white goats are not available, then one should sacrifice a black goat, and not, for example, white flowers, because it is the 'goat' universal on which the meaning of the text relies. Another difference lies in that a quality is contained by the thing it is the quality of, while a universal, in Bhartrihari's view, is independent of any of the phenomena that manifest it. More than that: these universals form a hierarchy. Higher-order concepts are entailed in the lower-order concepts, and in turn they themselves also entail yet higher ones, so that finally all concepts are contained in one, a primary Meaning, which is the equivalent of the Absolute in religious thinking. According to Bhartrihari, the universe thus has a conceptual, logical structure, ordered as neatly as Pāṇini's grammar – which is precisely why grammar is in his view the most direct way to cognizing the absolute, the 'door to salvation' and the foundation of philosophical reasoning. The theory of universals was later developed and acquired an even more prominent role in the Vaisheshika school of philosophy.

Words and sentences. Bhartrihari also proposed a philosophically more solid ground for the phonetic selfsameness of words. Similarly as things, he argued, words also have universals, ideal phonetic shapes to which they, in principle, should conform, but do not, in actual speech practice, which in Bhartrihari's times had evolved from a range of dialectal variations into a multitude of languages incomprehensible to each other's speakers. And the relation of meaning obtains precisely between the word-universal and the thing-universal, both being integral elements of the abstract, conceptual sphere. No wonder thus that as single things of the same general kind are different from each other, so are the ways people pronounce the words indicating them.

It is with the discovery of Sanskrit and its grammatical tradition that European linguistics began to evolve towards the form it has taken today. Ferdinand de Saussure, the most crucial figure in formulating modern ideas about language, wrote his dissertation on Sanskrit grammar and lectured on the subject for the remainder of his life. Thus we can be fairly sure that he was thoroughly familiar with Indian linguistic thought. Leonard Bloomfield studied Pāṇini's work and considered him one of his models, and so did his most ardent critic, Noam Chomsky, who also considered Pāṇini's grammar to be the first generative grammar 'in essentially the contemporary sense of this term'. Thus the influence of Indian linguistic thought, even though rarely highlighted, has been constant in the development of Western linguistics during the twentieth century.

Early legal and political thought. Towards the end of the Vedic period, India became increasingly diverse in the political sense. The eastern parts of the sub-continent started to be dominated by monarchies, where the position of power was inherited, while in the north-west the clan societies evolved into a more dem-ocratic (in the Athenian sense of the word) model of governance, where political decision-making was shared and negotiated among a fairly large group of noble houses. The term *rājā*, usually translated 'king', thus had different meanings according to the region: in a monarchy, it meant the ruling family, in a republic, anyone with the right to participate in the political process. The monarchies tended to uphold the Brahmanist orthodoxy, while the republics were less strict about it, and therefore the reform movements originated in them.

To ensure the support of the royal families, the caste of priests had to concoct a new narrative that would enable the rulers to stand out among the rest of the war-rior estate. Several myths, presumably dating from that time, tell about the divine choice of a ruler from many candidates. However, the most thorough effort to ground monarchy in the emerging Hindu tradition is made by the epic poem **Rāmāyana**, one of the most influential texts in India and throughout South East Asia. Relating the adventures of the righteous prince Rāma, the text also claims that he is an *avatar* of the god Vishnu, who gradually takes on the role of the preserver of the cosmic order. This led to the emergence of a new doctrine of legitimation, according to which royal power itself had a divine source and thus it was the king who guaranteed that cosmic order prevailed on Earth. This doctrine of *devarājā* ('divine ruler') spread together with the Hindu tradition to South East Asia, where it is influential to this day, for example, the kings of Thailand still bear the official title of Rama.

The Brahmanist tradition has also produced several other prominent legal and political texts. One of these is the **Mānava-dharmashāstra**, or 'Laws of Manu', also known as *Manusmriti*, a compilation that most probably emerged in its extant form around the end of the second century CE at the latest, after several centuries of textual development, and also draws on a large number of earlier sources. Some scholars, however, believe in a single authorship and an even earlier date. The text belongs to a larger group of *dharmashāstras*, or legal treatises, none of which is actually a code of laws in the proper sense, but only articulates what its authors believe to be just and correct. The judges appointed by particular kings therefore had much more freedom in considering particular circumstances than the treatise (and others of the same tradition) would lead us to believe. The *Mānava-dharmashāstra* was translated into English already in 1794 and became very influential during the colonial era, as the British used it to craft the so-called 'Hindu law', or a legal code that would apply to the indigenous population of India under their rule.

The *Mānava-dharmashāstra* is attributed to Manu, the Indian Noah who survived the mythical flood, and claims to derive its content from the Vedic tradition. The treatise formulates unambiguously the doctrine of the four castes and four stages of life, going on to stipulate in extreme detail what the desirable conduct of particular people should look like – up to saying that women at least two months pregnant should be granted free passage on a river-crossing ferry.

When a Shūdra has sex with a guarded or unguarded woman of a twice-born class – he loses a limb and all his possessions, if she was unguarded. If she was guarded, a Shūdra loses everything; Vaishya is imprisoned for a year and all his property is confiscated; and a Kshatriya is fined 1000 and his head is shaved using urine. If a Vaishya or a Kshatriya has sex with an unguarded Brahmin woman, the Vaishya is fined 500 and the Kshatriya 1000. If any of these two has sex with a guarded Brahmin woman, he should be punished in the same way as a Shūdra or he should be burnt with a straw-fire. A Brahmin who has forcible sex with a guarded Brahmin woman should be fined 1000; for sex with a willing partner, he should be fined 500.

(*Manu's Code of Law* VIII: 374–378, trans. Patrick Olivelle and Suman Olivelle)

Punishments for misdeeds become more draconic the lower the caste, while they are rather lenient for Brāhmans, thus in their case even the death penalty is replaced by shaving their head, while for others it is real, and neither is the property of criminal Brāhmans to be confiscated when they are exiled. But non-Brāhmans have to be mercilessly persecuted for whatever crimes they have committed. Indeed, upholding the law, the 'eradication of thorns' from the body of the society is one of the principal obligations of the ruler. The book also describes in minute detail all other duties and routines of the king, including the schedule he should follow every day, what his administration should look like and how the fortress, his site of government, should be built. And obviously he should respect the Brāhmans and listen to what they have to say.

Possibly the most important early Indian political and economical text by way of its theoretical impact is the **Arthashāstra** ('The Science of Wealth'). This book was discovered by chance in 1905, when an anonymous Brāhman presented a manuscript to the newly opened Mysore Oriental Library. The extant text of the *Arthashāstra* is most likely more or less contemporary with the established text of *Mānava-dharmashāstra*, but the text similarly draws on a long and even older tradition of 'wealth science'. It quotes from numerous authors whose work has not survived, possibly because it was considered outdated after the success of this treatise. However, most likely its initial version has been supplemented and significantly amended by later copyists. Credited to the Machiavelli-like figure of Kautilya, a wily Brāhman and kingmaker who stood behind the empire-building effort of the first Mauryan ruler Chandragupta (reigned 321–297 BCE), the treatise discusses in detail everything a king needs to know about economy, politics, and governance, which, in the Indian view, are inextricably intertwined.

By way of political stability, the *Arthashāstra* recognizes the merits of the early Indian republics, governed in solidarity, while monarchs always had to fear treason and rebellion. However, as an economic formation, monarchy is seen to be much superior – it is able to tax and centralize large resources needed for any ambitious and socially beneficial economic endeavour: the building of infrastructure for public needs as well as aesthetically excelling palaces, the enforcing of laws and standards on larger territory, the maintaining an army capable not only of self-defence, but also of expansion. The latter is also one of the righteous king's duties. Four principles of foreign policy are enumerated: conciliation and gifts for the friendly, 'sowing dissent', and use of force for the hostile neighbours. Of these, only the principle of 'sowing dissent' would help to subdue a republic.

The king also needs to uphold a large army of spies and agents, because among his officials, no one would tell him things he does not want to hear. The spies would also need to perform 'black ops' if necessary. However, even though the doctrine of the *Arthashāstra* is immensely practical at the expense of moralizing, the previous tradition, if anything, must have been even more cynical. For example, the treatise quotes earlier authors as saying that wayward princes should either be introduced to drinking and whoring so that they would not mature into political opponents, or tempted by agents to mutiny and liquidated, if they agree. The *Arthashāstra* opposes such practices decisively and recommends only instruction in political science as a cure for seeds of insubordination: by learning, any prince would come to agreement with the principles according to which a sage-king governs – if indeed he does so. However, if that does not bring about the desired result, the king is obliged to surrender control of the state to someone else and thus to forfeit his dynasty, rather than transferring the throne to a wicked only son.

The centralized politics of an ideal state also imply strong economic intervention. For example, prices should be regulated so that neither would the trade of the artisans be undercut by too low prices that endanger their livelihoods, nor would the profits of the merchants grow too high at the expense of their clientele. Thus the economic policies of the state should benefit the population as a whole, not a certain class or group. Similarly, taxation should not be too high – the share of the king should normally amount to one sixth of agricultural produce and between one tenth and one fourth in other spheres. The king had the right to raise extraordinary taxes should the situation require that, but also the duty to provide tax relief in times of famine, drought, and other calamities. Unlike the majority of legal systems across the world of that time, the *Arthashāstra* also considered crime to be an affair of the state: even though one citizen may have done wrong by another, the conflict between them was not a private matter, but an insult to the public order, which was guaranteed by the king, and therefore indirectly a transgression against him. Punishments should be proportional to the crime, and masterminding criminal activity was considered a bigger offence than actually carrying someone else's plans out.

While such views might leave a rather favourable view of the *Arthashāstra* as an early political theory, it should not be forgotten that the treatise is a practical 'science of wealth', not a moral teaching: it is simply the case, according to the text, that prosperity, its ultimate aim, is easier to achieve and maintain in a balanced and stable society, where no one needs to fear the whims of the powerful and can rest assured of the continuance of their livelihood. It is in that sense that the social superiority of the early republics is being dismissed in favour of the more efficient governance of monarchy. Indeed, history has proved the *Arthashāstra* right – soon enough, the republics were conquered by the emergent kingdoms, which remained the dominant political form on the subcontinent until the end of the colonial period.

Reform Movements: Jains and Buddhism

Background. There were quite a few teachers active during the period of reform movements, proposing alternatives to the orthodox Brahmanist tradition and trying to recruit disciples. Two of these traditions remain alive to this day: the Jains, who are still active in several regions of India, and Buddhists, whose main foothold on the subcontinent is Sri Lanka, but who are more influential in South East Asia, Tibet and Japan, and even in the West, where Buddhist teachings also continue to attract new followers. At present, we can speak about the Jains and Buddhists as full-fledged independent and institutionalized worldviews, but at the time of their emergence this was not necessarily the case. Even though the Buddha and Mahāvīra were not Brāhmans and did not uphold the orthodoxy in their own practice, their intent most likely was not to displace the Vedas entirely; they used the same concepts and re-interpreted them for the purposes of non-Brāhman spiritual seekers. These people of other castes who, accepting the doctrine of the *upanishads* that the goal of existence is to break free from the cycle of *samsāra*, relinquished their householder status and became wandering ascetics, were collectively called 'strivers' (*shramana*), and most of them came from the republics.

Jains. Apart from Buddhism, the only tradition that traces itself to these reform movements and is still alive is that of Jains. The word derives from *jina* 'conqueror', and refers to the effort of breaking out of the cycle of rebirths to achieve omniscience. The Jains uphold the principle of non-violence in the extreme, and this can be seen as their principal contribution to Indian thought as a whole.

The Jain religion is divided into two major branches called the Digambara and the Shvetambara. Apart from some differences in the teaching and their canons of scripture, the minority branch of Digambaras also distinguishes itself by radical forms of asceticism: male Digambara ascetics renounce the wearing of clothes and bathing, for fear that water might hurt some insects living on the body, whose life is also sacred. This has led to the formation of a prejudicial Hindu stereotype of Jains as filthy and indecent. The majority of Jains lead a lay life, however, perfectly able to unite their views and a normal social existence. Currently they make up about 0.4% of the population of India, and about one third of them live in the state of Mahārāshtra. Among all the religious groups of India, Jains are the most literate.

The 'fordmakers'. We know the historical founder of the faith as **Vardhamāna Mahāvīra**, but neither of these names occurs in the earliest strata of Jain scripture. He was nonetheless a historical person and an older contemporary of the Buddha. Current research places his death around 425 BCE, although the Jain tradition prefers a date about a hundred years earlier. His traditional biography is replete with legends, including an episode where he, as a foetus, was accidentally placed in the womb of a Brāhman woman and then miraculously transferred into a lady of the warrior caste. What we can assume, however, is that he was indeed born into a warrior clan, had an experience of religious awakening, performed austerities and achieved some sort of enlightenment, which he then preached to an increasing following.

The Jain tradition does not view him as its founder as it considers itself the uncreated reflection of everlasting universal history. According to the canon, Mahāvīra was only the 24th and last of the so-called 'fordmakers', teachers who help people to cross to the 'other side' and who appear now and again to re-establish the Jain faith. The first of these were cultural heroes, extraordinary in size and longevity, who taught people not only the correct teaching, but also brought to them fire, agriculture, writing, and social institutions such as marriage. All fordmakers followed the same pattern of warrior birth, austerities, and enlightenment. As the positive period of history was drawing to a close, the intervals between them became shorter and soon humanity is to enter the 'downward' cycle during which the true faith will be forgotten, until the wheel of history starts turning upward again and new fordmakers will appear.

Scriptures. The Jains claim for their own scriptural tradition the same kind of authority as the Vedas possess for orthodox Brahmanism – they are eternal truths, not created, but transmitted. However, the status of scriptures in the Jain tradition is quite different: they are sacred objects rather than material to be studied by the devout, and in some branches the reading of the scriptures is explicitly forbidden to lay people. Quite a few of these texts were only worshipped, not read, also by priests, who had even lost the ability to understand the script in which the texts they venerated had been written down. One text, the *Kalpasūtra*, is recited during an annual festival, but in a manner that makes it impossible to understand even if you know the language in which it is written (a middle Indian language supposedly spoken by gods in heaven). Different branches of the tradition also dispute the authenticity of each other's texts. However, this reverential attitude to scriptures has also induced Jains to highly value literacy and to establish India's oldest manuscript libraries. The attitude of Jains towards scripture is thus twofold: most of them do not know the contents of their holy books and have never read them, while they think of them with devout reverence.

Ideas: a realist cosmos and sticky karma. While the scriptural canon does not really serve as a source of information for the mostly directly transmitted Jain teachings, a text called 'Scripture on the Meaning of the Real' (*Tattvārthasūtra*) from around the fourth and fifth centuries CE, accepted as correct by all branches of the tradition, sums them up neatly. However, later developments have added substantially to the doctrine, and scholars representing different branches of the Jain tradition continue to debate the teachings to this day.

The three central blocks of the Jain tradition are 'correct teaching', 'correct knowledge' and 'correct behaviour'. The word 'teaching', sometimes also translated as 'faith', is **darshana**, the same term that is used for the Hindu philosophical systems, and means a correct attitude to reality rather than blind faith, while 'knowledge' denotes argumentative reasoning, without which such an attitude would be insufficient.

The Jain view of reality is realistic and relatively commonsensical. It does not posit supernatural beings in control of the universe – while it recognizes Brahmanist gods, these are viewed not as powerful deities able to impose their will on the course of things, but rather as capable helpers of pious believers, who are themselves also subject to the same laws of causality that hold humans and other living beings in samsaric bondage. Their divine status is not eternal, but the result of accumulated good karma. When that will be used up, they will also revert to the cycle of rebirths. The same applies to those condemned to hells – after their bad karma is exhausted, they, too, are reborn somewhere else. The same view is also held by Buddhists.

The doctrine of karma is perhaps one of the most original features of Jain thought. Karma is considered to be a material substance that somehow sticks to the immaterial soul-monads and makes them suffer. There are several forms of it, with different colours. It is produced even by involuntary actions and can only be burned off by ascetic practice. The glue that attaches the material karma to immaterial souls is passion, especially hatred and desire, but it remains unclear how something immaterial can actually be united with something material. At one point, an idea was even developed that material objects could also accumulate karma – for example, an axe used for killing – but this was dropped by later Jain theorists.

The soul-monads themselves are eternal and similar to each other in their pristine state. It is karma that causes them to take up different material existences, during which they transform themselves so that they have the same size in their immaterial form as their material bodies have – thus, the souls of elephants and ants are essentially of the same size, but differ while they occupy these respective bodies. Immediately after the death of one body, the soul-monad enters another. Karma determines the kind of rebirth, its future life span and social status within its species, but it does not limit the actions of the individuals, who can improve their status by abstaining from bad deeds and performing good ones. The soul-monads continue to exist separately even after liberation, when they occupy the uppermost level of the universe, in eternal, perpetual bliss. However, there are also souls incapable of achieving this state, who will remain in the samsaric cycle forever.

This final liberation is distinguished from enlightenment, which can be attained by a person while still alive, although not at present, when the world is going through an era of decline. Enlightenment, for Jains, means omniscience – actual knowledge of all things present, past, and future. Mahāvīra is supposed to have reached this, and so are some of his followers, but a disciple of one of them was the last one to attain this level for the present world cycle. Omniscient teachers are able to live on and expound the doctrine for a period, but they do not generate new karma.

Jain ethics. As there are soul-monads everywhere and they are all essentially equal, causing suffering to any one of them is a grievous offence. This is why the Jains uphold the principle of **ahimsā**, or non-violence, which initially distinguished them most sharply from orthodox Brahmanism with its animal sacrifices.

---

ahimsā   complete abstention from any kind of violence towards other living beings

---

In theory, the Jains also credit plants with consciousness and feelings (a story even tells of a greedy tree that wrapped its roots around a buried treasure chest), but the principle of *ahimsā* rather sensibly does not prohibit using them for food. The principle also includes passive transgressions, for example, not giving food to anyone who is starving is considered an act of violence. All Jains have to take a vow to uphold this principle, along with four other vows of speaking the truth (except in cases where this could lead to violence, such as telling hunters how to find their prey), not taking anything without permission, staying chaste, and not acquiring more possessions than needed. The last one also includes 'internal possessions', or passions and attachments. These vows had a stricter meaning for ascetics than laymen – for example, staying chaste meant complete celibacy for an ascetic, and appropriate sexual behaviour for the common people. The latter, however, had to take additional vows, such as only eating their own food after having fed the ascetics and not sending anyone else to a foreign country to conduct their business. At the end of their lives, laymen had to take one final vow of non-attachment to life and its pleasures, thus voluntarily accepting their death.

In practice, the principle of non-violence is upheld rigorously – not only do some ascetics renounce clothes or washing themselves, some lay people also prefer to wear veils so that their breathing would not harm any insects. *Ahimsā* is the major contribution of Jainism to Indian thought, as other Indian religions also took it in, albeit not so rigidly, and it was proclaimed by Mahātma Gandhi as one of the ethical principles of India's struggle for independence.

Kundakunda. There is a rich tradition of Jain scholarship, but not much of it has had broader influence. However, one Jain thinker of later ages deserves special mention. It is **Kundakunda**, traditionally dated around the second or third century CE, while some scholars place him as late as 750 CE. He is the foundational figure of Jain mysticism who, in particular, reinterpreted the doctrine of omniscience as the full cognition of one's own soul.

Kundakunda disagrees with Jain orthodoxy on the subject of karma: according to him, nothing can actually modify the soul, only distort its point of view and delude it so that it forgets its own fundamentally omniscient nature. Everything else in the universe is provisional and ultimately worthless, including the upholding of Jain rituals and the observance of vows, unless this is done with the correct attitude of directing one's efforts towards one's soul. Later Jain thinkers have made efforts to accommodate this fairly subversive doctrine in mainstream thought, and quite possibly interpolations have been added to Kundakunda's works to reduce its impact. In any case, Kundakunda's 'two levels' view of the world echoes the developments in Buddhist philosophy around the third century CE, and some scholars even claim it might have been Kundakunda who initiated this train of thought, provided, of course, that his traditional dates are indeed correct.

Buddhism. One of the major world religions, Buddhism currently claims more than 500 million practitioners around the world, with an estimated 7 million in Western countries. However, although all the branches of Buddhism claim their descent from **Siddhārtha Gautama Shākyamuni**, its historical founder, it might be argued that it is more appropriate to characterize Buddhism as a family of worldviews, similarly to the 'people of the Book' that comprise Jews, Christians, and Muslims, who all share the narratives of the Old Testament and a number of doctrines from monotheism to the immortal soul. The differences between the pragmatic Theravāda, the devotionalism of Japanese Pure Land schools, and the esoteric mysticism of Tibet are indeed quite comparable to what distinguishes Islam from Christianity, for example.

Buddhism originated in India during the period of reform movements and initially its goals were similar to other such movements. While the teaching of the historical Buddha did indeed reinterpret the key concepts of Brahmanist heritage and formulated quite a few radical innovations of its own, its initial purpose was most probably not to reject the tradition entirely, simply to broaden its horizon. Due to its success, however, in particular the support of the Mauryan monarch, Ashoka, Buddhism spread quickly and transformed from a community of spiritual 'strivers' into an institution capable of managing a mainstream worldview. This development naturally led to splits and divisions, the most important of which was the separation of two branches: **Theravāda**, the 'way of the elders' (also derogatorily called *hīnayāna*, or 'small vehicle', by its critics), centred on the monastic community, and **Mahāyāna**, 'the great vehicle', which also acknowledged the capability of lay people to attain liberation. Both schools developed their own, rather sophisticated philosophies, which soon started to compete with the Brahmanist scholarship.

Ashoka is reported to have sent Buddhist missions to other countries during his time already, and in the first centuries CE the teachings indeed started to spread to neighbouring areas. Soon enough, Buddhism attained a strong position in China from where it spread to Korea and Japan, and later it also appeared in the kingdoms of South East Asia and Tibet. While Buddhism in India experienced a decline before and during the Muslim invasions, it still retained a strong spiritual presence in these other countries. However, as mentioned before, the different forms of Buddhism differ from each other considerably.

The historical Buddha. The founder of Buddhism – without doubt the single most influential thinker of the period of reform movements in India, and one of the greatest religious leaders of all times and places – was given the name **Siddhārtha** by his parents. He adopted the name of **Gautama** as a wandering ascetic, and also earned the sobriquet of **Shākyamuni** ('the sage of the Shākya clan'), but most importantly he is the **Buddha** ('the awakened one') – initially the only one of his kind, but later literature treats him only as the latest in a long row of Buddhas. All Buddhist schools recognize his authority. However, not all of them consider him to be the most important of his kind.

The tradition places the death of the historical Buddha at 483 BCE (the Burmese and Thai favour even earlier dates), while recent scholarship favours a later date around 400 BCE. Legends would have him born as a prince and raised carefree in a magnificent palace, while actually his childhood home may have amounted to a station for changing horses at a crossroads. Nonetheless, his father belonged to the warrior caste and had the right to the title of rājā, which meant 'king' in a monarchy, but little more than a voting citizen in the republics. According to the legend, the young prince was taken on rides by his charioteer and encountered someone old, someone sick, and finally a corpse during these outings, which depressed him so that he decided to find a cure against these conditions. The latter half of his life probably corresponds more closely to what the tradition has been saying about him: he left his home and family, wandered around and studied with renowned ascetics, was dissatisfied with all of them, finally joined a group of independent shramanas, and, after a period of prolonged meditation, went through an enlightenment experience, which he then communicated to his fellow 'strivers'. They acknowledged his superior achievement and became his first followers. He continued to roam around for another 45 years, acquiring more support, including that of local kings, until he finally died as the head of a successful congregation. He was 80 years old and, just before his death, told his followers that no leader should take his place.

Scriptures. Like Socrates and Jesus, the historical Buddha did not write anything himself. According to the tradition, a meeting of Buddha's 500 disciples was convened some time after his passing, where they agreed on the contents of his teachings. Ānanda, one of those disciples, recited the teachings from his memory – this is why all Buddhist *sūtras* begin with the phrase 'Thus I have heard'. Another disciple recited the rules of conduct. These texts were accepted and memorized by everyone present, and, for a couple of centuries, the teaching survived in oral form. The teachings were finally written down in the first century BCE, in Sri Lanka, where the Theravāda branch has since established its base.

These texts were transmitted and written in Pāli, an artificial literary language based on the Middle Indian languages from the regions where the Buddha was active. It is still in use as the sacred language of the Theravāda branch of Buddhism, although the Mahāyāna adherents reverted to the use of Sanskrit. Throughout this book, Buddhist terms are normally given in their Sanskrit form, except for terms that are used mostly or only in Pāli.

Tripitaka (Sanskrit) or **Tipitaka** (Pāli)   the early canon of Buddhist scripture, consisting of *sūtras* (sutta), or the Buddha's talks; *vināya*, or rules for monastic life; and *abhidharma* (abhidhamma), Buddhist metaphysics

---

The canonical Buddhist scriptures are collectively called *Tripitaka*, or 'Three Baskets', one 'basket' comprising the talks (*sūtras*) of the Buddha, one for monastic rules (*vināya*), and one for metaphysical elaborations of the teaching (*abhidharma*), developed by some schools during the period between the Buddha's death and the fixation of the canon. Most scholars agree that nothing much was added to this Pāli canon by the Theravāda branch, which still abides by it. The Mahāyāna canon is quite different in content and is based on later scriptures, which were composed only in the first centuries CE. These have been preserved mostly in Chinese and Tibetan translations, but some fragmentary Sanskrit manuscripts have also survived.

In addition to canonical scriptures, early Buddhism has produced a significant amount of other literature. The *jātakas*, or 'birth stories', which started to circulate around the fourth century BCE in Pāli, are instructional tales that tell about the meritorious deeds of the Buddha in his previous lives, in both human and animal form. As soon as doctrinal divisions started to emerge in the community, treatises arguing for specific points of view as well as commentaries of accepted canonical texts also appeared.

One of the most interesting texts of early Buddhism is **Milindapañhā**, or 'The Questions of Menander', written between 100 BCE and 200 CE, which records conversations between a Greek king ruling over a successor state of Alexander's empire in north-western India, and the Buddhist monk Nāgasena. Menander is a historical person (coins with his portraits have been preserved) and he may indeed have had conversations with Buddhist monks, but otherwise there is no reason to believe that the dialogue is anything but fiction. It does, however, pose questions from within a rational frame of mind and the answers provided do not appeal to historical or transcendent authority, calmly, and reasonably arguing the points of Buddhist philosophy for an outsider.

Ideas: the Four Noble Truths. The core of the Buddhist teaching is summed up as the **Four Noble Truths**. The first of these is usually formulated as 'everything is suffering', but this translation is not entirely correct even though the word used indeed means 'painful' or 'unpleasant', it would be more correct to translate it as 'unsatisfactory', because it comprises both the pleasures and sufferings that life has to offer. The idea is that, while suffering is painful in itself, there is no real pleasure in whatever we enjoy as these things, too, will inevitably pass and sometimes we already feel this regret of passing when enjoying them. This is because all phenomena are impermanent and devoid of inherent self-nature. The second noble truth explains why this is the case: everything that exists comes about as a result of a strict causal nexus, starting with ignorance and ending with sickness and death. Buddhism has inherited from Brahmanism the idea of *samsāra*, or wandering through the cycle of rebirths, as it was simply regarded as common sense at the time, and one way to read the causal nexus is precisely as an explanation of the mechanism that leads a person to be reborn in another shape, in which sickness and death inevitably follow. However, the interim links between ignorance and death demonstrate the strong tendency of Buddhist teaching towards the psychological: we see how reality emerges from the point of view of the perceiver as the object of desire, something to be attached to, and these entanglements in turn cause the illusion of an independent selfhood.

While traditionally it has been held that the links of the chain describe the emergence of an individual over time, recent scholarship is inclined towards the view that the process of causation is constant, takes place at great speed and is a part of each of our acts of cognition. The view of reality as something not given to our perception as it is, but always already modified by our attitudes towards it, is a point that Buddhist philosophy has in common with Western post-structuralist and postmodern thinkers and indeed, in recent years, comparisons between them have started to appear.

anātman   the Buddhist idea that the view of selfhood as self-reliant, independent, and enduring is false; empirical selfhood is grounded only in the temporary co-occurrence of various factors, such as body and consciousness, themselves also transient

The doctrine of 'no-self' (*anātman*) is one of the most original as well as the most disputed and differently interpreted tenets of Buddhist thought. A classic explanation of this view is to be found in *The Questions of Menander*: when the king asks Nāgasena what does he mean by saying that his name is just a conventional designation, but there is no real self that it points to, Nāgasena in turn asks whether the king arrived to the meeting on foot or in a chariot. As the latter was the case, Nāgasena proceeds to interrogate what this 'chariot' is, and they agree that it is neither the wheels, the basket nor the axles, nor would a heap where all these lie together be appropriately called 'chariot'. What the word points to is the specific arrangement where all these relate to each other in a particular way. Similarly, Nāgasena says, the name 'Nāgasena' does not refer to a specific entity, but to the relationship of his body, his perceptions, his consciousness, etc., to each other so that a 'person' is seen to emerge, while that person has no reality of its own.

Not all early Buddhists were satisfied with such an explanation, and a school existed at least until the seventh century CE that stipulated the existence of a 'person'. It was also difficult to reconcile this view with the received theory of rebirths, which Buddhist doctrine endorsed: if there is no self, how can a person then be reborn? One way to answer this question was that the subject of rebirths was precisely the illusory self that emerged as a result of the causal nexus grounded in ignorance, and the overcoming of this ignorance would also result in the dissolution of this illusion and, accordingly, liberation.

The Buddhist idea of liberation, **nirvāna**, or 'extinction' is the subject matter of the third noble truth. While the Jain and Brahmanist doctrines tell us how it transpires that the individual soul exits the cycle of rebirths, in the Buddhist view it simply ceases to constitute itself. However, *nirvāna* is described both as a state of bliss and as a state empty of all cognitions, including blissful ones. The question of whether *nirvāna* itself exists in some form or not is again a matter of debate between various Buddhist schools.

The fourth noble truth provides us with a practical instruction on how to proceed towards liberation. This is the truth of the 'middle way' – between the enjoyment-oriented life of lay people and the ascetics such as Jains who subject themselves to all kinds of austerities, the Buddhist is expected not to opt for either extreme. This is because the austerities of the ascetic are similarly a matter of attachment, or perhaps competition about who is more austere and has therefore more merit, as are worldly desires. And it is this attitude of attachment that engenders the karma that binds one to samsaric existence.

The Four Noble Truths

1) The truth of pain: everything leads to pain, nothing in life provides satisfaction.
2) The truth of the origination of pain: everything we perceive is caused by desires causally grounded in ignorance.
3) The truth of the cessation of pain: it is possible to exit from the causal nexus and to cease to be determined by it, which is liberation.
4) The truth of the path to cessation: in order to achieve liberation, one should refrain from the two extremes of worldly pleasures and radical austerities, and follow the eight prescribed forms of behaviour.

Monks, all is burning. And what, monks, is the all that is burning? The eye is burning, forms are burning, eye-consciousness is burning, eye-contact is burning, and whatever feeling arises with eye-contact as condition – whether pleasant or painful or neither-painful-nor-pleasant – that too is burning. Burning with what? Burning with the fire of lust, with the fire of hatred, with the fire of delusion; burning with birth, aging, and death; with sorrow, lamentation, pain, displeasure, and despair, I say. ... Seeing thus, monks, the instructed noble disciple experiences revulsion towards the eye, towards forms, towards eye consciousness, towards eye-contact, towards whatever feeling arises with eye-contact as condition-whether pleasant or painful or neither-painful-nor-pleasant; experiences revulsion towards the ear ... towards the mind ... towards whatever feeling arises with mind-contact as condition ... Experiencing revulsion, he becomes dispassionate. Through dispassion [his mind] is liberated. When it is liberated there comes the knowledge: 'It's liberated.' He understands: 'Destroyed is birth, the holy life has been lived, what had to be done has been done, there is no more for this state of being'.

(*Ādittapariyāya Sutta*, adapted from the translation by Bhikkhu Bodhi)

Buddhist ethics. As a practical code of behaviour, the 'middle way' is spelled out as the 'eightfold path' of right views and correct behaviour. Just as most other ethical codes around the world, the eightfold path prescribes 'right speech', that is, not lying or gossiping as well as 'right behaviour', or abstention from violence, theft, and sexual misconduct. 'Right livelihood' refers to not possessing more than one actually needs. What is notable about Buddhist ethics, however, is the attention it pays to the psychological: the wishes to commit evil or licentious acts amount to little less than the actual performance of these acts, because the mind of the person is obsessed by the attachments and a certain amount of harmful karma is already generated. Four of the eight prescriptions of the path therefore deal with the states of mind: 'right views' are those of the Buddhist doctrine, 'right resolve' means the renunciation of pleasures for their own sake, 'right effort' means constantly staying on guard against a relapse into sensuality and 'right mindfulness' entails one being constantly conscious about one's situation. The eighth prescription is that of 'right meditation', or psychotechnical exercises aiming at the realization of the doctrine of no-self not simply rationally, but with one's whole being, which is the prerequisite of liberation.

Clearly, the 'eightfold path' was initially meant as a code of conduct for spiritual professionals who, without yielding to the temptation of showing off with austerities, also renounced worldly life and dedicated themselves full-time to the pursuit of liberation. However, it was soon reworked into a set of rules that could also apply to lay people who were able to abide by them simply through detaching themselves from the worldly environment in which they continued to live and work. This was a necessary prerequisite for Buddhism to become a lay worldview and notably for the emergence of Mahāyāna schools.

One item of controversy between various Buddhist schools was the concept of 'merit'. Some Buddhists said that pious deeds, which exceeded what could be expected from a normal person, would gain them merit able to wipe out negative karma. This idea was capitalized on by the community who used it for getting material support from lay believers led to believe they could improve their own position in this way. Others, however, opposed the idea and claimed it led to the formation of attachment to oneself and the idea of performance, which would relate to spiritual progress roughly in the same way as anorexia to losing excess weight. Nonetheless, giving alms and supporting the community was not discouraged and the critique applied only to the egoistic reasons for doing so.

The early community. Buddha, the doctrine and the community are collectively known as the 'three jewels' of Buddhism and a later code of conduct specifies causing a split of the community as one of the five 'heinous crimes' along with the intentional killing of one's parents or shedding the blood of the Buddha. Such crimes made it impossible for their perpetrator to attain any spiritual progress in the next lifetime.

This does not mean that the community would have stayed unitary for a long time. Monks normally wandered around during the dry season and for the rainy season they gathered to special places, such as groves donated by wealthy supporters. There they discussed and meditated together. These locations later developed into full-fledged monasteries active throughout the year. The word, **sangha**, used for the Buddhist community is the same that was used for the early Indian republics, and as the Buddha had not appointed a successor, indeed, had explicitly forbidden anyone to pose as such, we may imagine that the atmosphere of those places was fairly liberal and nobody was stigmatized for voicing differing opinions in the framework of the accepted. As the number of such places grew, they started to differ from each other both in their interpretation of the teaching and by the rules of common life. The latter caused the first splits, as some monks were more eager to regulate the behaviour of community members than others. Nonetheless it was customary even for monks representing different schools of teaching to live together in the same community and to argue with each other. It is therefore proper to use the word 'school' for these subdivisions of Buddhist thought and not 'sect', because they had none of the sectarian mentality of proclaiming one's own truth to be superior to that of all other co-believers. Unlike the Western monastic orders, then, these communities were perhaps more similar to academic faculties, where different trends in a field may well be represented within one department, but sometimes a department is composed of like-minded people.

Abhidharma. During the last centuries BCE, the discussions in various Buddhist communities took a decisively philosophical turn and a number of writings emerged that expounded the metaphysical and psychological foundations of Buddhist thought in a more systematic manner. These texts are collectively known as *abhidharma* and form the content of the third 'basket' of the Pāli canon. The prefix *abhi-* can have the meanings of 'taking possession of' or 'exceeding, surpassing' and applied to *dharma*, in this case 'teaching', it means both summing up and going beyond its surface message, similarly as 'metaphysics' means going beyond the science of things in nature. The goal of *abhidharma* thinkers was to systematize the ontological and epistemological premises on which the Buddhist message relies; the result is a very detailed and rather scholastic taxonomy of types of consciousness, minimal existents and so on.

Abhidharmic theory was not accepted uncritically. The most influential school of Buddhism it engendered is called Sarvāstivāda (literally, 'the theory that everything exists'), which credited all the minimal carriers of existence, including the past and future ones, with a certain ontological status. Otherwise, the

Sarvāstivādins argued, it would be impossible for them to participate in causal chains. Although the present reality is available to us in our perceptions, it is nothing more than a slice of a longer process, similarly as the picture on the screen of a cinema is the derivate of the film stored on some material medium. For others, this view implied too much reification. Another school, claiming to go back to the *sūtras* (hence Sautrāntika) rejected the reality of the past and the future dharmas and claimed that only what exists in the dimensionless present moment can be called really existing. In due course, this controversy led to the elaboration of the Mahāyāna doctrine of 'emptiness' as the characteristic of all forms of being, present included.

Politics. Although the Buddha himself came from a republic and called his community after this form of government, his teaching had more success in the monarchies, where it was able to enlist royal support. A major victory for Buddhism was the conversion of **Ashoka** (c. 268–c. 232 BCE), the third and most successful of the Maurya rulers. Devastated after a decisive battle (which he won), Ashoka sought spiritual comfort with a Buddhist monk and subsequently embraced the faith wholeheartedly, sponsoring, among other things, its first missions abroad. Ashoka has also left inscriptions all over India, which command his subjects to follow the 'teaching' or *dharma*, even though it is not precisely Buddhism that is meant, but simply any just and unaggressive lifestyle. Moreover, he presented an example of what someone who rules by the *dharma* should look like, by building roads, financing hospitals for both people and animals, and even providing short-term financial help to people recently released from prison so that they would be able to restart their lives.

Relations with such worldly rulers compelled Buddhism to devise a political discourse of its own, because the Brahmanist view that kings were legitimate by divine sanction was not compatible with its teachings. With their republican origins, Buddhists stressed that the legendary first kings of India were chosen as a result of social contract, and in order to have the legitimacy to rule, the monarch must behave like one who indeed bears the responsibility for those governed by him. Such a person merits the title of *dharmarājā*, 'ruler by teaching', or *cakravartin*, 'the one who sets the wheel in motion', and who conquers by peace and wisdom rather than military power. Sometimes translated as 'universal monarch', the term *cakravartin* indeed implies the right of such a king to govern the entire world because of his merit. Both the Hindu and Jain traditions have also adopted the term, but without the Buddhist ideas of leadership associated with it.

New developments. During the centuries after Buddhism's successful spread over India, several new developments took place. First of all, while Buddhism had initially constituted itself as a worldview for people who would withdraw from normal social life into communities of monks and nuns, this was soon no longer an option, as it was counterproductive for the maintenance of social life at large. A Buddhist lifestyle had to be devised for those who did not want to leave their homes and dedicate themselves to religious practice full-time. The growth of a supportive Buddhist laity also had a favourable effect on the development of monasteries, where monks could now dedicate themselves to meditation, discussion, and the study of scriptures without having to worry about their livelihood.

At the same time, the philosophical debates and controversies propelled Buddhist thinkers to develop increasingly more advanced theories and arguments in defence of their particular schools. For many, the scholasticism of *abhidharma* scholarship was not simply dry and unsatisfying, it also expressed a certain kind of attachment to the activity of conceptualization itself. The new theories that appeared posed themselves as radical critiques of such doctrines, and the conceptual apparatus they devised managed to revolutionize Buddhist thought for centuries to come.

The new developments in Buddhism thus paradoxically contained two contradictory tendencies – towards higher degrees of intellectual sophistication and away from it. At the same time when the Buddha was elevated to a transcendent object of worship and an emerging cult of ahistorical sacred characters provided the laity with more conventional channels of religious activity, the philosophical base of Buddhist thought reached new and unprecedented heights in such figures as Nāgārjuna (c. 150–250) and Vasubandhu (fourth–fifth centuries).

The rise of Mahāyāna. The seeds of the ideas we now call Mahāyāna probably began to ferment in Buddhist communities approximately around 100 BCE. At first, they did not entail an institutional split and supporters of the new trend lived together with their conservative colleagues in monasteries all over India. Some critics of the received tradition also downplayed the significance of the historical Buddha, placing him in a long line of Buddhas who had taught the world before him, mentioning also the next Buddha, who is currently waiting in a celestial abode for the time when it is appropriate for him to be reborn on Earth. Becoming a Buddha was thus no longer a singular feat, but something that, in theory, each follower of the teaching could expect to accomplish.

For a time, it remained possible to accept some of these innovations and reject others. However, when the new ideas began to be formulated in scriptural texts that claimed *sūtra*-level authority, things became more difficult. Soon enough the ideological division became rather heated. Some Mahāyāna texts started to explicitly criticize the older schools of Buddhism and to claim that their doctrine was inferior, or only a preparatory step for the higher message that they themselves claimed to possess. Yet a clear-cut split never occurred in India, though Mahāyāna had more success in its missions abroad, particularly in China. In the meantime, Theravāda continued to dominate in Sri Lanka and its missionaries finally managed to convert South East Asians, who had also embraced Mahāyāna, back to its doctrines.

Scriptures. The ideas of Mahāyāna first appeared in a group of texts which bore the generic title of *sūtra* and also followed the same pattern as the Pāli *sūtras* did, starting with 'thus I have heard' and going on to report a dialogue between the historical Buddha and one of his disciples. However, Mahāyāna *sūtras* sometimes contain episodes of magic and miracles and refer to the participation of supernatural beings in the assembly. They are not written in Pāli, but in Sanskrit, although not the highly sophisticated literary form of it, but a 'hybrid Sanskrit' mixed with colloquialisms and irregular use of grammar. Mahāyāna *sūtras* continued to be produced until the seventh century CE, but the most important among them come from the first centuries CE.

The anonymous authors of these *sūtras* used different tactics to bolster their authority. One way was to base them on revelations that they had in their sleep, another widespread claim was that the historical Buddha had indeed preached these texts, but their content was too advanced for the time and therefore the texts had been hidden until the people capable of understanding them appeared.

---

upāya ('skilful means')   teachings and practices which, in reality, were untrue or empty of meaning, but were adopted as beneficial for people who were unable to grasp the truth of Mahāyāna Buddhism without preparation

---

This reflected a doctrine that helped to reconcile the two mutually opposing tendencies within Mahāyāna thought – namely the idea of 'skilful means'. It was believed already in traditional schools that the historical Buddha was able to adjust his teaching precisely to the level of understanding of his listeners, so that they got the maximum out of it, while he never overwhelmed them with content they could not grasp. This view was now developed to include untrue, but beneficial teachings (something like Santa Claus, who induces children to behave correctly): certain parts of the established scripture could prove to be false when read on a higher level of interpretation, but nonetheless necessary as they helped the followers with a lower level of understanding to advance. This was obviously not something that the traditionalists were eager to accept.

Possibly the most influential Mahāyāna scripture is the **Lotus Sūtra** (*Saddharma-pundarika-sūtra*), which, among other things, explains this doctrine in detail. Most likely the text was initially written in verse, and prose renderings of the content were added later. It is a polemical text, which champions the superiority of Mahāyāna teachings over traditionalist ones and provides a number of parables to illustrate this thesis. Philosophically, it proclaims the important message that all living beings have the capacity to become Buddhas. Another important group of Mahāyāna scriptures is the *Perfection of Wisdom (**prajñāpāramitā**) sūtras*, of which there are a large number, ranging from the 100 000-verse long exposition to the *Diamond-Cutting Sūtra (**Vajracchedika-sūtra**)* of a few hundred lines and the **Heart Sūtra (*Hridaya-sūtra*)** of a few hundred words. The latter, which expounds the doctrine of emptiness in a condensed form, is often used in liturgy.

One *sūtra*, which deserves special mention even though its canonical status is not quite clear even in Mahāyāna circles, is the ***Vimalakīrti Sūtra***, which tells the story of a householder who manages to best all the members of the Buddha's retinue in debate (arguing for a number of subtle philosophical points in the process) and also presents the example of the ideal lifestyle. Such texts offered a discourse in which wealthy supporters of Buddhism were provided a more respectable paradigm of self-identification than merely the role of lay worshippers of relics and images.

Ideas: compassion and wisdom combined. The tendency to accommodate the lay world was also seen in the launching of a new ideal spiritual path for the follower. The ***bodhisattva***, 'enlightened being', was what the Mahāyāna adherent expected to become – not someone who had actually attained liberation and exited from *samsāra*, but someone who had indeed reached this level, but given up its perks for the benefit of all other beings still entrapped. The *bodhisattva* was thus opposed to the ***arhat***, a word initially denoting the disciples of the historical Buddha, but later the career model of traditionalist Buddhist schools – a person now allegedly selfish and caring only about their own liberation. This ideological thesis had no real ground in the reality of earlier teachings, as *arhats* were supposed to achieve their understanding of no-self through empathy with all others.

---

bodhisattva   the Mahāyāna ideal of a being who has attained enlightenment, but forsaken entry to *nirvāna* in order to help other beings still entrapped in the cycle of rebirths

arhat   the alleged ideal of traditional Buddhism striving only for one's own liberation

---

Even so, it is in the Mahāyāna that compassion (***karunā***) is elevated to one of the two distinguishing marks of the *bodhisattva* ideal. The other one is 'perfect wisdom' (***prajñā***), or a correct understanding of how the world works. Here,

Mahāyāna thinkers made a huge leap. While traditional Buddhist doctrine taught only the absence of personal selfhood, but credited the external world with an indisputable existence (which does not contradict the transience or finality of all things), Mahāyāna philosophy asserts that 'emptiness' (***shūnyatā***), the absence of an internal self-nature, is the characteristic of all existence. What exactly was meant by this claim was a subject of much controversy. In general, Mahāyāna thinkers agreed that the principal problem was our inadequate perception of the world that we think we inhabit – desires, attachments, and traces of past actions coloured our perception of it to a degree that made it impossible to see it for what it was. However, there were some who denied the self-same existence of the outside world completely, while others admitted of a self-identical outside reality, only contesting our ability to cognize its constant evanescent flux and to say anything tenable about it. This led to philosophical debates of extreme sophistication.

---

shūnyatā **(emptiness)** the primary characteristic of existence in Mahāyāna thought, the absence of self-nature of any existent, not just the perceiving subject

karunā **(compassion)** 'compassion', the extension of all protective feelings one has about oneself to all other sentient beings

prajñā **(perfect wisdom)** the in-depth comprehension of the empty nature of all reality

---

One way to describe emptiness was to point out that any actual thing was always composed of parts and materials, as were these in turn, so that all things were interdependent and similar precisely in their lack of self-sustaining identity. In this way a level of primary, enduring, self-sufficient substantiality can never be reached. The Buddhists started to use the word ***dharma*** not only for their teaching and the morality it implied, but also in its literal sense of 'carrier', in this case, of existence. Dharmas are neither material nor ideal. Their existence, as the 'perfection of wisdom' *sūtras* tell us, is dimensionless – they neither come into existence nor fade out of it, as this would imply a temporality. We can assume that each dharma is a flash, or perhaps something akin to how the foundation of being is described in quantum physics, which, in fact, has prompted comparisons between Buddhist philosophy and contemporary science. However, even though the dharmas literally mean 'carriers', they are not vehicles for loads or charges that can be thought separately from these charges themselves. And just like physics describes different substances by specifying the 'emptiness' separating the minimal particles of being in atomic structures – and not essential differences between the particles themselves – the Mahāyāna ontology similarly rejects the *abhidharma* qualification of dharmas and posits the emergence of different things through the emptiness that constitutes them. This resembles how coal and diamonds consist of the same kind of atoms and the difference comes about only through how these atoms relate to each other, that is, of how much emptiness there is between them.

A lived and transformative experience of such understanding is 'perfect wisdom' and its attainment enables the *bodhisattva* to see reality as it really is. Because *nirvāna* has become an egoistic goal to pursue, this experience of enlightenment replaces it in the Mahāyāna paradigm as the aim towards which the followers should strive. But the Mahāyāna *sūtras* go even further: because the exit from the cycle of rebirths has been identified as a trap for the egoist, it is now assumed that there is no *nirvāna* apart from *samsāra* – the difference between the two is simply that of one's attitude towards reality. Similarly, it is not necessary to posit physically existing hells or paradises – these, too, are nothing else than states of the perceiving mind.

Nāgārjuna (c. 150–250). Possibly the greatest Indian Mahāyāna thinker is **Nāgārjuna**, although nothing reliable is known about his life. Technically he is the founder or the Madhyamaka school, but his authority extends far beyond its borders. Historically, however, his legacy was overshadowed by other schools for nearly five centuries, during which the competing school of Yogācāra gradually gained prominence. A revival of his thought took place in the sixth and seventh centuries, when contradictory interpretations of his thought caused the school founded by him to split into two separate branches, both of which produced substantial literature to underpin their respective positions.

Nāgārjuna's main work, *Fundamental Verses on the Middle Way* (*Mūlamadhyamakakārikā*) is a verse treatise that scrupulously analyses, in 27 chapters, all phenomena for the logical possibility of their having an independent and enduring nature. He finds none. However, this does not mean he espouses a doctrine of philosophical nihilism – on the contrary, nihilism is ruled out just as naive realism is, which is why he calls his philosophy the 'middle way' between these two extremes.

Nāgārjuna's real target is not the nature of reality at all, but our views of it. In separate chapters of the treatise, he deconstructs causation, motion, senses, time, desires, compound phenomena, and so on, in other words, all ideas, which could theoretically be employed for the development of a discourse explaining how the world ultimately and self-reliantly is. His method is nonetheless not to judge these discourses by a constant standard he proposes himself – as this would again imply unwarranted reification – but to show that all of them, taken on their own premises, inevitably lead to conclusions that their proponents should be unable to accept.

Emptiness is thus primarily the lack of substantiality in anything that we can think or say about reality, which is why substantializing claims about it are all necessarily misleading. What Nāgārjuna proposes instead is a two-tiered view of truth: the 'ultimate' truth about how things really are cannot be articulated, but this does not disqualify the 'shared' truth of statements we can make about our lifeworld. From the fact that nothing is essentially, independently, and unconditionally a 'chair' and that 'flying' cannot be described without reference to things engaged in this kind of motion, it does not follow that it would be wrong to say that chairs cannot fly.

The view that truth has two levels actually goes back to earlier *abhidharma* scholarship, where it was used to reconcile apparent contradictions between different statements in the talks of the historical Buddha, and later conceptualized as a difference between the truthfulness of empirically verifiable and speculative statements. Nāgārjuna has developed this into an intellectual tool to reconcile the logical emptiness of essentialist statements about reality and the 'truth–false' distinction of simple sentences about situations we encounter in the world. On this view, 'shared' truths are not inferior to 'ultimate' ones, but just the expressions of a different perspective, just as we can speak of a glass of 'still water' even though we know that vigorous Brownian motion is actually taking place in it. Conveniently, this view also bolsters the doctrine of 'skilful means' – even as we know that a certain moralistic story, for example, is not strictly true in the referential sense of the word, the moral truth contained in it can absolve its falsity.

After their dissemination, Nāgārjuna's ideas became a topic of much debate and acquired an authority for a significant part of all Mahāyāna thought. Prominent Buddhist schools, including, for example, East Asian Chan/Zen and the Geluk-pa of Tibet, claim him as one of their predecessors and, in more recent times, his thought has been compared to such Western philosophers as Ludwig Wittgenstein and Jacques Derrida.

Yogācāra. The other dominant Mahāyāna philosophical school is Yogācāra 'yoga practice', also known by other names such as 'consciousness-only' or 'impressions-only', because its doctrine denies the reality of material objects. It arose in the fourth century largely due to the work of Asanga and **Vasubandhu**, two Brāhman-born half-brothers. In his youth, Vasubandhu studied traditional *abhidharma* and, in fact, one of the most reliable summaries of *abhidharma* philosophy is written by him (though some scholars believe it is by a different author with the same name). The connection to this tradition is also visible in his Yogācāra treatises, which carefully deal with arguments traditionalist thinkers might pose against his views.

Yogācāra takes as its starting point the position according to which we do not have direct cognitions of outside reality, only distorted mental impressions of it. To this view, Vasubandhu applies 'the principle of lightness', the Indian equivalent of Occam's razor, which states that if there are two theories of anything with equal explanatory power, one should opt for the 'lighter' one, which posits less about what is. The rationale behind this theory is that when we approach reality with our minds capable of distorting it, 'heavier' theories probably distort more. Accordingly, if mental impressions are the only thing accessible to us, the stipulation that there have to exist material objects that cause them is superfluous heaviness and should be rejected.

However, it would be a mistake to assume, as it is sometimes done, that Yogācāra denies the existence of anything external to the perceptive and self-conscious mind. What is negated is the reality of stable, continuous, self-same material objects that make up the world – these are believed to come into the existence that they exhibit only in contact with a perceiving consciousness to which their existence is exhibited. We know that physically, sounds exist only when there is an ear receiving them – the same applies, according to Yogācāra, to any phenomenon we believe to exist. Yogācāra does, however, admit the reality of 'constant becoming', which is what the enlightened being will have access to in the course of the disintegration of its own illusionary stability. The 'grasper' and the (stable) 'grasped' are interdependent – when one is gone, then so is the other. Therefore, we should also reject the idea that our desires are caused by something else than our own minds.

As a description of such internal contamination, Yogācāra proposes a reinterpreted earlier term, 'perfuming', which expresses a particular type of causation. When we normally think of the relationship of causes and effects as that between a pushing hand and a moving cart, or a seed maturing into a plant, Yogācāra proposes an indirect form of causality akin to the fragrance of perfume (or the stink of tobacco smoke) sticking to your clothes when you spend a lot of time in a room filled with it. The perfume or the smoke are not specifically directed towards your clothes, nor do they have to exist earlier in time, and two entities may also mutually 'perfume' each other. In the Yogācāra view, sense data and the effects of karma, stored in the consciousness of the individual, perfume each other and thereby bring karmic effects to maturation, creating deluded desires and producing new contaminating karma in the process.

To explain how this works, Yogācāra proposes a new view of the structure of the mind, in which there exist not six consciousnesses (Indian theory normally adds the cognition of mental objects to the five senses), but eight: there is also a seventh 'self-consciousness', which unites the activities of all others into a whole that it

Vasubandhu skilfully answers his imaginary opponents' critique, even though some of his arguments might not sound as convincing to us as they may have seemed to his contemporaries. For example, he discusses the ontological status of the demons who torture beings in hell. If these would be real beings themselves, they would have to be sent to hell for their own karma to suffer, but this is clearly not the case, as they thoroughly enjoy torturing others. It is therefore more likely that the denizens of hell only imagine what is happening to them. But if that is true, why should we also not be imagining what is happening to us? Vasubandhu does not, however, draw the consequence of solipsism from this, as he does not believe in the existence of a self. He therefore concedes the existence of separate individual consciousness bundles, which are able to interact and produce impressions for each other, or even terminate each other (which would correspond to what we normally call killing). At this point, however, his theory actually becomes heavier than expected, because it needs to account for the structure of the karmic laws that produce these sense impressions, bearing in mind that the origin of these may be in consciousnesses that have since ceased.

believes to be real and continuous. This is the source of our delusions. Finally, there is the eighth, or 'store consciousness' in which karmic seeds are stored and germinate into the impressions we believe to deliver reality to us. This concept has been sometimes compared to the Freudian and Jungian unconscious, which also stores impressions of past experience and transforms them into impulses that influence present behaviour. In both Yogācāra and psychoanalysis, this process is subject to natural, mind-independent laws.

According to Yogācāra, an enlightened being experiences the 'reversal' of the store-consciousness so that it is freed from karmic seeds and only reflects 'thusness' or 'constant becoming'. The mind is thus not the locus of whatever might be considered ultimately real, but the obstacle that an individual has to overcome in order to attain liberation.

Buddha-nature. One of the new notions Mahāyāna thought introduced to Buddhist doctrines is the idea of **Buddha-nature**. This concept evolved from two separate ideas. On the one hand, the extension of the capacity to attain liberation from monks to all humans naturally led to its further broadening to all living beings. The practice of the 'eightfold path', on this view, only led to liberation because beings already possessed an innate potential for it. On the other hand, theories of mind had started to analyse the mechanism of rebirths in more detail. Abhidharmic scholars had already posited the existence of a deep-level conscious flow that ensures the continuity of the individual even while in coma or deep sleep. It was concluded that it is this flow that continues after death and ensures rebirth. The Yogācāra idea of 'store consciousness' assumed a similar, if not more efficient function, as it was the repository of karmic effects.

Soon enough, these two ideas conflated into a core potential to evolve, something that all living beings have. This capacity came to be called Buddha-nature. It is stored in the foundation of our mental structures and ensures our ability to evolve spiritually, whatever the circumstances of our birth. Most schools believe that each individual is endowed with it, but there are exceptions. Notably Yogācāra assumes that there is a class of individuals who do not possess Buddha-nature and are thus unable to become enlightened, ever, no matter what happens. Some Mahāyāna scriptures, admitting that such persons exist, nonetheless state that they can be saved by the Buddha, who can transfer his own merit to them and emancipate them from this position.

Buddhist logic. The debates between various philosophical positions raised a practical need to be able to articulate one's views and arguments coherently and rationally. Soon enough, Buddhist monasteries included Hindu treatises on logic in their curricula for the monks to learn this art from. However, Hindu logic relied on an ontology that was quite incompatible with Buddhist thought. A theory of Buddhist logic emerged in due course, which was able to resolve the paradox between the limited nature of language, its inability to express the final truth about things, and the need to derive correct and acceptable arguments from theses about how things stand.

The system of logic was first developed by **Dignāga** (480?–540?) and brought to perfection by his commentator **Dharmakīrti** (sixth–seventh century). In order to overcome the gap between our inability to say anything final about the world and the need to speak about it coherently, Dignāga suggested an ingenious device called *apoha*, or 'exclusion'. It is true, Dignāga concedes, that we cannot claim that our words refer to the things they designate in their totality. 'Apple' does not translate into the complete and exhaustive list of all the properties a particular apple has, as this list is ineffable and keeps changing constantly. Moreover, all the properties on that list cannot be defined unambiguously either. So when we point to an object on the table and say '*this* is an apple', we are overstepping our bounds in the strictly logical sense, as 'apple' cannot completely describe '*this*'. What we can do, however, is to say '*this* is not a non-apple'. This is because a 'non-apple' only refers to something that does not have all the properties on the complete and exhaustive list. Dignāga's point becomes more understandable, perhaps, when we apply it to an abstract concept such as 'justice'. It is impossible to define 'justice' in a way that all people would accept and that would help us to judge all past, present, and future cases unambiguously. However, there would be any number of cases in which people with different views of justice might agree that justice has not been served. Buddhist logic has thus developed a discourse of argumentation that makes much weaker claims about reality and is in accord with its ontological commitment to the transient and empty nature of all things. On this basis, further sophisticated theories of logical modelling were elaborated and put to practical use in scholarly debate.

Mahāyāna ethics. Traditionalist Buddhist ethics of the 'middle path' had been based on the assumption that by gaining control of one's consciousness it is possible to extricate oneself from the entanglements of desires and hatreds and, consequently, to attain the state of mind necessary for exiting the *samsāra*. This option now left behind, Mahāyāna thinkers had to solve the difficult task of how to reconcile the idea of ultimate emptiness with the need for regulated behaviour. After all, if everything is ultimately empty and devoid of substantial foundation, what is the basis on which good and evil could be distinguished at all? More importantly, what would be the benefits of abiding by moral precepts, when there is no self and nothing ultimately real with respect to which one could restrain oneself? This question appears now and again and is indeed a difficult one with which many Buddhist thinkers have had to wrestle, providing different answers.

A mechanistic and somewhat circular answer is extracted from the definition of the *bodhisattva* itself. Compassion for all living beings is one of the two principal aspects of the ideal, so consequently it is also impossible for anyone practising (or striving towards) this ideal to do anything harming other living beings. But this has been countered by the idea that violent and apparently harmful 'shock therapy' can indeed be more beneficial to those beings than treating them in the frames of traditional morality. The Tibetans have even devised the idea of 'merciful killing', without hatred, to prevent someone from committing harmful acts, and indeed, an evil king was killed by a Buddhist monk for this very reason. However, if this view were adopted as a general principle and people allowed to commit seemingly evil deeds allegedly out of compassion for other living beings, havoc would surely result.

A more productive approach is suggested by the *Vimalakirti sūtra*, which turns the question around: it is precisely the baselessness of ethical acts that makes them ethical. A *bodhisattva* upholds precepts and performs good acts while knowing that the goodness of those acts is based on a deluded understanding of reality – but this is why these acts are good, and not self-serving behaviour oriented towards rewards or escape from punishment. Thus the Mahāyāna considers blindly followed moral discipline and exercise useful on the 'skilful means' level and not grounded in objective reality, while the genuinely ethical person practises virtues without an external reason for doing so.

Mahāyāna practice. The new developments also led to many innovations in the practice of worship. First of all was the appearance of a multitude of *bodhisattvas* and Buddhas other than the historical Shākyamuni. Their number grew very quickly into a veritable pantheon and came to resemble the European medieval cult of saints, with the difference that the Mahāyāna version was not based on historical persons or connected to particular places. Nonetheless we may assume that quite a few pre-Buddhist local practices found their way into these new forms of worship, and very likely Mahāyāna and emergent Hindu practices mutually influenced each other. The *bodhisattvas* and new Buddhas also started to make regular appearances in believers' dreams, thus providing further ground for religious innovation.

Ritualistic worship of sacred figures loosely organized into a complicated hierarchy thus became a characteristic of Buddhism that it had not previously had. The discourse for the legitimation of such practices was grounded in the ability of the Buddhas and *bodhisattvas* to transfer the merit they had acquired to people who needed it to emancipate from their current situation and embrace more serious practice. As compassion was one of the two key attributes of *bodhisattvas*, they would not deny a fellow living being this, and worship at temples became a way to attract their attention as well as establish a channel of communication needed for such transfer. This coincided with the development of Buddhist art. The code of monastic conduct in the Pāli canon initially forbade the depiction of the Buddha or the use of human figures in religious practice, but Mahāyāna abandoned this requirement and Theravāda soon followed suit. Already starting with the first century CE, Buddhist sculpture began to develop, first under the influence of the realist Greek aesthetic still influential in the north-west of India, and later exhibiting its own characteristic styles.

Monasteries. The intellectual efforts of Buddhist thinkers depended strongly on such institutional support that the early community would have been unable to provide. Buddhist monasteries gradually developed into centres of learning, with huge libraries, lectures, and debates constantly going on. During the emergence of Mahāyāna, the number of monasteries also increased quickly, and it is believed that between 100 BCE and 200 CE, approximately 1000 monasteries were built. Some of these appeared on particularly significant sites, such as the birthplace of the historical Buddha, the place of his enlightenment, and so on, others appeared near prosperous towns on the crossings of trade routes. Some monasteries were even built into caves that provided relief during the hot season. A proper monastery included living quarters for monks and nuns, while a lesser temple might be built just adjoining to a **stūpa**, a pillar initially built for containing relics, but later simply as an architectural element. Gradually, monasteries split into Theravāda and Mahāyāna centres, with the latter housing (as well as producing) many images and objects of veneration, while the former were more austere.

Probably the greatest Buddhist monastery was Nālandā in the north-east of India. Some sources claim that it had a longer history, was possibly founded by king Ashoka, and many celebrated Buddhist thinkers taught there, including, for example, Nāgārjuna, but its credible history started with the royal patronage of the monastery in the fifth century CE. Subsequent kings sponsored new buildings and the monastery attracted more and more talent, soon becoming the major centre of learning, where pilgrims from as far as China, Korea, and Tibet chose to study. The example of Nālandā inspired other rulers to set up competing centres of their own, all of which contributed to the flourishing of Buddhist scholarship until the Islamic conquest, when many of the monasteries were destroyed and monks either killed or forcibly returned to lay life.

The Development of Hinduism

Background. The present form of the religion that started out as Brahmanism is commonly called Hinduism, and it is clearly distinct from its previous stages of development. However, it would be a mistake to assume that there exists a systematically ordered orthodoxy, coherent in all details, that all Hindus share. Like all great religions, Hinduism is diverse, and the word serves as a vague label for a variety of traditions with a common core rather than a designation of one clearcut worldview. It is also futile to look for full systematicity in any one version of it, because each particular, lived form of Hinduism also acknowledges certain narratives possibly at odds with it, and individual practitioners may also have diverging opinions about them. Believing in one's own version of the truth still does not make the Hindu think of those who believe otherwise as heretics, but merely as people who similarly believe in their own version of the truth. This, of course, concerns only the members of the broader community, and Hindu zealots can be very aggressive towards the representatives of other religions, particularly Islam, with which it has a long-standing and politically coloured feud.

Perhaps we might define the end of Brahmanism and the starting point of Hinduism as the shift of focus away from sacrifice. Even though rituals of sacrifice exist to this day and the Hindu tradition mentions it commendably in many of its scriptures, the actual attitude towards animals gradually started to change and accordingly modified the mechanics of how the relations worked between this world and the higher one. The *Mānava-dharmashāstra* includes passages which discourage Brāhmans from eating beef, but on the whole this seems to apply only to such meat that has not been offered in sacrifice. But the Hindu scripture of *Bhagavata-purāna* already explicitly forbids animal sacrifice, saying that it is not allowed in the present 'dark age' of history. This may have occurred under the influence of the Jain tradition and its stress on total abstention from violence. Gradually, the idea of 'sacred cows' started to emerge. At some unidentifiable point in time cows started to be associated with feminine divinity and fertility, the idea of the mother goddess, and were thus not to be harmed. However, it is also possible that the resolute form of bovine sanctity only emerged during the Muslim conquests, as a protest against the slaughter of cattle that Islam allowed. 'Cow protection laws', pushed by Hindu politicians since the nineteenth century, have been one of the main sources of Hindu–Muslim conflict, given the importance of beef in the Muslim diet.

Another new development of Hindu thought during the classical period was the de-monopolization and de-ritualization of the communion with the gods, which now was no more the domain of the priestly caste alone, nor only available through the ritual of sacrifice. This brought Hindu deities closer to their worshippers and endowed them with a presence in the world of the devout. This presence is acutely felt and ritually enacted. For example, the figures in which gods are supposed to dwell can be touched and handled, thereby establishing a contact with the higher spheres that Brahmanic rituals did not provide for the lay people.

While the Hindu tradition upholds the hierarchy of castes against which the social challenge of the reform movements was directed, the three higher castes of 'twice-borns' (priestly, warrior, and the self-employed) developed a certain solidarity and started to be collectively opposed to the lower strata of hired labour and untouchables. The term 'twice-born' refers to the initiation ceremony that the male members of these castes went through and which qualified them for the study of scriptures, no longer the exclusive domain of the priests. Yet they maintained the idea of hierarchy and the duty of each person to live out their own destiny in the general order of things.

The changes in the pantheon. Another important development that occurred in this period is the eclipse of the most important Brahmanist deities by new figures. Brahmā, himself a late arrival, retains a position also in the new

The *Bhagavad-gītā* tells us the story of the warrior hero Arjuna, who falls into despair on the eve of a decisive battle because so many of his former friends and relatives will be fighting for the other side. He goes on a chariot ride through the territory between the two camps to think about things, and engages in a conversation with his charioteer. But that happens to be none other than the god Krishna, who teaches him the true nature of things, including that it is his duty as a warrior to fight, and that refraining from killing his friends would be an immoral violation of this duty. Similarly, everyone else also has to abide by the destiny they were born with and to fulfil their role in this life, in anticipation of a better chance in the next. This principle has been enshrined in ancient texts on political and legal thought and will later be elaborated into a full-fledged philosophical doctrine by the proponents of the Mīmānsā system.

pantheon as the creator of the universe, but the two central figures of **Vishnu**, the keeper of order, and **Shiva**, the destroyer of evil, now occupy central stage. Each of the two gods plays the main role in the two distinct branches of Hinduism, named **Vaishnavism** and **Shaivism** according to them. Though these two branches are sometimes called monotheistic in their excessive devotion to one god, this is not correct, because both of them recognize the other's god (as well as a host of minor deities not mentioned here), they just revere their own particular god ahead of all others. Historically, they have coexisted peacefully and acknowledged each other, so that only minor conflicts have emerged, and even those because of political rather than ideological reasons. Collectively, the three gods are known as the ***Trimurti***, embodying the three divine powers of creation, preservation, and destruction. Frequently religious symbols (such as fertility-denoting phalluses) have three distinct parts jointly symbolizing the Trimurti.

Each of these gods also has prime consorts, who appear in narratives, but are also independently manifested as divine carriers of female creative power. Each of the male gods also has a designated animal or bird vehicle, thus Brahmā rides a swan, Vishnu the mythical *garuda* bird, and Shiva a giant bull.

We met Vishnu briefly as one of the companions of Indra in the Vedic pantheon, and as the source of royal power in the legitimation discourses of early Indian monarchies. Now his role is becoming more and more central. In a Rigvedic hymn, Vishnu is mentioned to take three steps on his way to cover the earth, the ether and the entire universe and establish himself as its keeper, 'who alone supports heaven and earth in their three parts and all living beings'. Even though the rest of the *Rigveda* does not credit him with such status, with the shift to Hinduism he indeed became the supreme being for a large number of believers. A characteristic of Vishnu is a large number of *avatars* – the most prominent among these are Rāma and Krishna – the god who expounds the doctrine in the *Bhagavad-gītā*. The historical Buddha is also considered an *avatar* of Vishnu by many Hindus. Around the tenth century CE it was agreed that Vishnu had 10 main official *avatars*, though some texts mention 39 and others speak of innumerable ones. Not unexpectedly, there is an abundance of literature, scriptural and apocryphic, about their miraculous deeds.

Compared to Vishnu, the origins of Shiva are not so clear. As an adjective meaning 'auspicious', this word has appeared in the Vedas as an epithet of several deities, but it has also been proposed that it derives from a Dravidian word meaning 'red' – the latter explanation supported by his connection with the sun. He may be an amalgam of several divine figures, including the gods Indra and Rudra of the Vedic pantheon, with elements inherited from pre-Aryan deities. Rudra's rise to prominence started in the *upanishads*, where he is sometimes credited with the creation of the universe and even described in the same terms as Brahmā/*Brahman*, the absolute inherent in everything. Certain devotionalist texts follow this view, but the more widely accepted narrative sees him as one of the three main gods. Unlike Vishnu, Shiva does not have many *avatars*, but some texts claim that certain mythological personages, such as the monkey king Hanuman, a powerful ally of king Rāma in the *Rāmāyana* epic, is his incarnation. Another frequent way to symbolize Shiva is the phallus, or *lingam*, often representing him in temples.

Shakti. Special mention deserves to be made of the Hindu goddesses, or more precisely the collective goddess personified as **Shakti** or Devi (Mahādevi), because the consorts of Brahmā, Vishnu, and Shiva are all identified as her in different texts, and in other narratives she is also the mother of all three the Trimurti gods. The word *shakti* means 'power' or 'energy' and in a personified shape refers to a supreme female sacred figure. This is the term/name mostly used for female divinity in devotionalist practice, which is often identified as the third branch of Hinduism (beside Vaishnavism and Shaivism) called Shaktism. The word *devi* simply means 'goddess', and there are many narratives associated with her, as well as rituals not necessarily associated with *bhakti*-type worship. Scriptures that credit the female with a cosmic energy sustaining all creation and identifying her with the unchanging absolute have already appeared in the sixth century CE, and soon afterwards various devotional movements dedicated to the goddess started to proliferate, continuing to this day.

> The gods beheld a dazzling concentration of light, like a mountain ablaze, pervading all directions with its flames. Then that incomparable light, born from the body of all the gods, pervading the three worlds with its brilliance, coalesced into the form of a woman ... Honored by the gods, she roared on high with a boisterous laugh over and over, filling the entire heavens with her dreadful bellow ... The demon Mahishāsura [rushing towards the roar] then saw her brilliance pervading the three worlds, her feet trampling the earth while her crown scraped the sky. The twang of her bowstring jolted the underworlds. Her thousand arms reached out in all directions.
>
> (*Devi-Mahātmya* 2.12–2.13, 2.32, 2.37cd–2.39ab, trans. C. MacKenzie Brown)

But the goddess also has a much more frightening aspect, which is manifested in **Kālī**, the destructive feminine power. The origin of this can be traced back to some of the historically first depictions of the goddess as the personalized wrath of the gods, who victoriously destroys an attacking demon. While the good and benevolent goddess is associated with meeker qualities, Kālī is the untamed female, who is often depicted dancing on the prostrate body of Shiva. The word *kālī* can be traced back to 'black' and 'time', and she is usually depicted with black or blue skin, while the idea of time is connoted in her destructive capacity, as everything perishes over time. However, her tremendous energy can still be harnessed by the respectful devotees for their own purpose: addressing Kālī as 'mother', they invoke her caring instincts and so she destroys threatening evils on their behalf.

It should also be pointed out that the respect for the divine female energy in Hinduism did not manifest itself as an attitude towards actual women. Even though femininity is sometimes credited with the highest possible status and power, this is mostly done from the male point of view and for the spiritual emancipation of male worshippers. It is only relatively late that the authority of female teachers came to be accepted in devotional practice, while in lay life the idea of female power has not managed to disrupt the male-centred social order to any significant degree.

Scriptures. The Hindu tradition recognizes the orthodox status of the Vedic canon, or the *shrūti* ('what is heard', authorless, orally transmitted texts), which is retained in it, similarly to the Christian Bible containing the Judaic Old Testament. However, more central to the new form of the faith are the *smriti* ('what is remembered', texts ascribed to particular authors). Possibly the most influential Hindu scripture is the **Bhagavad-gītā**, a section of the **Mahābhārata** epic, traditionally credited to its legendary author Vyāsa. The text has most likely developed over centuries, starting not earlier than the fourth century BCE and achieving its present form no later than the fifth century CE, with the bulk of the composition originating from around the second–first centuries BCE. A dialogue between the warrior Arjuna and the god Krishna (who is actually none other than Vishnu), the *Gītā*, as it is called for short, touches on many aspects of the emerging Vaishnavist branch of the Hindu doctrine.

Other Hindu scriptures include the *āgamas* ('what has come down'), a diverse group of texts of mostly devotional nature that have been reported to exist (though not necessarily in their present form) by the seventh century CE at the latest, and *purānas*, mainly mythical and historical narratives containing a certain amount of philosophical speculation. These, too, have been credited to Vyāsa, while they are in fact collective works of various authors – the earliest sections date perhaps from the third century CE, the latest to the end of the first millennium, and minor alterations may have been produced even later.

The last group of texts, which forms a tradition of its own in Hindu culture, is called **tantras**. The term (literally 'weaving') means 'theory' or 'method' and denotes a category of scriptures, which is not restricted to Hindu traditions, but also appears in Buddhist and Jain traditions. The tantras are esoteric teachings, which claim to provide the follower with technologies for mobilizing the energies of the body to the pursuit of perfect knowledge. Most notoriously, some of the advocated techniques concentrate on the sexual drive, and tantras indeed abound in sexual imagery, starting with the casting of the creation of the universe in terms of divine intercourse. Other techniques to emancipate the self include the recitation of mantras, which were supposed to bring about the unity of the mind of the follower and the cosmic divine consciousness, and the practice of **mūdras**, specific significant gestures or poses with spiritual meaning, which were used by followers in order to manipulate the psychophysical processes believed to take place in their bodies. One further practice was the contemplation of **mandalas** and *yantras*, or symbolic representations of the universe through religious imagery.

Tantra practice has later split into 'right-handed' and 'left-handed' tantra – while the first sees the sexual imagery as metaphors, the second encourages the followers to actively use sex as well as other sensual pleasures, according to detailed methods, for attaining spiritual progress.

Ideas: internal renunciation and discipline. The Hindu worldview retains much from its Brahmanist past (including the idea of rebirths and liberation from them as its goal), but reconfigures many of those inherited elements just as it does with the Vedic pantheon. One of the tasks the emerging faith has had to face is how to reconcile the more advanced society of its age with the inherited understanding of the world. A prime example of this transformation is the treatment of the heritage of the Vedas and *upanishads* in the *Bhagavad-gītā*.

Nominally the *Bhagavad-gītā* (or *Gītā* for short) is the account of describing how Krishna convinces Arjuna to overcome his existential crisis and to fight, even though the opposite camp contains friends and relatives. However, the text covers much more ground: it presents a model of self-development for the individual, which bridges the gap between the two contradictory ideals of living in the world and renouncing it. The solution proposed by the *Gītā* is striking: one should carry out one's destined duties in the world, but without attachment or desire for their results and rewards. In other words, one should live in the world as if one had already renounced it, because the real renunciation is internal and not an 'external' withdrawal to a hermitage. After all, as we know well from many Western religious testimonies, one can go on to pine for worldly pleasures even while living the life of a recluse. What the *Gītā* recommends is precisely the opposite: to have the mind of an ascetic but the life of a regular member of the society.

yoga   a practical discipline aimed at harnessing the psychophysical resources of an individual for attaining spiritual progress

One of the key concepts of the *Gītā* is *yoga*, and each of its chapters is called the exposition of a specific form of it. The root of the word is cognate to the English 'yoke' and refers to the harnessing of one's psychophysical resources, which are considered to form an integrated system. Perhaps the most adequate equivalent for yoga would be 'discipline' in a sense which unites an academic discipline as a systematized body of knowledge with an order imposed on one's life in pursuit of certain goals. For yogas of different stripe, this goal is always spiritual progress. In due course, Yoga, written with a capital letter, also advanced into a distinct system of Hindu philosophy. In our times, the word is mostly associated with the physical exercises used for shaping the body into a more harmonious state, but fitness was never the goal of yoga practitioners, even if desirable for its positive effect on the mind. For the follower, however, the entire life is converted into yoga in the sense of keeping oneself in check and advancing towards higher mental states.

Acts of sacrifice, giving and austerity are not to be given up, but rather should be performed, as sacrifice, giving and austerity purify even the wise.

My final judgment, Pārtha, is that these actions should be performed out of duty, abandoning attachment and interest in their fruits.

One's prescribed duty should not be renounced; when one renounces his duty out of delusion, that renunciation is to be considered of the nature of darkness.

When one renounces his duty for fear of bodily difficulties, thinking it too troublesome, his renunciation is considered to be of the nature of passion, and thus he does not reap the fruit of his renunciation.

When one performs his prescribed duty having abandoned any attachment and desire for fruits whatsoever, considering only that it ought to be done, his renunciation is of the nature of goodness, o Arjuna.

(*Bhagavad-gītā* 18.5–18.9, trans. Ithamar Theodor)

Practice. Unlike the early Buddhists, the Hindus saw liberation not as 'cessation' or an exit from the cycle of rebirths, but a reunification with the absolute in total bliss. On a practical level, this developed into devotionalism, or *bhakti,* of certain branches of Hinduism that include constant chanting and dances seeking spiritual communion with the god who is worshipped in this way. Different sects proclaim different deities (mostly Vishnu or Shiva or one of their forms) to be the most important object of such devotion, but in practice their approach to these gods is fairly similar. This devotionalism is not a very early phenomenon, but only started to evolve towards the end of the classical period and gained impetus after the Islamic conquest.

---

bhakti devotionalist religious practices (including chanting, dancing, etc.) seeking communion with the absolute, which is personified in a particular deity

---

In the life of most Hindus, however, the divine occupies much less space than for the enthusiastic devotionalist. It is considered proper to offer homage to the gods on a daily basis, but it is not strictly necessary to visit a temple for the purpose – most Hindu homes have an altar where the preferred deities of the family are enshrined, and daily worship can be conducted just by washing them and offering them food and gratitude.

Temples. Another characteristic feature of Hindu religious life is the importance of temples, which in smaller places serve as central nodes for local communities, while larger and more awe-inspiring structures attract pilgrims from afar and contribute to the economy of urban centres often dependent on them.

Given the precision with which Vedic rituals had to be carried out in order to be efficient, the site used for them could most certainly not have been a small matter. However, nothing reliable is known about the precise shape and form of early Brahmanist temples, nor even whether these actually existed as permanent structures or were just sacred enclosures constructed for the purpose, as altars for fire rituals are to this day. (Considerations of safety suggest the latter.) Fragments of Vedic texts provide us with some information about the cosmogonic principles that have to be reflected in the construction of altars, and these became the basis of Indian architectural theory, which was systematized into a special body of knowledge probably in the first centuries CE. One reason for moving towards permanent temple structures was the shift from the Brahmanist idea that gods dwelled in the heavens and messages would reach them by smoke from fire rituals, to the Hindu view that gods can be invited to inhabit images in temples or on the home altar.

During the Gupta empire (third–sixth century CE), Indian architecture started to develop into a refined art form, which was practised both in the building of palaces and elaborate sacred structures that resembled each other as royal and divine power were essentially the same. Still, architectural theory has survived only in fragments and the first extant treatises of Indian architectural theory come from the sixth century CE.

According to these texts, the Hindu temple is a model of the macrocosm, and a sacred site where gods are believed to physically come down and enter the sacred images of various sizes. This makes them available for direct worship, which involves also a physical relationship – from visual contact to bathing, clothing, and offering food to the sculptures of the gods. For the devout, it was important not only to see the images, but also to be seen by the deity residing in them, which is why the statues often have really big eyes. The art of producing these images was strictly regulated and brought great spiritual merit on the artists, if they were successful – an image had not only to conform to the rules, but also be aesthetically pleasing in order for a deity to decide to inhabit it. The procedure of purifying and consecrating the image also involved numerous rituals, for example, covering it with honey and 'opening its eyes' with a special golden needle.

The construction of a temple has to take careful note of the cardinal directions, the trajectory of the sun and other matters that might influence the actual experience of the visitor in the temple. The manner in which temples should be built is spelt out in detail: a site likely to attract divine attention has to be cleared from the local spirits that inhabit it, a circle drawn on the ground, and a small treasure buried in its centre. This will be the site of the inner sanctum of the temple, topped by a tower and only accessible to the priests. A walkway will be built around it, so that the worshippers can circumambulate the sanctum where the god resides. A hall is built in front of the sanctum, where people can worship images and singing and dancing can take place for divine entertainment.

A parallel development to the construction of temples was the local spontaneous emergence of sacred sites. Certain trees were venerated as the abodes of village deities, and offerings were brought to them in hope or gratitude. Some other trees were seen as the Hindu trinity, with Brahmā as the roots, Vishnu as the trunk, and Shiva as the leaves on the branches. Quite often small shrines were erected by such sacred trees, and even after the tree died, the spot was still considered sacred and sometimes commemorated with the erection of a more solid structure. At this point, the principles governing the building of temples had to be observed, which accordingly raised the prestige of the site.

With the higher status came stricter rules. Hindus are obsessed with ritual purity. Strong caste and hygienic restrictions were imposed on the visitors to the temples, thus untouchables (and sometimes even members of lower castes) as well as menstruating women were barred entry to temples because their presence was considered polluting. These rules have been officially abolished in modern India, but reports that the practice is even now still upheld by some temples are being published in the media.

Pilgrimages. Temples had to be built on grounds which had the potential of becoming attractive for the gods, yet they possessed no internal sanctity of their own. However, numerous places in India are traditionally believed to be so-called 'crossing points' (*tirtha*), where the divine world is directly accessible. Millions of Indians flock to these places every year as a visit to a *tirtha* provides great spiritual merit and has a purifying effect on the person. Other reasons to perform pilgrimages include vows or obligations taken on oneself in case of answered prayers, penance for committed misdeeds, and mourning. Many of these 'crossing points' are hard to access and the pilgrims have to endure real hardships during their travel, which have the same cleansing effect as austerities performed by an ascetic. Other, more accessible sites include holy cities such as **Vārānasi**, where there are 84 paved landings on the banks of the Ganges for performing ritual bathing and communion with the gods, some of them reserved for cremation and the dissolution of ashes brought by pilgrims. Incidentally, Vārānasi is revered also by the Jains and Buddhists – the Jains consider it to be the birthplace of two fordmakers, who appeared in this world prior to Mahāvīra, while the historical Buddha is supposed to have delivered his first sermon in this city. Vārānasi thus deservedly enjoys the reputation of the spiritual capital of India, but there are other sacred cities similarly flocked by Hindu pilgrims all around the country.

Philosophical Systems

Background. The Indian philosophical tradition contains six so-called *darshanas* or 'ways of seeing', orthodox philosophical systems that nominally derive from the Vedic tradition. However, it should be pointed out that these systems also often present claims that are far from what the scriptures seem to mean – and some thinkers in some schools explicitly adhere to certain sections of the scripture while rejecting others. Since the textual tradition itself is far from monolithic, such controversies are not unexpected at all.

Most of the *darshanas* claim to rely on foundational texts traditionally dated to the age of the *upanishads*, but may come from a later age, and in any case, their systematic development into separate schools occurred during the classical period, from around the fourth–fifth century CE. Subdivisions occurred later, and in the case of Vedānta, this led to the development of three independent schools with little overlap but for their name. In most cases, however, the branches of particular *darshanas* disagree with each other only on relatively minor points.

Even though the *darshanas* are interesting to us primarily as philosophical systems, the aims of the thinkers who have developed them have not necessarily been philosophical in the strict sense of the word, but much more practical. For example, the need to perform rituals following the Vedic instructions as accurately as possible soon led to speculations about the nature of language, which then developed into theories about the nature of truth, and from there to logic and to ontological commitments about what exists and what does not. Most of the Hindu systems adhere to a belief in an underlying soul or self, but the Buddhist challenge also compelled their proponents to think their theories of personhood through more precisely. As a result, rich and intellectually stimulating discourses have emerged, which continue to inspire philosophical discussion to this day.

Most of these systems have a long history with uncertifiable beginnings, but the majority have acquired the form in which they are known during the classical period, the high tide of Indian culture from approximately the third century CE until the twelfth century. One of the characteristic features of this period is an infatuation with theory. There had to be a theory of everything, and any phenomenon had to be precisely classified in a taxonomical scheme of things. Thus, there were nine mental states, each of which had a colour of its own and a link to a certain deity, as there were six proper ways to conduct politics and eight correct ways to scratch your partner with fingernails during sex. The more philosophically inclined thinkers developed similar taxonomies for all phenomena that they were discussing, and sought to define as precisely as possible the relationships between them. For example, Kumārila (c. 700) of the Mīmānsā school distinguished between four different kinds of non-being.

This long development also means that the Hindu philosophical systems were all subjected to varying degrees of influence of Buddhism, which remained the other dominant intellectual trend of the era. Indeed, many philosophers dedicate a significant proportion of their work to the repudiation of Buddhist arguments that are incompatible with their Hindu convictions. Each of these schools also has a history of internal dispute. Some of these schools have a tradition that has remained alive to this day, others, however, have become extinct.

Common topics. The exposition of Indian philosophical systems frequently follows the line of reasoning of the proponents of these systems themselves. The problem with such an approach is the resulting difficulty in comparing their ideas to each other. Similarly, it makes it harder to spot the problematic aspects of these systems, at least unless they are a reason for debate within those schools themselves or have elicited forceful critique from the outside. However, all *darshanas* address a number of common topics, even though some systems pay more attention to only some of them. These include the *nature of existence*, as it is quite obvious that the concept of being, or being real, may have a different meaning for different thinkers. For example, Shankara of the Advaita Vedānta school admits that objects of perception exist, and can constitute separate links of causal chains, while they are ultimately unreal, because only the unchanging, eternal, absolute consciousness called *Brahman* is real in this sense of the word. If something can exist without being real, there is certainly reason to look at the issue more closely.

Second, we should address the question of *what exists*, real or otherwise, because here, too, the discrepancies between the systems are numerous. A closely related issue is that of *categories* or *qualities* that entities have – each *darshana* has its own system of them, and quite often the lists of categories are debated between the adherents of one school. What we should perhaps be more concerned with, however, is how these categories/qualities relate to the way the world is and the form in which it appears to us. This, in turn, leads to the problem of *causality* and *change*: accounts of how these are possible and come about also differ between systems.

The next item to be discussed is that of the *mind* – the ego, the self, consciousness, person, or whatever substratum is proposed for the role of the perceiver of reality and the agent of good and bad deeds. Indian philosophy offers far more sophisticated constructions of psychological processes than Western philosophy does, and uses a much broader range of terms for mental phenomena. Some of these terms have different meanings in different *darshanas*. A subtopic of this is the *cognitive process*, the status of perceptions, logical inferences, memory, and knowledge. Some of these debates are resemblant of the issues that are currently debated in Western neuroscience and philosophical discussions of artificial intelligence. Is the cognitive process fully describable in physical terms? Does it matter whether the cognitions are carried by a live consciousness? What is the ontological status of the elements of that process?

Another aspect of personhood that all *darshanas* take up is *agency*, or the status of acts. In order to remain orthodox, they have to accept the teaching of transmigration and the concomitant doctrine of karma, or the influence of persons' acts on their future destiny. However, here, too, the *darshanas* offer a range of possible interpretations, dependent on the rest of their doctrine. Finally, each *darshana* also has a vision of *mental emancipation*, or liberation from the unenlightened view of reality. Some of these are bleak and unappealing, others more inspiring, and some schools, such as Mīmānsā, seem to have incorporated the idea unwillingly as an alternative to a plain pursuit of the pleasures of a paradise.

There are not only differences between all six systems (and sometimes between branches within them), but also significant similarities, in particular between the Nyāya and Vaisheshika, on the one hand, and the Sānkhya and the Yoga, on the other hand. Mīmānsā and Vedānta form a pair in a different way – although there is not much in common in their teachings, they are considered to be parts of the same endeavour of 'investigation' (which the word *mīmānsā* stands for). Thus what is usually known as Mīmānsā is technically called Pūrva Mīmānsā, or 'prior investigation', dealing with the texts of the Vedas and other sacred texts, while Vedānta is also known as Uttara Mīmānsā, or 'ulterior investigation', which systematizes the message of the *upanishads*. As said, the name of Vedānta is itself an umbrella term for three mutually incompatible systems, each of which presents its own, original, and coherent view of how to interpret the scriptural heritage.

Nyāya and Vaisheshika. These two systems provide the most convenient point of entry into Hindu thought for the Western reader, since they present an effort to posit a common-sense worldview that would not contradict Vedic scripture.

Both systems assume the reality of the external world, which is composed of self-identical objects that can be divided into constituent parts, until we come down to the indivisible atomic level. Both schools also assume the reality of the perceiving subject, even if the cognitive process itself is described slightly differently than what we might expect. The difference between the schools lies primarily in their focus: the **Nyāya** is more concerned with logic and the correct ways of ascertaining what we know about the world, while the Vaisheshika addresses more metaphysical questions.

Ideas: the world as a logical structure. The criterion of being real, or existing, which are synonymous terms for these schools, consists in a continuity independent of observation. Nyāya and Vaisheshika believe that the world has a logical structure, and the goal of intellectual inquiry is to understand it. Vaisheshika, in particular, has developed an atomist theory of minimal entities, which can be combined into substances that have qualities, some of them general, others particular. All of these are parts of the objective world, which changes according to objective rules. Objects have essences which are separate from the essences of their constituents. Being something entails belonging to a logical kind, a universal. Nyāya and Vaisheshika were 'realist' in the medieval European sense of the word in that they credited these universals with a real existence. Thus a pot is a 'pot' because it partakes of 'potness'. This is also the reason why an object is more than the sum of its constituents – each existing thing has its own emergent quality of 'beingitselfness'.

There are also objective laws or principles that regulate the relationships between such essences. Particular things can interact according to these laws and produce causal chains. However, the result always inheres in the cause from the beginning – this is precisely how these objective essences of things form the comprehensive logical structure of reality.

Whatever divine agency can be observed in the world consists in precisely the enactment of these natural laws – any omnipotence as the capacity to suspend natural laws is inconceivable. Therefore, the blueprint of the world according to Nyāya and Vaisheshika is largely mechanistic, which provides cause for optimism: liberation is supposed to be reached through objective knowledge, and since the order of things follows clear rules, these can be discovered and known.

Nyāya and Vaisheshika share the belief that, to a large extent, the process of cognition also follows such a mechanistic blueprint. According to this view, cognition equals consciousness, which always has a content – it has to be a consciousness of something and not consciousness just by itself. A material object causes the appearance of a cognition of it, which is also material. However, these schools distinguish between 'mind' and 'self' in a different way than most others. Nyāya and Vaisheshika consider the capacity to process cognitions to be a quality of the 'self', or *ātman*, rather than the 'mind' (*manas*). The latter is simply a bit of mental machinery that delivers cognitions for the self to organize and process. Selfhood therefore comes with a distinct mental agency, it is an instance, a mental thing, and its history – the memory that it carries – affects its actions. In other words, it cannot be trusted always to deliver correct judgements on its own.

Whatever the self processes into a mental representation therefore has to undergo a further process, that of validation by logical proof. This is where Nyāya excels. Its logic was recognized as a major achievement also by thought systems that did not accept its metaphysics – even Buddhist monks were required to read Nyāya treatises during their studies.

Sānkhya and Yoga. The terms *sānkhya* and *yoga* predate the actual systems bearing these names. Both terms are met in the *upanishads* as well as the *Bhagavad-gītā* as distinct forms of knowledge and practice, and – perhaps in order to ground their authority in the tradition – the philosophical systems also pick up and develop some of the key concepts that the *Gītā* associates with them. The first texts summarizing the positions of **Sānkhya** as a distinct school most probably come from between 200 and 350 CE, while **Yoga** is grounded in the *Yogasūtra*, composed most likely sometime before or around 400 CE, although the tradition credits it with a much earlier date.

These two systems also form a pair and share most of their metaphysical positions, which have been developed mostly by Sānkhya thinkers, while the representatives of Yoga have dedicated their attention to practical ways of extracting an individual from the chains of being.

Ideas: the two tiers of existence. Existence, as these schools understand it, is strictly two-tiered: on the one hand, there is matter – divided into crude and subtle sorts – on the other, there are individual souls. Unlike some other schools of Indian thought, which posit the fundamental unity of consciousness, it is the souls that are many in Sānkhya, while crude matter is only of one kind, just organized into a variety of forms by the multiple combinations of three types of subtle matter called *guna*. This word points to qualities or categories in most other thought systems, but here its varieties are thought of as physical, even if invisible. They correspond to the three mingling elements mentioned in the

Bhagavad-gītā – the good, the passionate and the dark. In principle, everything exists from the very beginning, and anything that is produced as the result of some activity, has to be inherent in at least one of the elements of that activity, which is its cause. As a result of such processes, a material and physical plurality emerges that has some structural similarity to how souls are. That similarity causes the entanglement of the souls in a world with which, in principle, they have nothing in common.

This process takes place in the sphere of cognition, which, according to these systems, is a mechanical process, as the intellect is physical and so are sense impressions – just as some contemporary neuroscientific and physicalist explanations of consciousness also see them. The soul, interspersed with materiality, starts to take the cognitions of the material intellect as its own, a little like the consciousness of a person might naturalize an artificial limb or teeth implants as parts of their organism. The mind in the two systems is thus also dual: the non-material soul has a physical counterpart, with which it starts to mistakenly identify itself. Agency takes place on the material level, and the intermingling of the three types of subtle matter bears the traces of individual karma, which predestines the soul to reincarnation. Liberation, accordingly, consists in the separation of the individual soul from the material entanglement, resulting in pure bliss uncontaminated by sensual perceptions.

While the two systems mostly share this metaphysical foundation, there is a difference between them that consists in their attitude towards the divine. Sānkhya is atheistic and does not rely on an absolute that is independent of matter. Yoga, however, is theistic, and posits an ideal soul of the Lord, Īshvara, which is free from material entanglement, neither the creator nor the absolute, but a guide for the follower towards spiritual emancipation.

Mīmānsā and Vedānta. The last pair of Hindu philosophical systems is Mīmānsā and Vedānta. These two have very little in common in content, but have been paired as complementary – while **Mīmānsā** is sometimes also called Pūrva Mīmānsā, or 'first philosophy', **Vedānta** goes by the parallel name of Uttara Mīmānsā, or 'final philosophy'. The idea of finality or an achieved goal is also implicit in the word *vedānta*, which literally means 'end of Vedas/knowledge'. However, the label of Vedānta actually comprises three quite different systems, the non-dualist (*advaita*), the unity-in-complexity (*vishishtadvaita*) and the dualist (*dvaita*) schools, among which the non-dualist version is the most influential.

Mīmānsā ideas: finding your place in the sacred order. The word *mīmānsā* actually means 'investigation' or even 'exegesis', rather than 'philosophy', and the school emerged from the need to investigate the texts of the Vedas for their ulterior meaning. However, the gods glorified in the Vedic hymns are, for Mīmānsā theorists, of relatively little importance. Instead they focus on the eternal and sacred order of dharma that the Vedas express in their view. To exist means to occupy a place in that order. Reality is in constant change, but the change is far from random, it is governed by rules, which are derived from that same order. Karma, or the trace of actions, operates in the framework of these rules. Therefore, the Mīmānsā view of causality regards results as not only inevitably following from causes, but already inherent in them, as an oak is inherent in the acorn. Each individual thing is charged with its own energy (called *shakti*, but unrelated to female divinity) that has led it to develop from its initial form towards a mature result.

Mīmānsā also presents us with a rather original theory of cognition. While other schools usually stress the distorted character of the reality that reaches us in the form of sense-data, Mīmānsā views cognition as an act undertaken from the part of the individual subject, a movement in the direction of the universal order. Therefore, at the moment of its occurrence, each act of cognition is truthful and provides us with valid knowledge. Errors occur, of course, but only as a result of distortions that are already present in the mind. As to selfhood, this was a matter of controversy between different Mīmānsā thinkers. What they agreed upon was that the self had to be eternal and, from the point of view of individuals, the entity that united their various bodily forms and states of mind for the entire duration of their life from birth to death. But whether it was to be identified with the whole of consciousness or separated from the apparatus of cognition, and whether it was itself conscious, remained a topic of debate.

Early Mīmānsā was not very much concerned with liberation, as it did not ascribe much importance to the *upanishads* in comparison with the earlier layers of the Vedic corpus. Its ethical views were limited to instructing people to perform their duty within the universal order, which would lead to a better rebirth or, eventually, paradise. When liberation became the common topic of Hindu schools, however, Mīmānsā thinkers proposed their own, rather uninspiring versions of it. Depending on their view of the self, the exhaustion of negative karma would have the result of either eternal abiding in pure consciousness or a state where consciousness, too, had been left behind.

Advaita Vedānta. In modern times, **Advaita Vedānta** has evolved into the most influential orthodox Indian thought system and, in many ways, it is the source of Western ideas about Hindu philosophy, which is why it merits a little more attention than other *darshanas*. Though Advaita Vedānta is the oldest of the three schools of the Vedānta family, it is still relatively young compared to other schools. Its most important systematizer and proponent was **Shankara**, who most probably lived in the eighth century CE, was born in a Brāhman family of South India, and travelled extensively during his life, meeting various teachers of different persuasions and studying the Vedic tradition with them. Traditional biographies end his life at the early age of 32, while some scholars think this must be untrue, given the large number of probably authentic works ascribed to him. While it is true that he inherited a few of his philosophical positions from his teacher, and the teacher of his teacher, it is nonetheless Shankara who raised the school of Advaita Vedānta to its prominent position among the Hindu *darshanas*, where it still remains.

Ideas: existence, reality, and superimposition. One of the most characteristic features of Advaita Vedānta is the separation of existence and reality, which is presented to us as the rather counterintuitive idea that to exist is not enough in order to be real. Evidently, we need to accept that 'existence' and 'reality' do not necessarily mean the same thing for Indian thinkers as they do for non-Indian thinkers. But the difference may not be so crucial or incomprehensible after all. For example, in our own lifeworld, we admit that quite a few things are socially or culturally constructed and not 'real' in themselves, even though they exist and play a part in our life. Thus 'money' is what we call pieces of paper or metal, or even certain ways how electrons are organized in a certain element of server hardware, and yet it can be the cause of many things. Evidently its 'moneyness' is something we collectively superimpose on these objects (for the sake of clarity, let us talk only about cash), and even these objects may lose their 'moneyness', in financial reforms or when the states that have issued them lose power. If we say that money 'exists' because of this moneyness that has been superimposed on it by our minds, but 'really' we are only dealing with pieces of metal and paper, we are getting closer to the difference that Advaita Vedānta thinkers make between these concepts, except that with them, the distinction goes much deeper. Superimposition (*adhyāsa*) of an ignorance-based illusion on the absolute reality is what ultimately lies behind any particularity that exists for us. 'Materiality', for example, is no more solid than socially constructed 'moneyness': all things in our world are not real, nor are we ourselves as the perceiving and acting subjects, even though we exist. The only real thing is the pure, contentless, eternal, uncon-ditioned consciousness that pervades everything, everywhere and forever, and which cannot really be captured by words, but is called *Brahman*, because it has to be named somehow. Just as it has been told in the *upanishads*, it is this *Brahman* that the inner core of each individual, or *ātman*, is identical with. But even though *Brahman* and *ātman* are both contentless consciousness, this does not mean that *ātman* is restricted only to conscious beings. On the contrary, what we normally consider to be our consciousness, is the mechanical working of superimposed appearances and not the real thing itself. Most beings are too entangled in these appearances to be able to free themselves from them, but it is not impossible. From within the illusory materiality, when we try to grasp

Brahman with the same sensory apparatus that we use for the world, we fail, of course. What we are able to conceptualize, however, is a sense of divinity – not really *Brahman*, but our mistaken understanding of it. Although this divinity, or **Īshvara**, is no more real than we are, it is able to drag us out of the ignorance that has produced the world for us. Thus, religious practice and veneration of gods (Vishnu in particular) was not quite pointless.

The origin of illusions. The concept of ignorance is the least satisfying aspect of Advaita Vedānta as an intellectual achievement. We are told that it is ignorance (*avidya*) that is to blame for the emergence of all these superimposed illusions of particular existence, but we are never told where this ignorance comes from or how it works. For Shankara, the *Brahman* itself is emphatically not its source. The world just is, because there is ignorance. Nonetheless, the theory of causation that Advaita Vedānta proposes credits *Brahman* with the only real causality. Similarly to most of the systems reviewed until now, Advaita Vedānta believes that the result inheres in the cause, and the only real cause is the only real existent, that is, *Brahman*. However, *Brahman* is not actively involved in the production of these illusions. The simile often used for the purpose is that of a rope mistaken for a snake. The rope is the cause of alarm in the person who thinks it is a snake, but it is that person's ignorance, not the rope itself, that has produced the illusion. Just as the rope has not changed or done anything, when it seems to be a snake, so is the *Brahman* without agency and unchanging.

Some later Vedānta thinkers started to re-evaluate this position and to impute to *Brahman* a greater role in the appearance of the illusory world, especially because some passages in the *upanishads* have lent credibility to such assertions. The concept of Īshvara has helped to bridge the transition, and in the school of Vishishtadvaita Vedānta the role of the absolute as the basis of the world that we perceive has been clearly formulated.

Shankara and Buddhism. The idea of the phenomenal world emerging for us because of ignorance is very similar to the position of Buddhism and, indeed, Shankara has, not without some reason, been accused of being a crypto-Buddhist. Doubts in his orthodoxy can also be supported by his selective view of Vedic scriptures: he did not accept all of them unconditionally, but only those that conformed to his own understanding of the self and the Absolute. The rest was not necessarily untrue in Shankara's view, merely inefficient: someone who would want to spend time in paradise could, indeed, learn the procedures from them of how to accrue good karma through rituals. However, Vedānta was a higher-order truth meant for those whom paradise did not interest. This, too, was a view that he shared with the Buddhists.

And yet, the differences between Shankara's philosophy and Buddhism are more significant than their similarities. First of all, the belief in an unchanging Absolute is quite alien to Buddhist thought that is grounded in the transience of everything without exception. This is a point Shankara himself often underscores in his writings. Given that he wrote after a multitude of sophisticated Buddhist thinkers had provided their worldview with detailed philosophical defences, it is understandable that he also had to face their counterarguments. We can perhaps say that Shankara's relation to Buddhism is comparable to that of the later (post-Buddha) *upanishads* to the initial teachings of Buddhism: a reasonable gambit that incorporated some of the insights of the opponents in order to strengthen one's own argumentation without compromising on core issues.

Vishishtadvaita Vedānta. Literally, the word *vishishtadvaita* can be interpreted as 'qualified non-duality', but it has been pointed out that such a translation is misleading. A better equivalent would be 'unity-in-complexity', as the system grants the status of reality to both the ultimate and the empirical. The school was developed in the eleventh–twelfth centuries in order to provide devotional religious practice with a reliable philosophical basis. The tradition grounds itself in the work of earlier thinkers, but probably in order to enhance its authority rather than because of actual mentionable intellectual debt to them.

For the Vishishtadvaita Vedānta, empirical reality is real. It is dependent on the absolute, yet distinct from it. And the absolute is not without qualities, as existence without qualities is considered to be a contradiction in terms. The absolute also has a will, and wills empirical reality, which is its ongoing, constantly changing creation. In this way Vishishtadvaita has removed many issues with which the Advaita model presented us, such as how the world comes into existence if the *Brahman* is not to be held responsible for it, but yet the only causality of whatever is caused. The Vishishtadvaita model of causality is different: the result is inherent in the cause, but only as a potentiality, which may or may not be actualized and become real. As an actual reality, the result is different from its cause. We thus have a plurality of phenomena on the one hand, and an unchanging primary cause (*Brahman*) on the other. They are inseparable, but the relationship is not symmetrical. Phenomena depend on the absolute, while the absolute does not depend on them. (Even though the term *Brahman* is retained in Vishishtadvaita theory, for all practical purposes the absolute is identified with the god Vishnu.)

Something similar can be said about individual souls. They are particular, substantial, and independent of the bodies that they inhabit. Embodiment, which occurs as a result of past karma, is something without which souls cannot really express their dedication to the absolute. Karma, in the meantime, does not operate as a law of nature like, for example, Sānkhya thinkers believe, but is always and only effectuated by the will of the absolute god. And yet the decision of the god is never wrong, it is absolutely just and corresponds to what the past actions of the soul have merited. The relationship with the self and consciousness is also fairly simple: consciousness is something that the self has, not what it is. Thoughts are its acts, its properties, not its parts. And our perception of ourselves as persons is not a distorted view that has to be corrected through liberation – we see ourselves as we really are. The relationship of souls to the bodies they inhabit is analogous to the relationship of the absolute to these souls – a particularization, an unsymmetrical dependence. Liberation for Vishishtadvaita is the realization of this dependence by the soul. It is not something it can achieve on its own, though – it is only available through the will, or grace, of the absolute. But it is only bestowed on those who practise *bhakti*, and thereby bring themselves nearer to god.

Dvaita Vedānta. This last 'dualist' school of the Vedānta family was developed in the thirteenth century. Critical of both Advaita and Vishishtadvaita, this school claimed that the souls and the absolute are different in their nature. Similarly to Vishishtadvaita, Dvaita distinguishes between the independent reality of the absolute and the dependent phenomenal reality (sentient souls and non-sentient matter), but differently from its predecessors, Dvaita claims that the dependent reality is also essentially different from the absolute, its cause. But the absolute is in this case not an active, pre-existent cause or creator, it is just the necessary condition for the existence of the universe, which is constantly sustained by it. Even though the universe is caused by the absolute, it is also without beginning and end, and its existence is independent of consciousness. Creation, in this sense, is ordering and organizing rather than producing the world *ex nihilo*. This school, too, identifies the absolute with Vishnu.

From the point of view of contemporary philosophy, Dvaita Vedānta advances an interesting theory of positive, constitutive difference. The difference from everything else is the constitutive feature of each particular object, its individuating form. It is also this difference that assures the entity of its continuity, as it continues to be different from all other entities in the same, individual way. Dvaita distinguishes between kinds of differences on a general level, but this does not mean that the differences between things are essentially similar: each entity has its own way of differing from the rest of reality. This is also how individual souls differ, both from each other and from the absolute, and this difference is not given up even in liberation. The latter is only possible through an act of love by the absolute: while those who do not express their devotion to Vishnu through the practice of *bhakti* will never achieve it, those who do are not contributing towards it either, as only the absolute is able to provide it.

Kashmir Shaivism. Although traditionally not listed among the *darshanas*, the philosophical schools developed in Kashmir in the eighth to eleventh centuries also deserve our attention. While neighbouring areas were already fighting back the onslaught of Muslims from the West, the successive mountain kingdoms of Kashmir kept their independence and the region remained the centre of rich intellectual life, both Hindu and Buddhist. A key characteristic of Hindu thought in Kashmir was its reliance on esoteric tantras and *āgamas* rather than mainstream texts. Even though some followers of the teachings now collectively called 'Kashmir Shaivism' believed that one should observe the traditional duties associated with one's caste in daily life, this was only conducive towards a better rebirth, while ultimate liberation could only be attained by an initiated few, with the help of secret teachings. According to one influential version of these, release from karmic bondage is an effect of the actions of Shiva on the soul. By its nature, the soul is equal to god, but impeded from realizing this unity by 'dirt', which is material and attaches itself to the soul, and has to be removed by action. The goal is thus the recognition of Shiva in oneself, realizing one's own divinity, rather than the dissolution of one's self in an external absolute, as *upanishad*-based philosophies have taught.

Perhaps the most influential thinker among the Kashmir Shaivites is **Abhinavagupta** (tenth–eleventh century), a scholar of a radical tantric school, which rejected all conventional morality as illusory. Unlike other schools, the initiation ritual of his cult was supposed to remove caste membership and other earthly connections from the follower along with any obligation to keep precepts and uphold taboos. The initiates worshipped the goddess Kālī in her most frightening shape, as well as other female divinities, whose supernatural powers they aspired to acquire by offerings of impure and powerful substances, such as blood, alcohol, and sexual fluids. While this may sound rather eccentric, the philosophy they professed was intellectually sound and coherent. Abhinavagupta authored a number of treatises containing detailed critiques of other traditions and commentaries to the works of his own predecessors, in which he defended a philosophy of extreme idealism, rejecting the reality of material objects as well as the unmoving absolute of Advaita Vedānta and the impermanence of being as theorized by Buddhists. According to him, reality was one, conscious and characterized by internal dynamism, symbolically represented by the copulation of Shiva and Shakti. This reality is only partially accessible to human cognition in the guise of mental representations. However, it is emphatically not the product of individual minds, but perhaps more like the Platonic world of ideas without a real material world manifesting them. These ideas are not self-reliant, but themselves expressions of the universal consciousness which, in its natural state, constantly abides in the kind of bliss human beings experience during orgasm.

Kashmir Shaivism went underground soon after the Mongol conquest of the area in the thirteenth century, and in the fourteenth century Kashmir converted to Islam. It is thought that the tradition continued in secret, but it was openly revived in the twentieth century by scholar-practitioners and soon started to attract academic interest.

Cārvāka. The last to be mentioned among the classical philosophical systems is the heterodox and materialist school called **Cārvāka**. Nothing reliable is known about its proponents and the original works of the school have been lost. But critique of Cārvāka continues well into the sixteenth century, as supporters of other traditions judge their own views to be superior to that school on moral grounds, so at least on hearsay level the teachings of that school must have persisted. Not acknowledging the authority of the Vedas, Cārvāka thinkers are supposed to have held that only perception presents us with valid knowledge, while inference and other mental operations necessarily distort it. As a result, they claim that any positing of beings or powers that cannot be perceived is groundless and the same applies to the human soul. Theories about what happens after death cannot be verified because of the same reason. As a result, Cārvāka thinkers reportedly propose a hedonist ethics, saying that the maximizing of pleasure in this life is the only reasonable strategy. This is also the reason why they are criticized by other schools as preachers of immorality and egoism.

Indian Worldviews Under Muslim Rule

Background. Neighbouring Muslim rulers started to invade the north-western regions of the Indian subcontinent in the eighth century, but a more permanent Islamic polity was established there only in 1206 as the Delhi sultanate. Successive conquerors overthrew each other until the last of these, Babur, the founder of the Mughal empire, arrived in 1526, retreating from his previous kingdoms of Fergana and Samarkand that fell to invaders from the north. The Mughal rule proved to be the most persistent and was overcome only by the British in the nineteenth century. Under Mughal emperors, India was again mostly united and enjoyed a period of economic growth as well as a cultural revival, exemplified in the splendid architectural monuments of the age such as the Taj Mahal, the mausoleum erected in 1632–1653 for the favourite wife of one of the Mughal rulers.

However, the Muslim conquest also signified the end of the classical period of Indian culture, even though the initial hostile attitude of the Muslim rulers towards Hindu symbols, resulting in the destruction of many temples, was soon replaced by a more tolerant attitude of cultural coexistence. Sanskrit nonetheless lost its prominent position as the main vehicle of literary expression, because Arabic, the sacred language of Islam, and Persian, the literary language of the conquerors, claimed their share of the intellectual space. Arabic needed to be studied by Muslim scholars because the Islamic scripture of the Qur'ān was believed to contain direct divine revelation, dictated to the prophet Muhammad by the archangel Gabriel, which might become distorted in translation. Persian was the language of the administration and secular culture, as it had the capacity to culturally unite the diverse tribes of Turkic and Indo-Iranian origin, who made up the body of the conquering armies and their elites, and it naturally retained the position in the newly established Mughal imperial court. At the same time, the retreat of Sanskrit also gave an impetus to modern Indian languages to develop, especially when one of the spoken idioms, now called Urdu, started to be written down in a modified Arabic script from the thirteenth century onwards. Those emphatically defining themselves as non-Muslims began to use the native devanāgarī script for the same spoken language, calling it Hindi, around the same time. The two languages started to develop separately – for new concepts, Hindi created words using Sanskrit roots, while Urdu used Persian and Arabic borrowings for the same purpose.

Another strong blow to the tradition was the destruction of the Buddhist institutions. After centralized rule had declined during the period before the Muslim invasion, much of aristocratic patronage had switched from Buddhist institutions to the emergent Hindu schools. This did not affect the Buddhist monasteries of northern India, however, as these were situated on major trade routes and benefited from the traffic of people, goods, and ideas. Monasteries and universities, great centres of learning and debate, were attracting intellectually minded people from far and wide, and over the centuries they had acquired large libraries of manuscripts as well as other treasures. Many of these were ransacked by Muslim chieftains and the residents were killed or dispersed. The role of Buddhism in Indian intellectual life became virtually negligible as a result for many centuries until it was revived in modern times.

Islam is a strictly monotheistic religion in the same tradition with Judaism and Christianity. It mostly accepts the narrative of the Old Testament and also recognizes Jesus as one of its prophets, but denies his divinity. The last and most important prophet of the religion is Muhammad (570?–632), who managed to convert a sizeable number of Arabs to his faith and mobilized them into building a new world-state. In the fourth generation of rulers, Islam split into two opposing factions, Sunni and Shi'a, and this division is a major cause of conflict in the Muslim world to this day.

Islamic thought developed in dense contact with the inheritance of ancient Greek philosophy and is predominantly rational, consisting largely of successive efforts to combine monotheistic theology with Aristotelian thought and polemical responses to these. It is indeed the influence of Islamic philosophy that produced the revival of ancient Greek philosophy in Europe, following the theory of Ibn Rushd (Averroes, 1126–1198) that divine and rational truth are two forms of the same thing, and if revelations seem to be in conflict with rational argument, they need to be reread as metaphors for the expression of hidden meaning, and not verbatim. However, Islam also has mystical undercurrents such as Sufism, sometimes accused of heresy, but widely influential in devotional poetry.

Islam prohibits the forceful imposition of the faith on believers of other religions, but encourages voluntary conversion. During the early centuries of Muslim rule, Hindus were able to follow their own religion and taxes on non-Muslims were not regularly imposed, although many poorer Hindus converted because of economic reasons. The Muslim rulers depended heavily on the support of upper-class Hindus and also had many capable non-Muslims as officers in its army, for whom separate facilities were provided for their religious needs. Efforts to convert were undertaken, but without significant results. The success of Islam as a mass religion in India started in the thirteenth century, first with the outcasts and lower castes, who were excluded from social mobility by the Hindu system, but also as a result of interfaith marriages in the merchant class. By the time of the Mughals, India had a sizeable population of Muslims of local origin, even though exact numbers are unknown as a population census was first carried out in India only in the nineteenth century.

As to Islamic thought, India has contributed less to its development than might perhaps be expected. One of the reasons for this might be that the conquest of the subcontinent was finalized more or less at the same time that the Mongols destroyed Baghdad (1258) and subdued the caliphate, putting an end to the bustling intellectual life in the heartlands of the Islamic world. Indian Muslim scholars were mostly content with commenting on earlier works, composing technical study aids and writing for their local audiences. They had no ambition to engage in a wider dialogue with the rest of the Islamic world and therefore produced little of lasting influence.

The same cannot be said about syncretic movements, which sought a common ground for the religious aspirations of people as human beings, apart from their being Muslims and Hindus. It has been pointed out that the Islamic stress on strict monotheism and the equality of worshippers has had a strong impact on the *bhakti* movement, which indeed increased its influence in Hindu circles under Muslim rule. Identifying the absolute with a particular god did bring the foundations of the Hindu faith closer to monotheism, as the other gods, although retaining their divinity, were now reducible to the main one, and thus became something like the angelic figures that also abound in Islam. Many religious visionaries in India tried to find a common ground between the two faiths. The greatest of them was **Kabīr** (fourteenth–fifteenth century), whose name signifies just that ('great'). We know little about his life except that he was born into a recently converted Muslim family, studied with a Hindu teacher, and became critical of both religions. Although the worldview expressed in his poetry draws on both traditions, he belongs to neither, nor is it a synthesis of Hindu and Muslim thought, but an emancipation from both, which is what he recommended to his followers. The popularity of his devotional poetry grew quickly, many of his texts were set to music and sung by *bhakti* worshippers. During his lifetime, he was supposedly also abused and hated by Hindu and Muslim zealots alike, but after his death he was claimed by both traditions as their own. His poetry has been preserved in several collections and it has contributed in a major way to the emergence of the Sikh faith.

> The Hindu says Ram is the Beloved,
> the Turk says Rahim.
> Then they kill each other.
> No one knows the secret.
> They buzz their mantras from house to house, puffed with pride.
> The pupils drown along with their gurus. In the end they're sorry.
> Kabir says, listen saints:
> they're all deluded!
> Whatever I say, nobody gets it. It's too simple.
>   (Kabīr, *Bījak* I: 4, trans. Linda Hess and Shukdeo Singh)

The attitude of tolerance and mutual recognition became the official policy of the Mughal empire under its greatest ruler, **Akbar** (1542–1605; the name also signifies 'greatest'), who occupied his throne for the same period as Elizabeth I in England, plus a few more years before and after, and with a similarly positive effect. Having inherited the empire amid rebellions and strife, Akbar soon established himself as a just ruler, who was able to pardon his erstwhile enemies, and the same generosity was extended to the common people. He abolished the tax that non-Muslims had to pay as well as pilgrim taxes for Hindu holy places. He promoted those loyal to him, fairly and without regard to their faith. But he did not endorse Hindu customs wholesale, for example, he prohibited the self-immolation of widows (*sati*) who had not consummated their marriage (that is, very young girls) and strongly discouraged the custom also for older women.

Akbar was very interested in cultural and religious matters, looking for an ideology that would suit the needs of his religiously diverse empire. Thus, for example, he commissioned a large translation effort of scriptures (as well as secular literature) from Sanskrit into Persian. He also organized a hall of debates on religious matters, initially reserved only for the Muslim clergy, but as the leading mullahs were unable to agree or even behave in an orderly manner, he opened the debates to other religions, including not only all domestic ones, but also Zoroastrians and even Christians, whom he invited to his court from the Portuguese mission in Goa. Akbar also met with the leader of the Sikhs and reportedly even gave their community a large donation of land, on which the Golden Temple was later built. Yet nobody convinced him. Scholars disagree whether he finally really decided to establish a new religion of which he was himself the central figure, as his traditionalist Muslim critics have claimed, or only a religious order of people committed to the same kind of tolerance he held dear. In any case, nothing much came of it. After his reign, his followers mostly continued a similar policy of tolerance and coexistence, even though certain political conflicts, for example with the Sikhs, have retrospectively been given religious colouring.

The Sikhs. The syncretic tradition of the Sikhs was established by **Nānak** (1469–1539), an approximate contemporary of Martin Luther, who was born in a merchant family near Lahore in Punjab (now Pakistan). As the Sikh scripture came to include many texts by or attributed to the poet Kabīr, and there is some evidence of Nānak belonging to a group of his followers, it is sometimes said that the Sikh faith came to embody the philosophy expressed in Kabīr's poetry, a claim disputed by other scholars who insist that the ideas behind Nānak's reform movement were primarily his own. The Sikh tradition has filled Nānak's biography with incredibly auspicious events from early on, but we do actually know some things about his life, for example, that he was married and had two sons. Shortly after the birth of his second child, he evidently had a religious experience. After that, he began teaching and travelling around the country and even beyond its borders, expounding his new faith. Towards the end of his life, having gathered a following, he again settled down in Punjab and established a religious centre in the village that he chose for his new residence.

Thus Nānak became what the Sikhs call their first *guru*, or 'teacher', the spiritual leader of the new community. Altogether, their tradition counts 11 gurus, but only 10 of those are people. The eleventh and final one is the Sikh scripture entitled *Ādi Granth* ('first book'), a collection of around 6000 hymns, mostly by Nānak and his successors, but also including many texts by Kabīr.

Even though the message of Nānak had been one of solidarity and transcending all religious boundaries, the emerging Sikh community had to contend with the hostility of outsiders. The fifth guru, the compiler of the scripture, was arrested,

The scripture of *Ādi Granth* is the final authority on the teaching and, as decreed by the 10th guru, there should be no other leader of Sikhs after him, except for this text. There is supposed to be a copy of it in every Sikh home, every morning the book is opened at a random page and the first passage is read aloud as the message for the day. Every evening the book is closed again. For the global Sikh community, a daily message is presently sent out from the Golden Temple of Amritsar.

Ādi Granth is written down in the Gurmukhi ('facing the teacher') script, one of the two alphabets now used for the Punjabi language, but the text is, in fact, written in a mix of languages, including not only Punjabi, Hindi, Sanskrit, and Persian, but also a number of non-literary languages spoken in the region at the time of its composition. About one sixth of the hymns are by Nānak, but almost one third of the book is written by the fifth guru, who was also its editor. The main body of the book is organized according to types of music, according to which the hymns are supposed to be performed. The section best known to Sikhs is the beginning of the book, a short mantra condensing the essentials of the faith followed by a hymn that is to be recited daily.

tortured, and killed on the orders of Akbar's son and successor on the Mughal throne. Narratives differ whether this was because the guru had blessed one of the monarch's enemies for rebellion, or because of the increasing influence of the Sikh community in northern India. In any case, the sixth guru, who was also the son of his predecessor, established the rule that Sikh men had to carry arms and be able to defend their community against aggression. A century later, the tenth guru upped the stakes by establishing the order of 'the pure ones' within the Sikh community – dedicated warriors ready to die for their guru without asking questions. From those times onwards, Sikhs have been trusted allies for some and feared enemies for others, until the Sikh kingdom of Punjab was defeated by the overwhelming forces of the British after two bloody wars in 1849. At present, Sikhs are just below 2% of the entire population of India, and about one third of them live abroad.

Doctrines. The verbatim meaning of the word *Sikh* is 'learner, disciple', or someone who follows the teachings of the teacher, the guru. The philosophical foundations of the Sikh worldview are straightforward and simple to grasp. The most important concept in the teaching is 'the One', a concept of the absolute that is analogical to both the Muslim monotheism and the Hindu idea of *Brahman*, even though at the time the latter tended to be equated with one of the personalized gods, Shiva or Vishnu. For Sikhs, the One has no definite characteristics, no human or other form, no beginning or end nor can it be represented adequately in any way. All particular faiths and forms of worship are accepted by the teaching as worshipping the same One in principle.

The One has two important qualities: its will, which brings about creation and order in the world, and its grace, its permanent gaze on things that affirms its benevolent presence. The One is equated with truth, and truth resides deep in the soul of every human being. A further notion is 'the word', which is the channel through which Sikh truth is activated in the consciousness of the individual – it is not real speech though, but rather the understanding that religious experience produces in a person, a 'soundless word', as it is called in the scripture. It is only humans who are capable of understanding this 'word', which makes human life very precious.

Sikhs believe in reincarnation, and egoism is considered to be its cause. An individual who is obsessed with oneself and one's personal interests is so full of egoism that the divine word cannot be heard. The Sikh views of social order are strictly egalitarian – there are no hierarchical differences of caste and gender, no permissible boundaries between ethnic groups. Reportedly even emperor Akbar, when visiting the Sikh community, had to stand in line for food during a jointly shared meal.

Practice. The Sikh faith is adamant that spiritual advancement has to be achieved in the middle of an active life, dedicated to the service of the community, and not as a result of recluse practices or other forms of specifically spiritual activity. A devout Sikh has to rise early, take a bath and recite passages from the scripture while meditating on the One, work during the day and recite other hymns in the evening. A Sikh has to be in possession of five symbols, which initially indicated membership of the community of the Pure, but are now worn by everyone regardless of gender. These are uncut body hair signifying continuity, a comb for neatness, a bracelet as a sign of the unbroken circle of the One, a sword or dagger indicating a readiness to fight against injustice, and specific trousers that stand for sexual propriety.

Voluntary work for the benefit of others is valued much more highly than rituals, which are considered by the gurus to be distracting and pointless. Still, the Sikhs celebrate the Hindu holidays, but they have created narratives related to the tradition of the Sikh community to legitimize them – for example, the Hindu harvest festival is celebrated as the anniversary of the creation of the order of 'the pure ones', and new initiates are accepted to the order on that day every year. These festivals are also occasions for thousands of Sikhs to undertake pilgrimages to the Golden Temple or other sacred sites of Sikh history.

The Sikhs also do not have a special clergy, only people who have been trained to read aloud the *Ādi Granth*, but maintain a normal life apart from that duty. Although there are temples, these are considered to be larger versions of communal rooms that also exist in Sikh homes – places where the *Ādi Granth* is stored, and where people can gather and recite hymns together as well as discuss communal affairs and enjoy a shared meal, which is an important part of Sikh life.

The rites of passage are also fairly simple in their core content, even though celebrations associated with them can be as pompous and joyful as those of any other community. The marriage ceremony, for example, consists only of someone reading from the scripture (a copy of which has to be present) and the couple circumambulating the book four times. A name is given to a child when the parents come to a communal room and the scripture is opened at random. The first letter of the left-hand page is what the child's name must begin with. Every Sikh also has a middle name, which tells their gender: Singh ('lion') for all boys, Kaur ('princess') for all girls.

Modern Indian Thought

Background. In the seventeenth century the Mughal empire started to fall apart because of internal tensions and outside pressure. Wars of succession weakened the ruling house, local chieftains asserted their independence from the central power and European nations showed up on its borders, demanding, and being granted, trade agreements that quickly led to their economic domination. Soon, the real struggle for control continued between the Europeans, as no Indian party could muster the necessary strength to emerge victorious from the political chaos. The Portuguese, the Dutch, the French, and the British were all interested in establishing themselves as the rulers of India, and it was the British who finally succeeded in attaining this goal. Negotiations and wars placed more and more territory under the control of the British East India Company, which was technically a private enterprise, but enjoyed the full backing of the government. By the middle of the nineteenth century its sphere of domination included practically the entire subcontinent. After a rebellion in 1857, Indian territories were placed under direct control of the British crown and the company was dissolved. In the following years, British expansion continued eastwards and the Anglo-Burmese wars brought Burma (now Myanmar) under British control as well. Parts of the Malay peninsula had been acquired previously. Only Thailand, which embarked on a modernization campaign of its own, managed to resist.

The colonial regime had a twofold effect on Indian society. On the one hand, it brought harsh racist discrimination and overbearing administration, on the other hand, it also mediated European thought to India, which included Enlightenment ideals of emancipation as well as Herderian national romanticism. Colonial policies elicited a variety of Indian reactions, conservative and liberal, moderate and extremist, which finally led to an independence movement that was crowned with success after World War II – albeit at the price of the country's partition into mostly Hindu India and Muslim Pakistan. Since 1947 India has been the largest secular democracy of the world, where all religions are at least nominally equal and many of the oppressive traditional prejudices declared to be a thing of the past. Nonetheless, old thinking habits have proved to be remarkably resilient and religious conflict and caste feud have still not become completely extinct.

Colonial modernity. Much of modern Indian thought is defined by its relationship with the colonial system, which is far from unambiguous. First of all, we should note that the Hindu society had been accustomed to foreign rule during centuries of Muslim domination, which they had not accepted as their own, so British rule did not present them with an entirely new situation of losing their country to a conqueror. British colonialism always sought to identify figures of influence in subdued territories, and to co-opt them for administrative purposes, thereby securing a certain degree of legitimation to its power. A system of education and recruitment of Indian officials was set in place. Influential Hindu families soon realized the possibilities of the new system and collaborated with the British towards such ends to the extent that it suited them. For example, in 1817 some prominent Hindus of Calcutta (Kolkata), the capital of Bengal and the administrative centre of British rule, established an English-language school for raising a new Indo-British elite. This and other similar projects brought about what is now called the **Bengali renaissance**, a movement for the restitution of the cultural identity of the educated Bengalis as a modern nation. Especially among the younger generation, many were captured by a mix of European ideas – British liberalism, French revolutionary ardour as well as German national romanticism. The last one led them to a re-evaluation of their own, Indian heritage. A vision emerged of a culture that was Indian in spirit, but cleansed of the backward and socially oppressive traditions such as the self-immolation of widows (*sati*) and caste prejudice. This was the ethos of the 'Brahma Society' (***Brahmo Samaj***) founded in 1828 by **Ram Mohan Roy** (1772–1833), one of the central figures of the Bengali renaissance, who attracted a large following, but also a lot of critique from traditionally minded Hindu clergy. Roy proposed a version of a rationalized, monotheist Advaita Vedānta combined with the triple ideals of liberty, equality, and fraternity of the French Revolution. He was convinced that British rule would help India to achieve social progress and help it to overcome the dark sides of its heritage. Roy was multilingual and wrote some of his texts in Persian, thus addressing also the Muslim community, as well as English, in order to bring the Indian ideas to a broader arena.

While the ideas of Roy attracted a large following, there were also other interpreters of the tradition who were far less optimistic about the British influence. Indeed, while the British saw themselves as the carriers of a superior civilization when they abolished the sati and raised the age of legal sexual maturity for girls from 10 to 12, they were also openly racist and disdainful of a number of Hindu cultural practices, such as vegetarianism. However, the Hindu opposition to such racism often did not make a distinction between racist prejudice and social advancement. Thus the raising of the sexual maturity age was met with violent protest and some patriotic writers glorified the sati as a courageous and noble act.

Re-interpreting the tradition. Inspired by the ideas of Johann Herder, Indian intellectuals started to look for the roots of their identity in the tradition, producing novel and occasionally surprising interpretations of ancient works. Just as Ram Mohan Roy had interpreted the *upanishads* to show that modernity and social justice are compatible with the traditions, others turned to the *Bhagavad-gītā* for the justification of a violent response to the British rule. In that work, as we know, Arjuna the warrior is persuaded by Krishna to follow his warrior's destiny in spite of the violence he must inflict on his own friends and relatives. The nationalist thinkers took that to mean that aggressive action does not produce undesired results if it is not undertaken because of selfish motives, but instead directed towards a goal benefiting the whole community. Others turned to the Vedas, which predate the development of the caste system, in order to justify a more communal form of Hinduism, as well as to divorce it from ethnicity and turn it into the base of a more universal religion which everyone could embrace regardless of their provenance.

One person stands apart in the large group of Hindu reinterpreters as the one who probably contributed the most to the development of contemporary Hinduism. This is **Swami Vivekananda** (1863–1902), the grandson of a scholar and the son of a well-to-do lawyer. He received a European-style education and entered the circle of Bengali intellectuals. Vivekananda was interested in both the religious Hindu heritage and Western esotericism, which at the time sought active contact with Indian thought. He also studied Sanskrit along with Western philosophy and science, and the modernized Hinduism of the Brahmo Samaj appealed to him. But a chance encounter with Ramakrishna, an illiterate guru of a Kālī cult, inspired him to the extent that he gradually fell completely under the mystic's spell and became his disciple, and eventually spiritual heir.

Vivekananda managed to combine his broad-ranging knowledge of Western philosophy, his command of the English language, and his devotion to the tradition of his guru into the single pursuit of establishing a new form of the Hindu faith, and a modernized version of its philosophy, loosely based on the Vedānta. The goddess Kālī had to give way to the masculine Shiva, and the trance-based mystical visions to a teaching that could co-exist with Kant, Hegel, Darwin, and Spencer – Vivekananda had translated works by Spencer and had been corresponding with him. In due course, Vivekananda embarked on a global mission, visited the United States, and spoke at the 'Parliament of Religions' in 1893. This was a conference of oikumenic mysticism convoked to demonstrate the fundamental unity of all religions. Vivekananda's short, but inspired speech established his reputation in the United States, and opened to him the possibility to tour and lecture in America and later in Europe. He was offered academic positions, including a professorship at Harvard University, which he declined in order to pursue his spiritual goals. Upon his return to India, he was celebrated as the spokesperson for his country, and received with pride. His stature now made it possible to start raising issues of social critique, yet never questioning the legitimacy of the traditional order itself. He continued to travel both in India and abroad until his death in 1902.

Another influential figure in the making of modern Hinduism is **Aurobindo Ghose** (1872–1950), who started his career as a political activist and was imprisoned on charges of terrorism, but released when a prosecution witness was murdered. After that, he decided to abandon politics and to dedicate himself to spiritual pursuits, gradually attracting followers and publishing his writings on yoga. Like Vivekananda, Sri Aurobindo, as he was now known, was also conversant with the ideas of Western philosophy and admired Plato, Nietzsche, and Bergson. Recent scholarship has also pointed out his affinity with Hegel, notably his appropriation of the Hegelian 'absolute spirit', which he reinterprets as an ecstatic supramental awareness. However, Aurobindo's concerns were primarily spiritual and his lasting influence comes from the reformulation of traditional views in terms suitable for the modern age. In this, he has proved remarkably successful as his books on integral yoga are still in print and continue to appeal to spiritual seekers worldwide.

Moderates and extremists. Imported enlightenment values and the spirit of traditionalism gradually developed into two conflicting ideologies that consolidated themselves on two wings of the Indian reform movement. The 'moderates', building on the ideas of the Bengali renaissance, were interested in social emancipation and relied on the effects of British rule which they considered beneficial, and the 'extremists' were interested in the revival of the Hindu ideas which they saw as suppressed by racist British oppression. The moderates preferred the legal political channels available to the advancement of their cause, while the extremists wanted to take the struggle to the streets and did not shun away from political violence. The moderates were content to project the realization of their goals into a more remote future, while the extremists wanted results immediately. The more astute among the British administrators realized that the shifts in society required the establishment of a new balance, but there were also headstrong conservatives, driven by racism and a sense of superiority, who saw their colleagues' willingness to concede anything as a weakness, and they were often supported by like-minded politicians in London. As a result, the colonial regime always proposed too little and too late, which gradually shifted popular support towards the extremist wing. A case in point was the disastrous effort, in 1905, to partition the province of Bengal into a Hindu and a Muslim part, which was opposed by both communities and sparked a ferocious wave of protest. But even when the partition was revoked a few years later, it was done in a way that satisfied neither community.

In 1907, the moderates and extremists had reached a point where unified and coordinated resistance to oppression was no longer possible. Extremists had resorted to violence and the British cracked down on them, which the moderates considered a damaging development to the reform movement, as loyally presented demands of justice could now also be dismissed as terrorist ultimatums. Both wings continued the struggle on their own, until the movement was reunited under Mahātma Gandhi's leadership after 1915.

---

swaraj 'own rule', the government of India by Indians elected by Indians

swadeshi '[produce] of own country', a shorthand for the boycott of imported goods as a means of political protest

---

Two concepts emerged during those debates, which are often left untranslated: *swaraj* and *swadeshi*. The idea of *swaraj* ('own rule') means the government of India by Indians who are elected or appointed by Indians, even if India itself would still remain a part of the British empire. *Swadeshi*, in turn, means 'of own country', and the word came to be used primarily in the context of a boycott of British imports, notably as a protest against the partition of Bengal. At the time, India had become one of the main markets for British industrial products, such as cotton cloth, and the boycott of these products hit the British economy quite hard: during 1905–1906, for example, the imports of British cotton fell by 44% and the imports of footwear dropped by 68%, because Indian consumers stopped buying them. This was also a boon to the rising local industries which acquired the market share.

The caste question. The extremist wing of the movement was also resolutely committed to all elements of the traditional Hindu heritage. This precluded low-caste and untouchable activists from joining their ranks. But moderates were not very eager to welcome them either, as their movement was also primarily driven by the traditional elites. And yet the oppressed gradually managed to make their voice heard. One of the early activists was **Jotirao** (Jyotirao, Jotiba) **Phule** (1827–1890), for whom even a reformed and modernized Hinduism seemed too oppressive. He belonged to the hired labour caste by birth, but his family had done quite well. After attending an elementary school, he continued his studies in an English-language school run by Scottish missionaries. This institution combined a strict and non-compromising Christian spirit and complete intolerance for Hindu beliefs with a democratic attitude that did not respect caste differences and a broad curriculum that included natural science and other disciplines. Enlightenment authors were readily available, and their criticism of Christianity convinced Phule and many of his friends that all religions were wrong in their specifics, only what they shared could be believed.

In 1848, Phule reportedly had a life-defining experience, when the parents of a Brāhman friend rebuked him, as a low-caste Hindu, for attending his friend's wedding procession. When he returned home, shaken, his father endorsed the rebuke and said that in earlier days, things might have taken a much worse turn. At the same time Phule had been reading Thomas Paine's critique of traditional social institutions, which extremistic anti-British Brāhmans were propagating as an ideological foundation for resisting British domination. The ideas of Paine inspired in Phule a social radicalism of a different kind. He became active in promoting social reform, established schools for women as well as low-caste and untouchable students and protested Brāhman oppression, which soon led him to conflicts with his friends of the Brāhman caste as well as his own parents. One point he stressed were the common interests of all oppressed groups: at the time the caste system had become increasingly complicated because of separate qualifications for children of inter-caste marriages and a further division according to inherited professions. Slightly higher-standing groups in this hierarchy often sided with those still higher and shared their disdain of those below them. Phule tried to convince them of the wrongness of such views, insisting that the Brāhmans were responsible for all social injustice, and emancipation from the caste system would be in the interests of all oppressed groups. However, Phule did not oppose British colonialism, as the British sided with him in his condemnation of the traditional hierarchy.

Phule's work contributed towards the emancipation of many single individuals, including some of India's first feminists, but did not manage to overturn the system itself, as the majority of educated Hindus were of Brāhman descent. However, he managed to raise social awareness – among other things, he is credited with the introduction of the (still used) word ***dalit*** ('broken') as the designation of untouchable social groups into the parlance of reformers who spoke out against their oppression.

The gender question. The patriarchal norms of the traditional Indian society came to be questioned by the new, English-educated middle class, as the men who saw themselves as the new elite were not content to accept the old model of arranged marriages to illiterate, uneducated women. In this, they were supported by the colonial administration, which also considered the Indian traditional view of women as backward. Since the second half of the nineteenth century, efforts were made to raise the status of women and to provide them with a level of education that would help them to advance in the world. Women's magazines promoted the ideal of an educated and domestically competent lady of the house, who could be the ideal companion for an Indian-born British civil servant.

This was very much in accordance with the views of the moderates, but rejected by the extremists. For example, when in 1891 a law was passed raising the age of marriage consent from 10 to 12 years for women, a Bengali paper wrote that 'the Hindu family is ruined' as a result. Moderates, who welcomed the law, were painted as traitors to their own nation and supporters of the oppressing racist colonial regime. Similarly, while the British had prohibited the self-immolation of widows in 1829 (largely because of the campaigning of Ram Mohan Roy), the women who committed the act in spite of the prohibition were now praised by extremists as the true daughters of the nation.

Such was the atmosphere in which the first women thinkers and activists emerged. One of these was **Savitribai Phule** (1831–1897), the wife of Jotirao Phule and the first teacher of the first Indian-run school for girls, many of whose pupils later grew to be important figures of the women's movement themselves. Another prominent early feminist was **Pandita Ramabai** (1858–1922), the daughter of a progressive Brāhman family. She was well-educated and not forced to marry at an early age, but lost her parents and had to move to Calcutta at the age of 20. In the Bengali capital she became acquainted with the ideas of social reformers and was welcomed among them as an intellectual of her own right. She was widowed after a brief marriage and then travelled to England where she converted to Christianity. Having been involved in the promotion of women's equality already before her travels, she opened a 'Home of Learning' for high-caste widows (as she herself had been one) after her return to India in 1889. In a book, written in English, she speaks about the conditions of high-caste Hindu widows, but also about the oppression of women more generally.

Ramabai, however, soon became the target of critique by extremist politicians. Even though her conversion to Christianity had presumably been not much more than a gesture of emancipation from the Hindu social structure (and Indian religious controversies), she was attacked as a zealous Christian missionary and started to be distrusted by the very women she tried to defend. As a result, she did then start to move more towards Christianity and opened a chain of missions open to anyone in need. These, too, are reported to have been run by women and evolved into centres of a women's movement.

The Muslim question. The British constantly made efforts to pit the Hindus and Muslims against each other. In some cases, as with the partition of Bengal, they did not succeed, but some of their measures produced real discord. For example, when a delegation of Muslims petitioned the British authorities in 1906 to grant them separate voting constituencies which would ensure that a number of Muslim deputies were elected even in regions with a Hindu majority, support was assured to them, but not necessarily because the British considered such a solution more democratic. A more likely explanation is that they anticipated that Hindu–Muslim debates might cripple the elected legislative councils and prevent the formation of a unified front against the British. The All-India Muslim League was established soon after, and confrontation between the religious communities grew. In the following years, in spite of a few rather successful efforts to collaborate, Muslim and Hindu leaders kept to separate paths of resistance. Eventually this led to the split of India as a nation into two opposite camps, enshrined after the achievement of independence in the partition into India and Pakistan (including the present Bangladesh, which seceded from Pakistan in 1971).

The idea of partition itself evolved from the thought of the poet and mystic thinker **Muhammad Iqbal** (1877–1938), who rose to prominence as an advocate of pan-Islamism in the 1920s. In his youth, Iqbal had been an Indian patriot, glorifying his homeland and opposing British rule in Urdu verse. At the same time, he was strongly inclined towards mysticism. In 1905 he continued his studies of philosophy in Europe, and the experience changed him: at the time, no love was lost between the European powers and the Ottoman empire, which had tried, but not succeeded, to implement modernizing reforms. Iqbal developed a sense of solidarity with the Islamic powers and was disappointed in secular enlightenment ideals. After his return to India in 1908, he no longer believed in the idea of the nation as the basis of an integrated community and as the solution for the political future of his country. He now took to writing in Persian, which educated young Muslims of India could read, but which would also be understood by people in Iran and Turkey. In his poetry he expounded a philosophy influenced simultaneously by the mystical traditions of Islam and the work of Bergson and other Western thinkers, while in his political statements he voiced the concerns of Indian Muslims who were growing increasingly wary of the nationalism of the Hindu reformers. Iqbal was no traditionalist, the Islam he endorsed was, he believed, capable of acting as a modernizing and emancipating ideology. For him, the positive programme of Islam was universal and could not be subjugated to the particular domination of one nation. On a more practical level, he understood that Hindus, the majority in each administrative unit, would easily be able to dominate the Muslim minority.

In 1930, in his presidential address to the Muslim League, Iqbal stated for the first time that the Muslims of India constitute a separate nation and therefore should have their own territory to live in. At this point, the idea was not to divide the state into two, only to ensure that there would be administrative units in India in which Muslims would be at the helm. During the following years this idea matured into the demand for partitioning India into two separate states, which indeed became a reality in 1947.

Views from the West. The rise of Indian self-consciousness coincided with several important developments in the Western world. One of these was the progress of humanist scholarship. The success of comparative linguistics established the relationship among Indian, Iranian, and most big European languages on a scientific basis and beyond any doubt. Studies of Sanskrit became an essential part of historical linguistics, and Western scholars were soon astonished by the level of scholarship of early Indian grammarians, which was superior even to their own current understanding of the nature of language. Translations of other Sanskrit and Pāli texts, including Brahmanist and Buddhist scriptures, inspired Western scholars of religion, who were quickly emancipated out of their previous limits of critical studies of the Bible and related texts. The academic discipline of Indology gained momentum, scholarly societies were established and some of the pioneer work accomplished at the time has not lost its importance to this day.

The second important development was the renewed interest in paranormal phenomena, accompanied by the increased faith in science and its capacity to explain everything. Movements such as theosophy emerged, which claimed to provide scientifically valid theories of the supernatural, seances, and mediums also attracted the attention of people with a rigorously rational frame of mind. The idea that all religions expressed, on an intuitive level, realities that can now be tackled with scientific rigour, enjoyed wide support. Many leading figures of the movement, including **Helena Blavatsky** (1831–1891), the founder of the Theosophical Society, were very interested in Indian thought, as they imagined that corroboration for their own theories can be discovered there. Blavatsky travelled in many parts of India and claimed to have reached Tibet in search of ancient wisdom, which endeared her to gullible Western sponsors and ensured her writings a large audience.

One person whom she managed to convince in her truth was **Annie Besant** (1847–1933), a passionate Irishwoman, who had already established a strong reputation as a champion of the disenfranchised and an advocate of women's rights, and had been arrested for promoting birth control and involvement in the organization of strikes. After meeting Blavatsky, she soon became interested in theosophy, moved to India, and became involved in politics there, eventually becoming the president of both the Theosophical Society (1907) and the Indian National

Congress (1917). Her opposition to the British raised her popularity in the political circles and her experience of the Irish independence movement was certainly helpful for Indians in planning their own actions of resistance.

In 1909, Besant met the son of a clerk of the Theosophical Society and became convinced the boy was the incarnation of the Buddha whom the doctrines of theosophy were predicting to arrive. This boy, **Jiddu Krishnamurti** (1895–1986) grew up in the custody of Besant and her associates and though he rejected any claims to supernatural descent or an inspired mission in 1929, he maintained a warm relationship with Besant until her death. Krishnamurti did not receive any academic education, but developed an eclectic worldview of his own, which he continued to publicize in talks, discussions, and writings. His influence was far-reaching – over the years his interlocutors included the Dalai Lama, Jawaharlal Nehru, and Aldous Huxley, as well as several prominent natural scientists. Some of these dialogues have been published and continue to enjoy a wide readership.

The path to independence. After 1916, Hindu and Muslim leaders abandoned their disagreements for a while in order to work together for the common purpose of constitutional reforms. This was made possible because two leaders of the younger generation had appeared on the scene – **Mahātma Gandhi** (1869–1948) on the Hindu side and **Muhammad Ali Jinnah** (1876–1948) at the head of the Muslim League. Both of them were English-educated and had adopted a British lifestyle, including clothing and eating habits, something that Gandhi later dropped for an altogether different image. Both of them had also studied law, initially in India and later in London. Jinnah became a successful lawyer after his return to India and he joined politics ostensibly for quite pragmatic reasons. His aim was to overcome the dissent in the ranks of Indians opposed to British rule, and he was quite certainly no religious fanatic, just someone looking out for the interests of his own community. The Muslims and Hindus who were opposed to British rule, according to Jinnah's views, should focus on what they had in common rather than on what divided them. This is why he was critical of all political groups and thinkers who stressed religious identities, including Muhammad Iqbal. However, his pragmatic line had little success. For a time, Jinnah even quit active struggle and went to live in London, but still retained his connections to Muslim politics in India. When in 1937, the Muslim League did not win any seats in the elections even in the provinces where Muslims were a majority, Jinnah realized that in a united India the interests of his community would not be duly represented. He now became inclined to accept Iqbal's doctrine of two nations and even radicalized it into the demand of two separate states. After the partition of India, he became the first leader of Pakistan.

Mahātma Gandhi (1869–1948). Mohandas Karamchand (Mahātma) Gandhi is probably the best-known Indian political ideologist and leader of the twentieth century, whose tactics of non-violent civil disobedience proved to be more efficient in pursuing the aims of the liberation movement than the conciliatory efforts of the moderates or the violent opposition of the extremists of the previous generation.

Gandhi's goal was to forge an Indian identity that would include also Muslims and he remained opposed to the partition of India until it happened. Yet, on a different level, his own views of India were very much Hindu-centred. He did not succeed as a lawyer on his return from London, and took a job in the British colonial administration of South Africa instead. He was thinking of himself as primarily British at the time, but his ideas soon changed when he experienced racism first-hand. He read widely and even corresponded with Leo Tolstoy, whom he greatly admired. Soon enough he started to put his philosophy into practice. One of the chief notions he developed was the idea of *satyagraha* ('insistence on truth'), a form of civil disobedience, which implied ignoring morally wrong acts of power and peacefully suffering the punishments inflicted because of this, while still not submitting to the pressure. The idea of *satyagraha* was to be combined with the Jain idea of *ahimsā*, or complete abstention from violence. In Gandhi's view, the idea of *satyagraha* was derived from the traditional idea of dharma as a moral order, which is intuitively known to the individual, and thus the 'truth' to be insisted on was a shared understanding to begin with. And the British discrimination of people based on the colour of their skin had nothing to do with it.

However, in South Africa Gandhi was only concerned with the British racism directed against the local Indian community, ignoring similarly oppressed native Africans. He is even quoted as evoking the shared Indo-European heritage of Indians and the British as an argument against racism, thus implicitly leaving Africans out of the equation.

---

satyagraha   'insistence on truth', a form of civil disobedience combined with the principle of non-violence, inducing protesters to peacefully suffer the punishments inflicted because of their refusal to bend to oppressive laws and regulations

---

Gandhi returned to India in 1915 and joined the political struggle. He proved to be remarkably efficient as a tactician, forging, among other things, a temporary alliance with pan-Islamist Muslims (whom Jinnah opposed because of their fundamentalism) and organizing a campaign of non-cooperation with the British as a result of the massacre of protesters in the Sikh temple grounds of Amritsar. Gandhi now became markedly anti-British, wearing only Indian traditional clothing. As his popularity grew, he was able to convert the protests into mass politics involving more and more of the population and turning local grievances into national concerns. In the meantime, he remained true to his commitment to non-violence. Thus, to the dismay of many of his colleagues, he called off the non-cooperation campaign after a group of protesters killed policemen in a violent clash.

But his ideas also included a few blind spots. One of these was his decisive opposition to modernization. According to Gandhi, the future of Indian economy should consist of small-scale rural artisanal production. He was opposed to industrialization and urbanization, and in a letter written in 1909, he even argued that railways, hospitals, telegraphs, and lawyers 'had to go' after India would be able to control its own destiny. Upper classes, too, would have to learn to enjoy simple, happy, and religious peasant life. This vision may have endeared him to the simple and religious, but not yet happy peasants. However, India was lucky to have other leaders actually designing its economy after independence was regained.

Another oddity in Gandhi's thought was his support for the caste system, even though he opposed the oppressive social practices directed against lower castes and untouchables. This led him to conflict with some of his collaborators, notably Bhimrao Ambedkar, who, coming from the untouchable group himself, was committed to the eradication of the whole notion of caste from Indian society as a source of social evil.

Gandhi continued the struggle for an independent and united India, leading massive popular protests, negotiating with the British and trying to appease the Muslims until the very end. It is ironic that after independence was finally achieved, but at the cost of the partition of India, Gandhi was assassinated by a Hindu nationalist, and the tensions he tried to overcome – some of them with roots deep in his own worldview – persist to this day.

Independence. It has been argued that India finally gained its independence at least as much due to the problems into which the colonial administration had run as to the activities of Indian politicians. According to the British's own laws and regulations, the crown had accumulated a massive debt to India during World War II, which it was unwilling to pay back. After long and difficult negotiations, the British instead conceded their power in India to the new constituent assemblies of the two new countries of India and Pakistan. India's leadership was assumed by an interim government led by **Jawāharlāl Nehru** (1889–1964), a prominent activist of the independence movement, only recently released from prison to participate in the transition negotiations. Nehru had been a close ally and collaborator of Gandhi, but his vision of independent India differed significantly: he pushed for a quick industrialization under the auspices of the state, thus combining a version of state socialism and ancient Indian political theory. Nehru did not endorse Soviet-style communism, however, and he was also hostile to Indian communists. In foreign politics, Nehru followed the politics of non-alignment, which raised India's profile as a moderator in conflicts likely to be accepted both by the West and the Soviet bloc.

The position of the minister of law and justice in the first post-independence government was held by **Bhimrao Ambedkar** (1891–1956), a professor of economics and law with two doctorates, one from Columbia University and the other from the London School of Economics. Ambedkar was born as a member of the untouchable (*dalit*) group and one of his lifelong aims was to eradicate the basis for the social evils that *dalits* had to suffer. His best-known work from the pre-independence period is a monograph, published in 1936, entitled *The Annihilation of Caste*, in which he systematically argues against the traditional social system, demonstrating its incompatibility with modern statehood. The constitution of India, of which Ambedkar was the chief architect, indeed posits the equality of all citizens, granting everybody the same civic rights, as well as the secular character of the republic. Ambedkar also almost single-handedly revitalized Buddhism in India, converting to it in 1956. As Buddhism did not acknowledge any caste differences, this became an attractive way out of the still-persisting social structure for *dalits*. Indeed, about 500 000 of them followed Ambedkar in his conversion and the number of converts has risen to millions afterwards. Ambedkar's revivalist movement was remarkable in that it specified negative vows that new converts had to make, stating that they will not worship Hindu gods, believe in their incarnations, and, specifically, that they will renounce the idea that the historical Buddha was an *avatar* of Vishnu.

Another influential intellectual who was involved in the creation of the Indian state was **Sarvepalli Radhakrishnan** (1888–1975), the first vice president and the second president of the new republic. Radhakrishnan had studied at a missionary school where his teachers were critical of Hinduism and he accepted the critique as a challenge. His confidence in his faith was restored by Vivekananda's interpretations, and his subsequent engagement with the philosophy of Hegel already took place in the context of Advaita Vedānta and its understanding of the absolute. Proving that Indian thought was not just a spiritual endeavour, but also intellectually equal to Western thought and productive in a modern society, became one of Radhakrishnan's lifelong goals. His voluminous writings on Indian philosophy and translations of classics as well as his participation in the rising movement of comparative philosophy have made a lasting contribution to intercultural dialogue. After a successful academic career, which culminated with a professorship at the University of Oxford, Radhakrishnan entered politics, as his international reputation and academic mind made him an ideal spokesman for his country.

The role of Hindu nationalism in Indian politics. The radical wing of Indian anti-colonial ideologists of the nineteenth and early twentieth centuries fashioned the future worldview of their country as a return to the dominant position of the Hindu faith. This spirit of religious national identity has retained its strong position in contemporary India, which is constitutionally secular, that is, the state power positions itself at equal distance from all the religious communities represented among Indian citizens. Nonetheless, the overwhelming majority, around 80% according to official data, identify as Hindus, and political forces who claim India for Hindus have been active throughout the history of the Republic of India. A right-wing political party with such a programme, allied with a paramilitary Hindu organization, was formed a few years after the achievement of independence, and its descendant, the Bhāratiya Janatā Party (BJP, 'The party of the people of India'), is one of the two major political forces in today's India, claiming to be the biggest political party in the world. This party has led the government of India since 2014 and also holds the positions of chief ministers in a number of Indian states.

BJP is a right-wing party based on an ideology called **Hindutva**, or 'Hinduhood', developed in the 1920s by V. D. Savarkar (1883–1966), a London-educated radical Brāhman. Savarkar opposed the view of Hindu faith espoused by such thinkers as Gandhi and Radhakrishnan – a personal, individual way of life in harmony with society, nature, and the universe, without any claims on anyone else. Hindutva, in contrast, purported to construct a doctrine of communal life based on principles derived from scripture, and envisioned for India a political structure that recognized the superiority of Hindus over all other identities. Some proponents of Hindutva acknowledge the right of Indian inhabitants of other cultural backgrounds to merge into the group of Hindus, which, they claim, is primarily a cultural and patriotic self-identification. Opponents, however, have compared the Hindutva ideology to fascism and consider it incompatible with a democratic, secular form of government.

Contemporary Indian thought. The social and cultural institutions of contemporary India are modelled on a Western blueprint, which means that philosophy has become an academic discipline and religions have been divorced from politics, at least in the eyes of the law. And yet traditional thinking retains a strong foothold on many levels, from the daily cultural practices of the common people to the minds of religiously engaged politicians who try to enlist their communities for their particularistic agendas. India has also kept its appeal for the spiritual seekers from around the world, looking for charismatic gurus and cult leaders such as **Sai Baba** (1926–2011), whose organization currently has branches in 126 countries. Moreover, conversant with both the Western tradition and their own,

Indian thinkers such as Daya Krishna (1924–2007), Bimal Matilal (1935–1991), and Jitendra Mohanty (b.1928), to name but a few, have continued their efforts to synthesize Indian thought with other conceptual systems and to analyse it for its philosophical significance. No longer constrained by a need to prove the legitimacy of their work, and happily divorced from any type of spiritual quest, the work of these thinkers has laid the foundation of a modern Indian philosophy, which develops as well as questions both its own traditional origins and the insights of global thought. A younger generation of Indian thinkers is active in universities worldwide, bringing the dialogue to the doors of Western philosophy departments in which it will hopefully soon find a more permanent abode.

2

China

Introductory remarks. As the world's second biggest economy, China has demonstrated a momentum of development over the last decades, unmatched by any other country, and has asserted itself as one of the global powers. Even though it officially continues to be the people's republic established by **Mao Zedong** and is defined in Western terms as an autocratic state ruled by a single political party, it has in many ways reverted to its traditional form of statehood, as the present official ideology has incorporated large parts of the same tradition that has in the past been proclaimed by most Chinese ruling houses. Similarly, the Communist Party has all but taken the place that the learned officialdom has had during the millennia of imperial rule. The same Confucian heritage, once famously claimed by Max Weber to be unable to generate a productive modernity, has been propelling the development of quite a few other countries of East Asia, in particular the city-state of Singapore, where Chinese cultural influence has been predominant. It is, of course, open to debate how the selective adaptation by autocratic powers of certain elements of an internally contradictory tradition should be evaluated, but a claim can nonetheless be made that a historical continuity is again outweighing the effects of the cultural ruptures of China in the twentieth century.

Economic success and the rise of political influence have been accompanied by increased cultural self-confidence, which is entirely justified, as China is home not only to industries and trading hubs, but also to an impressive aesthetic, philosophical and literary culture as well as scientific advances that have significantly contributed to the development of various disciplines. For example, it was only due to historical coincidences that the technocratically minded faction of Wang Anshi lost out to the conservatives in Chinese politics of the eleventh century, thus putting a stop to what might have been a technological revolution. An inward turn of the Ming empire again changed the course of history, when the government effectively called off the Chinese navies from the world's seas, which they

Asian Worldviews: Religions, Philosophies, Political Theories, First Edition. Rein Raud.
© 2021 John Wiley & Sons Ltd. Published 2021 by John Wiley & Sons Ltd.

had been dominating under the guidance of admiral Zheng He in the fifteenth century, thus leaving them for the European powers to take over.

The hallmark of the Chinese civilization has been its meritocratic nature that, on the one hand, has divided the population into the dominating educated elite of state officials and the dominated masses, but, on the other hand, has also ensured to a certain extent that hereditary aristocracies have not been able to block the possibilities for social advancement for the worthy commoners. This feature has been admired by many European intellectuals since the seventeenth century (including, for example, Voltaire), when characteristics of the Chinese society became better known in the West through the writings of Jesuit missionaries such as Matteo Ricci (1552–1610). It is also important that the loyalty of the Chinese officials is not given personally to the ruler, but to the principles that a proper ruler has to embody. Thus betraying a tyrant was not an immoral act, but, on the contrary, proper behaviour. Another feature of the official elite was its shared base of education, which included philosophy and encouraged aesthetic activities: poetry and music were more prominently on the agenda of the scholarly tradition than, for example, discussions of the supernatural. The remarkable resilience of this power-structure has made China a unique civilization and the brief periods during which it has strayed from these principles in its history (including Mao's rule) have, in retrospect, all proved to be the least successful on all counts.

Periods of cultural history. Chinese cultural history is usually divided into periods according to the ruling dynasties and interregnums: from the mythical beginnings of statehood in China until the end of the empire and proclamation of the republic in 1912 there has always been a ruling house in power, even though at times these have been very short-lived and not really in control of much territory. But others have ruled longer and constituted a specific cultural climate that has had enduring influence on the cultural environment. From the times of the Zhou dynasty (1046–256 BCE) Chinese thought has been advanced by wandering political scholars, of whom Kongzi/Confucius was, in retrospect, the most illustrious and important. But there were others, and in the dialogue between them a multitude of philosophical schools emerged. Politically, China was divided into de facto independent states at the time, and the leaders of these often sought the advice of such scholars on how to survive and prosper in this atmosphere of political and military rivalry. Various responses developed into philosophical schools, and thus the 'Warring States' period is also the classical age of Chinese philosophy, or the 'Hundred schools'. A short-lived unification gave way to the emergence of the rule of the Han dynasty, an era of relative peace and prosperity.

During the Han dynasty (206 BCE–220 CE) the Ru teaching based on the views of Kongzi consolidated into the ideology of the officialdom, while the anarchistic undercurrent of the Lao-Zhuang school developed into a distinct worldview of its own right. The end of the Han dynasty and the subsequent period of the Six Dynasties (220–589) present us with a long period of disunity, which witnessed the influx of Buddhism of various kinds from India in the midst of ongoing political turmoil. The Tang dynasty (618–907) ruled during an era of cosmopolitan and multicultural flourishing – international trade through the Silk Road prospered and remote intellectual trends, such as Christianity and Islam, were present in Tang China along with a multitude of Buddhist and indigenous views of the world.

After the decline of the Tang and a brief interregnum the Song dynasty (960–1279) assumed power, which soon led to another period of boom. In addition to the development of cities and economy, this period is interesting from our present perspective as the beginning of a period of the great synthesis of worldviews usually called **Neo-Confucianism** (accompanied by the gradual decline of Buddhism). The Mongol dynasty of Yuan (1271–1368), the subsequent Chinese dynasty of Ming (1368–1644) and the Manchu dynasty of Qing (1644–1912) all had their own cultural flavours, but none of them introduced very strong structural changes into the architecture of Chinese worldviews: new currents of previous thought systems emerged occasionally, but their nomenclature remained largely the same.

Towards the end of the Qing dynasty, this edifice began to crack between conservative isolationism and Western pressure, until the country started to fall apart, a process accelerated by several rebellions. The model of Japanese modernity inspired Chinese intellectuals also to aspire for a new form of statehood, which finally appeared with the republic. Subsequent internal and external conflicts, in particular the Japanese aggression and mass murders, rattled China to the extent that a strong-handed warlord such as Mao Zedong was able to take the power into his hands. After his death, the track of modernization was resumed and the China of today, with its successes and contradictions, is the result.

Even though both India and China have been governed by foreign invaders for long periods of their history, there is a substantial difference: in India, these invaders kept their culture and some fusions emerged only in the long run, while in China, most of the conquerors, from the Tartar rulers of northern China during the Six Dynasties period to the Manchus of the Qing dynasty, acknowledged the superiority of Chinese civilization and did not seriously try to replace it by their own culture. This gives China a stronger sense of historical continuity, which is further supported by the unity of the written language.

Notes on the Chinese language. There is significant linguistic diversity in China, with various minority languages spoken by populations of millions, and even the dialects of Chinese are mutually unintelligible. Nonetheless, the written language shared by the official estate – an acquired skill for all of its users, similarly to Sanskrit in India or Latin in medieval Europe – was the same everywhere all over the empire. Spoken Chinese gradually started to make its way into written texts from the Tang dynasty onwards, but it only managed to replace the classical language as the official form of written Chinese towards the end of the nineteenth century, during the course of the modernization drive, centuries later than Sanskrit met with a similar fate in India. This stability – or conservatism – has much to do with the development of the Chinese cultural paradigm.

Compared to Mandarin, which is the language used in most of China at present, its ancestor, Classical Chinese, is even more different from Western languages. It conveys meaning with the help of discrete units, each of which takes the form of a syllable and corresponds to a character. The Chinese writing system has historically made use of up to 50 000 characters in total, but it suffices for a literate person to know 2000–3000 in order to understand most of any text – the rest has to be looked up in a dictionary just as we occasionally do when we encounter a rare word in our own languages.

Each of the characters normally has one, occasionally two, but very rarely more than two ways to be pronounced. When there are more than one, each of them has a particular meaning, but it is not at all unusual that a character with one pronunciation has more meanings. These units cannot really be divided into parts of speech, which would behave differently as do our nouns, verbs, adjectives, and so on. On the contrary, most words (this is what they will be called for the sake of simplicity) can act as any of these, depending on their position in the phrase, like both words in the expressions 'good make' and 'make good' mean different things in either case. Nor do any words change for grammatical reasons, as grammatical relations are also mostly expressed by word order. 'Big fish eat small fish' looks like a sentence in classical Chinese, except that in the English version it is clear that 'big fish' are many, and it would be even closer to the logic of classical Chinese if the word 'fish' were be used as a verb in this case ('big fish fish small fish'), as it can be in the context of fishing. As a result, Chinese phrases are often ambiguous. For example, the English sentence 'time flies like an arrow' is normally understood as a poetic image about the passing of time, but can mean literally also that certain insects, called time flies, have taken a liking to a piece of weaponry. In daily practice, this latter reading is blocked out by the mind as absurd. In the Chinese case, however, this often cannot be done. In order to minimize the possibility of misunderstanding, the earliest extant texts in Chinese already demonstrate a certain rhythm, a repetition of sentence patterns that makes it easier for the reader to discern which particular role each word is currently performing. Even so, Chinese texts can be extremely ambiguous and, especially in cases where such a rhythm is not strictly maintained, open to multiple legitimate interpretations. The most notorious of such texts is probably the **Daodejing**, or *The Scripture* *of the Way and Vigour*, one of the main classics of the Lao-Zhuang school. More than 300 English translations exist of this book, presenting sometimes quite incompatible and contrary readings of the same passages, and the same is true of many other languages, albeit usually on a much smaller scale.

Another difficulty is added by the change in the meanings of characters. Quite often a term may have signified something during one period, and something else during another one, but this would not be immediately clear to the people reading and discussing texts of previous eras. This led later scholars to read the earlier texts in correspondence with their own conceptual world, and, sometimes on purpose, to attribute the ideas of their times to previous authors. As the Chinese culture is inherently conservative and arguing by precedent is a well-accepted rhetorical strategy, such retroactive transformation of earlier texts has proved to be a way of introducing novelties. Opponents of such novelties may have, in turn, rejected them by pointing out the conceptual mismatch.

This situation has given rise to an early and well-developed tradition of textual criticism as well as commentaries, which are meant to aid the reader to understand important texts correctly. Kongzi himself engaged a lot in such study, and the early canon of his teaching consists mainly of the fruits of this work. However, later commentators have often been overzealous in discovering hidden meanings, often in places where these had clearly not been intended. But when perplexed novices are inclined to accept such explanations by their teachers, and also learn from them the method of interpretation by developing all chains of association, however spurious, schools of thought and traditions of understanding are born that may continue over centuries and then require true intellectual courage to be challenged and criticized. Yet there is also a characteristic beauty to the way in which new meanings are invented and concepts generated in this way, which then take on lives of their own, with considerable results for social practice.

Religions, philosophies, ideologies. While Indian thought distinguishes between specific subfields such as *artha* or the *darshanas*, in the Chinese case it is much more difficult to separate different 'disciplines' within the edifice of worldviews from each other. All Chinese worldviews have direct implications on the daily behaviour of people who follow them, all of them also have a political dimension and the latter is, in turn, always grounded in deep-level ontological and cosmological beliefs. Under the circumstances, the task of political theory is to bring what happens on Earth into harmony with what goes on cosmically, which is also automatically taken to be beneficial for the society and conducive towards the well-being of people. All currents of Chinese thought also share a certain amount of presuppositions, even though they give them different interpretations and draw different conclusions from them. These grew out of the earliest beliefs and ritual practices, described in the next sections, and have remained influential to this day. Thus, even if the bigger part of urban Chinese population has converted to a more modern worldview, a certain amount of residue of such views is still to be observed in their understanding of the world and social relationships, including their behaviour in practical situations. Whenever we encounter such deeply embedded phenomena, this should only remind us that the strict Western division between religion, philosophy, and ideology – as well as the understanding of religions as worldviews structurally similar to the Abrahamic creeds – is not justified in the context of other cultures.

Another aspect to be noted is the non-exclusive nature of Chinese beliefs and religious practices. Unlike in the West, or even in India, where the adherents of different worldviews draw clear boundaries between each other, in China, as well as in other areas of East Asia where Chinese cultural influence has been prevalent (Korea, Japan, Vietnam), the traffic of ideas and practices between sets of beliefs with different labels has been normal, acceptable and widespread, and a single individual can easily and seamlessly combine, in their mind, elements of what are classified as different worldviews. This does not preclude debates on the doctrine, of course, and the criticism of the adherents of one school of thought by those of another – it is just that beliefs and practices are not the property of one group by default, and an innovation perceived to be efficient may spread across the group boundaries quite easily.

The Beginnings

Background. Little can be said with precision about the origins of the Chinese civilization. The earliest written sources that present us with historical data are fairly late, ideologically biased in favour of the political regimes of their times, and also blend mythological material with possible historical fact. Archaeologists continue to debate whether certain excavated sites correspond to the power centres of semi-mythical early rulers and dynasties mentioned in these sources, and it cannot even be established which of these cultures were created by people linguistically related to the ancestors of the contemporary Chinese. Fairly sophisticated ancient cultures existed in the Huanghe and Yangzi valleys already in the fourth millennium BCE, but some scholars claim the civilization goes back even further. Signs that may have been pictographic writing, dating back 7000–8000 years, have been discovered on the cliffs of Damaidi and signs resemblant to characters have also been inscribed on archaeological finds dating back 5000 years ago, but again scholars are not in agreement whether these indeed constituted a writing system. What we can assert more or less with confidence is that the territory we now know as China was culturally and linguistically diverse and dominating regional powers supplanted each other. It is with the advent of the Shang (Yin) dynasty that we get on a stronger footing. This dynasty ruled the Huanghe valley and adjacent territories in the second millennium BCE, had an advanced economy based on agriculture, a strong military as well as a network of outposts and allies. It built several capital cities with large and strong buildings and had a developed culture, attested by the skilled craftmanship of objects found in royal tombs as well as by the presence of musical instruments.

Ancestor worship, divination, and sacrifice were the main elements of the Shang religion. Just as the Shang kingdom was highly centralized around the figure of the monarch, so was the pantheon organized around the figure of Shang Di, the Supreme Celestial Ruler. And just as the king was unreachable for his subjects, the Supreme Celestial Ruler was also not directly addressed in worship. Luckily the ancestors of the king were able to speak to this god, which is why the monarch had to participate in one rite or another almost on a daily basis.

The Shang were overthrown in 1046 BCE by the Zhou, a rival, culturally less developed, but linguistically close state of agriculturalists with their power-base to the north-west of the Shang territories. According to historical records, the main reason for the fall of Shang was the character of its last monarch, a cruel tyrant given to sensual pleasures, who enjoyed to watch the humiliation and torture of his subjects and had even his uncle killed when he dared to reproach him for his behaviour. Shang divination and ritual professionals defected to Zhou and even the military leaders betrayed their king. The capital was razed to the ground and a new dynasty began. The Duke of Zhou, the architect of the new political system, is a highly esteemed figure in Chinese political history and must have indeed been a very capable statesman. The Zhou house, with a relatively less advanced cultural background, soon adopted the better part of Shang culture, together with its rites and divination arts. For example, the Supreme Celestial Ruler soon became one with Heaven (Tian), an anthropomorphic Zhou deity who also supposedly resided in the sky and actively interfered in worldly affairs.

Technically, the dynasty established by the Zhou lasted longer than any other in Chinese history, but during the subsequent centuries, the rule of the Zhou was plagued by rebellions and the central powers weakened to the degree that different states under Zhou rule became independent. This is why the latter half of Zhou rule (475–221 BCE) is called the 'Warring States' period. Different powers vied for supremacy and tried to adopt different political doctrines to attain their goal. The situation was resolved by the most efficient and also most ruthless military power among them, the Qin, whose leader proclaimed himself the first emperor and in 221 BCE had unified all of what was then China under his rule.

The policies of the first emperor, **Qin Shi Huang-di**, were indeed radical – for example, in 213 BCE he ordered all possibly subversive books to be burned, so that history could begin anew. But his rule also brought with it some benefits that only a centralized state could implement – for example, the Chinese script was standardized on the orders of his government so that from that time onwards, educated people from different parts of China had a common written medium at their disposal. Measures and currencies were also standardized, which greatly simplified trade. The emperor also ordered the construction of the Great Wall, which eventually reached about 3000 km in length, to protect his territory from northern barbarians and relieve his subjects from constant danger of attack. As tyrants often are, the Qin emperor was wary of competitors and therefore left a power vacuum behind him when he died, and the throne was soon won by an insurgent group that founded the Han dynasty.

But his empire was short-lived and soon replaced by the Han dynasty, which lasted, with a short interregnum, for more than 400 years (206 BCE–220 CE). It is according to this house that the Chinese are known as the 'Han' people, and indeed Chinese society acquired many of its most typical institutions and traits during this period.

Shamanism. The role played by shamanism in the officially sanctioned world-view of Shang China remains open to speculation, but it had a firm base in the worldview of the Zhou. There were two types of shamans. First, there were those who allegedly departed from their bodies and embarked on 'spiritual journeys' to meet otherworldly beings and consult (or cohabit) with them. This tradition is reflected in early poetry, where accounts of such journeys have been preserved. Second, there were also medium-shamans, who received visits from such beings in their bodies and gave voice to them. Shamans of the latter type were usually young women, and it was believed virginity makes one vulnerable also to hostile intrusions from the otherworld.

These two discourses were later combined in the **Dao creed** so that the 'spiritual journey' was supposed to take place within one's body: regions were identified within it, such as the 'cinnabar field' just below the navel and the 'purple chamber' within the head, where one had to move one's spirit with the help of psychotechnical exercises in order to make contact with deeper realities.

The cult of ancestors. Available archaeological evidence suggests that the central role in the early Chinese system of beliefs was played by ancestral spirits. Family ties were strong and extended beyond the grave – the dead depended on the living for care through sacrifices and offerings, and the living depended on the dead for advice and otherworldly interferences on their behalf. Deities worshipped by bigger groups were the ancestral spirits of the ruling houses. During the Han dynasty the role was taken over by abstract astral deities identified with concrete celestial bodies, although a heavenly connection of the ancestral spirits had been gradually emerging during earlier times.

Mortuary rites during the burial had the function of installing the spirits of the dead in their proper place in the otherworldly system of lineages and hierarchies. Many kinds of ritual objects have been found in aristocratic tombs, including weapons, carved ivory and jade indicating the wealth of the dead person, as well as amulets and statuettes of guardian spirits, such as dragons and ogres. Later, rituals dedicated to ancestors were performed regularly and may have involved shamanistic practices, in which one of the descendants of the worshipped spirit had to perform the role of the dead ancestor receiving the sacrifice, and it is supposed that they also had to speak on behalf of the dead delivering answers to questions. The practice of asking the ancestors for advice soon developed into a system of divination, a corpus of knowledge guarded and utilized by religious professionals.

Oracle bone divination. The earliest surviving textual information about Chinese worldviews is contained in the so-called 'oracle bone' texts of the Shang dynasty, which are also the oldest universally recognized samples of Chinese writing from which the current Chinese script has evolved. It is assumed that the Shang also used brush and ink for writing on bamboo, as the characters for 'writing brush' and 'bamboo book' are met in oracle bone inscriptions, but no such texts have survived.

During later Shang, oracle bones were used in a procedure that began by formulating a question to the divine ancestors, for example, about whether there will be rain or whether a military expedition would be successful, and the bones were then treated with heat until they cracked. The procedure was carried out in the presence of the ruler, or by the ruler himself, as it was his ancestors who were addressed. Divination professionals then studied the cracks in order to determine what the answer to the question was. Sometimes a verification was later added to the bones stating that what was prognosticated had indeed come to pass.

The use of tortoise shells for divination has a much longer history, but checking the probability of specific statements by writing them on the bones is a Shang innovation. Gradually, a body of knowledge arose when professionals trained each other and specific patterns of cracks started to be associated with 'omenverses' that divination professionals formulated and passed to each other. Little by little, this lore evolved into a 'science' of divination that started to formulate broader cosmological claims in order to establish a more systematic basis for itself.

Patterns of reality. While Western philosophy has, from the start, usually expressed a preference towards substance as the foundation of being, the Chinese have developed a consistent process philosophy since its very beginnings. The first written expression of such views is the **Yijing**, or *The Book of Changes*, a manual used by divination professionals.

The *Yijing* makes use of 64 symbols called hexagrams, each of which consists of six lines, straight or broken. The lines correspond to the two fundamental principles of **yin** and **yang**, female and male, darkness and light, flexible and rigid, passive and active, static and dynamic. However, it should be noted that unlike Western binary oppositions, these two principles are not exclusive of each other, but intertwined in various ways.

The Book of Changes has evolved considerably over the centuries and consists of several layers, the earliest of which may date as far back as the tenth century BCE, but were later appended with layers of commentaries that clarify the short cryptic statements of the initial text and explain the worldview behind them. It also contains a few short treatises that elaborate on the most important hexagrams once again and also state the book's philosophical premises in more general terms.

According to these, reality is not a stable structure, but a process of constant change in which various types of combination of yang and yin are constantly transforming into each other. The 64 hexagrams describe the typical and recurrent patterns of entanglement, which characterize any given situation. For divination purposes, someone in harmony with the present could access the cosmic process by using a random number generating system, which would show whether a line of the hexagram is straight (odd number, *yang*) or broken (even number, *yin*). These were further subdivided into 'old' (likely to change) and 'young' (just emerged, less likely to change) *yin* and *yang*. In early practice, the division of a group of yarrow stalks into smaller bundles according to a complicated procedure was used for this purpose. At about the times of the Tang dynasty, a simpler method was introduced with three coins, the combinations of which yielded old and young *yin* and *yang*. Finally, the easiest method of one coin toss appeared, with heads signifying *yang* and tails standing for *yin*. In such a way, before taking a decision, anyone could try to establish which hexagram applies to their particular situation and take this into account when making up their mind.

The onto-cosmology of change. Already at a relatively early stage, Chinese thinkers started to emphasize that it is not the divinations for which the *Yijing* is important, but its discussions of principles and virtues. The later layers of the book indeed present an onto-cosmology, or a theory of being and cosmic order, that has influenced virtually all currents of Chinese worldviews by stressing the processual, complementary, binary, and non-transcendent nature of all reality.

Yang and yin are not polar opposites in conflict with each other (and therefore cannot be aligned with ethical categories such as good and evil), but form a unity in which neither can exist without the other. In the simplified popular version of the *taiji* symbol, the border between the yang and yin halves of the circle is not a straight frontier line, but a wave, and each half contains a dot of the other.

But yin and yang are not primary creative principles. In fact, they are two aspects of an energetic force field called **qi** that makes up the whole, beginning-less and endless universe. Just as humidity, *qi* can condense and form solid matter, but it can also expand and become imperceptible. *Qi* can also have various degrees of purity, and humans, endowed with the capacity of feeling and thinking, consist of the purest kind. *Qi* is in constant change and reconfiguration, and patterns of yin and yang can be used to describe its momentary states, which are nonetheless always transient.

---

qi   the energetic force field that makes up the whole universe; condensations of *qi* form matter in various states

yin* and *yang   two characteristics of *qi* that represent the female and the male, darkness and light, flexibility and rigidity, rest and activity respectively, and all existents are characterized by constantly changing patterns of their mutual entanglement

---

Particular properties of things thus consist in the arrangements of yin and yang; things themselves arise as the bundles of such properties. The idea that everything has a dominant male or female might strike us as odd, but it must have seemed natural to the early Indo-Europeans, who assigned a grammatical gender to each noun, as many languages, such as French, Spanish, or German, still do. For the Chinese, however, the male and the female always existed in mutual entanglement, and this applied to things (such as medicines, which could correspondingly strengthen the yin or the yang in one's organism) as well as abstract principles and qualities. For example, the virtue of humaneness contains a yang element in its power to actively produce good, and a yin element in its quality of caring. The virtue of integrity, in contrast, is yang in its unyielding adherence to what is right, and yin in its egalitarianism. In this way, all qualities are just expressions for particular configurations of balances. Moreover, every yang element in an array gradually changes into yin and vice versa. Such change is not viewed as a violent loss of identity, but a natural process that affects all things. On the contrary, it is the resistance to change, the clinging to a state that should otherwise pass, that is considered unnatural and violent. Spontaneity cannot be achieved as the result of conscious effort, but harmony is spontaneous by definition.

This onto-cosmology is also flat in the sense that it does not recognize a controlling principle that is external to it. The patterns according to which reality changes are naturally spontaneous and a part of the changing reality, not a divinely established law or the dictate of a transcendent will.

Ritual behaviour. In Shang religion, magnificent rituals with sacrificial feasts, dedicated to the king's ancestors, held an important place and the Zhou adopted many of these ceremonies, which were also occasions for dance and music. However, while the Shang used such rituals to manipulate the divine will, the religious professionals of the Zhou soon turned the mechanism around and started to conceive of such rituals as a technology of bringing people into harmony with the cosmic process, which was also political in that it was the duty of the ruler to ensure such harmony in his state and a just and happy society was impossible without it.

---

li   a concept that initially designated rituals, but gradually came to mean proper, conventional, socially acceptable, and morally commendable behaviour that is in accordance with the cosmic order

---

Even the significance of the word *li*, which initially signified just rituals, gradually changed, first into the designation of court etiquette, and then into 'propriety' or polite behaviour that was considered to be the external manifestation of a spirit harmoniously aligned with the cosmic process and accordingly capable of making sound decisions. Still later, as a philosophical concept, *li* started to signify something we might even compare to the current use of the term 'procedure' (as something that should be followed especially in critical situations or in the handling of interest conflicts, etc.), in other words, the proper, legally prescribed way of doing things that guarantees every participant the necessary respect and safeguards their position, helps them to 'keep' or 'save face', if necessary. More critically, we might also characterize *li* as convention, the unquestioned way of how things have always been done, which resists innovation and idiosyncratic behaviour.

From the designation of events the concept thus evolved towards a characteristic of a self-regulated person-in-process, the backbone of a successful and harmonious relationship of the individual with their environment. This change also brought with it an additional requirement of sincerity: it was not enough to observe the procedure or to follow propriety mechanically – *li* was real only if enacted with deep personal commitment and belief that what it prescribed was indeed the only right thing to do.

The mandate of Heaven. Unlike the Shang, who claimed to rule on behalf of a heavenly lord, the Zhou did not derive their political and spiritual authority from the celestial order alone, but claimed to enact the will of the people. Soon after the overturn of the Shang, this was formulated as a political theory that became one of the central tenets of Chinese thinking for millennia. This was done by the Duke of Zhou, one of the model rulers of antiquity, who, instead of seizing the throne for himself after his brother's death, safeguarded it as a regent during the minority of his nephew, the rightful second king of the dynasty. According to this doctrine, the right to rule over people is correlated with the ability to do so for everyone's benefit and in concordance with the cosmic moral order. Heaven, which in the worldview of the Zhou was an anthropomorphic deity, selected the appropriate ruler and gave him the task of bringing the world to order and maintaining it. His descendants then had the right to continue his work – but only until they abided by the rules. A lord was accountable for his actions, and his task was to keep the society stable and harmonious. If he failed to rule virtuously, Heaven would decide that it is time to assign the mandate to someone else, who would then lead a just and victorious rebellion. This is what had happened when the Shang dynasty overthrew the previous, mythical dynasty of Xia, and now came to pass again, since the last Shang king was a cruel tyrant. Consequently, the Zhou kings pledged to rule virtuously and care for their subjects, because otherwise, they, too would lose the mandate of Heaven.

This doctrine has justified nearly all dynastic changes throughout Chinese history. It is convenient as the victors of civil wars are always justified as the representatives of 'natural order', which was what Heaven soon started to mean. The doctrine is, coincidentally, also compatible with the Hegelian-Marxist idea that it is not particular people who can arbitrarily change the course of history, but that historical processes create circumstances for suitable personalities to appear as leaders capable of implementing necessary changes.

More importantly, however, the doctrine of the mandate of Heaven held rulers, to a certain extent, responsible to the people. One way to check whether the ruler still possessed the mandate of Heaven was by studying folklore: if the songs that the people were singing were happy and joyous, the ruler had been doing his job, but if the tone of the songs turned sour, it was time for change. The collection and study of folk songs was one of the tasks of the Music Bureau, a government office responsible for the organization of music- and poetry-related activities of court life, and *The Book of Songs*, the earliest anthology of Chinese poetry, is supposed to have been compiled from material collected in this way.

Ethical charisma. The way in which the possession of the mandate of Heaven manifested itself in a leader was called *de*, which is another difficult and ambivalent term. It is often translated as 'virtue', which has indeed become its standard meaning in modern Chinese, but this is misleading inasmuch virtues are often thought of as ideals that are superimposed on natural reality rather than derived from it. *De* is also not divided into different kinds, as the virtues of Western ethics normally are. More precisely, an underlying meaning of *de* would be the manifestation of the natural order in a particular individual, and the ensuing capacity to act in accordance with it and to the perpetuation of it. This underlying sense can be said to unite various schools, even if they give it particular hues. 'Ethical charisma', suggested by some scholars, is thus a more appropriate translation of the term, as the characteristic of a natural leader who inspires followers to do what each of them individually agrees is just and right. Another nuance of the meaning of the term is 'vigour', as the possession of *de* invigorates, empowers, and enables to do things. Even though the usual connotation of *de* is positive, the word is originally morally neutral and has been, in some texts, also used for the evil powers that a charismatic villain might have.

In practical politics, then, the loss of the mandate of Heaven is notable also in the lack of ethical charisma and failure to inspire followers, particularly as the motivation of the ruler is compromised. Again, the theory is convenient for prospective rebels, because, if they are able to gather support, their cause is likely to be just. On the whole, it ensures the capacity of a centralized system to self-correct by removing from the position of leadership any persons who are unfit or unable to hold it. During a period of instability or turmoil, however, it is likely to produce multiple bids for power that would continue until a genuinely charismatic leader is able to re-establish the 'natural order' and social stability, which would always entail a reasonable level of support among the people, or at least among the intellectuals needed to maintain this order for a longer time.

Classical Chinese Thought: The Hundred Schools

Background. With the start of the Warring States period, or the final part of nominal Zhou rule, the intellectual climate of China changed considerably. Just as different political centres started to fight for power, different traditions and schools of thought also engaged in fierce polemics against each other and splits occurred even within the borders of one school. Later historians distinguish six distinct schools or 'houses' of thought (even if they are collectively called 'a hundred'), but only two of them, the Ru and the followers of Mozi, developed into organized institutions. The tradition of the divination professionals, whose services continued to be sought for by the powers that be, has also been credited with the status of a school. The anarchistic and anti-institutional Lao-Zhuang tradition of thought did not participate in the struggles for political appointments, and the scholars of logic, or 'the school of names', did not form a distinct, interconnected group. The last group of 'legalists' emerged from among the disciples of the Ru scholar Xunzi, and it was them who provided advice to the first emperor that led to his ruthless subjugation of the entire political field.

The early Ru school. While the Western tradition calls the mainstream Chinese worldview 'Confucianism' and the central authority of Confucius, or **Kongzi** as he is called in China (551–479 BCE), is underscored also by many current Chinese thinkers and politicians, he should nonetheless not be credited with the establishment of this tradition. The Chinese word for it, **Ru**, means 'scholar, an educated person' and thus designates the shared worldview and textual tradition of the literati class. It may have originally referred to religious professionals and even ritual dancers, but this group would also have been responsible for the preservation of knowledge related to these rituals. Given the importance that Kongzi assigned to ritual behaviour, the transfer of the term to the followers of his tradition was only natural, and using the term of 'scholars' in order to oppose themselves to another influential school of thought, the followers of the egalitarian Mozi, can also be seen as a claim to a superior intellectual standing. Since the Han dynasty, this group has dominated the executive strata of the Chinese political system and has also managed to establish its values as a more general norm. These values included the idea of a stratified meritocratic society and have contributed to the status of learning in the whole of Chinese society as something to be aspired and looked up to.

Kongzi himself lived in the 'spring and autumn' period (771–476 BCE) immediately preceding the Warring States, during which the central authority of the Zhou dynasty was already weak. He belonged to a large group of wandering scholars, professional political advisors called *shi*, who sought employment with various local rulers whom they promised success if they followed their admonitions. In this endeavour Kongzi himself was not particularly successful. He did have a brief military career in his youth, but was disappointed with the affairs of his native state and left in pursuit of more worthy appointments, which he never found or kept, sometimes because his employers were not capable of living up to his standards. He was more popular as a teacher, however, numbering as many as 3000 disciples in all, if sources are to be trusted, among whom about 70 are known as the primary followers of his doctrine. He was also famous for his learning and is credited with the authorship or editorship of a number of classical works, including *The Book of Songs*, an anthology of poetry, *The Book of Documents*, a compilation of speeches and dialogues of rulers from mythical times to his day, and *The Spring and Autumn Annals*, a history of his native state, according to which the historical period of his life is now known. Together with *The Book of Changes* and *The Book of Rites*, a compilation from various sources, these texts started to be called 'The Five Classics' and became required reading for all educated people. With time, it became customary for scholars and politicians to use examples from them in debate and as reference to historical precedent, when arguing for the implementation of some specific policy. Kongzi's own ideas are recorded in one of the most important Ru texts, the *Analects* (**Lunyu**), which contains brief sayings and bits of dialogue with his disciples, not organized according to any thematic principle. Traditionally this text was considered an authentic transmission of the master's words, but more recent textual scholarship has established that quite a bit of it is of later provenance and thus not an accurate reflection of what Kongzi has actually said. However, as some scholars have also pointed out, the text does not contain any polemical passages and it is therefore very likely that it was complete before the Warring States period with its intense intellectual debates had started.

In the *Analects*, Kongzi is reported as saying that he did not create, but only transmitted, and to a certain extent that is true: his values are conservative in that he viewed an imaginary past, depicted in history books, to be the political ideal from which his current times had deviated. However, this imaginary past was to a large extent his own creation, as he idealized certain rulers and practices at the expense of others, and set up certain precedents, often mythical, as examples to be followed. What Kongzi can certainly be credited with is the organization of these values and ideas, extracted from his views of history, into a mostly coherent discourse, a system of concepts and standards by which particular behaviours and events were to be judged, as well as a description of the human ideal, 'the superior man', to whom the prerogative of political decision-making should belong, not as a birth right, but as a responsibility earned through the cultivation of virtues. It was this ideal to which the majority of the best minds of China have been aspiring from those times to the present day.

Ethical teaching, religion or something else? Up to the present, Western scholarship has not come to a consensus about how the Ru teaching should be classified. Some argue that it is a religion, others that it is an ethical philosophical teaching with no views about the world beyond our reality, yet others claim that the teaching defies such Western classification in principle. The Ru classics contain statements that can be interpreted to support each of these claims, especially as they can be read in a variety of ways.

Those who argue for a fundamentally religious nature of the Ru teaching are convinced that Kongzi had inherited the Zhou belief in **Tian** (Heaven) as an anthropomorphic, personalized deity who supervises the present world from high above and has an arbitrary will. Such a belief is indeed met also much later among the supporters of Mozi. Others, however, argue that Kongzi already understood

'Heaven' as a convenient term to designate a natural order of things, a combination of physical and moral laws, which had the same degree of validity. Observing the patterns of behaviour and change in both nature and society – as well as the results these processes brought about – gave one the benchmarks needed to evaluate the propriety of someone's behaviour. By the end of the Warring States period this was certainly the prevalent view among Ru scholars. Frequent denials by Kongzi to say something about otherworldly beings or to comment on afterlife support this view of the Ru teaching as not relying on the authority of a transcendent supreme being.

It is also quite clear that the main stress of the Ru teaching is on proper behaviour that brings about social harmony, in other words, it has a central ethical and political component. And yet this social harmony is not something to be constructed, but has to be discovered and emulated. 'Studying' in the Ru parlance meant not only learning the facts from historical texts and analysing them, but also studying the internal workings of one's own mind and bringing it into accord with the natural order. And though ritual behaviour was not advocated as a manner of worship, on the one hand, it was also not understood simply as a conservative tradition of identity maintenance on the other. Ritual, in the Ru tradition, was a psychotechnical tool for the nurture and maintenance of the proper dispositions of one's personality. Similarly, it can be said that the Ru classics had scriptural authority: one could debate what had been meant in them, but one could not express the opinion that the classics themselves were wrong on some account. The combination of all these features suggests that what is usually called 'Confucianism' cannot adequately be characterized as a religion or as a philosophical theory, but a 'teaching', which has elements of, but cannot be strictly defined as either of these.

When the ancients wanted to shine their shining charisma over the whole universe, they started by bringing their own states to order. When they wanted to bring their own states to order, they started by managing their families. When they wanted to manage their families, they started by perfecting their own persons. When they wanted to perfect their own persons, they started by straightening their minds. When they wanted to straighten their minds, they started by establishing honesty in their thoughts. When they wanted to establish honesty in their thoughts, they started by perfecting their knowledge. And the perfection of knowledge lies in the investigation of the nature of things.

(*The Book of Rites*, 'The Great Learning', ch. 42)

Ideas: the 'Way' and 'non-striving'. The word 'way' (*dao*), which, similarly to English, signifies both the paths and roads on the ground and the ways of doing things, has been mostly associated with the anti-institutional Lao-Zhuang school, which is usually called Daoism in the West for this reason. However, it is in fact Kongzi and his Ru followers who turned the word 'Way' into a philosophical concept. In short, its meaning stresses that although there may be many ways for doing certain things, there is only one proper Way among them. This, of course, means following the natural order and an ensuing commitment to ritual propriety and moral excellence, which will not fail to produce a harmonious society. A polity can therefore have the Way or stray from it, and it is the duty of loyal subjects to do what they can to restore it. For the Ru, the Way is thus a category related primarily to social and political practice, and only secondarily to the larger 'order of things' in which it is allegedly grounded. This is the view later criticized by the Lao-Zhuang school, who elevated 'the Way' to an ineffable cosmic principle, which cannot be enforced by conscious action.

Indeed, 'non-striving', 'non-doing' or 'non-action' (***wuwei***) is another concept that is actually taken from the *Analects* but later adopted by the Lao-Zhuang as one of the cornerstones of their teaching. For the Ru, 'non-striving' signifies the ideal political situation, where all the rules have been internalized by all political agents to the extent that no conscious effort is needed on the part of the ruler to keep the state running smoothly. Action is thus only required when the state, for whatever reason, has started to stray from the Way. Again, the Lao-Zhuang considered such action to be just as pointless, because any forceful effort would only push one further away from the cosmic Way.

The rectification of names. When asked by a disciple what would be his first task if he were assigned a position of political responsibility, Kongzi famously answered that it would be 'the rectification of names'. This is related to the traditional belief that language and socio-cosmic order were reflections of each other, indeed the word *dao*, or Way, could also be used as a verb meaning 'to speak'. An analogy easily comes to mind with the ancient Greek concept of *logos*, also met in the initial verses of the gospel of John, which identifies 'the Word' with god itself.

The socially oriented thinker that he is, Kongzi connects language primarily to the human world, not the cosmic order, even though this is where everything has its roots. Indeed, the same role that the Way plays as the natural order is fulfilled on the social level by what primarily means 'patterns' (*wen*), but is used by proxy also for 'literature' and 'culture'. As it happens, the word for 'culture' in contemporary Chinese as well as several other East Asian languages can be broken down as 'change of patterns', an intellectual is 'a person of patterns' and so on. The logic behind this view is obviously that only ordered thoughts and literary self-expression both confirm and conform to the norms that guarantee the correct functioning of the human world and the sustainability of civilization.

The word 'rectification' or 'correction' has, in Chinese usage, also strong moral implications – what is right, is also necessarily proper. The actual examples of what 'the rectification of names' means for Kongzi all refer to ranks, titles and other designations of social status. Kongzi thus points out that confusions in language use will necessarily cause problems in the organization of daily life, with dire consequences, including the disruption of the 'natural' moral order. Later Ru scholars, such as Han Yu (768–824), have also called upon their colleagues to restrain themselves from artificial flowery rhetoric, in favour of a plain and clear style. The order of the pattern should take precedence over accidental beauty. Another tendency in Asian languages is to follow elaborate conventions for expressing politeness and humility, something that may also occasionally obscure what is being talked about for anyone but the seasoned courtier: for example, at the time when the *Analects* were written down, it was customary for a woman, regardless of her position or marital status, to use the word 'concubine' in polite talk instead of the pronoun for the first person, thus 'the concubine thinks' instead of 'I think'. Such usage was most likely not the primary target of Kongzi's criticism, but the attitude to life that had produced it may well have been.

---

wen ('**patterns'**)   in a narrower sense, literature and culture, or practices that on the social level fulfil the same role that *dao* accomplishes in the cosmic totality

---

If names are not rectified, then speech will not be in correspondence with the order of things; if speech is not in correspondence with the order of things, then projects will not be completed; if projects are not completed, then rituals and music cannot flourish; if rituals and music will not flourish, punishments and penalties will not be appropriate; if punishments and penalties are not appropriate, people will be unable to move their hands and feet. Therefore, the words of the superior man have to be fit for speech, and the speech of the superior man has to be fit for practice.

(*Analects* 13.3)

The 'superior man' and the 'sage'. While the Ru school was egalitarian in the social sense, at least regarding the right of every talented person to education, and indeed made it possible, at least in theory, for people from humble origins to advance in society, the teaching was strictly hierarchical in its view of the 'quality' of particular individuals. Those capable of study, self-cultivation, and the development of their virtues were considered superior to those who were not talented enough or inclined to pursue this calling. In a nutshell, the Ru solution to all social problems was to put superior people in charge. The term for 'superior man' (**junzi**) has originally meant 'son of a prince', which demonstrates how aristocratic birth right has come to be replaced by an ethical ideal in Ru theory. However, even if the capacity to become a superior man might be a characteristic of an individual from birth, this result is never achieved without rigorous training and self-cultivation. It is an ideal that needs to be emulated, not a type of person that naturally occurs.

> The superior man is an expert of what is right, the petty people are experts of what is profitable.
>
> *(Analects* 4.16)

The *Analects* constantly oppose the description of the superior man to the petty people, who do not deserve political authority. Concerns of economic efficiency, for example, guide the decisions of petty people, while the superior man is motivated by social justice and harmony. Most certainly the superior man should also not desire personal prosperity at the expense of others, nor should he be restrained by fear for the results of just actions. This is why the criticism of rulers (or refusing them service, if they do not heed) has been a time-honoured practice in Chinese politics, meant as it is to ensure the preservation of the mandate of Heaven by the criticized ruler, who is otherwise in the danger of losing it.

However, while the superior man is judged according to his abilities and actions, or the practical application of this superior nature, the ultimate human ideal is nonetheless that of a sage, or a master, who not only enacts the teaching in his practical behaviour, but also perpetuates it by articulating it and transmitting it to disciples. The paradigmatic sage is, of course, Kongzi himself. This difference of ideals reflects, perhaps, the relationship between people in power – whom the Ru would prefer to be 'superior men' – and the wise men whose advice they should listen to, or the Ru themselves.

Harmony, culture, music. All in all, the superior man is not someone who imposes their vision on the world, but dedicates their efforts to the achievement of harmony and the creation of an environment, where a moral order would ensure the dignified coexistence of all. The Way cannot be imposed, it must be discerned by careful study and followed as a route that leads to this goal. Such study entails the internalization of cultural patterns. Self-cultivation has always been a central practice for Ru scholars, and although the term has been given different meanings over centuries, these have always included the idea that ritual propriety is encapsulated in cultural patterns, which need to become an organic part of one's personality.

Even though poetry was valued by Kongzi as an expression of people's feelings as well as their collective political sentiment, the highest rank in his hierarchy of cultural practices is nonetheless allocated to music. Many passages in the *Analects* reflect Kongzi's admiration for superior music and his annoyance with new trends that have the potential to undermine one's efforts to become a better person. Music also has a prominent role in ritual behaviour, which is an even bigger reason for it to reflect the cultural values that the tradition holds dear.

> When character triumphs over cultural patterns, the result is a country bumpkin. When cultural patterns triumph over character, the result is a clerk. When character and cultural patterns complete each other in harmony, what results is a superior man.
>
> (*Analects* 6.18)

The main virtues: humaneness. The *Analects* discuss at length the qualities that the superior man must possess and cultivate. The first among these is *ren*. This is the first and foremost quality of the superior man, so it is no wonder that it is constantly discussed in the *Analects* between Kongzi and his different disciples. As Kongzi was in the habit of appraising the character of his disciples and modifying his answers accordingly, it is often that the definitions of *ren* he gives are at variance with each other.

In English, *ren* is most often translated as 'benevolence'. It is also tempting to translate it as 'virtue', as some of the early translators did, for two reasons. Originally, *ren* had been used for the characteristic of 'aristocratic manliness', just as 'virtue' derives etymologically from the Latin *vir*, 'man'. The transformation of the term in early Ru thought into the soft values of empathy and caring was as radical as the gradual shift of 'virtue' from the soldierly to the civil in ancient Rome. The second reason is that *ren* is the first and primary among virtues, and the efficacy of all others depends on its presence. However, this translation would be misleading as some of the strong traditional connotations of 'virtue' (such as chastity and dedication to a code of honour) are not part of the concept of *ren* at all. 'Benevolence', the usual equivalent, has the disadvantage of being normally associated with what someone in a hierarchically higher position should feel about those in a lower situation, while *ren* is first of all the relationship between peers, which should also be extended to those below and above.

For these reasons, 'humaneness' is a better way to translate the term. The character denoting *ren* consists of two elements signifying 'human being' and 'two' and thus refers to the principle that ought to be at work in ideal interpersonal relationships. It also indicates that the human condition is grounded in sociality, and cannot be perfectly realized by just one person. It is also well known that Ru thought is strongly human-centred: for example, on hearing about a fire in the stables, Kongzi was only concerned with whether any people were hurt, but the fate of the horses did not interest him. (We should note that 'humane' in its Western usage does not really describe such an attitude.)

> Only someone with humaneness can truly like another human being or truly despise another human being.
>
> (*Analects* 4.3)

'Humaneness' is the attitude towards one's peers that entails wishing them well, understanding their situation and problems, and taking them into account. Empathy is one of its key components. But such empathy does not entail the indulgence of the others' weaknesses. On the contrary: *ren* also means treating others with the respect they may sometimes not grant themselves as responsible social beings. Thus, *ren* can also manifest itself as criticism – caring and constructive, but criticism nonetheless.

Wisdom, integrity, filial piety. Kongzi has often underscored that virtues cannot occur in isolation and need to be enhanced by each other. Wisdom or integrity would be invalid without underlying humaneness, and humaneness in turn cannot be practised without the support of other exemplary qualities. In particular, wisdom (***zhi***) is needed in order to discern the particular needs of a situation and to assess the character of other people.

> Study without thinking, and you will be caught in a trap, think without studying and you end up in peril.
>
> (*Analects* 2.15)

> Should I explain to you what knowledge is? Knowing what you know, and not knowing what you don't know – that is knowledge.
>
> (*Analects* 2.17)

> The wise delight in being like water, the humane delight in being like mountains. The wise are in movement, the humane abide in tranquillity. The wise attain harmony, the humane live long.
>
> *(Analects 6.23)*

Wisdom is therefore neither derived from facts that can be memorized from the classics, nor achieved through argumentative speculation, but arises from the combination of both. In order to be real, wisdom needs to be practised; its worth is expressed in the way it can make the world a better place. Similarly to the compassion and wisdom of Mahāyāna Buddhists, the humaneness and wisdom of the Ru make up a binary that joins them as mountains and waters are joined into a landscape.

> For the superior man, there is nothing/no one that pleases him as such and nothing/no one rejected by him as such – if something/someone is right, that he will follow.
>
> *(Analects 4.10)*

Integrity (**yi**) is another of the main Ru virtues, the quality that ensures that the actions of the superior man are just and unbiased. In later Ru thought integrity rose nearly to the same rank as humaneness. Also often translated as 'righteousness' or 'rightness', this virtue emphasizes above all the commitment of the superior man to his duties and moral principles. This also means the superior man does not care for the opinions of the world and can side with the underdog, if their cause is just.

> The Duke of She had a conversation with Kongzi and said: 'In our clan, the character of the people is straight. If someone's father steals a sheep, his son will denounce him'. Kongzi said, 'In our clan, what is considered straight character is something different. A father will cover for his son and a son will cover for his father. This is where we find straightness'.
>
> *(Analects 13.18)*

Finally, filial piety (**xiao**), even if not listed among the 'cardinal virtues' of the Ru teaching, is one of its central values nonetheless and has even a scripture dedicated to it. The Ru teaching emphasized the role of the family as the model for the whole society, with a strong, but caring father at the top of the hierarchy and everyone else knowing that it is just as beneficial for themselves as for the whole family to know their place. Proper family relationships are the standard for solidarity and trust, and in a 'well-ordered' family there is no reason to doubt the propriety of other family members' actions. On the contrary – it is still possible to uphold the Way within the family even if society as a whole has strayed from it, in which case the morally justified actions of other family members may be in conflict with the laws. In totalitarian states (such as China under the rule of Mao Zedong), for example, children have often been encouraged to denounce their family for dissident views, harbouring fugitives and persecuted people and so on. This is something to which the Ru ethics would strongly object.

Over millennia, obedience to and caring for one's parents has become one of the hallmarks of Chinese civilization. Historical texts about rulers considered especially virtuous often stress how they took care of their aged parents, and such examples have become the norm of proper behaviour.

Mengzi (372–289 BCE). The Ru school continued to enjoy a high reputation throughout the Warring States period, even if actual rulers seldom took its advice. However, it also had to respond to theoretical challenges from other strands of thought, in particular, the followers of Mozi (see below), and debates on how to interpret certain crucial ideas of the teaching emerged also within the Ru school itself. The man who managed to establish his vision in these polemical debates as the orthodoxy, to the extent that he has been considered second only to the Master Kongzi himself, was called **Mengzi**, or Mencius in Latinized form. According to his legendary biography, he was raised by his widowed mother in great poverty. Initially Mengzi was not inclined to study, but obeyed his mother's caring instigation and acquired an outstanding education. He then wandered around China and was finally accepted as a member of a prestigious academy of learning established in one of the states, which he left to mourn the death of his mother for three years and thus demonstrated his exemplary filial piety. His teachings are gathered into a voluminous book that bears his name and has been included, together with the *Analects* and two shorter texts, in the list of 'Four Books' that supplemented the 'Five Classics' during the Neo-Confucian revival of the Song dynasty.

Mengzi on human nature. One of the biggest unsolved questions in the Ru teaching at the time was the character of human nature. Kongzi had said almost nothing on the topic, except noting that by nature all people are similar, but grow different as a result of their acquired habits (*Analects* 17.2). This indicated the need for proper education, which would ensure the habits acquired are indeed those that foster social harmony, but said nothing about the fundamental character of human nature itself. This led one of Mengzi's contemporaries to saying that human nature is morally neutral and just as indifferent to good and evil as water is to the direction where it flows. For Mengzi, this was unacceptable. According to him, human nature is fundamentally good, just as water always flows downwards.

> Suppose someone sees a child, who is about to fall into a well. Anyone would be alarmed at this sight and feel compassion within their hearts. This would not be caused by their relationship with the child's parents, and they would not save the child in order to be praised by their community and friends, nor because they would fear voices blaming them for no action. Therefore we see that a mind without compassion is not human, a mind without shame is not human, a mind without modesty is not human, a mind without the feeling of right and wrong is not human. The feeling of compassion in the mind is the sprout of humaneness, the feeling of shame in the mind is the sprout of integrity, the feeling of modesty in the mind is the sprout of ritual propriety and the feeling of right and wrong in the mind is the sprout of wisdom. It is just as natural to have these four sprouts in the mind as it is to have four limbs to one's body.
>
> *(Mengzi* 2A6)

Moreover, human nature contains within it the 'sprouts' that proper education would address and develop. Without the four sprouts, there would be nothing to cultivate and education would have no results. It also appears that the Ru virtues have, according to Mengzi, their roots in one's natural *emotional* responses to the world, rather than rational deliberations about what is good for oneself and the community. However, it is the capacity to rationally reflect on things that is needed for bringing these natural responses to maturation. This is the capacity human beings are endowed with by Heaven – in other words, the natural order of things – and which separates them from animals. The superiority of human civilization over other domains of nature is constituted precisely by the human ability to develop the four emotional sprouts into full-fledged virtues and order the lives and relationships of human beings according to them.

Xunzi (310?–235? BCE). The views of Mengzi were challenged by **Xunzi**, a Ru thinker of the next generation, who also discussed and refuted other Warring States philosophers in the book known by his name. During his lifetime and directly afterwards, Xunzi was rather influential, especially as some of his alleged disciples, who broke with the Ru school, developed some of his ideas into a distinct school of 'legalists' that formed the ideological basis of the short-lived Qin dynasty. Later, however, and perhaps because of that very reason, Xunzi's ideas were eclipsed by Mengzi and he has been for long considered to be a 'heterodox' Ru thinker, while Mengzi was claimed to represent the orthodoxy. At present, however, the rationalism of Xunzi is again attracting more philosophical attention.

> What is it that makes a human being truly human? I say that it is their ability to make distinctions. To desire food when hungry, to desire warmth when cold, to desire rest when tired, to like comfort and to dislike calamities – these are characteristics that people have by birth and need not to be waited to develop, these are what sage-king Yu and the tyrant Jie had in common. But what makes a human being truly human and different from a biped without hair, is the ability to make distinctions. ... Wild animals also have parents and children, but there is no parental affection between them; they also have males and females, but there is nothing like the difference between men and women. This is why the human Way consists in nothing but making distinctions.
>
> (*Xunzi*, ch. 5.4)

Xunzi lived in times when the political situation had further deteriorated and Mengzi's optimistic views of human nature seemed a bit off the mark, as the majority of politically active people shamelessly pursued their own gain. On the whole, Xunzi's philosophy is realistic with an inclination towards the cynical, and averse to superstition. He was critical of pseudoscientific doctrines, such as astrology and physiognomy, and tried to purge the Ru teaching from any residue of the supernatural, even though he considered the rituals of ancestor worship as an essential component of civilized life, just without the belief that the ancestors are actually existent somewhere as the recipients of this worship. He may also be considered one of the world's first proponents of social constructionism, as he pointed out that gender roles in human society are based on the human ability to make distinctions rather than a natural order. Similarly, rites and proper behaviour are imposed on human society by sages, who thereby create the conditions for civilization, which is not the expression of inborn human abilities.

Xunzi on human nature. By far the best-known contribution of Xunzi to Chinese thought is indeed his theory of human nature. According to him, human nature is bad – not actively evil, but also not good in its inclination to seek instant gratification, profit, and pleasures as well as the simplest solution to any problem. Only by purposeful effort can the mind be dragged out of this condition and be made to see things in terms of moral value and long-term perspective. Xunzi criticizes the view of Mengzi as naive: a newborn baby is naive and simple, and if proper education would consist in developing the characteristics that human beings possess at birth, it would mean that this naivety and simplicity should form the moral backbone of the adult, while in fact the opposite is the case.

> Human nature is bad, and its goodness results from purposeful effort. People are born with a desire for profit in their nature, and if they follow these cravings, an all-out war will ensue, while politeness and humility will go under. People are born with hatreds and aversions in their nature, and if they follow these inclinations, mockery of humaneness and breaches of integrity will occur, while loyalty and trustworthiness will go under. People are born with a capacity for pleasures by ears and eyes, and they will enjoy melodies and forms, but if they follow these cravings, lust and immorality will rule, while propriety, integrity, cultural patterns, and principles will go under. Accordingly, if people are allowed to pursue their nature and follow their feelings, the result will necessarily be violence and disorder, ritual principles will be abandoned, and society will return to chaos. Therefore it is necessary that teachers impose character-transforming laws on them, and the Way of propriety and integrity, so that politeness and humility will result, cultural patterns and principles reassembled and order restored. When we look at it this way, it is obvious that human nature is bad and goodness results from purposeful effort.
>
> (*Xunzi*, ch. 23.1)

While the position of Xunzi may indeed have seemed more realistic in his own times, the tradition has sided with Mengzi. Xunzi's views, however, were developed further by two scholars, who are supposed to have studied with him – the Qin minister Li Si (280–208 BCE) and Han Feizi (280?–233 BCE), who later became one of the key figures of the legalist school.

Xunzi on the rectification of names. True to his social constructivist outlook, Xunzi also offered a new interpretation of Kongzi's 'rectification of names'. In Kongzi's view, social hierarchy was ideally co-dimensional with the natural order, and that was what authentic language reflected. Therefore, an effort to rectify names was needed when designations of social hierarchy and the moral standards that corresponded to the respective positions were not in accord with each other. For Kongzi, the rectification of names thus primarily consisted in bringing deviant individuals to heel.

For Xunzi, however, 'names' were established by social convention and did not reflect an eternal order, which is why the 'rectification of names' should consist in making all used terminology consistent with the current situation. The reason why Xunzi started to think about names in the first place is that legal terminology had come into disarray since the 'old sage kings' and this gave cause to constant litigations and was bad both for business and for the general behaviour of people who were perplexed by the multitude of available discourses. So the future true ruler should standardize the terminology by keeping some of the old and creating new where necessary. (We might remember that a standardization of Chinese did actually take place under the Qin emperor.)

But such a task cannot be undertaken without a proper understanding of how language works, which is why Xunzi sets forth a rather detailed description of the cognitive process and semantics. A functional language needs to be in accordance with sense data and can come into being only when that is already ordered; names have to reflect the hierarchy of classes into which things naturally organize themselves. So Xunzi's idea of language is both natural and conventional at the same time: on the one hand, it is something that can be devised or altered at (the ruler's) will, but, on the other hand, it has to follow the logical structure that the world manifests to us in perception.

This is why he is rather dismissive of logical systems that derive from language, and address reality afterwards: the categories that we create have to follow the principles that operate in reality and not vice versa. As said, Xunzi's perception of nature was far from mysticism and 'Heaven', for many others a benevolent controller of what happens under it, amounted to little less than the totality of natural laws in his view. The task of the ruler is to carry out efficient policy that manages people and resources, within the confines of these laws, in the best possible way. No good things happen without effort, and good people only appear as a result of good education, so it is important for Xunzi that the language one uses is up to its task. Which, in its available form, it is not.

> Names do not have fixed links to their referents. They are assigned by convention and when that convention becomes a standard, we say that the link is fixed. If a name differs from that convention, we say there is no fixed link. Names do not have fixed natures. They are assigned by conventional [ideas about] nature and when that convention becomes a standard, we say this name is natural. Names do not have fixed quality. When a name is straightforward, easy to use and does not contradict its object, we say it is a good name.
>
> (*Xunzi*, ch. 22.2)

The development of the Ru school: from political turmoil to official ideology. Towards the end of the Warring States period, the Ru school was eclipsed by the 'legalist' school, which lent itself to the justification of the ruthless political action that led to the violent unification of China under the rule of the Qin emperor. However, the short span of the dynasty and the ensuing troubles suggested that while such policies might serve well for seizing power, they are not necessarily the best for keeping it. The Han dynasty, which emerged victorious from the troubles and continued to rule, with a short interregnum, for more than 400 years, came to choose the Ru teaching for its ideological basis. Its founder, an illiterate, but resourceful officer of peasant background, was initially suspicious of scholars, but soon realized their importance in building a successful administration. He preferred to recruit advisors not associated with the previous dynasty, and the Ru were the obvious choice. Even so, only during the rule of Han Wen-di (179–57 BCE) was the role of Kongzi recognized on the imperial level and adherence to the Ru tradition and a system of civil service examinations was established as one channel of advancement to public office. The content of the examinations was not just Ru teachings at the time. In 136 BCE, the Ru teaching was proclaimed to be the official state ideology. An academy of scholarly training founded a few years later in the Han capital had a curriculum based on the classics of the Ru tradition, and this was also reflected in the content of civil service examinations. Little by little, Ru scholarship became the primary uniting characteristic of everyone involved in all levels of Chinese government.

Mozi (470?–391? BCE). A distinct change of style is visible between the early Ru writings and the texts of Mengzi and Xunzi – arguments and thought experiments have replaced the authoritative statements of the Master, which the *Analects* consist of, or the expounding of theories and comments on verse and cryptic divination texts in other treatises. The man responsible for this change was **Mozi**, a contemporary of Socrates, who lived during the onset of the Warring States period. Nothing is reliably known about his life, but some things can be inferred from the transcripts of his teachings. He must have studied with a Ru teacher, as he is well versed in Ru doctrines. He may have come from among craftsmen, as examples to his arguments are usually drawn from that world, and he has no feelings of solidarity for the scholars, nor does he accept their intellectual authority. Nonetheless, while he rejected the Ru teaching in general, this did not stop him from approvingly quoting Kongzi on those occasions where Mozi considered him right.

It is also probable that most of Mozi's disciples had a similar background, which would indicate a certain change in the Chinese society, with previously subdued groups becoming intellectually more active. Considering the overall outlook of Mozi's teachings, we can say that he gave voice to the views and concerns of the 'petty people', despised by the Ru scholars, who nonetheless had a coherent worldview of their own and a vision of a more just society derived from it. While Mozi took over quite a few Ru concepts, he often gave them a different meaning and also showed why certain Ru goals, in his view, could not be attained with proposed methods. He was also extremely critical of the Ru scholars as a social group, considering them lazy, parasitical, and arrogant. It is therefore understandable that the Chinese intellectual tradition, controlled as it has been by the Ru since the beginnings of the Han dynasty, has looked down on the thought of the Mo school, labelling it intellectually shallow, stylistically uncouth and morally suspect. This view was first promoted by Mengzi, whose polemics against Mozi were instrumental in the school's eventual demise, and is shared by many Chinese intellectual historians almost to this day.

Mozi's teachings are partially preserved in a book that goes by his name, but is most probably compiled by his disciples on the basis of their transcripts of his speeches. His seminal essays are recorded there in three different versions, which differ also in their degrees of radicality, and may reflect the character of the three different disciples who have written them down. The book also contains additions from later centuries, the so-called 'late Mo' thought. However, such appendages should not be considered falsifications of the original – the early Chinese were simply not so much concerned with individual authorship and the authenticity of texts and were inclined to lump together into one 'book' the writings of various origin that carried the same basic message.

What is innovative in Mozi's writings is their argumentative and polemical character. He is very critical of the Ru, but always provides detailed and logical reasons why he disagrees with them, and has thus also provoked the responding Ru scholars to engage in similar reasoning. It has therefore been suggested that whatever else might be the worth of Mozi's contribution to Chinese thought, a turn from the simple presentation of one's views to consistent rational argumentation is certainly creditable to him.

Ideas: utility and equality. One of the targets of later Ru critique of Mozi was the characteristic utilitarianism of his thought. He looked at all social phenomena from the point of view of their utility, an attitude considered vulgar and self-seeking by Ru thought. But the term the Ru interpreted as 'privately profitable' meant 'socially beneficial' for Mozi. In his view, expensive and elaborate funerals, for example, were a waste of resources, as was the prescribed three-year period of mourning after the death of one's parents. During this period an upright person was supposed to withdraw from public life and refrain from work. Similarly, Mozi condemned both music – too expensive and too refined a form of entertainment that contributed little to the common good – and aggressive warfare – the gains of which could never outweigh the loss of life it inevitably caused. He did approve of defensive war, however, and developed techniques he and his followers shared with those under attack; the idea was that if every state and city would be able to defend itself efficiently, this would dissuade aggressive rulers from attacks, as chances of success would be minimal. Thus defensive warfare was socially beneficial not only as a way of ensuring the continuation of the present political situation, but also as a means of minimizing aggressive warfare in general, and indirectly the reason for directing the resources needed for war to worthier purposes.

Another central feature of Mozi's thought is strict egalitarianism. He accepted quite a few premises of Ru thought (as well as the sociopolitical implications of the previous Chinese onto-cosmological tradition), including the hierarchical nature of the decision-making mechanism, but his standards for just decisions differed greatly. For Mozi, any judgement must rest on impartial, objective, and measurable data. According to him, there would be a difference in the quality of the product of a skilled craftsman and an unskilled one, but there would be no difference in the measurements they would obtain with a yardstick. There were three components of what Mozi considered useful, or indicative of the efficiency or well-being of a society: the level of material wealth, the size (and growth trend) of the population, and the level of social order. (It should be noted that 'wealth' was understood as a basic living standard for everybody, and not luxury, which Mozi rejected.) And these three criteria of social efficiency could indeed all be measured: the levels of wealth (as in gross national product per person), the size of the population and the social order (as in a low crime rate) were all objective. Any important decision that affects the life of many should, according to Mozi, be based on this kind of objectivity. In his view, such objectivity must also have been characteristic of Tian, or Heaven, who would judge each individual directly according to their behaviour and input to society, instead of delegating this task to all levels of rulers. Therefore, as a premise, we should consider each individual equally valuable.

Impartial concern. This conclusion leads to the central tenet of Mozi's philosophy, or impartial concern. The term is often translated as 'universal love', which is literally correct, but misleading, as the majority of scholars agree that emotional attachments were not a part of this idea. On the contrary, impartial concern is 'cold' rather than warm: Mozi and his followers insisted that our relationships with other people should not be defined by any personal attachments to them. Therefore, they opposed the Ru notion of filial piety as particularistic and therefore detrimental for social harmony. Mozi presents the example of a thief who steals, because he values his own family more than the family he steals from, and by criminally relieving the hunger of those close to him he causes the same kind of hunger to others. In another example he asks to whom it is more reasonable to entrust one's relatives when going to war – to a proponent of particularism or an advocate of impartial concern? Suggesting that only someone committed to impartial concern would take care of people who are not their own family, Mozi concludes that we are all implicit universalists.

Similarly, aggressive warfare results from a ruler valuing the wealth of their own state more highly than the welfare of their neighbours. This is why Mozi also rejects the Ru idea that social harmony can be achieved by extending the private attachments to increasingly broader circles, as proposed in *The Great Learning* – such extension does not create a universalist and impartial totality, but only pushes the limits of private, particular attachments to their natural limits. A nationalist view may extend kinship solidarity to the whole ethnic group or population of a country, but denies the same kind of sympathy to people of other countries or groups. As nationalism has been a cause of destructive conflict throughout history, it presents a good example of how the Ru idea fails from a Mo viewpoint.

The idea of 'impartial concern' – that we are morally obliged to everyone in the same degree – was the target of the attack by Mengzi and other Ru scholars, who emphasized that the care for 'one's own' must always come first. It is quite possible that the polemics against Mozi actually raised filial piety to a more central position in the Ru moral system – for example, a text called *The Book of Filial Piety*, claiming to be a conversation between Kongzi and one of his disciples, was written approximately at that time. Some recent scholars have also argued that the 'cold' universalist reading of Mozi's argument is not doing it justice, but presents it through a critical Ru prism.

'Compasses' of thought. If things are to be judged only by completely objective standards, then it is obvious that opinions can be either right or wrong and that right opinions are better than wrong ones. This is why Mozi is intolerant of the plurality of opinions and freedom of thought in general. Argumentation, for him and his followers, is a method for finding out what the truth is, but once the problem is solved, there is no room for dissent. Human nature, according to Mozi, is completely malleable and rulers can bend it in whatever direction according to their will. This is why social hierarchy is useful: it is up to the ruler to establish the truth and the correct opinion, which must then be strictly followed by the populace. Rulers, in turn, are competent if and only if the opinions they establish are in accordance with the Heaven's impartial view of things. In this respect, Mozi's social ideal is more reminiscent of totalitarian regimes than of modern democracies. In practice, Mozi advocated an impartial system of rewards and punishments that would ensure that the ruler's 'correct' opinions would be endorsed by everyone – a concept later taken over by the legalist school.

There are three rules, or 'compasses' ('gnomons', to use the precise term) that should be used for determining whether an opinion should be endorsed:

historical precedent, empirical observation, and the practical utility of its conse-quences. The last was the main among the three, so even if an opinion satisfied the first two, but failed the third, it was still considered wrong. Positive historical precedent referred to the practice of the sage kings of the past, but Mozi often evokes more recent precedents, and not only for good examples. Empirical obser-vation also included the testimony of other people. Therefore, for example, the belief in ghosts and spirits was supported by Mozi and his followers, because there were stories about vengeful spirits in the past, sightings of ghosts were reported by his contemporaries, and the consequences of neglecting the spirits would be more harmful than paying one's respects to them. Even if ghosts would ultimately turn out not to exist, Mozi says, anticipating Durkheim's sociology of religion, the cer-emonies organized in their honour would still provide occasions for villagers to convene and socialize and strengthen their spirit of communality. It can therefore be asked whether Mozi's endorsement of spirit beliefs, an odd feature of his teach-ing in view of its overall stress on rational argument, can perhaps be a concession to the popular worldview still prevalent among his followers.

The Mo school. It is likely that Mozi had hundreds of followers and they were organized as a strict fraternity with authoritative masters in charge and observing a disciplined and frugal lifestyle. For quite some time, they com-peted rather successfully with the Ru in seeking the favour of rulers. Especially smaller states often sought their technical advice in defensive warfare, which they shared willingly. Their coherent views and the argumentative style used for dissecting their opponents' opinions must also have made a strong impres-sion on intelligent audiences. Later Mo scholars concentrated in particular on the logic of argumentation and engaged in a debate with the 'school of names', which had similar concerns. They also re-evaluated the earlier teach-ings critically with their newly developed analytical tools at hand. Unfortunately, the writings of later Mo scholars have not been preserved very well and are therefore difficult to decipher.

The counterattack of the Ru mounted by Mengzi and his followers was none-theless successful in undermining the school's authority and finally defeating it so that no Mo writings remain after the third century BCE. Its influences linger, how-ever, and can be discerned, for example, in the thought of Xunzi and the legalist school, but also in the overall style of Chinese philosophy from the late Warring States period onwards.

Laozi and the *Daodejing*. One of the most influential and controversial texts of the entire Chinese intellectual tradition, usually called *Laozi* in China and *Daodejing* in the West, challenges the fundamental assumption of both the Ru and Mo schools, namely, that conscious effort is needed to realize a sociopolitical ideal. This view is grounded in a sophisticated metaphysics bordering on mysticism, which is presented in a cryptic and aphoristic style very different from the usual writings of the Warring States period. This is why it was believed for a long time that the text is much older and predates most Ru writings, but its polemical references to both Ru and Mo texts let us date the traditional text approximately to the third century BCE. Other versions of the text from about the same period have been excavated from tombs during the last decades of the twentieth century, which testify to the dynamism of the textual development. It is a collective work with some internal inconsistencies, and our best guess is that it was written during a longer period of time by a number of authors, who shared their basic worldview, but may have had different opinions on details, and later generations were also able to edit and adjust the aphorisms of the earlier textual layers.

The text is ascribed to a mythical person called **Laozi**, or 'Old Teacher', an older contemporary of Kongzi, who almost certainly did not exist, and even if he did, he definitely did not write the book that took his name. First references to him in historical sources appear well after the text itself was in circulation, and the figure described in them is supposed to give the text greater authority. Supposedly a wise man working in Zhou archives, Laozi allegedly had a meeting with Kongzi, after which Kongzi acknowledged his intellectual superiority. Dismayed with the declining ways of the world, Laozi is reported to have travelled westwards into the wild, riding on an ox, but as his reputation preceded him, the border guard was reluctant to let him depart together with his wisdom, and asked him to leave something behind. This is when Laozi, we are told, produced his book, which is about 5000 characters long. The title of *Daodejing*, or *The Book of Way and Vigour*, is composed of the two characters with which the two parts of the book start.

Reading the *Daodejing*. While many Asian philosophical texts are difficult and prone to multiple interpretations, the *Daodejing* is definitely in a league of its own. A large number of translations of it exists, over 300 into English alone, and a further 400 or more into other languages. Some of them are misleading or just plain wrong, but even the best of them are not indisputably correct. The best way to approach this text is therefore to read several different translations simultaneously. This is because the key concepts are all ambiguous and difficult, and often convey at once several ideas that the Western intellectual tradition habitually considers distinct and separate. This may partially be due to the different inclinations of different authors in the collectivity, writing at different times. Some translations appear to us as closer to the 'standard', because they endorse the prevalent view of the Chinese scholarly tradition and therefore also resemble each other more closely. This does not necessarily make them more precise, as some of the more idiosyncratic interpretations seem, from the perspective of the present, to capture the tone and message of the original more adequately. The 'standard' follows, for most part, the interpretation of Wang Bi (226–249), a scholar combining Ru learning with 'dark learning', a syncretic teaching that appropriated and reinterpreted quite a few of the concepts of the Lao-Zhuang school. Wang Bi was certainly a conscientious scholar, but he worked on the text centuries after it had entered circulation and occasionally altered the text so that it would better match his idea of it. He was also inclined to foreground the mystical aspects. So, in spite of the historical chance that his interpretation has become for us the 'standard' text, his reading of it is just one among many possible ones.

For those readers who have to rely on a translation, such a particular perspective may change the text quite a bit. For example, the famous first sentence of the *Daodejing* is usually translated as something like 'the *dao* that can be spoken about is not the eternal *dao*', meaning that the world is guided by a transcendent metaphysical principle that cannot be captured in words. In fact, the character *dao* ('way') appears three times in this sentence, and 'to speak' is indeed one of its meanings. This interpretation suggested by Wang Bi is therefore certainly legitimate, but not the only or even the primary one. It is just as correct to translate this as 'the way that can be taken is not the constant way', meaning that any particular behavioural strategy opposes itself by its very particularity to the general process of being as a whole.

Ideas: the Way. Curiously, the term *dao*, when it occurs in Ru texts, is normally translated as 'the Way', but left untranslated (and often capitalized), when the *Daodejing* is discussed. This helps to underscore the traditional interpretation of 'way' as a transcendent metaphysical principle, possibly with creative powers of its own. Another, and perhaps more adequate approach would be to see the treatment of the term in the *Daodejing* as an effort to hijack and redefine the Ru understanding of 'natural order'. What the text emphasizes is that the way how things are in themselves cannot be captured, rigidly defined, reified, and enforced as the basis of a social system. Any effort to do so is actually straying from how things are in themselves. Something like a '12-step programme to attain sincerity' would never result in sincerity, only a different kind of artifice. And just as it is impossible to become sincere deliberately, one cannot also achieve an accord with natural order otherwise than by abandoning oneself to it.

The way that can be taken is not the constant Way
The name that can be named is not a constant name
Nameless is the beginning of Heaven and Earth
Naming is the mother of myriad things
Therefore:
  Constant absence of desires
  Turns into seeing its subtlety
  Constant presence of desires
  Turns into seeing its limits
  These two have a common origin
  But differ in name
  Together we call them the mystery
  The mystery behind all mysteries
  The gate of all wonders

(*Daodejing*, ch. 1)

Within the Way, there are really no distinctions, not to mention opposites. Concepts such as 'beauty' or 'profit' are the product of the discriminating mind, which generates its own order and imposes it on how things are in themselves. In reality they have no importance. But assigning a higher value to some things over others produces desires and thereby fosters crime and disorder. The same applies to the virtues of the Ru. What we are concerned with here are conventions and distinctions rather than 'natural order', which the Way is supposed to embody.

While there are some sections in the *Daodejing*, which could be read to speak of the Way as an entity, most of the text makes more sense if we think of it as the fundamental character of the world, its *processual* nature, which indeed matches the architecture of Chinese thought in general. The Way is constantly present as an absence of stability, and this is what makes the world go round. 'Thirty spokes are united at the hub, but it is the emptiness within it that lets them be used for a carriage', the *Daodejing* says (ch. 11), and 'The Way is an empty vessel – be careful not to fill it in use' (ch. 4).

Vigour. The other character in the title of *Daodejing* is usually paid much less attention in discussions of the *Daodejing*. It is the same word the Ru tradition inteprets as 'ethical charisma', but while the *Daodejing* keeps its basic meaning of 'the force that makes things happen', it has stripped it completely from any moral connotations. Matters are actually more complicated, as on occasion the text also uses the word in a negative way, in its original Ru sense ('vigorous virtue').

In the positive sense of the term, we might translate it as 'vigour' – 'virtue' would be misleading, because this is a Ru concept criticized in the *Daodejing*, and 'power', which is also sometimes used, works between entities rather than within one thing. Just as the Way itself, vigour is neutral and cannot be harnessed for individual goals.

> Greater vigour is not 'vigorous virtue', therefore its vigour is present
> Lesser vigour does not stray from 'vigorous virtue', therefore its vigour
>   is absent
> Greater vigour engages in non-action and has no motivation to act
> Lesser vigour acts and has a motivation to act ...
> Therefore:
>   Stray from the Way and 'vigorous virtue' will follow
>   Stray from 'vigorous virtue' and humaneness will follow
>   Stray from humaneness and moral integrity will follow
>   Stray from moral integrity and ritual propriety will follow
>
> (*Daodejing*, ch. 38)

> The sage has no constant mind
> He lets the mind of the people be his mind
> Who is good to me, I am good to them – who is not good to me, I am good
>   to them as well; this is the vigour of goodness
> Who is sincere with me, I am sincere with them – who is not sincere with
>   me, I am sincere with them as well; this is the vigour of sincerity
> The sage is in the world and inhales the entirety of the world as his mind
> People look at his ears and eyes
> He looks at the people as his children
>
> (*Daodejing*, ch. 49)

Anything that produces natural change is vigour, other types of creatures and things have it just as people do. In this sense, vigour is the dynamism of the Way at work in one particular thing. 'The Way generates things, vigour grows them', the *Daodejing* says (ch. 51). To be in possession of vigour therefore means to be in accord with the Way. From the habitual Western point of view, it seems good to be 'in control' of one's inner resources, but the very opposite is meant here – it is the inner resources, which make up the capacity to be in the world and to change in accord with it, that should help one to find one's natural place in the greater scheme of things.

Non-action. 'When high-rank scholars hear about the Way, they do their utmost to practise it; when middle-rank scholars hear about the Way, they sometimes practise and sometimes forget to; when low-rank scholars hear about the Way, they laugh at it – if they wouldn't laugh, it would not be the Way', the *Daodejing* says (ch. 41), seemingly to convince us that it is a sign of human quality to take its teachings seriously. But this might as well be a trap: the idea that people can be ranked according to their achievements is so alien to the *Daodejing* that endorsing the division of scholars seems quite out of place. So maybe it is the laughter, as some scholars suggest, the expression of joy and happiness, that is the most adequate reaction to the teaching? This seems indeed to be in accord with one of the key concepts of the *Daodejing*, that of non-action.

> In studying, days are spent in expansion
> In practising the Way, days are spent in self-limitation
> Self-limitation and then again self-limitation
> Until the point of non-action is reached
> Non-action – and no action is left undone
> Taking the world always happens without effort
> But when efforts are made to that end – it will never suffice for taking the world
>
> (*Daodejing*, ch. 48)

Originally, this is a Ru idea expressing a Weberian ideal of governance – the rules are in place and internalized by all parties concerned to the extent that no effort is needed to enforce them. For the *Daodejing*, however, the internalization of decreed rules is the actual root of the problem. Things take their course and no procedure can foresee everything that might happen, and there will inevitably be occasions when 'poetic justice' is morally superior to what the laws prescribe. It is therefore unwise to try to regulate all aspects of human behaviour instead of just letting things take their course. Similarly, sticking to detailed action plans fails to deliver expected results, when something unexpected occurs – and something always does. Non-action therefore means not refraining from any kind of action whatsoever, but only from deliberate efforts, strict timelines and benchmarks and other kinds of administrative excess, especially in managing state affairs: 'The Way is constant in non-action, therefore no action remains undone – if nobles and kings would maintain this principle, the myriad things would change by themselves' (*Daodejing*, ch. 37).

The political ideal. While non-action is pictured as the way that a sage acts in daily life, it is primarily advocated for rulers as the best strategy for success. Just as for other thinkers of the period, the social and political concerns are central also for the authors of the *Daodejing*. Their vision of what social order looks like is nevertheless remarkably different from the Ru and Mo schools. Even though the simple lifestyle described in the *Daodejing* is more resemblant of the Mo political vision than the Ru view of culture and civilization, the Mo ideal of a populous and technologically advanced state attracting immigrant workforce (a goal which many rulers set themselves in those days) is explicitly rejected. The *Daodejing* advocates a sort of a communal agrarian utopia with no drive for technological innovation or intellectual advancement, a lifestyle perhaps akin to such closely knit religious communities as the Amish or the Mennonites.

> Let the state be small and the population scarce
> Let there be weapons for tens and hundreds — never to be used
> Let death be a weighty matter, let travels lead no one away
> There would be boats and carriages
> But no one would board them
> There would be armour and halberds
> But no one would deploy them
> Let the people again remember things by knotted cords
> Let them think their food is sweet enough
> Let them consider their clothes are beautiful enough
> Let them appreciate their houses as peaceful enough
> Let them find their lifestyle as pleasurable enough
> You can see the neighbouring state
> You can hear each other's fowls and dogs
> But people will grow old and die
> And never go to visit each other
>
> (*Daodejing*, ch. 80)

It is difficult to imagine that this vision could result from letting things take their course. Even the text itself acknowledges that such a utopia could not be achieved except by promoting illiteracy, ignorance and indifference to the ways of the world. Knotted cords should be enough to keep track of things, and even the affairs of the neighbouring village would not arouse anyone's curiosity.

In practice, this ideal would probably be even more difficult to enforce without resorting to the very same strategies of deliberate action that the *Daodejing* condemns. It is therefore understandable that these teachings have never had much political success, except when mistakenly connected to the promises made by the Dao creed, which combined the authority of Laozi with alchemical and psycho-technical practices pursuing immortality. We may also speculate as to how much this social vision is actually derived from the metaphysics of the Way – as the *Daodejing* is not a work of single authorship, it is a meeting place of different strands of thought and its metaphysical and sociopolitical components can also be evaluated separately.

Zhuangzi (369?–286? BCE). The *Daodejing* might have remained a cryptic text read by eccentric hermits and not become a classic of a philosophical school, were it not for the second major text of its tradition, the book of **Zhuangzi**. It is true that the term 'the school of the Way' was first used only during the Han dynasty and that there was no such formal organization or even a discernible group of like-minded scholars around in previous times about whom we would know. And yet, with the appearance of the *Zhuangzi*, we can speak of the beginnings of an articulated and influential strand in Chinese thought that opposed itself to other schools, had a shared vocabulary and central ideas, and soon became something with which the Ru mainstream had to reckon. Usually this 'school' is called Daoism in Western academic literature, but the mystification of the concept of the Way and the ideological character of an -ism are both inappropriate to describe this current of thought, which is why it will be here called the **Lao-Zhuang** school, a term favoured by many recent authors.

Zhuangzi, or Zhuang Zhou by his proper name, is a historical figure, a contemporary of Mengzi, who was unaware of him. Of the book that circulates in his name, only about one fifth, the so-called 'inner chapters', is believed to be actually written by him. Just as with Mozi's book, later writings influenced by him and developing his ideas were appended to the book, so that we should make the difference between the historical Zhuang Zhou and 'Zhuangzi' as the collective author of the entire book.

Zhuangzi's style is lively and diverse, and he often makes his point by parables and illustrative little stories, in some of which he features himself. Another central figure of the book is Kongzi, to whom Zhuangzi ascribes many of his own views, often presenting them from a standpoint of someone actively engaged in worldly affairs – something Zhuangzi himself neither advocated nor practised, but, unlike the authors of the *Daodejing*, did not criticize. We also often find Zhuangzi in conversation with Huizi, or Hui Shi of the 'school of names', and these passages are possibly based on actual debates. But more often Zhuangzi engages his quite substantial literary skills to create characters and situations that convey his point, and many of these have become stock references all over the East Asian cultural area.

Ideas: the change of perspective. The best-known story in Zhuangzi's book is probably about himself and a butterfly, who cannot figure out who is dreaming of being the other. Zhuangzi concludes the story with saying that this is an illustration of what is called, literally, 'the change of things'. However, earlier in the chapter he has used the word 'thing' as something that is never essentially 'this' or 'that', but always answers to either of these depending on the perspective of the speaker. The character 'change' can also be read as 'changeability' and refer to such a difference. Similarly, a 'yes' can become a 'no' from a different point of view, and what is 'right' for some is 'wrong' for others. Indeed, the butterfly story also makes more sense as an argument against essences, against the view that there should be a ground for each of us to stand on firmly and claim as properly our own, than an ironical account of how changes in reality should be understood.

Zhuang Zhou once had a dream that he was a butterfly, a happy butterfly enjoying itself and contented in spirit, with no knowledge of Zhou. Suddenly it woke up and realized with astonishment that it was Zhou. What it did not know, however, was whether it was Zhou who had dreamed he was a butterfly, or whether it was a butterfly now dreaming it was Zhou. But between Zhou and a butterfly there necessarily has to be a difference. This is what we call the change of perspective.

(*Zhuangzi*, ch. 2)

But this means that although persuasive arguments can be voiced in a philosophical debate, Zhuangzi argues, it can never be settled for good what the actual truth is. More than 2000 years of philosophical history in both Europe and Asia only confirm his thesis: being persuaded by arguments is not tantamount to being correct. However, Zhuangzi does not deny their usefulness, but suggests we should only use words as instruments to foster understanding, instead of clinging to them as the unchanging expressions of eternal truths. We use nets for catching fish, he says (ch. 26), leaving them when the fish is caught, and the same should apply to words.

And yet we stay anchored in our perspectives, bound to them by agendas and desires. In another story Zhuangzi encounters a strange bird in an enclosed forest and pursues it to a scene where the bird is about to eat a praying mantis, which in turn is attacking a cicada; both of them are concentrated on their prey and therefore oblivious to their surroundings. But when Zhuangzi is trying to use the situation and shoot the bird with his bow, he is himself targeted by the forest warden. Each of the participants of the chain could have escaped danger by not fixing themselves on the perspective they were holding, and the same applies to philosophical views as well.

Zhuangzi on non-action. While the Ru advocated non-action in the ideal situation, where natural order has been internalized by all and the *Daodejing* promised that things take care of themselves when one is able to refrain from participating in their management, Zhuangzi offered an innovative and influential perspective on non-action as non-effort. Instead of removing action from oneself, he recommended removing oneself from the action. While we are anchored in our particular perspectives, we may indeed act consistently and even attain the goals we have set ourselves, but Zhuangzi compares such life to that of a galloping horse, who cannot be stopped and does not know where it is going, until completely worn out (ch. 2). As an alternative, he offers stories of superior craftsmen, whose results are achieved by non-action. The most famous among them is probably the cook Ding who has carved up thousands of oxen without having to replace his knife (while some of his colleagues changed them once a month). Instead of seeing himself as the cutter and the ox as his object, as he did at the start of his training, he has learned to give up what the senses tell him and to let his spirit act freely. His knife naturally finds the gaps in the flesh and never touches a bone or knuckle, which is why it is just like new after years of use (ch. 3). By leaving the particular perspective behind and feeling oneself as a part of the process, one is able to harmonize oneself with what is taking place, and thereby blend one's directed action with what would naturally happen. This view has later been combined by Chan/Zen Buddhists with the *anātman* theory and has, for example, influenced the training psychology of martial arts: until a practitioner stays focused on winning at all costs, they will not be very successful, and the first step towards mastery is the internalization of the art, until it becomes second nature and spontaneous action will guide the person, not vice versa.

This is also how we might interpret Zhuangzi's ethical stance: there is a consensus among scholars that he does not advocate ethical nihilism, even though his perspectivism does not allow him to endorse any standards of 'good' and 'evil'. Wholesome action is what is in accord with the natural order and accord with the natural order cannot be attained by deliberate effort, which is why we must trust our intuition rather than imposing artificially devised standards of behaviour onto real-life situations.

The Lao-Zhuang school. The ideas expressed in the *Daodejing* and the *Zhuangzi* attracted a considerable following among Chinese intellectuals, but due to their anarchistic nature they did not provide a sound basis for establishing an organized school, nor were they seriously looking for practical outlets in political life. Zhuangzi reports an effort by a ruler to recruit him as an advisor, which he declined, and this must have been the general sentiment of similarly inclined thinkers, many of whom have remained anonymous and are known to exist only by their contributions to the later *Daodejing* textual layers and the inauthentic chapters of the *Zhuangzi*. One of the reasons the Lao-Zhuang tradition has been identified, since the Han dynasty, as one of the 'schools' of classical Chinese philosophy, may even have been the fact that the historian who composed the first compendium on the various schools was himself an adherent of this tradition and put the Lao-Zhuang above all others in his treatise.

Apart from the *Daodejing* and the *Zhuangzi*, some other works of the Lao-Zhuang tradition have also survived. One of these is a book attributed to Liezi, a master mentioned in the *Zhuangzi*, but quite certainly inauthentic. Another one, ascribed to a student of Laozi called Wenzi and also considered a late forgery for a long time, has recently been re-established after the discovery of an early manuscript. Gradually, comments on the *Daodejing* also started to appear, as the text was becoming more popular, and quite a few among its readers also engaged in alchemy and the occult in their pursuit of the 'natural order'. After a few centuries, this trend of thought developed into various schools of the Dao creed.

Yang Zhu (440?–360? BCE). Even though some scholars associate the solitary figure of **Yang Zhu** with the Lao-Zhuang school, this is probably because his work has survived primarily in some of the later chapters of the *Zhuangzi* and as an appendix to the apocryphal book of Liezi, in addition to being briefly summarized in refutations of his ideas by Mengzi. Yang Zhu is known for his unabashed egoism and hedonism. He did not care for fame or riches – these, according to him, were goals for the foolish, who did not understand the joys of instant gratification. Neither was long life, with pain and sickness towards the end, worth striving for. Therefore, he concluded, one must dedicate oneself to entertainment and the pleasures of the body.

> The people of ancient times knew that we come to this life for a short time and death will arrive quite soon, therefore they followed their hearts in whatever they did. They did not stray from what naturally seemed good to them and what brought pleasure to their bodies, but eschewed what led them away from such things. Therefore they did not act in order to acquire fame and respect, but followed their nature and had fun. From the myriad things, they denied themselves nothing that was good, nor was a posthumous reputation something they sought.
>
> (Yang Zhu in *Liezi*, ch.7)

These views presented him for Mengzi as a good other extreme against the Mo school and its impartial caring for others, placing the Ru conveniently at the balanced midpoint. Some followers of the Lao-Zhuang ideas might indeed have felt inclined towards his view of life, but more probably he was associated with this school by critical Ru scholars who used him to highlight what they saw as the weakness of Lao-Zhuang ethics, or the presumption that people will behave well if left to their own devices or if they only follow their instincts.

The school of names. When argumentation and debate became a necessary component of not only philosophical discussions, but also of daily life, for example in court politics, it was inevitable that the status of arguments and the capacity of language to articulate truth started to be questioned. This was done by several thinkers grouped together as the 'school of names'. As some scholars have suggested, these people have taken the Ru ideas of the 'rectification of names' further to question the basics of reference, anticipating some of the central concerns of analytical philosophy. In any case, they disprove the widespread claim that classical Chinese thought had no inclination towards logic – it is true, however, that this logic was seen with suspicion, was not developed much further, and never acquired such a position as it has in Western thought.

Similarly to the ancient Greek school of Sophists, the 'school of names' in Warring States China had a strong connection to legal argumentation, but soon developed into a strand of paradoxical thought perceived as a threat to rational debate as such. Indeed, if language can be used to defend both incompatible opposites in a dispute, legal or otherwise, how can it be trusted at all? We saw that for Zhuangzi, the conclusion was that it cannot, and every argument is necessarily anchored in a particular perspective. Other thinkers, such as those of the late Mo school, tried to undermine the threat by showing how such paradoxes can be dissolved.

Just as with the Lao-Zhuang tradition, the school of names was not properly a school and some scholars have even opposed to each other the two main figures associated with it. These figures were Hui Shi, a contemporary and alleged friend of Zhuangzi, and Gongsun Long, a thinker of the next generation. **Hui Shi** was most likely a minister in his home state, which he was forced to flee after its military defeat. His works have been lost, and only a handful of theses credited to his name have been preserved in the *Zhuangzi*, as well as quite a few conversations between them. **Gongsun Long** was also famous as a skilled disputer and advisor to politicians. A short treatise by him survives. Both men were known for their pacifist views and as advocates of an impartial view of everyone and anything, which suggests Mo influences.

Hui Shi (370?–310? BCE). One of the later chapters of the *Zhuangzi* lists 10 theses that Hui Shi is supposed to have successfully defended in arguments. Nothing is recorded of his reasoning, but some of it can be inferred. For example, when Hui Shi says 'Today, I started out for Yue and arrived there yesterday', he is most likely questioning the referring power of context-related terms, as both parts of the sentence can indeed be uttered as true by the same person at different moments. Therefore, all words do not refer to realities in a similar manner. The thesis 'What has no length cannot be added up, and yet a distance of a thousand miles consists of these' speaks about the relationship of points and lines, which Aristotle in his *Physics* allocated to two different registers of observation. Other theses seem to point to different logical categories such as natural kinds and type-token-relationships: 'When things very similar to each other are opposed to things less similar to them, we call this the small scale of similarity and difference, but when all things are both similar and different to each other, we call this the great scale of similarity and difference'. Hui Shi's final thesis sums up his ethical views: 'When all the myriad things are loved in the same way, heaven and earth will become one'.

These sentences, although mostly paradoxical on the surface, may well be the provocative formulations of a coherent worldview. However, as none of the argumentation survives, any further discussion of Hui Shi's views is only speculation.

Gongsun Long (320?–250? BCE). We stand on a firmer ground with Gongsun Long, famous for his assertion that 'a white horse is not a horse'. In a treatise written in a style very similar to Socratic dialogues, he argues that a compound term such as 'white horse' unites two concepts and therefore is interchangeable with neither of its components. For example, were someone to go to the stables and ask for 'a horse', they might as well be presented with a black one, while a request for a 'white horse' would not have the same result. If the terms are not interchangeable, their meanings are consequently also not identical. The opponent argues that horses with no colour do not exist, which is why it is incorrect to require the interchangeability of a general term and a particular one. To this, the proponent replies that a group of horses of different colours can, in fact, be called 'horses' without the specification of colour.

From this, we can see that what Gongsun Long is actually discussing are the limits of reference. In the culture of debates prior to the appearance of the school of names, the identity of the two parts of a correct proposition seems to have been taken for granted, and the treatise is directed against such a naive view rather than meant as a critique of language in general.

Later Mo responses to the school of names. The ideas of Hui Shi and Gongsun Long did not receive much further attention. Evidently many of the Ru scholars found philosophical debate a frustrating exercise that would lead people away from ethical concerns rather than strengthen their moral backbone. The Mo school had a different view and the somersaults of logic have indeed been subjected to detailed critique in later Mo writings, but with the decline of the Mo school this tendency, too, died out.

The late Mo thinkers were keen on resolving the paradoxicality of the 'school of names' claims either by demonstrating that there was a fallacy underlying a particular thesis, or that it expresses a correct and therefore non-paradoxical insight in an exaggerated and puzzling manner. For example, they countered Hui Shi's view on points versus lines by defining a point in a relationship to other points, that is, as the endpoint of a hypothetical line. As any point on a line can be the endpoint of another line, there is no paradox involved in the relationship. Similarly, they accepted his view of relational terms, but pointed out that the use of a contextually embedded term such as 'this' or 'today' comes with a set of truth conditions that must be applied wholesale to the situation under consideration. It is therefore correct that the same person can truthfully say they 'left for Yue today' and 'arrived in Yue yesterday', but not in the same sentence.

They also addressed the critique of reference of Gongsun Long in an example that resonated with the Mo concern with population growth and a low crime rate: 'A thief is a person. But "many thieves" is not the same as "many people" and "no thieves" is not the same as "no people." What is unclear here? Adversity to a large number of thieves is not adversity to a large number of people, and wishing there were no thieves is not wishing there were no people' (*Mozi*, ch. 45.5). In other words, there is no contradiction between thieves – people who steal – being a subset of the set of 'people', while propositions about the subset or its members may be correct even if they would be wrong about the set as a whole.

Late Mo advances in logic also included quantification, or the application of limiting conditions such as 'all', 'some', 'at least one', to propositions so that these might alter their truth-value – a development which only entered the discourse of Western logic with the work of Gottlob Frege towards the end of the nineteenth century. It is truly a pity that history was so unkind to this school, which could have provided a significant component to Chinese thought also in later ages.

The legalist school. The idea that the social ideal could be achieved by laws and regulations, and strictly enforced rewards and punishments was promoted by a number of philosophers, but it found its most systematic and best-articulated expression in the work of **Han Feizi** (280?–233 BCE). He synthesizes a large body of practical and realistic political thought that concentrates on penal codes and administrative techniques rather than the Ru concerns of ethics and social well-being. Another influence on him was a strain of thought called Huang-Lao, which blends the political ideas of the *Daodejing* with practical discourses of managerial manipulation.

Han Feizi is reported to have had a stutter, which is why he did not do well in public debates, but excelled in writing. Traditionally, Han Feizi is supposed to have studied with Xunzi together with Li Si, another legalist, who later became an advisor of the Qin emperor and the architect of many of his ruthless policies, including the burning of subversive books 'to let history begin anew'. During their studies, Li Si had acknowledged Han Feizi's intellectual superiority, but nonetheless invited him later to enlist in the service of Qin. But when the Qin emperor was much taken with Han Feizi's ideas, Li started to fear he would be pushed out of favour and falsely accused his friend, who was then arrested. Again at the instigation of Li, Han Feizi committed suicide in prison to avoid the shame of public execution, without knowing that the emperor had actually ruled in his favour.

The downfall of the Qin dynasty also signified the end of the legalist school. The Ru were quick to ingratiate themselves with the Han emperors and associated the end of the previous dynasty with the immorality of the politics it had pursued. Nonetheless Han Feizi continued to be read by both thinkers and practical politicians of subsequent generations, and some of his stories have even generated idiomatic expressions in the Chinese language. His lively, accessible style and witty stories have made him a popular classic even though some of the ideas he propagates are usually considered morally insensitive, if not downright repulsive. Often aptly compared to Niccolò Macchiavelli's 'Prince', Han Feizi's treatise indeed rejects conventional morality in favour of political efficiency.

Ideas: efficiency, law, and the ruler. The word 'legalism' is a translation from the Chinese *fajia*, and *fa* indeed signifies law, although it can also have a wider sense of 'standard' (as in Mo texts) or 'method' (as, for example, in discussions of military strategy). Therefore, even though the legal system held a central importance in legalist thought, we might also consider it in a broader sense as a methodology of efficient statecraft. Composed towards the end of the Warring States period, in utter political chaos where nothing could be relied on, the treatise of Han Feizi is not looking for good government, but just any government with a potential to achieve stability. Similarly, his advice is not directed to the ideal ruler or even a ruler with the potentiality of becoming ideal, but to anyone who has happened to land in the position of power and seeks to maintain it. Realistically appraising the political situation of its day, it provides recipes for mediocrities to improve their efficiency as holders of power, while battling the 'five vermin' of treason, corruption, accumulation of private wealth, private armed security, and, most importantly, the preaching of virtues such as humaneness and moral integrity, which in reality only confuse the ruler who wants to enforce law and order.

To strictly enforce the law by a system of rewards and punishments, or the 'two handles' of the government was the central tenet of this method, bolstered by the principle of holding people accountable for their actions. Han Feizi speaks less about the relationship of the ruler and the populace at large, but concentrates mainly on the environment of the ruler and the governmental apparatus. 'The technique of administration' is another key idea in his focus, which consists in building an efficient and reliable bureaucracy with clearly defined 'job descriptions' and chains of command. This also implies putting people in charge of realizing projects they have themselves proposed and strictly separating the responsibilities of each person, punishing both neglect and excessive zeal.

Han Feizi often uses illustrative stories to make his point. For example, to show how it is the ruler who should take care of rewards and punishments himself, he tells the anecdote about a minister who advised his king only to deliver rewards and leave the unpopular punishments to him – and successfully usurped power, because it was the minister people came to fear. Another story tells about a noble who punished both his steward of caps and steward of blankets, when it turned out that his steward of caps had covered him with a blanket while he slept – a job that should belong to the steward of blankets. But some of his stories have actually entered the Chinese language. The best-known example is probably the Chinese word for 'contradiction' (*maodun*), which literally translates 'spear and shield'. This word derives from a story in Han Feizi, which tells about an arms dealer who claims to have among his wares both a spear that penetrates any shield and a shield that resists the thrust of any spear.

Han Feizi often uses military terminology, as the armies of the time must certainly have provided better examples of discipline and efficient management than the societies and the systems of government. One of his key terms is 'strategic advantage', which he uses to denote the position of power, strengthened if used skilfully and lost if taken for granted. Such attention to the attunement of oneself with the trends in patterns bears a certain resemblance to Lao-Zhuang's ideas of the Way, and Han Feizi is indeed the author of the first extant commentary on the *Daodejing*. But he develops these ideas according to his own position into something he calls 'Way of the Ruler', who is to remain unpredictable in his actions and opaque in his wishes, therefore immune to manipulation and servility.

Sunzi and 'The Art of War'. The military terminology employed in legalist discourse reveals the importance of another tradition of Chinese philosophy, which is often left unconsidered in its histories. This is the art of strategy, best known today by the name of **Sunzi** (544?–496? BCE), a historical general of the Spring and Autumn periods, although the treatise attributed to him comes from the late Warring States period, as textual research has made clear. Apart from its practical use as a manual for warfare, this short book is well known for its ideas of strategic

[The enlightened ruler is] void himself, and therefore knows the concerns of what is full; he is still himself, and therefore knows the directions of movement. When speeches are made, they name their agendas by themselves; when affairs are managed, they take their form by themselves. If the agendas correspond to the forms, the ruler has no need to be involved with them and can return to his own concerns. The ancients have said: 'The desires of the ruler should not be visible. If the desires of the ruler are visible, subjects will adjust themselves to these. The intents of the ruler should not be visible. If the intents of the ruler are visible, subjects will try to excel according to them.' ... By getting rid of 'wisdom', he attains clarity, by getting rid of 'virtues', he attains efficiency, by getting rid of 'bravery', he attains strength. The circle of his ministers looks after their respective duties, the hundreds of his officials follow stable courses of action – everyone will serve according to their abilities. This is what is called 'the maintenance of stability'.

(Han Feizi, ch.5, 'The Way of the Ruler')

thinking that can be extended into all areas of life that involve competition and possible hostilities.

The treatise of 'Sunzi' is often translated as 'The Art of War', but the word 'art' actually means 'law', so 'method' would be more appropriate. Unlike the Western tradition of chivalry, Sunzi has no appreciation for the glory of war as such. The best battles are those that need not be fought, as military action inevitably causes loss of life and damage to the living environment. War should be resorted to only when all else fails, and even then only if there is a realistic chance of winning. Most importantly, however, it is intellectual superiority and not martial valour that should form the basis of any viable strategy. The ability to outsmart the adversary is paramount.

Warfare is the Way of deception. Therefore, if you are capable, you should show yourself as uncapable, if you are functional, you should show yourself as dysfunctional, if you are near you should seem to be far and if far, you should seem to be near. Make the situation look advantageous for the adversary and invite his advance, appear disordered and then seize him. If he is stable, look out for him, if he is strong, evade him. If he is irritated, tease him, if he is humble, encourage his arrogance. If he is retreating, keep him on the move, if his forces are harmoniously organized, separate them from each other. Attack when he is off guard, appear where he has no idea. These are the rules that bring an army to victory, but never let it be known that you are following them.

(Sunzi 1.6)

Sunzi also stresses the importance of treating prisoners well and winning the respect of the rank-and-file of the adversary, while sowing dissent among their leadership. It is by such means that a good victory is brought closer. The skill of a general is never measured by the destruction he causes, but, on the contrary, on how small are the losses to both sides when the battle is over.

All in all, warfare is for Sunzi always a means to an end, and even that end must be weighed carefully against all the pros and cons of a particular situation. Moreover, the theoretical knowledge of military strategy can be undermined by the personal character flaws of a commander prone to rash decisions, excessive self-confidence or a tendency to humiliate his enemies. Just as the philosophical schools of the period, 'The Art of War' puts forward its own concept of the ideal decision-maker who can be trusted with the fates of other people.

From Han to Tang

Background. The end of the classical period of Chinese philosophy, or the 'Hundred Schools of Thought', ushered in an era of textual scholarship. This was inevitable because of the damage wrought by the Qin purges of scholars and the destruction of books. Hidden manuscripts had survived, of course, but much work was needed for the re-establishment of definite texts, and we may well assume that quite a few of the works we know now differ a lot from their original, pre-Qin form. The relative stability and prosperity provided by Han rule as well as imperial patronage of Ru scholarship, together with the establishment of institutions of higher learning and research as well as the rise of the general prestige of education – the only way to social mobility – contributed a lot to the success of this work. Nonetheless, the form in which the Ru tradition secured itself imperial patronage differed quite a bit from its previous shape. This was largely owing to the efforts of a scholar called Dong Zhongshu (179–104 BCE), who, on the one hand, is responsible for the promotion of Ru thought as the best basis for an official ideology of the Han ruling house, but, on the other hand, was the person who blended the Ru tradition with esoterica and cosmological ideas.

The Han dynasty also saw the demise of such schools as the Mo and the school of names, and the legalist school was discredited because of its involvement with the totalitarian policies of the Qin, even if their ideas remained influential. The Lao-Zhuang 'school' did not suffer as much, as it continued to appeal to free spirits not lured by the prospects of official careers.

Towards the end of the Han period, central authority again declined, until power was seized in the capital by an unscrupulous warlord. He made his son the emperor of a new dynasty, but this was not recognized by many and a civil war ensued. This is the era of the 'Three Kingdoms', made famous by the fourteenth century novel of the same name, which has, in our times, inspired retellings and films as well as graphic novels and strategy games. A longer period of disunion followed the brief unification of China at the end of the Three Kingdoms, during which northern tribes captured large areas of China and short-lived dynasties replaced one another in the southern part of the country. This is the Six Dynasties period of political instability and cultural and intellectual excellence. During this period, Buddhism became prominent in China, influencing and developing not only new schools of Chinese thought, but also stimulating the institutional development of the Dao creed and having a large impact on Chinese literature.

The period of the Six Dynasties was followed by another unification, which led to a more stable political era under the rule of the Tang (618–907). Considered the golden age of Chinese culture, the Tang times opened the country up to foreign influences arriving both by sea routes and through the Silk Road, and combining them fruitfully with domestic traditions. Literary genres flourished from poetry to popular stories, foreign music was played, and foreign foods and spices enjoyed. These happy times were punctured by a rebellion, however, and though it was crushed, the dynasty was no longer the same and central authority once again gave way to about 50 years of political upheaval, until the all-out civil war was brought to an end by another successful dynasty, the Song.

The Tang dynasty was mainly tolerant of foreigners and foreign worldviews. Both Christian churches and mosques were present in the Tang capital, and Muslims, in particular, formed a sizeable community: many merchants travelling along the Silk Road were Muslims, and quite a few of them settled down in the Tang capital and married local women, but kept their faith and formed a separate cultural group by keeping to their ways. In the cosmopolitan atmosphere of the capital, this was never a problem. In fact, the inaugural myth of the Islamic community of China features an alliance with the imperial house: the emperor had allegedly seen a dream with a monster attacking his country, and only the help of a turban-wearing Western sage could defend him. The sage was interpreted to be prophet Muhammad, and an imperial envoy was supposedly sent out to invite him to China. The prophet declined the invitation, but sent his uncle instead, who then remained in China as the leader of the local Muslims. Historically, this story is untrue (with even the mentioned uncle safely buried in Mecca), but testifies to the feeling of multicultural integration that the Muslim community enjoyed.

Towards the end of the dynasty, however, nationalist feelings and calls to return to a purely Chinese cultural norm started to increase. Some influential intellectuals continued to view Buddhism, in particular, as a threat to authentic Chinese culture. But while in 819 a prominent Ru scholar was exiled for voicing criticism over (in his opinion) excessive attention given to a Buddhist relic, by 845 the tables had turned and an emperor passionately dedicated to the Dao creed even organized a purge of Buddhism, forcing hundreds of thousands of monks and nuns to return to lay life, burning down the buildings and confiscating the property of about 40 000 temples and monasteries. Muslims and Christians were, however, not affected by this purge, probably because their communities were largely turned inward and did not influence mainstream Chinese intellectual life very strongly.

The Dao creed. One major development during the period from the Han to Tang dynasty is the gradual emergence of the Dao creed. This eclectic new tradition combined elements of folk religion, alchemy, classical philosophy, and also started to include Buddhist ideas, when these became known in China. The resulting tradition is usually called 'religious Daoism' in Western literature, although it became a full-fledged religion only towards the end of this period.

In the Dao creed, the philosophical 'Way' of earlier times gradually acquired the status of a transcendent entity, or the will of such an entity, who could also be called the 'Great One', or sometimes 'Heaven', as in the early religion. Also, in this tradition the figure of Laozi gradually acquired an increasingly elevated status and developed first from the wise author of the *Daodejing* to a leading successful practitioner of immortality techniques, then further on to become the 'Old Lord', a deity able to interfere with earthly destinies, and finally identified with the Great One or Dao itself. But the pantheon of the Dao creed included many other figures, incorporating spirits and demons from the local lore whenever it seemed practical to do so.

From time to time 'celestial masters' emerged who claimed to have received revelations from Laozi himself and therefore to merit the leadership over all followers of the Dao everywhere. The Dao creed nonetheless remained an eclectic movement with no orthodoxy for a long time, and different versions of it were spread in different parts of China. Local cult leaders were sometimes remarkably successful in mobilizing their followers. Indeed, often such leadership went hand in hand with political activism, and a Dao-inspired millenarian peasant uprising, known as the Yellow Turban rebellion of 184–205, contributed significantly to the downfall of the Han dynasty. At the same time, the Dao creed also attracted disconcerted intellectuals who saw no point in pursuing an official career in the Ru tradition during politically unstable times, and preferred a bohemian lifestyle or a quiet retreat to some mountain hermitage. Many of the leading poets of the time, for example, have openly proclaimed their preference for the Dao creed, the most famous of them being Li Bai (701–762), one of the best-known Chinese poets of all times.

Early efforts to systematize the teaching were not recognized by the majority of practitioners, and only towards the end of the Six Dynasties period, together with the establishment of a stronger imperial authority, the Dao creed also acquired a systematic form. This followed the blueprint of Buddhism probably more than it inherited from the Chinese folk religion. During the Tang, the Dao creed attained the status of an officially recognized religion, complete with its own temples, priests, and canonic scriptures and was favoured by several emperors, including the ill-famed initiator of the purge of Buddhism.

The Five Phases. One of the components of the emerging Dao creed was a cosmological vision that developed from the divination theories and tried to provide them with a broader protoscientific context, which would also have political implications. It may have originated in the work of *Yijing* scholars already in the third century BCE, gradually gained currency, and became the standard account of things. According to this view, the universal order relies on the patterned sequence of five 'phases' or 'elements' of wood, fire, earth, metal, and water. Each of these represented a different type of condensation of *qi* (the universal energy-field of which all matter consisted), comprised a direction (from among the four directions and the centre), a colour, a season, a planet, an animal, a body part, a flavour and so on, and they followed each other either through generation of the following phase (wood generates fire, earth generates metal, and so on) or overcoming (metal destroys wood, water destroys fire, and so on). All processes from cosmic transformations down to the functioning of the body were subject to these patterns, and thereby inextricably linked. After all, everything consisted in the movement of *qi*.

A body of knowledge soon emerged that developed the details of this theory, and was shared by a group of esoteric professionals called *fangshi* ('masters of method'). Their services were sought by both powerholders and the broader populace, who needed advice on a broad range of questions from arranging the affairs of the state to personal health. A separate branch of knowledge soon emerged from this source, called *fengshui* (literally 'wind-water'), initially a theory of how tombs should be constructed in order to provide maximum benefit to the ancestors buried in them, but soon developed into a full-scale geomantic teaching, applied to all spatial arrangements and architecture in particular. The goal of fengshui was to construct an environment for the people to live in, which would be in agreement with the patterns ruling over the cosmos, and thereby to ensure their safety, longevity, and prosperity. Fengshui principles have become deeply rooted in Chinese understanding of space and remain influential to this day.

The Five Phases theory also had its political implications, as it tied particular policies more directly to cosmic processes and furnished the theory of the mandate of Heaven with a protoscientific context. Moreover, the theory also prompted that natural disasters (of which the last period of the Han dynasty saw quite a few) or other extraordinary happenings were the result of political imbalance. Since each ruling house identified itself with an element, the one ascending at the time when its own bid for power was launched according to either of the sequence patterns, it also needed to fear the rise of the following element and to pacify the forces associated with it.

The Han imperial cult. Under the influence of the Five Phases theory and in response to other tendencies, the Han emperors sponsored the emergence of an imperial cult that would bolster their authority in the paradigm of the popular sentiment. This needs to be kept in mind when we assess the Han dynasty primarily as the period when the Ru tradition established itself as the ruling ideology – indeed it did, but not precisely in the pristine form inherited from the Warring States period. It should also be noted that the separation of traditions – the Ru, the Lao-Zhuang, the different esoterica and even Buddhism – into clearly delimited units is our concern more than it was a need for the Chinese, who viewed them as different kinds of knowledge, each of which was useful in its own way and an 'interdisciplinary' mixture of all these was quite compatible with common sense.

The advocates of the Ru at Han court, such as Dong Zhongshu, thus comfortably blended their ethical and political teachings with onto-cosmological theories that were gaining popularity. From a purely philosophical point of view, this may seem like profanation, but in fact this was a politically wise move. For example, by including certain popular sacrificial ceremonies in the imperial cult, the court also appropriated their symbolic capital. Already the Qin emperor had always paid his respects to local spirits, whenever he was on the move, and one of the Han emperors initiated sacrificial ceremonies both for Laozi, who was on his way to become a divine character, as well as for the Buddha.

Another important addition to the Han imperial cult was the Five Celestial Emperors, each one associated with one of the Five Phases. Among these, the Yellow Emperor (Huang-di), associated with earth and centre, quickly became the most important. The Yellow Emperor was associated with wisdom and knowledge as well as medicinal practices. This mythical figure did not feature among the sage rulers of antiquity venerated in the Ru tradition, but the belief in him was widespread already during the Warring States period, when he also represented the idea of the centralized state.

By adopting the Yellow Emperor into its political and cosmological scheme of things, the Han imperial cult also co-opted an increasingly important stream of thought, which is called **Huang-Lao**, combining the first characters of Huang-di and Laozi. Differently from the philosophical Lao-Zhuang tradition, Huang-Lao thought is primarily practical and combines the *Daodejing*'s political ideas with practices of individual self-cultivation. The Huang-Lao political vision is strongly influenced by the legalist school and contains also some Ru elements. It has been speculated that the social base of Huang-Lao thought consisted of influential non-imperial clans, who were interested in maintaining as much political autonomy as possible. Co-opting Huang-Lao ideology into the imperial cult could therefore also be seen as a move to undermine such separatist tendencies. This idea is supported by historical sources, which tell us that those emperors who favoured Huang-Lao thought also eradicated local cults and destroyed their places of worship.

> Shining just as the sun and the moon
> Moving in the company of the five stars
> He comes and goes to the Cinnabar Hut
> Ascends and descends from the Yellow Court
> Leaving behind all fashions and vulgarities
> Abandoning his radiance and hiding his form
> He contains the primordial spiritual transformations
> He inhales and exhales the ultimate essence
> The world has no grasp of his reach
> And looks up to him as to eternal life
>
> *(The Bian Shao inscription in the honour of Laozi, c. 165 CE)*

The *Huainanzi*. These syncretic developments also produced philosophical efforts to attain a synthesis of different trends of thought on a Huang-Lao basis. The most important among these is probably the ***Huainanzi***, a collection of essays resulting from the work of scholars gathered into an academy by Liu An (179?–122? BCE). Liu An was the prince of Huainan and advisor to the emperor, and his involvement in philosophy pursued the goal of combining various ideas into a comprehensive system. The authors of the *Huainanzi* demonstrate their learning by quoting extensively from earlier literature of various schools, and their take on their heritage is often innovative and original. The result remains eclectic, however, and precisely therefore indicative of the way in which Chinese thought was going at the time.

One of the main goals of the work is to base philosophical and political reasoning in a cosmological framework. The Five Phases theory and yin-yang cosmology feature prominently, organized into models of how the universe works. The best theory of government is one that is in accordance with it, and therefore does not have to resort to strenuous effort. A ruler should rule not by interfering with the course of things, but by representing it. This is an idea shared by Lao-Zhuang thought and Han Feizi. However, the *Huainanzi* also incorporates elements of Ru thought into its system. Unlike Warring States Ru scholars, it does not present a clearly defined view of human nature, thus rejecting efforts to describe its primordial form in terms of virtues, but neither does it dismiss the Ru virtues such as humaneness and integrity altogether: these are considered important principles for the functioning of a harmonious society. Nonetheless they cannot be achieved by overzealous activity, which does not let things proceed according to their course.

While the *Huainanzi* documents an important phase in the formation of the Han synthetic thought, it nonetheless failed in establishing itself as its base. The syncretic Ru-based system of Dong Zhongshu (179–104 BCE), advanced at the same time, managed to do what the *Huainanzi* could not: to integrate the yin-yang cosmological ideas, the theory of the Five Phases and philosophical thought into a system that could serve as the officially endorsed worldview of the Han empire. In the centuries to come, this resulted in the retreat of Lao-Zhuang ideas to the margin, which simultaneously increased their appeal to those intellectuals who were less inclined to pursue official careers.

Immortality and alchemy. Little by little, the attention of Huang-Lao thought turned to another important aspect of the emerging Dao creed, namely the pursuit of immortality. This also gave rise to a cult of immortals. It was believed that by following a lifestyle in accordance with the cosmic order, anyone could minimize the harmful effect that certain disorderly processes have on their bodies. Prominent figures of the Huang-Lao tradition were credited with immortality, and figures of immortals were enshrined as objects of veneration. More successful 'masters of method' gained the ear of emperors and other aristocrats, who often sponsored their activities in search of elixirs of immortality. This involved alchemical experiments, and alchemy therefore quickly became an important part of the Dao creed.

Soon enough, however, the so-called 'outer alchemy', which involved actual study and combination of substances, was overshadowed by an 'internal alchemy', or the psychotechnical manipulation of one's consciousness and body. It was believed that the body is not only a replica of the cosmic order, but also populated by a multitude of spirits. With the help of certain technologies, which included breathing exercises aimed at controlling the *qi*, diets, callisthenics, and also sexual practices, it was possible to manipulate these spirits to one's advantage, in order to prolong one's life and to achieve higher states of consciousness. In particular, the 'cinnabar field', a region around the navel, was considered to be the locus of concentration of *qi*, and by gathering one's consciousness in this region one was supposedly able to become one with the pattern that regulated the movement of fundamental energies.

'Dark learning'. Towards the end of the Han dynasty and during the disorders that followed, many intellectuals did not feel tempted by the official career path and were drawn to a bohemian lifestyle instead, engaging in the arts, philosophical discussions, drinking and sensual pleasures, and preferring elegant aestheticism to the dangers of the political roller-coaster. For example, the Seven Sages of the Bamboo Grove, a grouping of late Han intellectuals, included one Li Ling, an affluent man, who constantly had two servants with him – one of these carried a jug of wine and had to pour Li Ling a drink whenever he wished it, the other one carried a spade and had the instructions to dig some soil onto Li Ling should he drop dead. A bit more than a century later, in 353, another group of aesthetes gathered on the banks of a river during the famous Orchid Pavilion banquet, and lifted winecups off lotus leaves that were floating by.

This was the backdrop against which a new trend of thought emerged, called 'dark learning', which combines ideas of the Dao creed with traditional cosmology and the idea that the world is in itself semiotically significant and decodable. Things have hidden essences, but these reveal themselves to an appropriately prepared observer. Being and Nothingness are not just philosophical concepts, but concrete realities with which one can engage.

This way of thought also had a strong influence on Chinese aesthetics. The idea of representation in Chinese art does not mean the representation of surfaces, but precisely these hidden essences, and therefore it need not be exactly realistic – the artist should observe the landscape to be painted at length and absorb it, become mentally one with it, and will thereafter be able to depict it out of memory. A treatise on painting from the ninth century mentions an artist who wandered around in the mountains, got drunk, and then put his head into a bucket with ink and dried his hair with a silk canvas so that a painting would appear on it as a result – all of this a testimony of his superb ability to fuse with nature.

Quite a few scholars associated with 'dark learning' wrote treatises and commentaries on earlier texts – for example, Wang Bi, the author of the most authoritative commentary on the *Daodejing* was a prominent representative of this school.

'Great Peace' and Dao rebellions. All the above-described components contributed to the emergence of what we now know as the institutionalized Dao creed, but the beginning of this phenomenon should still be identified with the two theocratic semi-independent polities that were established as counter-powers to the disintegrating Han empire towards the end of the second century CE. One of these, the movement of **Great Peace** in north-east China that ultimately led to the Yellow Turban rebellion was crushed by the imperial armies, while the other, or 'the Way of Celestial Masters' in south-western Sichuan, survived and gained the recognition of the political elites. Both of these were led by charismatic healers with considerable skills of leadership, ability to muster and maintain popular support, and intellectual capacities. Both made use of public ceremonies of healing, where followers had to publicly confess their sins and were relieved of their ailments through blessings. Both organized and held a large territory for a considerable amount of time. But while the 'Great Peace' movement chose a direct confrontational course with the authorities and sought to replace the Han dynasty with itself, the 'Celestial Masters' opted for political manoeuvring that ultimately granted them success.

The 'Great Peace' movement (*Taiping*, not to be confused with the nineteenth century Christianity-inspired rebellion of the same name) was founded by Zhang Jue (d.184) and his two brothers. The ideal of 'great peace' had been articulated as the end goal of their activities by many others, including the Qin emperor, and Zhang Jue took it up as his own slogan during a time when the Han dynasty was plagued by corruption, mismanagement, and neglect of the people, all of which pointed to the loss of the mandate of Heaven. In an anonymous text entitled *The Scripture of Great Peace* (*Taipingjing*), which entered circulation roughly at the same time, social criticism directed against the situation is blended with a doctrine of collective salvation by restoring the natural order in the individual bodies of followers and the society at large. Efforts had been made to present versions of this scripture to the throne, but without success. It was nonetheless read among worried intellectuals and followers of Huang-Lao thought. Zhang Jue combined these ideas with the common superstitions widespread among the people, gained authority among them for his reported healing abilities and organized them into an army of 'yellow turbans'. The yellow colour was, according to the Five Phases scheme, the ascendant one that would defeat the purple of the Han dynasty, and a rebellion broke out in 184. However, the Zhang brothers had severely underrated the military power of the court and were quickly defeated and killed, though calls to arms on behalf of the 'yellow turbans' continued to be issued by Dao-inspired millenarian rebel leaders for another couple of decades.

The Way of the Celestial Masters. The Way of the Celestial Masters is also known as the way of 'five measures of rice', as its adepts were required to donate an amount of rice (about 50 litre) to the movement to gain acceptance. Not much is known with any certainty about its mythical founder, so we should consider the central figure of this movement to be Zhang Lu (d.216, not related to Zhang Jue), the grandson of the alleged founder and the third leader of a small, de facto independent state. Unlike Zhang Jue, Zhang Lu secured for himself an official appointment and later, when his rule was perceived as a nuisance by the military, he negotiated a peace with the new leaders of China that involved the recognition of his spiritual authority. Many of his followers, however, were forcefully moved from Sichuan to the capital area, which, in fact, contributed to the spread and rise of the Dao creed. The Way of the Celestial Masters is a revelational religion and claims to be based on a transmission that the mythical founder had received from the deified Laozi himself on a mountain peak, where he was practising religious austerities. The doctrines of this group are laid out in a commentary to the *Daodejing*, which was raised to the status of a scripture and one of the practices consisted in a public recitation of the *Daodejing* text. The interpretation given to this text was rather particular, however, as it was credited with magic powers that helped to control and subdue spirits. The Celestial Masters led their followers to believe that spirits were everywhere and reported all misdeeds to them. Each member of the cult also had personal 'spirit generals' under their command, given to them by their teachers, first as 'invisible friends' to children who later increased in number. A regular follower of the cult could amass as many as 75 spirit generals, and a sexual ritual called 'merging *qi*' would combine the invisible servants of the participating man and the woman into a joint spiritual army of 150 generals.

The cult was hierarchically organized and each member had to know their place. The territory under its control was divided into parishes and governed by a bureaucracy that included both earthly and heavenly officials. These organized the gatherings and recitals of the *Daodejing* and oversaw the health of their subjects – any illness was considered to be an offence as it signified a breach of the natural order, which could have caused more serious disruptions. Talismans and petitions to spirits to take care of the problem were the main remedies used for their removal. Meditation was another method, and 'quiet chambers' were established in which it could be practised.

Syncretism and orthodoxy. The Celestial Masters completed the process of Laozi's deification and unification with the Dao as well as the Great One. However, their main ambition was not to create a systematic orthodox teaching and spread it over the country, but to devise an ideology that would invigorate their community, provide their followers with practical guidance in their lives and ensure discipline. For the purpose, they borrowed anything that fit from anywhere.

The situation changed considerably when the Way of the Celestial Masters in fact did spread over the country and also gained prominent followers among the elites. Many of these were followers of the Ru tradition and did not break away from it, even if they received initiations into the Way of the Celestial Masters, as they did not think the two were incompatible. However, the intellectual and ethical concerns of the Ru spread also to the Dao creed and efforts were undertaken to systematize the teaching and clarify issues that had not bothered the charismatic early masters and their often illiterate followers.

One of the most important attempts to bring coherence to the Dao creed was undertaken by Ge Hong (283–343/363?), whose ideas are gathered in a text called *Baopuzi*, or *The Teacher Embracing Simplicity*. Ge Hong is a typical intellectual of the time in that he divides his work into chapters dedicated to the Dao creed, and another set of chapters written in the Ru tradition. A high-ranking official with significant military merits, Ge Hong travelled widely and read a lot, and studied natural sciences – that is, alchemy – in addition to the philosophical and historical texts any educated person had to know. He also wrote on psychophysical techniques to enhance one's living potential, from breathing exercises to the 'arts of the bedchamber'. Later Dao tradition has claimed him for itself, but it is probably more correct to characterize him as an intellectual with broad interdisciplinary interests, who was trying to construct a systematic worldview for himself, taking the best from all traditions.

A more successful effort to construct the Dao creed as a systematic worldview was undertaken by the fifth–sixth century polymath, scholar, calligrapher, and musician, **Tao Hongjing** (456–536). A childhood friend of the founding emperor of one of the short-lived dynasties (incidentally, the same man with whom Bodhidharma, the founder of Chan Buddhism, supposedly met on his arrival in China), Tao Hongjing came from a scholarly family and served under three dynasties in various roles, including the position of the tutor of the emperor's children. His education and artistic skills were widely recognized and in recent times he has even been called the Leonardo da Vinci of China. In 492, Tao Hongjing retired to the Maoshan mountain, which had been previously known as a site of Dao creed revelations, and with brief intervals spent most of his remaining years there, systematizing Dao texts and writing new ones, which involved inventing and describing new deities. These became the basis of the Way of Supreme Clarity (*Shangqing*), one of the most influential versions of the Dao creed.

In the works of these intellectuals we also see the gradual transformation of the concept of immortality as the goal of a Dao creed follower. While the teaching continued to be preoccupied with longevity, its aim was no longer to achieve a terrestrial state of being where death would not come – 'immortal' became a designation of a celestial spiritual form into which alchemical and meditation procedures would gradually transform the practising individual, and immortality on Earth started to refer to the ability to live out one's predestined life span, the lowest form of spiritual perfection an individual could achieve.

Later developments. The Way of Supreme Clarity introduced a new element into the Dao creed. Namely, it invented a superior level of knowledge, hitherto unrevealed and therefore unknown to any previous practitioner, but claiming to be more valuable than the previous tradition. A similar move was made by the proponents of another branch of the creed, the Way of the Numinous Treasure (*Lingbao*), which borrowed heavily from Buddhism, introducing the ideas of reincarnation, the model of Buddhist cosmology and even some Sanskrit terms, to which new meanings were assigned. The term 'numinous treasure' referred to the material form taken by a spiritual entity or abstract idea, thus its scriptures were claimed to have emanated from the Dao itself and to be older than Heaven and Earth.

During the Tang dynasty, both Shangqing and Lingbao creeds won favour with the court. Some emperors even tried to base their government on Dao creed principles, and the *Daodejing* was placed on the list of works that were required for civil service examinations. Again borrowing from Buddhism, the Dao creed also developed institutionally: it introduced a monastic system, a hierarchy of initiations and also produced an imitation of the more sophisticated Buddhist meditation techniques. It is believed that the ambition of the Dao masters was to replace Buddhism, an alien thought system, with the Dao creed as the primary metaphysical teaching and technique of spiritual emancipation. Other innovations included a sacred geography that conceived the territory of China in religious terms, and the recasting of Laozi, whose alleged surname was the same as that of the Tang emperors, in the role of the progenitor of the imperial family.

It can be said that during the Tang dynasty, the Dao creed managed to wholly distance itself from the worldview of rebel peasants and the political radicality that had once characterized its earlier versions. What it did not lose, however, was its eclectic character and its ability to adopt borrowings and invent new teachings.

Chinese Buddhism. The encounter between Buddhism and Chinese thought is probably the most interesting intellectual synthesis in East Asian history. Buddhism entered China at about the same time when Christianity started to spread in the Roman empire, and it became one of the dominant worldviews towards the end of the fourth century, again when Christianity had established itself as the primary religion of Europe. Unlike Europe, however, Buddhism never displaced the Chinese indigenous thought traditions, even though it was occasionally viewed with suspicion by Ru scholars. But – again as in Europe – the result of this cultural development was domestic rather than foreign, and just as the thought of St Thomas Aquinas or Martin Luther is a European phenomenon, the philosophical systems of Zhiyi and Fazang are Chinese, even though in both cases the basic vocabulary is imported from a foreign tradition.

The incompatibility of Sanskrit and Chinese linguistic structures produced serious difficulties of translation and even inspired conceptual innovations. As the texts had scriptural authority for Chinese Buddhists, they obviously needed them rendered into their native tongue with absolute precision, no word omitted, and some particles of Sanskrit could even evolve into full-scale philosophical terms as a result. Initial efforts to use Lao-Zhuang vocabulary for Buddhist terms soon turned out to be confusing and gave way to the development of a properly Chinese Buddhist discourse. A by-product of this process was an in-depth analysis of Buddhist concepts and the reinterpretation of Indian ideas in the Chinese context. Several schools emerged as a result that had no counterpart in India, even though they were based on originally Indian texts (or Chinese translations of them). This increased the level of theoretical sophistication (or complication) of Chinese reasoning considerably, as the detailed Indian metaphysical classifications of types of consciousness or levels of being now found their way into Chinese thought.

A different kind of impact was produced by Buddhism on Chinese culture in general. The monotonous way of reciting Buddhist texts alerted the Chinese to the tonal character of their language, as meanings were lost when tones were neglected. This produced a wave of poetic reform, in which tonal schemes were regulated and new patterns of poetry introduced. In contrast, the stories about the previous rebirths of the historical Buddha lent a certain respectability to the fantastical and the imaginary, which in turn inspired Chinese writers to turn out entertaining popular literature. Last but not least, the Buddhist institution with temples and monks provided a development blueprint for the indigenous religion, which appropriated the Lao-Zhuang sages and created a further host of scriptural works in the course of their institutionalization as the Dao creed.

Texts and translations. The bigger part of the intellectual efforts of Chinese Buddhists consisted in making sense of the original texts, both through translation and the production of commentaries. Acquisition of reliable source materials was not easy. One of the most famous classical Chinese novels, 'Journey to the West', written about 1000 years later than the events it claims to describe, tells the story of **Xuanzang** (602?–664), a Chinese monk who undertook a pilgrimage to India, visited many Buddhist sites, studied in the Nālandā monastery, and finally returned to China with a huge collection of texts. The novel provides him with the company of the monkey king, a fighting pig (in reality, a celestial general banished to this form for excessive lust, which has not left him) and a sand-eating river demon (another banished celestial general). These characters often have to rescue Xuanzang from various troubles in picturesque and miraculous ways. In an imaginative and exaggerated way, the novel has thus preserved the cultural memory of the perils and difficulties of early pilgrimages, and it is noteworthy that some of its characters – such as the monkey king, a central figure of the Rāmāyana epic – are themselves cultural imports from India.

As said, the translation of Sanskrit texts into Chinese was no easy task. Prior to the arrival of Buddhism, Chinese culture had been very much self-contained and seen other cultures with suspicion, if at all. Therefore the Chinese had no actual experience of translation of theoretical or artistic texts, especially on such a large scale. Moreover, Sanskrit is as far removed from classical Chinese by way of both grammatical structures and the semantic build-up as any two languages can be. It is therefore no wonder that initial translations did not do justice either to the source texts or the target language. With time, however, the situation improved considerably. In particular, the figure of

Kumarajīva (344–413), a Buddhist from Central Asia to whom both Sanskrit and Chinese were acquired languages, is responsible for the creation of a smooth Chinese Buddhist idiom, sufficiently precise theoretical vocabulary and stock translations of recurring expressions.

Mind and self, emptiness and nothingness, sudden and gradual. It is only logical that the Chinese reception of Indian ideas specifically high-lighted the concepts and problems that resounded with the concerns of the Chinese thought traditions. One of these was the question of human nature. The Ru debate about 'original' human nature – the existence of which was a prerequisite for it being either good or bad – and Zhuangzi's views on per-spective and non-action provided the background against which the Buddhist views on self were interpreted. The Buddhist view of the illusory nature of selfhood resounded well with Zhuangzi, while the idea of 'Buddha-nature' and 'original enlightenment' as its corollary resembled Mengzi's view of the 'sprouts' of virtues embedded in every human psyche. On the other hand, the 'absence as presence' of the Way – the empty hub that connects the 30 spokes to form a wheel (*Daodejing*, ch. 11) resounded well with the Buddhist doctrine of emptiness. The idea that there is a superior metaphysical princi-ple, the ultimate truth, corresponding to the Lao-Zhuang Way on the one hand and the conventional reality of 'myriad things', each without a self-nature of its own, may have been a distortion of the original Indian idea but, combined with the theory of Buddha-nature inherent in all beings, it became very influential in Chinese Buddhism and formed the basis of Tiantai and Huayan thought.

Proponents of Buddhism were quick to make use of such resemblances, which then quickly led to the Sinification of Buddhism, with its own debates and con-cerns. Some scholars have even argued that Mahāyāna, which was the dominant form of Buddhism in China, only came to form a coherent and independent system of thought in China, while in India it always existed in a dialectical symbiosis with Theravāda schools of thought. While this is probably an exaggeration, it is true that some issues that were central for Indians did not attract much attention in China, while new topics were raised. The Chinese, for example, were on the whole not very inclined towards reasoning represented by classifications of dharmas and consciousnesses, even though some efforts in that direction were also made. However, they were much engaged in debates relating to the nature of enlightenment.

Early Buddhist texts had repeatedly underscored that nirvāna could only be attained as the result of a long and strenuous effort, which emphasized the importance of monastic discipline. This view was supported by the classifica-tion of followers according to their stages of achievement: those who had just 'entered the stream' were inferior, for example, to 'once-returners', who only had to be reborn once more in order to be ready for the final leap. However, as early as at the beginning of the fifth century CE, the Chinese started to question this theory. First, if Buddha-nature is universal, they argued, and every being already has it from the start, it cannot be a capacity that is acquired as the result of training. Second, if there is a distinction between an unenlightened and an enlightened being, there must also be a moment at which the transformation from one to the other takes place. Accordingly, the experience of enlightenment must occur at a certain precise point in time. Training is, of course, necessary for achieving this experience, but it would not result in half-enlightened or three-quarters-enlightened minds, which is what the theory of gradual enlightenment would logically imply. This insistence on the momentary nature and character-transforming quality of the experience of enlightenment later became the hallmark of the Chan school.

Indian schools in China. Records show that the first divisions into schools that support one or another answer to some of these questions occurred in China quite early, but none of these became established traditions. A more solid basis for identifying particular monks and teacher–disciple lineages with schools appeared when Indian Mahāyāna thought was imported together with the *sūtra* texts. Kumarajīva, for example, studied Buddhism with a monk of the Madhyamaka school and his translation of Nāgārjuna was interspersed with comments, possibly by his teacher, which were inseparable from the original text for the reader. Madhyamaka became known in China as the 'Three treatises' school, combining Nāgārjuna's theory with Lao-Zhuang views and even some practices taken over from the Dao creed, so that the focus turned somewhat on the ineffable, mystical character of emptiness instead of the Indian stress on the logical deconstruction of all possible discourses on enduring identities and permanent natures of things. However, the influence of Nāgārjuna was not restricted to this school only, and his views were seminal also in the development of proper Chinese Buddhist schools.

Another, and just as influential, Indian import was **Yogācāra**, known in China as the 'Consciousness-only' school. The founder of this school in China was Xuanzang, who had studied it during his stay in Nālandā. Chinese Yogācāra differs from the Indian school in that it asserts more boldly that 'the three worlds [of desires, forms and the formless] are nothing but mind', and identified Buddha-nature with the 'true mind', the goodness of human nature in the sense of Mengzi, thus raising it from the status of unrealized potential to an actual presence inaccessible because of delusions. Just as with the 'Three Treatises', we find the ideas of the 'Consciousness-only' school soon entering broader circulation and influencing the newly emerging Chinese Buddhist schools, which gradually came to eclipse the Indian imports.

Tiantai. The first originally Chinese Buddhist school, **Tiantai**, has received its name from the Tiantai mountain in the Zhejiang province. This was the site of a temple where the actual founder – although technically the fourth head – of the school, **Zhiyi** (538–597), lived and worked. (The word 'head' of a Buddhist school is used in this book instead of the usual 'patriarch', with its Orthodox Christian and patriarchal connotations.) After his death, the temple was rebuilt and the school received imperial patronage and became one of the leading schools, a reputation it held with occasional setbacks until the Song dynasty, with many large temples and lots of support from high places.

The idea of a Buddhist school came in China to be associated with the in-depth study of a particular text, and Tiantai was the school dedicated to the studies of the *Lotus Sūtra* – and it is in a large part due to the reputation of Tiantai that this *sūtra* has been established in East Asia as the most influential Mahāyāna scripture of all. However, the actual teaching of the school has only a little to do with the parables of which the *sūtra* mostly consists. Thus, for example, while one of Zhiyi's major works purports to be a commentary on the *sūtra*, it does not get further than the first character of its Chinese title, meaning 'subtle' or 'wonderful', and expounds Zhiyi's own views instead.

Ideas: three truths. The central and radical contribution of the Tiantai school is the idea of three truths. Nāgārjuna had introduced the idea of 'two truths' in his work, separating the conventional truth – as a sentence about something can be correct or incorrect – from the ultimate truth of emptiness of all things, and not claiming that the ultimate truth is superior or somehow more true than the conventional, or shared truth. Tiantai took this idea further and interpreted a verse of Nāgārjuna to say that this equality of the two truths is itself a third one, the 'middle' truth. This third truth came to mean that every true proposition is true only from a certain perspective, and more than that, even a conventionally false proposition is true from some perspective in which its truth conditions are met. In other words, the truthfulness of any sentence is relational to the perspective from which it is uttered. The legacy of Zhuangzi and the debates around the 'school of names' is clearly a part of this assertion.

'Three thousand worlds in one thought-moment'. But if there is no perspective from which we can see reality without distortion – at least none available to us unenlightened beings – then it would be a mistake to dismiss all others and we should, instead, try to relate to them. Zhiyi constructs a sophisticated

The relationality of truth in the Tiantai view can perhaps be best understood through an argument on essences. Many philosophers, including a large Western tradition from Aristotle onwards, hold that the properties of a thing can be divided into essential and contingent ones, and a thing remains itself as long as its essential properties do not change, while contingent ones may. If we now take two things that can be metaphorically compared to each other, this implies that they have at least one property in common. A person, for example, can be compared to a doormat if they let everyone else figuratively wipe their feet on them. But what if this very property would be the only essential one? After all, it is easy to see that what we call 'essential' properties of things are so primarily from our very particular human perspective, and even different human perspectives, say, that of a rich snob and a hungry child, may produce quite different divisions into 'essential' and 'contingent'? We can very well assume that there is a perspective from which the world is divided into (actual or metaphorical) doormats and non-doormats and no other classification has any importance, just as from the perspective of a mosquito the environment is divided into 'warm-blooded animals' and 'other' entities. Therefore, pointing to a piece of coal and saying 'this is a diamond' may be conventionally false, but true from the perspective in which only the chemical element from which an object is composed has any relevance.

metaphysical edifice showing how the 10 perspectives of being (the six realms of being, from hell-dwellers to humans and celestial beings, and the four perspectives associated with the stages of development of the Buddhist insight) are all contained within each other, as they are states of mind rather than actual, physical ways of existence. This view originates in one of the Lotus Sūtra's core teachings, namely the identification of *samsāra* and *nirvāna*, or the cycle of rebirths and the exit from it. Both, according to this view, are but states of mind, and there is no nirvāna that exists separately from this very reality. The extension of this attitude to all perspectives that a being may have in various forms of existence is only a natural development.

Ten types of existence all contained within each other makes 100 perspectives. Multiplied by 10 aspects of suchness, again listed in the *Lotus Sūtra*, we get 1000. And when these are applied to the three worlds of desires, forms, and the formless, we get 3000 perspectives from which reality could be observed. In practice, these perspectives are formed by multitudes of causal chains that lead up to the emergence of a particular way of being of a particular phenomenon at a single moment. No being, no entity is 'self-identical', neither in the sense of persisting through time, nor in the sense of containing all of its being within itself. A thing such as a loaf of bread usually consists of different materials (flour, yeast, water), these have histories of their own (flour comes from grain, which contains nutrients absorbed from soil, etc.) and have been processed with various means (ground in a mill) again with histories of their own, by people with histories of their own and so on. The claim of Tiantai is that if we follow these causal chains, we find all of them interlinked at some point, so that each phenomenon in the whole universe has a chain of connections to absolutely every other phenomenon that ever existed, exists now, or will exist in the future.

Therefore, the aim of Zhiyi in this is not to confuse us with the multitude of perspectives, but, on the contrary, to say that each single thought-moment we might have actually contains them. The entire universe is constantly reproduced by any minute flicker of mental activity by any entity. This also underscores the fundamental sameness of all ways of being-in-the-world, to use a Heideggerian term, and consequently of all entities – an attitude of inclusiveness extended by later Tiantai thinkers also to non-sentient beings, so that even stones and grass came to be viewed as having Buddha-nature. Conversely, any mentally active entity has potential access to the entire universe at any moment, and to realize this is tantamount to enlightenment. The goal of meditation practice is precisely to attain such an experience of oneness with the universe.

Tiantai doctrines exercised a profound influence on nearly all later Chinese and Japanese Buddhist schools and were also very influential in Korea and Vietnam. Moreover, focusing on a single detail in order to mediate a cosmic experience became a crucial element of East Asian aesthetics and artistic practice. In China, Tiantai survived the purge of 845 and its temples were restored, but still the school gradually went into decline and over the next centuries became extinct as an independent tradition of learning and practising.

Huayan. During the Tang dynasty, the Tiantai school was for some time eclipsed by another Chinese innovation, the **Huayan** school, which was based on the study of the *Avatamsaka* (*Flower Garland*) *Sūtra*, or *Huayanjing* in Chinese. Fragments of this text had been translated into Chinese already in the second century CE, but it became an object of serious study only in the seventh century CE, evolving into a distinct philosophical strand of thought under **Fazang** (643–712), formally the third head of the Huayan school. Fazang, the son of wealthy immigrants, studied briefly with Xuanzang, but disagreed with him and turned to the study of Huayan. Eventually he became the Buddhist teacher of a powerful empress and dedicated a treatise to her, which established the reputation of his school as one of the intellectual peaks of Chinese thought at the time. He was followed by a few other prominent scholars as heads of the school, who engaged in vigorous debate with the Tiantai.

However, Huayan was severely harmed by the purge of Buddhism in 845 and vanished in China soon after that, even though unsuccessful efforts to resuscitate the school were made repeatedly and its texts continued to have influence. Thus, for example, it has been argued that the Neo-Confucians of the Song dynasty and Zhu Xi in particular were indebted to Huayan thinking in their discussion of the interrelationship of the 'principle' and the phenomenon. The school had also been exported to Korea, Japan, and Vietnam before its demise in China. It held a strong position in Korea until the end of the fourteenth century and continues to exist in Japan to this day, even though it has lost much of its former influence.

Ideas: the interpenetration of things. One of the central metaphors of the *Flower Garland Sūtra* is 'Indra's net', the image of a huge net in which all knots contain a diamond so that each of these diamonds is able to reflect every single one of the others. This view has often been compared to the monadology of Gottfried Wilhelm Leibniz, even though, in the case of Leibniz, each monad is a separate entity, complete in itself, and not affected by others. Huayan, however, accepts and develops the Tiantai view of each entity being related to every other one in the universe to its logical endpoint. For this purpose, it adopts a term from classical Chinese thought, 'principle' (*li*), which it contrasts with 'phenomenon' (*shi*). The idea of 'principle' is first used by Han Feizi in a similar sense as the unique mode in which the Way manifests itself in each particular thing. In Huayan thought, it comes to signify an underlying reality uniting all things, more similar in its meaning to the 'Way' of Lao-Zhuang – possibly because 'way' in Buddhist discourse had been appropriated for the teaching itself, the way leading towards enlightenment. In Huayan, this underlying reality principle is understood as creative non-being, or emptiness.

Accordingly, we can look at reality on four different levels. First, there is the realm of things as forms and phenomena, like the waves on the sea or the shape of lion that a sculpture made of gold has. Second, there is the realm of principle, like the water of the sea or the gold the lion sculpture is made of. Third, there is the realm of non-interference and interpenetration of the principle and phenomena. This is supposed to correspond to the Tiantai view: phenomenon and the principle are both interdependent and separate, one cannot be without the other, but neither is completely exhausted by the other: waves are dependent on water, just as water is dependent on the form of waves it inevitably takes. To this, Huayan adds a fourth, and highest point of view, the realm of non-interference and interpenetration of all things. While Tiantai linked all things to each other through causal chains, that is to say, through the 'principle' in operation, Huayan posits a level of reflection on which all things interpenetrate each other directly.

If you look at the form of the lion and the lion only, there will be no gold. Accordingly, the lion is manifest and the gold is hidden. If you look at the gold and the gold only, there will be no lion. Accordingly, the gold is manifest and the lion is hidden. If you look at both of them, then both are hidden and both are manifest. Hidden means mysterious. Manifest means obvious. This is called the gate of the mutual becoming of the mysterious and the obvious.

Gold and lion together are either hidden or manifest. They are either a singularity or a plurality. They are determined either as pure or mixed. They either have power or do not. They are either here or there. The principal and the dependent shine on each other. The principle and the phenomenon are equally apparent and both of them completely contain each other, interfering neither with their independent existence or their distinction in details. This is called the gate of the mutual containment of independent existence of details.

(Fazang, *The Treatise on the Golden Lion* VII: 5–6)

This last viewpoint is perhaps better understood if we think of 'things' not in the Western sense of self-identical objects that somehow exist separately from the processes and situations they are involved with, but as the trajectories through time-space that each of them has. Someone can sit on a chair now; someone else sat on the same chair yesterday. These two people have occupied the same point in space, but this does not mean that they interfere with or exclude each other, as two things claiming the same space normally would. But their movement through the same point in space also means that on a certain level, they have interpenetrated each other, if we think of them as the totality of their movement. In this way, all things interpenetrate each other, because even if no object has occupied, during its lifespan, any point in space in which all other objects have been, a chain of such interpenetration can surely be established. Physicists claim that if we take a glass of water out of the ocean and then pour it back, then after a certain period of time any glass of water, taken out of the ocean anywhere in the world, will contain some molecules of the water of the first glass. This illustrates the Huayan principle of non-interference and interpenetration of all things quite well.

Chan. The best-known school of East Asian Buddhism is unquestionably **Chan**, or Zen, as it is called in Japan. Founded in the early sixth century by an Indian monk called **Bodhidharma**, it synthesized the teachings of many schools and combined them with a unique practice aimed at transcending ordinary logic in order to achieve the enlightened state of mind. Emphasizing a direct transmission from teacher to disciple, Chan officially downplayed the role of scriptures, even though it quickly developed a large body of writings of its own. The teacher–disciple relationships soon transformed into lineages of transmission, which contributed to the split of Chan into a large number of sub-schools. The main split was that between northern and southern Chan. Most later Chan lineages claim their descent from the allegedly orthodox and superior southern tradition inaugurated by **Huineng** (638–713), the sixth head of the school, although there is evidence that this narrative was created in retrospect by southern masters, perhaps in order to counter the imperial patronage that some masters of the northern lines had secured for themselves.

In a few centuries, Chan had become by far the most popular school of Buddhism in China, and although it was hurt by the 845 purge just as any other school, it was strong enough to survive and continue to flourish. Soon enough it had been exported to Korea, Japan, and Vietnam, and the temples in these countries maintained a relationship with Chinese masters over centuries. Due to the efforts of Suzuki Daisetsu, it became well known in the West relatively early, gained a lot of popularity as an alternative view of life in the 1960s, and the study of Chan/Zen has eclipsed most other East Asian Buddhist schools also in Western academia. However, even though a large number of serious studies and expositions exist, Chan/Zen has also been misinterpreted, simplified and commercialized by many of its Western (and contemporary East Asian) proponents.

The founding myth and early history. Chan writings often report a fictional episode, from which the school is supposed to have started. One day, the Buddha went on a walk with his disciples, but instead of preaching, he suddenly held up a flower to them. All of them were confused and puzzled, with the exception of one – Mahākāshyapa, who instinctively smiled. It is to Mahākāshyapa, the Buddha then said, that I will entrust the most secret core of my teaching.

The Chan tradition provides a fictional lineage of Indian Buddhist sages, through whom this secret core is supposed to have reached Bodhidharma. Predictably, these include some of the most prominent thinkers such as Nāgārjuna and Vasubandhu. When we reach China, we get to be on a more secure historical ground, although scant evidence exists about the first heads of the school, through whom the transmission reached the age of Huineng. All of what we know comes from Chan sources, which cannot always be trusted.

Bodhidharma is considered to be a historical person, but his life has also been retroactively embroidered with legends. The most famous of these is his encounter with the emperor, the founder of one short-lived dynasty in South China (Liang), who had recently converted to Buddhism from a life spent in the pursuit of sensual pleasures. The emperor had built numerous temples and took great pride in his achievement, so that when Bodhidharma had been introduced to him, he showed him around personally and finally asked, how much merit the guest thinks he has assembled through all these good deeds. None, said Bodhidharma, because deeds accomplished with the aim of assembling merit have no worth. So what is the meaning of the ultimate truth, then? the emperor asked, puzzled. There is no ultimate truth, answered Bodhidharma, just emptiness. Who are you who thus speak with me? the emperor now asked – losing his temper with the eccentric, we might think – and the answer of Bodhidharma was: I do not know.

Chan sources tell this story as an example of Bodhidharma's courage and superior knowledge, but it is not very likely that he was ever introduced to the Liang court at all.

At the time of Huineng, the Chan tradition had firmly established itself and had become economically self-reliant. Unlike other schools, which often depended on donations and sponsorship, as well as landownings, which allowed the monks to comfortably engage in practice and research, Chan monasteries required their inhabitants to work the fields and provide for themselves. Monks nevertheless were not attached to a particular monastery, so that when they felt that the instruction they had received was insufficient, they were free to leave and try the Chan of another place. More famous masters therefore amassed larger numbers of disciples, which produced some competition, and the prestige of certain lineages exceeded others, somewhat like universities are ranked in the present world.

Chan training. The focus of Chan was primarily practical. The name of the school is a Chinese distortion of the Sanskrit word *dhyāna*, 'meditation', and meditation was indeed the primary way of practice in Chan monasteries.

The teaching of Chan has been summarized in a brief verse attributed to Bodhidharma, but first recorded in the twelfth century:

> Transmitted separately, outside other teachings
> Does not rely on writings and letters
> Direct pointing to one's mind
> Seeing one's true nature, becoming a Buddha

As the topics of meditation, Chan gradually came to use so-called 'public cases' (*gong'an*, Jp. *kōan*), extracts from the conversations of famous masters and their disciples, which supposedly captured the essence of their teaching by transcending the limits of ordinary logic and formulating a paradox that cannot be solved by conceptual reasoning. After a period of such meditation, a monk was supposed to ask for an audience with his master, who tested his understanding and assigned another 'public case' to him. These tests often involved radical measures, such as slapping or shouting. When the realization of the disciple was such that the master was convinced that he had attained enlightenment, he acquired the right to take disciples of his own.

Collections of 'public cases' started to circulate more widely only in the eleventh century, but they were often based on earlier stories, true or fictional. Many of these were taken from *The Record of the Transmission of the Lamp*, a history of Chan that recorded the exchanges between famous masters and their disciples. Another source was the 'collected sayings' of famous Chan masters, collected by their disciples. Most public cases were also commented on by the compilers of the collections in which they appeared, even though the comments were not meant to clarify their content, but rather the opposite – to cut off any avenues that might have led to their rationalization. Thus, for example, the founding myth of the school, the story of the Buddha holding up a flower and Mahākāshyapa smiling in return, is included in one of such collections. However, the compiler has provided it with a comment asserting that the Buddha was no better than an impostor on the market, who sells dog meat for good mutton, and asking what would have happened if all the monks in the assembly would have rolled on the ground, roaring with laughter – or, if no one had smiled, would the core teaching have remained untaught. The aim of the texts is not to instruct the readers, but to perplex them further.

This attitude already reflects the tendency of later masters, such as Linji (d.866), to bring the paradoxical to its extreme limit so that it would unbind the adept's mind. Linji is famous for his dictum 'if you meet the Buddha, kill him, if you meet the head of the school, kill him' – obviously, this is not meant as an instigation to actual violence, but to the extinguishing or erasing the buddha-ness or the headness of a particular, actually encountered person in one's own mind, without letting any titles or status differences to interfere with the perception of that person.

Master Juzhi, whenever anyone asked him for instruction, always raised his finger. A boy was living with him. Once, a visitor came and asked this boy: 'How does your master instruct others in Chan'? The boy raised his finger. Juzhi learned about this and cut the boy's finger off with a knife. The boy was in pain, screamed and ran away. Juzhi invited him back. The boy turned around and Juzhi raised his finger. At this moment, the boy became enlightened.

When Juzhi was about to leave this world, he addressed the assembly and said: 'I received this one-finger Chan from my teacher Tianlong, and I could not exhaust it during my entire life.' These were the words he said, and then he was dead.

Wumen says: Neither Juzhi's nor the boy's enlightenment would fit on the tip of a finger. If you get this, then Tianlong, Juzhi, and the boy will all be pierced through and thread on the same skewer.

The verses say:

Juzhi looks silly compared to old Tianlong –
Trying to bring the boy to heel with a knife ...
A river god would raise a hand just a bit,
And the great mountain Hua of myriad ridges would split!

(*The Gateless Barrier*, case 3)

Ideas: sudden enlightenment, undistracted consciousness. It would seem that this set of premises is unlikely to lead towards a deep level of philosophical speculation, nonetheless we find a lot of it in seminal Chan texts such as the *Platform Scripture of Huineng*, a fictional autobiography of the sixth head of the Chan school and exposition of the teaching attributed to him. This is another text with a complicated history and several versions in circulation and scholars differ in their opinion of how old and how authentic its contents are. What all of its versions have in common, however, is the emphasis on all people possessing Buddha-nature and an inherent potential for enlightenment, which means that conventional social distinctions between the powerful and the disenfranchised, the rich and the poor, the learned and the illiterate, the natives and the foreigners are all based on illusory criteria. The later versions of the text bring in a distinction between the people with naturally superior understanding and the dull and stupid, but the earlier versions do not discriminate between people on the basis of their talent either, pointing out instead that everyone can be both deluded and awakened.

The *Platform Scripture* brings to a logical conclusion the debate between adherents of 'sudden' and 'gradual' enlightenment and strongly argues for the direct teaching, a wholesale abandonment of conceptual commitments in favour of an unbound, undistracted flow of consciousness that may be in contact with ordinary realities, but does not become attached to, and distracted by them. The scripture takes the form of a sermon delivered from a 'platform' – an elevation or dais from where a teacher could address a crowd – in the context of conveying Buddhist precepts to followers. This is also what Huineng does, but his precepts are 'formless', in that they cannot be reduced to rules of life and restrictions of behaviour, as precepts normally were. Instead, Huineng advocates his followers to rely on their inner enlightenment potential, give up their commitments to external strictures – indeed, the servile following of rules is just as bad as doing whatever one pleases – and find their internal self, which is identical to Buddha-nature. And meditation is the way that leads to this. Unlike other schools, Huineng says, Chan does not advocate the contemplation of the mind, or a state of mind such as purity, because any such object of meditation is itself an illusion and deviation from what 'pure mind' should naturally be. However, Huineng does also not advocate a state of mind empty of *all* content, as is sometimes thought, only a state of mind empty of all *permanent* content. This is a mind that an enlightened Chan follower should be able to maintain at all times, simultaneously remaining fully functional – having a working relationship with one's lifeworld does not imply being entangled in it and defined by it.

In our school, from its very beginnings, attainment of enlightenment rests on the absence of thoughts as its core, the absence of [external] aspects as its form, the absence of foundation as its root. What is this absence of aspects? It means that you can relate to the aspects [of all phenomena], and yet distance yourself from them. The absence of thoughts means that you can relate to thoughts, but not think them. The absence of foundation is what we see as the root nature of all people. The stream of thoughts has no foundation. The thought of before, the thought of the now, the thought of after – all of these thoughts follow each other and there is no interruption. Whenever there occurs an interrupting thought, the body as total reality is separated from the body as form.

(*The Platform Scripture*, Dunhuang version, section 17)

Although the tradition describes Huineng as the illiterate son of a banished official, raised in extreme poverty, the text of the *Platform Scripture* leaves no doubt that its author(s) were thoroughly educated in previous Buddhist literature and quite familiar with the teachings of Yogācāra, Tiantai, and Huayan. A similar attitude persisted also during the next generations and many ideas of these and other schools were domesticated by Chan, if they were useful for the support of Chan ideas. The multiple lineages and fairly anarchistic view of institutions prevented a Chan orthodoxy from arising for quite some time, which also provided later Chan thinkers with a broader range of views as their own source of inspiration.

Other trends. Two other developments of Chinese Buddhism need to be mentioned: the fairly short-lived tradition of esoteric Buddhism and the teachings of Pure Land.

Esoteric Buddhism emerged in India as a reaction to the Hindu tantric teachings, which became increasingly popular with rulers and started to eclipse the position of Buddhism. Developing certain Mahāyāna ideas and combining them with ecstatic practices, proponents of esoteric Buddhism produced a corpus of Buddhist tantras and claimed to represent a higher level of the teaching, called the Vajrayāna, or Thunderbolt (Diamond) Vehicle, named after *vajra*, 'thunderbolt/ diamond', the mythical weapon of the Vedic god Indra, supposed to be as impossible to cut as a diamond and as forceful as a thunderbolt. Symbolic objects called *vajra* are still used in the rituals of esoteric Buddhism.

The tradition was imported to China during the Tang dynasty by several Indian practitioners and acquired a small following in the capital. Many esoteric Indian texts were introduced and the recitation of mantras and contemplation of mandalas started to spread. However, the tradition lost some of its vigour after the persecution of Buddhism in China and the transmission lines became extinct. Though the esoteric teachings again attracted some interest under early Song rule, this was mostly scholarly and the school was not restored as an independent institution. In 805, however, the third head of the esoteric school had named his Japanese disciple Kūkai to be one of his six successors, and the school survives in Japan to the present.

While the idea of mandalas did not survive the demise of esoteric Buddhism in the Chinese tradition, the recitation of mantras became quite prominent, especially in the **Pure Land** school. This school is based on several Indian texts featuring a buddha called **Amitābha** or Amitāyus, who had vowed to offer a safe haven to all beings who had faith in him and trusted him. For this purpose, he had created a 'buddha-field', an extension of his own consciousness, called the 'Pure Land' and situated abstractly in the West, where everyone who so wished could go after their death. For that to happen, the follower only needed to recite a mantra glorifying Amitābha's name. In China, this teaching was introduced as early as the second century CE, but did not consolidate into a school and remained the domain of mostly eccentric practitioners. Nonetheless, these people left behind a body of writing that developed a kind of a tradition, which evolved further in later ages.

The Buddhist institution. Apart from the ideas and practices that Buddhist schools imported from India or developed in China, Buddhism also introduced quite a few institutional innovations to worldview-related cultural practices. Until the spread of Buddhism, religious professionals were largely experts in certain techniques, such as divination, or the proper organization of events, such as rituals and ceremonies, and they operated either as officials of the government or freelancers. The institutions of monastery and monkhood were unknown to the Ru, although a site of sacrifice had been erected at Kongzi's birthplace soon after his death and similar structures appeared also elsewhere and these gradually took the shape of temples. However, nothing among the early Chinese cultural institutions resembled Buddhist monasteries in scope and scale.

The words that came to signify Buddhist temples originally meant 'government office' and 'garden'. The first term was probably borrowed from the designation of temporary quarters assigned to foreigners. Full-fledged monasteries were large architectural structures, complete with halls of worship, residences for monks, and spaces for public rituals and were usually built with government sponsorship. During political turmoil and division, rulers competed in such generosity, which provided them with cultural capital. Lesser-scale temples arose through local initiatives and were considerably more modest, but people often considered donating to such construction projects to be beneficial for their posthumous destinies. It is estimated that by mid-fifth century the number of Buddhist monasteries was over 6000 and monks and nuns numbered over 750 000, and a 100 years later the total of monks and nuns had exceeded 2 million, while the number of monasteries was about 30 000 and growing. Economically, they enjoyed a comfortable status, being exempted from paying tax, which may be one of the reasons for the 845 purge, the destruction of a large number of monasteries and the confiscation of their significant wealth, accompanied by the forcible return of a large number of people to the general workforce.

The Buddhist institution held a careful balance in its relationship with state power and the aspirations of other worldviews. In general, it did not try to compete with the Ru tradition for political influence, even though some Buddhist masters became spiritual advisors and teachers to rulers and must have had their ear also in other matters. The idea of personal salvation by enlightenment certainly appealed to many powerful people, and thus presented an alternative to the Dao creed, which claimed to be in command of techniques leading to immortality. On the other hand, the Dao creed also embraced the discontent of the poor, which Buddhist institutions were not very concerned with. Enjoying a tax-exempt status, the Buddhist institutions were happy to provide spiritual comfort and ritualistic services to the powerful, as well as a safe haven to the intellectually discontented, but during this period did not try to interfere with social processes on the larger scale.

From Song to Qing

Background. The cosmopolitan lustre of the Tang gave way to another interregnum, which was brought to its end by a general, who installed the Song dynasty. This is the time when urban culture started to develop in China – the economy was increasingly dependent on trade and technology, a literate middle class arose and a market for entertainment with it. The invention of woodblock printing increased the speed and accuracy of information dissemination. The Song dynasty was also the time of a major intellectual movement, the Neo-Confucian revival, that consisted in the reinterpretation of the classical Ru tradition and a mostly successful effort to curtail the influence of Buddhism and the Dao creed through the adoption of their seminal ideas into the canvas of its own views. Although both Buddhism and the Dao creed survived as independent institutions, the 'unity of the three teachings' has undoubtedly benefited the followers of Kongzi more than others, and from now on this tradition was the most attractive for talented intellectuals to join.

While this consolidation of thought systems took place in the intellectual spheres, Song is also the period when the folk religion of China, a syncretic practice that has combined the ancient tradition of ancestor worship with elements borrowed both from the Dao creed and Buddhism, most likely started to gain the form in which it is known today. The folk religion does not rely on scriptures, nor does it have an institutional form or a professional clergy, which is why it is difficult to trace its historical development. The state has also viewed certain folk religious practices, especially societies centred around certain cults, with suspicion, and occasionally these have indeed become vehicles of dissent and rebellion.

The rule of the Song dynasty was brought to an end by a series of wars with the Mongol army of Genghis Khan and his heirs, the conquest of China in 1276 by Khubilai and the installation of a new dynasty, the Yuan. Initially hostile to the Neo-Confucians, the Yuan rulers soon realized they would be unable to govern China without their help, but complete trust was never achieved and a nationalist sentiment continued to fuel rebellions, some of them led by Dao and Buddhist sympathizers. One of these finally proved successful, managed to overcome the Yuan in 1368, and inaugurate a new dynasty, the Ming (1368–1644).

During the 300 years of Ming rule, China was, after some short successful efforts at seafaring, turned inward. The capital was moved from the south to Beijing, education, culture, and trade were encouraged and with good results. New cultural forms appeared, from the characteristic blue porcelain to theatre and popular novels. Further aggression from the Mongols prompted the emperors to reconstruct the Great Wall into an efficient fortification. Communication with the outside world was not encouraged, but also not entirely cut off, and accounts of the China of the times have survived by some missionaries, such as Matteo Ricci (1552–1610), who travelled around in the country.

Bureaucracy was reinstated, and the literati were again able to lead comfortable lives in its service. By the Ming times, the civil service examinations had become increasingly difficult and threatened by corruption, which gradually started to eat the government from within. In the seventeenth century, the Ming were too weak to muster efficient support and fell to a series of mutinies and the invasion of another non-Chinese nation, the Manchus.

The last dynasty of Qing (1644–1912) was in many ways the continuation of Ming, as the Manchus quickly adopted Chinese customs and culture, although without assimilation, and became ardent supporters of the traditional imperial system of governance. Qing emperors recognized the superiority of Chinese culture and enthusiastically promoted the systematization and development of all branches of learning. Perhaps their non-Chinese origin was one of the reasons for their conservative tastes and admiration of the past, which was not their own. Nonetheless one half of civil service positions was reserved for people of Manchu descent, which made the competition harder for the Chinese and resulted in a clear division of officials into smart Chinese and less talented Manchus, who had a statistically better chance of success.

Towards the end of the eighteenth century, when Western powers became more active around China's shores, the country was forced to end its self-imposed cultural isolation. Restrictions on foreign trade were not effective, and the British East India Company, in particular, acquired a strong position. However, while Chinese goods such as tea and silk were in great demand, there was not much of British origin that the Chinese markets craved. In order to change the situation, the British East India Company recast itself as a drug cartel and very successfully started to import opium from its other Asian dominions. The Chinese government was naturally opposed to this, which resulted in the Opium Wars of 1839–1842 and 1856–1858, with devastating results for China.

The last decades of the Chinese empire saw incapacitated emperors, a powerful empress dowager with a limited mindset, increasing corruption and mismanagement, despaired scholars offering memoranda to the throne on how to reform the country, rebellions led by secret societies and one inspired by a weird misinterpretation of Christianity, efforts by foreign powers to force the Chinese government to do their bidding and, above all, a growing desperation among all strata of the Chinese population about the destiny of their society. All of this inevitably led to the fall of the Qing and the establishment of the Republic of China.

The development of the Dao creed. Even though the Neo-Confucian revival gradually evolved into the primary intellectual movement of the Song-Qing period, the other worldviews of China did not give up their positions completely. Especially the Dao creed enjoyed a revival during the Mongol conquest. None other than the Genghis Khan himself expressed his interest in the teachings and sent, in 1219, an envoy to invite the most famous Celestial Master, Qiu Changchun (1148–1227), for an audience. Qiu, although rather advanced in years, undertook the journey, which took several years, but paid off handsomely, as the Khan decreed that Qiu (and his tradition of Complete Perfection, founded only relatively recently by his teacher) would from then on be in charge of the entire creed and also their earthly possessions. The Complete Perfection tradition had abandoned the pursuit of immortality in all but name, as its goal was to liberate one's 'shining spirit' for eternal existence. Unlike earlier schools, the ideologues of Complete Perfection also prescribed strict moral rules for their followers, and all the sexual theories of previous schools were purged from the teaching. By the end of the thirteenth century, it is estimated that Complete Perfection managed over 4000 monasteries, and that in spite of the later Mongol rulers favouring Buddhism over the Dao creed.

Buddhist schools. Some Buddhist schools had not survived the 845 persecution, others were reduced in size, but Chan did not suffer as much damage as others. By the end of Tang, the multiple lineages of Chan had consolidated into what came to be known as 'five houses' of Chan, which differed from each other mostly in details and preferential techniques of instruction, but not in the central tenets of their teaching. During the Song dynasty, three of the five houses became extinct. At the time, what is called the 'literary phase' of Chan started, with a stress on the study and editing of earlier texts as well as an explosive increase in literary output by Chan practitioners themselves. The association with literature and art also brought more cultural prestige to Chan, and it enjoyed the status of the dominant Buddhist school during the later centuries.

During the Song dynasty, Pure Land Buddhism acquired a larger popular appeal and also contributed to the formation of an innovative social movement known as the White Lotus Society, a group propagating an eclectic egalitarian doctrine that inspired several rebellions against the Mongol rulers of the Yuan dynasty. In later centuries, Pure Land teachings gradually became mingled with Chan and during the Ming dynasty nearly absorbed the latter, largely due to the syncretic efforts of Zhixu (1599–1655), who tried to consolidate all Chinese worldviews into one whole that could then be opposed to the imported doctrine of Christianity. Still, the role of Pure Land thought in China is rather modest compared to the overwhelming success of Pure Land schools in Japan.

Wang Anshi (1021–1086) and 'New Policies'. The major political upheaval of the Song dynasty is connected with the rise and fall of **Wang Anshi**, the leader of a group of reform-minded politicians. He came from a family of scholar-officials and worked in the provinces for more than 10 years before proposing to the court a project of radical reforms, known as the 'New Policies'. Wang observed first-hand the tendency of large landholders to amass riches, while the poor had to bear most of the tax burden and the central power was also drained of resources.

Wang carefully formulated his reform policies in a discourse borrowed from *The Book of Rites* and presented them as a return to the just policies of the past sage rulers. What he proposed was quite unprecedented, however. His idea was to centralize the economy and to transfer it from a system of obligations to a monetary basis, with price regulations in place, to centralize taxation and to make the wealthy pay their proportional share, to eliminate monopolies and provide state loans to small enterprises and small-size, struggling households. He also proposed to introduce military conscription and to reform education along more technocratic lines, including mathematics, military strategy, law, and medicine in the curriculum. Although the rule of law had a bad reputation in Chinese political theory due to the unscrupulous policies of the legalist school, it was certainly one of Wang's goals.

It is difficult to say what China would have looked like after some time, had all these reforms indeed been implemented. In actual history, Wang's political activities were hindered by his opponents in many ways, until he was finally ousted from his position in 1085 by the opposing faction. His adversaries were led by a Neo-Confucian historian, an excellent scholar, but with conservative political views. Wang's own Ru credentials were also impeccable and his scholarly work includes comments on many ancient texts, which he often read in an innovative manner, as Neo-Confucians also did. Still, a creative attitude towards the tradition is probably the only feature they shared. The ethical teaching of Neo-Confucians in general favoured a trickle-down economy, believing that social hierarchy reflected the natural differences in abilities and the moral superiority of the wealthy compelled them to care for the destitute, even though reality did not offer any proof for such optimism.

The Neo-Confucian revival. The term 'Neo-Confucianism' is a Western concept for a range of new thought that is usually called 'Dao learning' in Chinese and comprises all the schools that reinterpreted and developed the Ru tradition during the Song, Yuan, and Ming dynasties. It has been argued that this term has less problems than 'Confucianism', as it does not refer to any historical school, and Neo-Confucians indeed raised Kongzi out from among all sages of the past to the status of the architect of their tradition. Some scholars also include Qing thinkers under this label, while others claim that they represent a new phase in this tradition, which should be considered separately. Neo-Confucianism has been often compared to European Renaissance, in that the distance between the cultures of Ancient Greece and Rome and the Italy of the late Middle Ages is approximately of the same order of magnitude, and the revival of certain Greek and Roman ideas did not mean a full-scale emulation of those earlier societies and cultural codes. In this way Renaissance culture was both a return and a step forward, and similarly is Neo-Confucianism the construction of something new.

The Neo-Confucian revival began with the work of a small group of scholars, such as the polymath Shao Yong (1011–1077) who sought to give new life to ancient texts, and to synthesize the competing various traditions into a holistic system. Shao was among the first to turn to the *Yijing*, or *Book of Changes* for inspiration, providing a new interpretation that integrated Ru, Dao, and Buddhist notions into a systematic vision. The official pedigree of the Neo-Confucian tradition downplays his role, however, possibly because of his excessive interest in numerology and other pursuits too close to the tradition of the Dao creed. History thus credits primarily the other members of the group (Zhou Dunyi, Zhang Zai, the Cheng brothers) with preparing the ground for the arrival of the towering figure of **Zhu Xi** (1130–1200), whose work turned the new way of seeing things into an orthodoxy. Zhu Xi's work remained almost unchallenged for three centuries, until **Wang Yangming** (1472–1529) introduced another reappraisal of the tradition, a turn of comparable dimensions and just as provocative. Through their combined efforts, Buddhism and the Dao creed lost most of their intellectual appeal.

Zhou Dunyi (1017–1073). In his retrospective reconstruction of the Ru tradition with which he identified, Zhu Xi saw the transmission as broken after Mengzi and restored only by **Zhou Dunyi**, an obscure minor provincial clerk who has left only two relatively short pieces of writing behind. These were transmitted to Zhu Xi by the Cheng brothers, who studied with Zhou Dunyi, even though they did not actually recognize him as their teacher. Zhu Xi, however, was of a different opinion and installed him in the line of orthodox transmission as the first figure of Neo-Confucian thought. Quite a few later scholars consider this move to be arbitrary and assert that Zhou Dunyi was, in fact, expounding an eclectic version of the Dao creed combined with decipherings of the cryptic messages of the *Yijing*, meant to explain the hexagrams.

The best-known work by Zhou Dunyi is a short treatise entitled *A Comment on the Diagram of the Great Ultimate*, a symbolic cosmological scheme of how the universe works, consisting of five circles, the first one of which represents the totality of being as a void, the second one pictures it as an interpenetration of the yin and yang principles, the third one introduces the Five Phases, and the last two are again void. The diagram indeed comes from Dao sources, but the reading Zhou Dunyi gives to it sharply contrasts with the ambitions of Dao followers to transcend the human form and become one with the cosmic principle. For Zhou Dunyi, the human perspective is central and superior to all others, and sagehood, conceived in the terms of traditional Ru virtues, is the paragon of human achievement.

> The Great Ultimate is originally the Ultimate of Non-Being. The Five Phases
> are generated out of it, and each of these has its own nature. The true core
> of Non-Being is subtly united with the essences of yin and yang and the
> Five Phases, and self-organization ensues. The pattern of Heaven becomes
> the male, the pattern of Earth becomes the female. The two kinds of *qi* are
> blended and their transformations produce the myriad things. The myriad
> things continue to produce and produce, and their changes can never be
> exhausted. However, only humans have attained excellence in this process
> and the superior level of spirit – when human form is produced, spirit has
> achieved wisdom. The five [moral] natures now feel and move, good and
> evil are distinguished from each other. Myriad affairs take place, and the
> sage regulates them according to balance, correct standards, humaneness
> and integrity.
>
> (Zhou Dunyi, *A Comment on the Diagram of the Great Ultimate*)

In this way, Zhou Dunyi can indeed be considered the first to articulate one fundamental principle of Neo-Confucian thought, namely the ontological identity of the universe as constant interdependent becoming and the moral potential at work in human nature, which synthesizes Mengzi's views with cosmological ideas appropriated from the Dao creed.

The Cheng brothers. The two men responsible for kickstarting the Neo-Confucian revival in earnest were the brothers **Cheng Hao** (1032–1085) and **Cheng Yi** (1033–1107). Both of them successfully passed the civil service examinations and attained high positions, attracting imperial attention, but soon fell to disfavour because of their views and character. Their lives coincided with the period of reforms initiated by Wang Anshi, which they both opposed. Wang was soon enough ousted from office by his adversaries and exiled, but the Cheng brothers did not get along too well also with the ascending group. It is said that they were different in character, the older Hao being better-natured, friendly, and tolerant, the younger Yi being more serious and strict. Scholars have identified also differences in their philosophical views, although their works have been preserved in a common collection, where the author of particular texts is not always identified. On the whole Cheng Hao is supposed to express his views in condensed propositions, and Cheng Yi in a more analytical manner. They had numerous disciples and established a lineage, which reached Zhu Xi and was established by him as the orthodoxy of Neo-Confucian thought.

Ideas. The thought of the Cheng brothers focuses on the concept of *li*, 'principle' or 'pattern', not to be confused with *li* 'ritual propriety', which is written with a different character. The concept of principle is first met in the Warring States philosophy and later adopted by Tiantai and Huayan Buddhist thought, where it is elevated to the position of the central metaphysical concept. This is an important development, as the concept of 'principle' has considerably more philosophical flexibility than 'the Way'. Indeed, the Neo-Confucian lineage that includes the Cheng brothers and Zhu Xi is often dubbed as 'the teaching of the principle'. For Han Feizi, the 'principle' had meant the particular manner in which the Way is manifested in a single thing; for the Buddhists, the underlying, all-pervading pattern of reality. For the Cheng brothers, the *li* was both of these, articulated as the 'single-rootedness' of all things in the thought of Cheng Hao and as the unity of opposites for Cheng Yi. Both of them thus agreed with the formulation that 'the principle is one, but its manifestations are many', but gave it a somewhat different meaning.

It seems that Cheng Hao was more concerned with developing the cosmological theories of Zhou Dunyi and other early Neo-Confucians into a metaphysical system, while Cheng Yi dedicated himself to grounding an ethical doctrine in these views. Cheng Hao had studied Buddhism and the Dao tradition between returning to the study of the Ru classics, and reportedly experienced something akin to enlightenment while reading these. As a result, he imported this experiential dimension of Buddhism also to the Neo-Confucian tradition and claimed that the attainment of sagehood takes place as a profound, personality-changing experience based on the realization of the unity of the Way of Heaven and one's particular human nature. The analogy with the idea of original enlightenment and Buddha-nature is not hard to perceive.

This ontological sameness, or 'single-rootedness' of Heaven, the human mind, and all other phenomena was Cheng Hao's fundamental contribution to Neo-Confucian theory. But it had some undesirable side effects. If all things were single-rooted, this also meant that 'good' and 'evil' are not distinguishable in a fundamental manner. This is indeed what Cheng Hao claimed, but he also tried to evade the consequences by claiming that goodness derives directly from the Way, while evil results from accidental intermingling of elements and is therefore secondary.

A more consistent moral philosophy was put forward by Cheng Yi, who identified morality with the essence of being human. He reads Kongzi to say that delight is an essential attribute of a sage, and real delight can only arise from moral actions. Besides, moral virtues cannot be acquired, but have to arise from one's internal nature. Therefore, human essence, morality, and delight are inextricably intertwined with each other. However, people are often confused and assume that selfish actions can lead to pleasures that qualify as delight, although they do not. Delight has to preclude strained effort, just as harmony comes naturally to music. Moreover, although the words 'delight' and 'music' are pronounced differently, they are written with the same character.

Cheng Yi's stern character and his view of morality made him insensitive to the plights of other people. For example, when asked whether widows should be able to remarry if they cannot support themselves and are likely to starve to death, he is supposed to have said that death by starving is a small matter compared to the loss of integrity that remarrying implies. The strict and often inflexible moralism of Neo-Confucian thought may be considered to be his main legacy. Indeed, his views were too much even for the imperial court and his work was prohibited for many years after his death even after Cheng Yi himself was pardoned for his quarrels with the ruling faction.

> Heaven I call my father, Earth I call my mother, and though I am such an insignificant creature compared to them, nonetheless I, too, have a place in their great interaction. Therefore: what fills the universe, I take for my body, what manages the universe, I take for my nature. All the people are brothers and sisters to me, all things complement me. The great lord is the eldest son of my father and my mother, and his distinguished ministers are the keepers of our house.
>
> (Zhang Zai, Western inscription)

Zhang Zai (1020–1077). An uncle of the Cheng brothers, **Zhang Zai** became a proponent of Neo-Confucian thought as well, adding an important aspect to it by connecting the cosmological with the sociopolitical. Just like his nephew Cheng Hao, he had studied Buddhist and Dao traditions before taking up Ru classics, and similarly to his nephews he was also both raised to high positions and dismissed from them for his critical views.

Zhang Zai was a prolific writer, but his most influential text remains a short piece entitled 'The Western Inscription', a summary statement of his views that he hung on the Western wall of his living quarters. In it, he proclaimed in Neo-Confucian manner that Heaven and Earth are his parents, the entire universe is his body and the laws that move it are identical to his nature. What is new in his views is that all people are his brothers and sisters, while the emperor is the eldest son of the same parents. Zhang Zai thus develops the idea of single-rootedness into a principle of comprehensive social solidarity, but also sets down the criteria for legitimate hierarchy and further elaborates on the distinctions of affection. The text became extremely popular – Cheng Yi is reported to have said that nothing of the same quality had been written since the times of Mengzi – and is often considered to be the founding statement of Neo-Confucian ethics.

Zhu Xi (1130–1200). With the work of these early Neo-Confucian thinkers the preconditions of a large synthesis had been put in place, but a couple of generations had to go by before the appearance of the thinker who would accomplish it. This thinker was Zhu Xi, a philosopher, textual scholar and intellectual historian of rare magnitude, whose contribution to the Ru intellectual tradition is considered by some scholars to rank second only to Kongzi himself.

Zhu Xi was the son of a provincial official, who also taught him classics at home, and, after passing his examinations, briefly held a minor administrative post himself. Approximately at the same time he befriended a philosopher who followed the tradition of the Cheng brothers and started to study with him. After about 20 years of mostly academic activity, Zhu Xi was again appointed to a number of official positions, but soon dismissed from all of these because of his uncompromising attacks on corruption and mismanagement, which earned him the wrath of quite a few influential politicians. His teachings were similarly attacked as misreadings of the Ru tradition, but gained in popularity, as they were systematic, coherent, and intellectually appealing.

A large part of Zhu Xi's work was dedicated to the editing and commenting of classics. Among other things, he is responsible for the demystification and rationalization of a large number of passages in ancient works, as he always trusted the source text rather than the interpretations attached to it over the centuries in between, thus, for example, reading some sections from the *Books of Songs* as straightforward love poetry rather than complicated allegories for family values relating to historical precedent, as bookish commentaries had treated them. Zhu Xi also established the text of the canonical 'Four Books' in addition to the 'Five Classics' of the Ru tradition, writing detailed exegeses of the *Analects* and the book of Mengzi in the process. From 1313 to 1905, Zhu Xi's interpretation of the classics was the standard required at civil service examinations.

Ideas: metaphysics. The goal of Zhu Xi's teaching was self-realization, or becoming as good a person as possible, which in the best case meant the attainment of sagehood. But sagehood is impossible without a clear understanding of the greater scheme of things, which is why a coherent metaphysical picture of the world is necessary, not as the satisfaction of intellectual curiosity, but as an immensely practical mindset without which ethical development would have no solid ground. A metaphysical system would thus inevitably result from 'the investigation of things', or the first step on the way to social and cosmic order. Zhu Xi's metaphysical views are not laid out in an orderly manner in a single treatise, however, but have been gathered by subsequent generations of scholars from his vast corpus of writings into a coherent whole.

As opposed to the Buddhist and Dao systems, the Neo-Confucian metaphysics of Zhu Xi assumes that the universe is not empty or void, but 'full' of reality, and is not very much concerned with the question of how this reality came into being. It is dualistic in that there is the most general natural order, or the Way, on the one hand, and the basic stuff from which the universe consists, or *qi*, on the other hand. The Western perspective identifies this basic stuff traditionally as matter, which is inert by default and brought into being by external stimuli, but the Chinese point of view emphasizes the energetic potential of *qi*, its internal dynamism. Sometimes *qi* is translated as 'vital force', but we should not assume that non-living things consist of anything else. This *qi* is not homogeneous, but varies in both composition (interpenetration of yin and yang-type qualities) and degrees of condensation, from solid to ethereal. It is also qualitatively uneven, some of it pure, some impure.

The actual concern of metaphysics is the sphere in which the dynamism of *qi* and the natural order interact, or the domain of 'forms', as Zhu Xi calls it. The manner in which the Way is manifest in the transformations of qi is what Zhu Xi calls 'the principle', or *li*. The principle is above 'forms', *qi* is below them. Much on what he writes on their relationship is indeed implicit in former Chinese thought, or at least seems so in retrospect after Zhu Xi has reinterpreted the ancient texts in his manner. *Li* and *qi* form a binary axis, in which the principle provides coherence to each of the 'myriad things'. In this, the principle acts as the definition of the natural state of these things – it does not differentiate between essential and contingent properties, but between the state of how things are and how they ought to be. A dog ought to have four legs; a dog with three legs is still a dog, but not in the state in which a dog ought to be. Similarly, the principle of being human specifies that humans are ethical, and if someone is not, they are still humans, but deviant ones, not conforming to the way how they ought to be. There is no gap, so to say, between their ontological and deontological status.

The Neo-Confucian axiom that 'the principle is one, but its manifestations are many' is valid for Zhu Xi in the sense that every single thing necessarily has a principle, the idea that every phenomenon is structured corresponds to the 'oneness' of the principle, while the differences between these singular structures account for the many manifestations. The oneness, or necessary structurality of the 'myriad things' (for Zhu Xi, these include acts and events) is what makes all of them in principle knowable to the person who investigates them.

The nature of things and the human mind. When such structurality is divorced from its general character and applied solely to the particularity of a thing (or event), it becomes the 'nature' of this thing. By this move, the nature of one thing can be opposed to the nature of another. For example, the nature of human beings is qualitatively different from the nature of inert objects in that they have consciousness and the ability to control what they do.

This can be described in the terms of yet another binary, usually translated as 'substance' (*ti*) and 'function' (*yong*). This opposition goes back in intellectual history to as far as Wang Bi's work, where 'substance' is the primordial vacuous stasis, out of which dynamic things emerge as its functions. Later authors have correlated any kind of stasis with 'substance', and 'function' with movement. But Zhu Xi gives these terms a different meaning: for him, both stasis and movement as manifest in things are functions, while the way how these things are in a not-yet-actualized state is their substance. For example, it is substantial for an eye to be able to see, but when it actually sees, this event is functional. Similarly, the substance of human beings makes them able to commit all sorts of acts, but what they actually do makes up their function. Accordingly, function can never be met without substance, which is always present within it. But the form a function takes is only made possible by its corresponding substance, not predetermined by it. Perhaps the closest pair of concepts in Western philosophy is the opposition, suggested by Gilles Deleuze, between the virtual (substance) and actual (function).

'Who exhausts their mind, knows their nature. Who knows their nature, knows Heaven.' These words [of Mengzi] mean a human being is able to exhaust their mind, to know their nature and to know Heaven. This is because 'Heaven' is the principle itself, in its spontaneous state, and also the reason that brings a human being into existence. 'Nature' is the completed substance, and also the realization that brings a human being into existence. 'Mind' is that by which a human being masters their body and actualizes the principle inherent in it. ... Only when chained by the forms and tools of egocentrism and bound by the superficiality of sense-data, the mind becomes clouded and cannot exhaust itself. A human being is able to get to the bottom of the principles of all things and affairs, until one day they penetrate every single thing and there will be no place they have not reached, and then, through the completion of their mind, they have restored their substance to its natural dimension.

(Zhu Xi, Explanation of 'exhausting the mind')

The mind, according to Zhu Xi, is precisely the instance that makes the decisions about which activities will be undertaken, a control centre that regulates the 'functions' that the substance of human being will be involved in, and mediates between the nature and the emotions, or the levels of principle and the stuff of *qi*. It is through the mind that the principle operates, but the mind is separate from the principle itself. The mind, as such, is in a state of balance and undisturbed by emotions. By its nature, it contains all the elements needed for the comprehension of reality. When it comes to contact with this reality, emotions arise that are capable of upsetting this balance, but when the moral capacities inherent in human nature are applied the result is harmony – both with itself and with the world.

This is the ideal that characterizes a sage, and also the manifestation of the principle in a particular mind, in other words, the way how the human being ought to be.

Early critics and the Goose Lake debate. Despite the growing popularity of Zhu Xi's ideas that resulted in their orthodox status, there were also scholars who were critical of his approach, considering it too bookish and concentrating on philological detail. These concerns were voiced during one of the most celebrated philosophical debates in Chinese intellectual history, the meeting of Zhu Xi and two brothers, Lu Jiuling (1132–1180) and **Lu Jiuyuan**, who is also known by his sobriquet Xiangshan (1139–1193) and considered to be the founder of the lineage of 'the teaching of mind'. This took place at the Goose Lake temple, where Zhu Xi had been invited by a friend and collaborator of his, who had also been Lu Jiuyuan's examiner in the civil service examinations. The records of this meeting stress the difference between Zhu Xi and the Lu brothers in their emphasis on either study or practice: Lu Jiuyuan famously claimed that Zhu Xi's approach results in a fragmented understanding and aimless drifting, unlike the single-minded practice advocated by himself. But the differences went deeper. Lu rejected in principle an approach based on binaries, and articulated instead a view of a unitary, mindful reality that is manifested in the individual human being by their own consciousness. Although his views have, in fact, been traced back by later scholars to arguments found in the work of Mengzi, the adherents of Zhu Xi's school have criticized him of being a crypto-Buddhist, because of his excessive stress on the mind as the only true reality. As a result, his position lost its status for centuries, until the appearance of Wang Yangming.

Another oppositional voice of the time was that of Chen Liang (1143–1194), a frustrated scholar who had repeatedly failed the civil service examinations and felt that disputes of philosophical nature contributed little to the solving of political problems that China was facing at the time. In a series of essays sent to Zhu Xi, Chen articulates a view that a flexible evaluation of the current situation should take precedence over blindly following the established norm, and that this kind of expediency is what integrity (*yi*) really means. Chen's views have recently been compared to utilitarianism, but Zhu Xi reportedly found them so disturbing that he did not even show the essays to his students, in fear that these might lose their sense of moral standard.

Wang Yangming (1472–1529). After Zhu Xi's death, his disciples managed to establish his teaching, together with that of the Cheng brothers, as the main line of the Ru tradition, known as Cheng-Zhu school, or 'the teaching of principle'. Very few scholars dared to radically challenge it until the appearance of the second major figure of Neo-Confucianism, Wang Yangming, during the Ming dynasty.

Unlike the early Neo-Confucians, Wang Yangming had a brilliant career as a military commander, provincial governor and vice minister; more typically, he was also exiled and forced into retirement several times in his life because of his criticism of powerful sycophants, and then invited back to undertake tasks he was deemed the best to handle. It is reported that during a time when he was banished to a province, where he had nothing to read or no one to talk to, he realized that all the resources he needed for understanding reality were actually there within himself, and this idea became the cornerstone of his teaching. The idea may have come to Wang from his study of Buddhism, even though he does not refer to Buddhist sources in his teaching – for obvious reasons, as calling one's opponent a Buddhist was a typical insult in Neo-Confucian polemics. In any case, such views are the reason why early Western interpreters were quick to cast Wang as a subjective idealist, a sort of a Chinese George Berkeley. More recent scholarly consensus rejects this view.

Wang Yangming's relationship to the inherited thought of Zhu Xi was difficult and ambiguous. At one point, he has said that from Mengzi up to his times there was no one mentionable except Lu Jiuyuan. At another point, however, Wang Yangming has expressed his admiration of Zhu Xi and even written a text stating the similarities of his own views with later views of Zhu Xi – unfortunately, his textual scholarship was not up to par and he mixed up quotations, resulting in critique from Zhu Xi's partisans. Nonetheless, both thinkers undoubtedly share a number of general Neo-Confucian views and differ on other points, and Wang is justly considered to be the classic of the second main Neo-Confucian school, 'the teaching of mind'.

Ideas: the principle and the mind. There are quite a few passages in Wang Yangming's work that let themselves be read as articulations of subjective idealism, as he has repeatedly asserted that there are no 'things' that exist outside the mind. When asked about the ontological status of flowers blooming on a cliff, Wang responded that before they are looked at, the mind of the looker and the flowers themselves are both in a dormant state, and the mind only registers the colour of the flowers when a connection is established. This example is quite similar to the famous question of whether a tree falling on a deserted island causes a sound, to which the scientifically correct answer is that it does not: the sound appears in the relationship of the hearing ear and the cause of the airwaves, but without the former the airwaves do not produce a sound. It has been argued that 'things', in the idiosyncratic philosophical language of Wang Yangming, actually refer to reifications of reality that are produced by thought – something like the intentional objects of Western phenomenology –, and not to self-identical mind-independent objects, the existence of which would be denied. As a result, we could say that a phenomenon acquires its thingly form in the interaction with the mind. The objects that make up our world are relational, as sound is, but this does not mean that the *qi*, or the basic stuff these objects ultimately consist of would not be ontologically independent.

Wang transfers this relationality also to moral categories. In an often-presented example, he claims that filial piety does not reside in the figures of the parents, but in the mind of the child, and loyalty is not contained by the figure of the ruler, but by the minds of the subjects. This is the reason why Wang identifies the principle – of which filial piety, loyalty, and other virtues are concrete instantiations – with the mind that is capable of initiating such relationships. In this, his views diverge sharply from those of Zhu Xi, for whom the mind was separate from the principle and only acted as the conduit for its activities.

> The absence of good and the absence of evil – this is the substance of the mind
> The presence of good and the presence of evil – this is the movement of thought
> Recognizing good and recognizing evil – this is 'pure knowledge'
> Doing good and abstaining from evil – this is 'the investigation of things'
> (Wang Yangming, *The Teaching in Four Statements*)

Unity of knowledge and action. One of the most famous theses of Wang Yangming is the unity of knowledge and action. Many scholars underscore the practical bent of his thinking as well as the fact that he arrived at his vision as a result of a long intellectual search, which this idea reflects.

Wang maintains that the 'mental clarity', characteristic of human and only human intellect, is the basis on which the multiplicity of phenomena, and their difference from each other, ultimately lies. However, this intellect is not human in origin, but in principle shared by all beings as the potential inherent in the qi they all consist of. The purity of the human *qi* – in case it is not tainted by selfish desires – makes it possible for this intellect to recognize the differences in things. But this knowledge is only the prerequisite of true knowledge, which appears when 'pure knowledge' (something akin to Kant's innate moral law) is applied to one's activities in practice. 'There has never been anyone who knows, but does not act', Wang says, 'and if there is someone who seems to know, but does not act, this only means they do not yet know'. Thus, for example, if you are aware of the fact that smoking is dangerous for your health, but still continue to smoke, this does not qualify as 'knowing' in Wang's sense.

The moral implications of this thesis are obvious. Learning ethical doctrines is pointless unless they are reflected in one's every activity. Moreover, ethical knowledge cannot be installed in one's mind by an outside source – it is inherent in the principle which the mind instantiates in every particular person. 'The investigation of things', the first step in the establishment of cosmic order, is therefore nothing else than clarifying one's relationships with all significant others.

Later developments. Wang Yangming did not encourage the establishment of an undisputed orthodoxy, but, on the contrary, urged his disciples to debate and argue, so that each of them would hone their own internal understanding of his teaching to perfection. Critical opinions were, of course, also exchanged with the followers of Zhu Xi's tradition. As a result, the Neo-Confucian field turned from an orthodoxy-oriented tradition into a lively discipline. However, a large amount of the debate was held over the interpretation of single phrases and concepts and soon declined into casuistry. The best Qing dynasty Ru scholars were able to combine textual criticism with original contributions. For example, **Dai Zhen** (1724–1777), considered by some scholars to be the first exponent of philosophical hermeneutics in the world, has theorized at length on the hermeneutic circle, or the dependence of the meanings of separate utterances on the context in which they occur, while the context only emerges from such separate meanings. He considered the goal of his philosophy to be a method that would help people to distinguish shared, general senses of text from their individual interpretations, inevitably biased as these are. To that end, Dai also developed a naturalistic theory of mind, arguing that human nature is primarily an extension of how all life is, which is why desires and emotions form its core and should be considered the manifestations of the morally good natural order, not contingent impulses that crop up to distort it. Moreover, one's body and mind form an organic continuity. However, desires and emotions should be in harmony both within this continuity and also with the world at large. It is the role of the mind, through knowledge and the cultivation of personal talents, to ensure this happens. Selfishness, according to Dai Zhen, arises from single-mindedness and the neglect of one's personality as a whole.

During Qing rule, the social position of Ru scholars continued to be high, learned literati were held in favour by the authorities and were mostly able to enjoy privileged lives. This, in turn, caused other problems, such as corruption: officials overseeing the civil service examinations, for example, became prone to bribery and started to give high marks to examinees who had paid their way and then employed certain pre-agreed phrases in their essays. As long as the empire functioned reasonably well, the internal decay was not manifest on the outside, but when foreign powers started to engage China during the nineteenth century, things quickly got out of hand.

The demise of the empire. During the nineteenth century, the legitimacy of the Qing rule gradually started to erode. Traditional administrative structures were unable to cope with the economic and political pressures, and Western presence, from trade representatives to missionaries, forced the Chinese to question many of their previously self-evident beliefs. The stagnation of the social system was linked by many intellectuals to the conservatism of the Zhu Xi-style Neo-Confucian orthodoxy, which inspired them to look for alternatives in other parts of their heritage as well as in the newly imported Western ideas. A vigorous movement of textual studies ensued, which cast doubts on the authenticity of the received versions of Ru classics and their dominant interpretations, accompanied by a renewed interest in other Warring States thinkers, in particular Xunzi and Mozi. Another school proposed a pragmatic recasting of old Ru thought as a motor of social innovation and reform. Other thinkers turned towards Buddhism and attempted to construct new versions of it. Ideologues of all persuasions presented efforts to consolidate the entire Chinese tradition on the basis of what they personally preferred. Most of them were agreed only on one point – that this should not be the Zhu Xi line of Neo-Confucian thought.

Contacts with the outside world increased considerably and took on various forms. Many Chinese intellectuals of the period travelled extensively, either because they had to flee the wrath of the imperial power or were sent abroad to represent it on foreign missions. In both cases, they were exposed to different social systems and ways of life, as well as to the sets of ideas behind them. In China itself, Christian missionaries, representing different confessions, started to acquire a local following. Many of them, such as James Legge (1815–1897) and Richard Wilhelm (1873–1930) were open-minded intellectuals, who engaged actively with Chinese traditions of thought. They are still remembered primarily as pioneers of Sinology and authors of many philosophical translations, so that in the end their accomplishment consisted less in promoting Christianity in China than bringing Chinese thought to the Western world. However, the missionary message also had its echoes on Chinese thought, sometimes in quite unexpected ways.

After the military superiority of the West was clearly established during the Opium Wars, the days of the empire were numbered, as new concessions had to be made to foreign powers for fear of new invasions – the memory of the destruction of the Old Summer Palace in Beijing during the Second Opium War was still fresh in memory. Russia and Japan soon joined the Western powers in their efforts to carve up China. Besides, Japan, which had until recently been another Asian empire with a mostly Neo-Confucian state ideology, also presented itself as an example of successful modernization that many Chinese intellectuals looked up to. Nonetheless, especially because of the strong conservative influence of the empress dowager Cixi (1835–1908), the Qing court was unable to go along with the times, conceded too little and too late, and thus gradually lost its hold on power altogether.

The Taiping rebellion (1850–1871). A series of rebellions hastened the downfall of Qing rule. The most notable among them was the revolutionary-religious movement of the 'Heavenly Kingdom of Great Peace', usually known by the Chinese name of **Taiping**. This movement was started by Hong Xiuquan (1814–1864), the son of a poor farmer, a member of the Hakka ethnic group from Guangdong province. He showed talent at an early age and so his family enabled him to get an education, but after initial success he failed the civil service examinations several times. However, he had been attracted to the sermons of a Christian missionary and soon embarked on an independent study of the Bible. That particular translation used the ancient term Shang Di, the Supreme Celestial Ruler, for the Christian God, and Hong gradually developed an idiosyncratic interpretation of Christianity as identical with the ancient, pre-Zhou Chinese religion. As the designation *di* ('ruler') was later incorporated into the title of the emperor, Hong considered this to be sacrilege and the Ru tradition, which endorsed the imperial rule, to be a distortion of the ancient ways. In time Hong's views developed and he started to consider himself a son of the Christian God, a younger brother of Jesus, and when his movement gained in popularity, he also saw himself as the king sent by Heaven to rescue China from imminent destruction.

Destitute peasants, many of them also Hakka like Hong himself, were impressed by his message and flocked to his cause. At the highest point of the movement, the Taiping 'heavenly kingdom', ruled from Nanjing as its capital, included the better part of southern China and its population was about 30 million people. The Taiping kingdom was a marching army: each citizen had to take military training, and everybody could be mobilized for armed struggle. The imperial armies indeed were soon dispatched against the Taiping and eventually won a bloody victory, but only after more than 10 years of Taiping rule. The Taipings had counted on Western support – after all, Hong was the brother of Christ himself – but did not receive any. On the contrary, Westerners actually helped the Qing army in this battle. The internal tensions and increasing corruption among the Taiping court was another reason why the morale of the movement decreased.

Both the rise and the failure of the Taiping movement were characteristic of the times. It also demonstrated that only a strongly modified, domesticated Christianity stood any chance of success in China, an effort largely undermined by the strict commitment to orthodoxy of all Western churches.

Kang Youwei (1858–1927). The sad state of the empire was recognized also by some of those at its helm, but the only effort to reform the country from top down was aborted almost as soon as it started and is therefore known as the 'Hundred

Days of Reform'. The architect of this move was an idiosyncratic scholar and utopian social critic called **Kang Youwei**, one of the most fascinating intellectuals of late Qing times. After his initial failure in the civil service examinations, Kang embarked on an intellectual quest, reading Western philosophy along with Buddhist texts. He also spent long periods of time in meditation and finally had an experience he considered to be Buddhist enlightenment. He nevertheless retained his status as a scholar in the Ru tradition, which, he decided, was in need of reforming. Just as the Neo-Confucians had included Buddhist and Dao ideas in their thought systems, Kang ventured a synthesis that would engage Western thought as well. In his early work, he tried to build a philosophical system that would follow the models of Descartes and Spinoza by deriving his conclusions from carefully formulated axioms, rejecting all other convictions, and aiming at the discovery of general laws that regulate social structures universally. He was also a prolific, albeit controversial textual scholar, promoting the image of Kongzi as a social reformer who had consciously invented historical precedents, legendary histories about sage kings, as fictional models to promote his own vision.

In 1898, a young emperor, eager to modernize the country, tasked him with reforming the Qing administration. China had recently suffered a humiliating defeat in the Sino-Japanese war of 1894–1895, in spite of having modernized its weaponry, but not touching the structures of the army. A military reform was therefore called for, as well as an educational one which foresaw the establishment of a university in Beijing for disseminating Western science, and reforming the curricula of all schools by introducing mathematics and science. Civil service examinations were to be abolished, trade, and agricultural schools created in the provinces. Bureaucracy was to be rationalized, sinecures abolished. The economy would function naturally, according to capitalist principles.

It is difficult to estimate whether China would have had a different fate if all of this had happened. But it did not, as the reform movement was stopped by a betrayal. In order to curtail the influence of the empress dowager Cixi, the reformers had enlisted the support of a general, who was to take control of her palace and remove her from power. That general was none other than Yuan Shikai, who later became the first president of the Republic of China and then tried to restore the empire with himself on the throne. In 1898, however, he decided to play it safe with the Qing, betrayed the reformers, and Kang Youwei had to flee for his life.

During the next 15 years, Kang travelled widely, visiting India, Europe, and North America (US, Canada, Mexico). His political vision evolved during that time, resulting in a curious mix of radical utopianism and conservative monarchism. On the one hand, he started to support the restoration of monarchy, when he returned to China after the declaration of the republic and even participated in a coup, on the other hand, however, he articulated a radical utopia for the entire world. This work, *The Book of Great Unity* (*Datong shu*), was not published during his lifetime, and yet he is mostly known to posterity because of its ideas.

'Great Unity', the title of Kang's magnum opus has been taken from *The Book of Rites*, where it refers to an ancient golden age. Kang uses it to designate a distant future, which, according to his own estimates, would not arrive sooner than after 200–300 years, and some aspects of his ideal society would require even more to appear. At the time all current social institutions would have been abolished except for a democratically elected governing apparatus. Nations and races would have disappeared, families extinct. People would indulge in a hedonistic lifestyle with no particular obligations. Marriages would have been replaced by temporary contracts, and children would be raised in public nurseries. Even cemeteries and care for ancestors would be there no more – dead people would be cremated and their ashes used as fertilizer. At the same time there would be censorship to ensure the undisturbed continuation of the social order. An educational system would also contribute to the same goals, where everybody would receive a humanistic and legal education, specializing in a profession only at the university level.

Kang had possibly been disappointed in the workings of capitalism during his travels. There is no place for private property in the Great Unity, everybody is equal and therefore there are no litigations, no criminals, and no corruption. Kang is less specific about how this ideal is to be reached, except for doing away with what is wrong at present. The key here seems to be the Neo-Confucian idea that the moral principle operates in everyone's mind, so when external constraints and distinctions are removed, it is only a matter of time until the onto-cosmological morality has taken over.

The Chinese enlightenment and Liang Qichao. The first wave of Western ideas that Chinese intellectuals learned about were those promoted by Christian missionaries. But when the need for access to Western science was recognized by the administration, students were taught English at vocational schools and some of them were sent overseas to study in England and the United States. A number of these students put their command of English as well as Chinese classics to good use in translating books related to political and social theory and Western philosophy into Chinese. These appealed to a younger generation of Chinese intellectuals and a movement now called 'Chinese enlightenment' started. It was influential in toppling the Qing, and continued as a cultural trend well into republican times.

An exemplary figure to represent the first generation of Chinese enlightenment thinkers is **Liang Qichao** (1873–1929), one of the most ardent spokesmen for social change at the time and one of the most popular public intellectuals. Liang was considered a prodigy in his childhood and did well in his study of Chinese classics, but, as a student of Kang Youwei, soon turned to Western thought in his search for an intellectual foundation for an ideology of reforms. After the short-lived reform effort of 1898, Liang had to escape to Japan, and also visited the United States, Canada, and Australia during his years of exile. He returned to China when the Qing dynasty fell and entered politics, holding even some ministerial positions before retreating to the safety of academia.

Liang's political thought formed during a period when survival as a nation was an existential question for China and no one could predict what would happen with an incompetent government and technologically superior Western powers striving to assert themselves on Chinese soil. It had gradually dawned on Chinese intellectuals that the traditional vision of the world as 'everything under Heavens' with China in the centre was deeply erroneous. Liang is therefore both extremely critical of the Chinese tradition and passionately committed to save China as a nation. This, he believed, could be achieved in changing the character of the Chinese people, which had been moulded over centuries by the political technologies of subjugation, seduction, control, and surveillance. As a result, the Chinese had become meek, docile, and indifferent to the incompetence and corruption of officials on all levels. Liang prescribed a new national character that the Chinese had to acquire in order to become a viable nation-state: they needed to cherish their liberty and be aware of their rights, be independent in judgement, be ready to take their fate into their own hands, and, above all, be conscious of the nation as a group, whose interests should stand above the private ambitions of any individual.

It is certainly correct to say that Liang was a nationalist, because the fate of China as a nation was the most important topic of his thought, but his nationalism had nothing to do with ethnic categories, as he often underlined the equality of all ethnic groups, nor with a feeling of cultural superiority. Liang's nationalism was therefore a defensive position, and indeed he retreated from it towards the end of his life, when the republic had been proclaimed and the question of Chinese survival was no longer imminent. After a visit to Europe in 1918, he became aware of the dangers of nationalism and its potential to provoke destructive wars. His late political thought is therefore more universalistic, in particular, he suggests that a vision of peaceful coexistence of a multitude of nations could be the Chinese contribution to world civilization.

The Boxer rebellion (1899–1901). While the intellectuals pondered what kind of balance of the Chinese tradition and the newly imported Western ideas would save their country from its ongoing crisis, the population at large developed much simpler and straightforward reactions to the changes that disrupted their regular way of life. A violent effort to put things back where they ought to be was undertaken by the cult movement of **Yihetuan**, usually translated 'The Righteous Fist' and often called 'the Boxers' movement', following a contemporary missionary. The Boxers were mainly poor rural youths, who trained in a network of martial arts clubs and opposed all signs of Western involvement in Chinese life, from railways, whose straight lines ignored the principles of *feng shui*, to electricity and telegraph. The Boxers considered themselves the recipients of Heaven's message to do away with all this, and also that Heaven had sent them invincible spirits to assist in that purpose, in a literal sense. Their martial arts training developed rituals of spirit possession, in the 'internal alchemy' tradition of the Dao creed, the purpose of which was to make the possessed individual invulnerable to Western weapons. Transformed into spiritual warriors, the Boxers would return China to its former glory and wipe out Western abominations. Christianity and missionaries were among their first targets. It is estimated that tens of thousands of Chinese Christians were killed during the rebellion, along with hundreds of foreign missionaries and their families.

This ideology spread by posters and started to dominate a wide network of sports clubs-cum-secret societies primarily in northern China. Initially, the Qing government was wary of them, as secret societies such as the White Lotus had often been sources of trouble for the authorities in the past, but in 1900 empress dowager Cixi changed her views on the Boxers and issued imperial decrees in support of their cause. Emboldened, the Boxers converged on Beijing and besieged the foreign legation area for almost two months. Cixi ordered the army to support them, and troops indeed appeared, but the general in command later claimed it was only to ensure the foreigners' security. In order to save their citizens, the foreign governments whose representations were in danger, assembled their own troops, entered Beijing and dispelled the Boxers, who proved to be not invulnerable to Western bullets after all. A heavy indemnity was imposed on China along with the requirement that the supporters of the Boxers in the administration would be chastised. Cixi herself, however, was able to keep her dominant position.

The humiliating defeat induced the Qing to now finally try to introduce some of the reforms Kang Youwei had proposed, and it also adopted a more conciliatory attitude to Western presence in order to avoid a full-scale colonization. But even though violence ceased for some time, the situation remained unsatisfactory both to intellectuals, who would have preferred a more radical overhaul, and to the people, who were now losing trust also in the monarchy as the guardian of their cultural tradition.

From the Fall of the Empire to the Present

Background. The Qing dynasty finally fell as a result of a popular revolution that engulfed much of China in 1911, and the last emperor, the six-year old Puyi, abdicated in February 1912. A political compromise between the republican ideologue Sun Yat-sen and the former Qing military leader Yuan Shikai led to the transfer of power to a newly constituted republic, with Sun conceding the presidency to Yuan. However, the ambitions of Yuan were not satisfied and after a few years he attempted to restore the monarchy, with himself as the emperor. He failed, but the republic still did not manage to get on a stable footing. For more than 10 years, parts of China were controlled by competing strongmen and no political vision managed to unite the whole country – a situation seen many times in history after the fall of a powerful dynasty such as the Han or the Tang. This so-called Warlord Era was brought to an end by Chiang Kai-Shek (Jiang Jieshi), an ally of Sun and the new leader of the Guomindang (The Party of the Nation), who gained control of the capital and brought most of his opponents to heel. The only remaining force to contend with was the Communist Party of China, led by Mao Zedong. These forces should not be regarded as political parties in the usual sense of the word, but rather as half-ideological and half-military formations, strictly organized mass movements, with command lines and information distribution channels, optimized for armed struggle.

During the Japanese invasion of 1937–1945, Chiang and Mao buried their differences for a while and formed a more or less united front of resistance. After the war, the conflict was rekindled and the initial success of the numerically superior Guomindang soon turned into a defeat. Chiang failed to attract popular support and had to retreat from all power centres. Finally, he had to flee to the island of Taiwan, which he initially considered to be a temporary base for a counterattack. On the mainland, Mao declared his victory and proclaimed the establishment of the People's Republic of China (PRC) in 1949, as opposed to the Republic of China (ROC), which Chiang claimed to represent. Both Chiang and Mao saw themselves as the legitimate authority over all of China. Chiang's claims were recognized by the United States, as the outbreak of the Korean War in 1950 signalled the expansionist ambitions of the communist government. The Republic of China thus enjoyed Western support and even kept its seat as a member of the United Nations until 1971, when Henry Kissinger orchestrated a reconciliation between the PRC and the United States. Most Western countries shifted their recognition from the ROC to the PRC during that time.

Both Mao and Chiang ruled their territories with an iron hand, although the ROC maintained a modicum of democracy to ensure Western protection. On the mainland, a communist-type state industrial complex was developed with Soviet support, Taiwan developed quickly into a more prosperous free-market economy. Delusional decisions and incompetent planning hampered Mao's campaigns to modernize China, such as the 'Great Leap Forward' (1958–1960), which was meant to change the predominantly agrarian country into an industrial society, but resulted in nothing but famine and environmental damage and was abandoned after just three years. However, the questioning of Mao's leadership only increased his paranoia and led to the alienation of even his close associates.

Finally, in 1966, Mao initiated a mass movement called the 'cultural revolution', a wholesale persecution of 'bourgeois elements' who were to blame for his failures, in other words, everybody at least minimally competent in management and economy. Bands of Red Guard cadres (*hongweibing*), mostly teenagers, were to seek out and neutralize everyone even remotely suspicious. Estimates vary about the number of people killed in the process, but it was at least 500 000 and may exceed 2 000 000. At the same time, Mao's personality cult reached previously unseen heights. Officially, the cultural revolution was declared to be over in 1969, but the process continued, albeit in a less intense form, until Mao's death in 1976.

The power struggle after Mao ended with Deng Xiaoping assuming the leadership, even though he never let him be appointed as the official ruler of the country. An erstwhile ally of Mao, purged during the cultural revolution and then again just before Mao's death, Deng had been responsible for devising economic policies, but had never before been able to realize his own vision. Through a series of quick reforms, Deng revitalized the Chinese economy and set it on the course of growth that has resulted in China's revival. He was, however, no democrat, and is responsible for the crackdown on students' protests on Tiananmen Square in 1989.

A search for a manageable balancing point between demands for more civic freedom (by many educated urban people) and the discomfort with too much of it (in the less developed rural areas) has characterized China ever since. Some rulers have leaned towards one direction, others towards the other, most of them tolerating no criticism of official policies and pushing for ethnic and cultural homogeneity, which has resulted in the suppression of minority cultures. A booming market economy has thus proved to be compatible with a disregard for human rights, severe restrictions on information traffic, and effective mechanisms of social control. After a long absence, China is also asserting itself as a regional power and world player, with ambitious and self-serving projects of development aid. All in all, China has resumed, after another interregnum, its historical pattern of government, with a single ruler at the helm, a body of councillors around him, and an apparatus of (at least, in principle) meritocratically promoted civil servants to enforce his will all over the country. The main difference is that the Ru have been replaced by a more strictly organized party, which remains communist mostly in name.

However, the road from the end of the empire to the present has been bumpy and full of historical contingencies. Imported ideas and earlier traditions of Chinese thought have sometimes opposed each other, sometimes searched for avenues of synthesis, and often achieved it in unexpected ways. None of the old schools has remained the same as the result, but neither has any of the Western imports survived the confrontation with Chinese ideas in its original form.

May Fourth movement. The early years of the republic were characterized by a strong feeling of opposition against everything traditional, especially among the younger generation, a movement that has retrospectively been named after students' protests on 4 May 1919 against the Treaty of Versailles and the government's concessions of territory to Japan. The term, however, is often applied to the whole period comprising roughly the years 1915–1921, and is also known as the 'new culture movement', during which the mentality of complete cultural innovation reigned supreme among urban intellectuals.

Many of the protesting students were followers of a new generation of academics and writers, who were well versed in the Chinese tradition, but thought it was no longer adequate as the value basis of their time. These included, for example, Lu Xun (1881–1936), the founder of contemporary Chinese literature, and, in particular, **Hu Shi** (1891–1962), a philosopher, diplomat, and educator, and at the time a professor of Beijing University. Hu had been inspired by Liang Qichao to question his classical education, and later became the first historian of Chinese thought who did not view it from the Ru point of view and tried to link the thinkers and their ideas to their historical contexts. While he was critical of the tradition – or primarily the uncritical attitude with which it had traditionally been received – Hu also promoted a re-evaluation of ancient thought and its application in the current circumstances. Thus, for example, he read the *Daodejing* to support a scientific approach to nature and treated the Lao-Zhuang view of the Way as something similar to the principle of natural selection.

Hu had studied with John Dewey in the United States, and was also strongly influenced by the ideas of Darwinism. His take on American pragmatism, which he dubbed 'experimentalism', consisted in denying the absolute character of any context-divorced truth, and insisting that intellectual endeavour inevitably reflects the environment in which it has matured. In 1919–1921, at the high tide of the May Fourth movement, Hu also organized a visit for Dewey to China, where he spent almost a year as a visiting professor in Beijing and thereafter toured other cities, which strengthened both the influence of pragmatism and the intellectual status of Hu, its foremost local representative.

Hu was also one of the first Chinese intellectuals to call for the abandonment of classical Chinese as the vehicle of written self-expression. A new literature should speak of the current events and use the language of the people, he claimed, and this indeed became the position of the entire May Fourth movement.

Other intellectual leaders of the movement included some prominent academics as well as social reformers, who later joined the communist camp. United more by what they did not like than by a coherent programme of cultural reform, the May Fourth leaders nonetheless contributed a great deal to the spread of liberal and democratic ideals, on the one hand, as well as the nationalist sentiment of an emergent new China, on the other hand.

Social emancipation and the beginnings of Chinese feminism. While the rest of China was in turmoil, certain areas enjoyed relative stability and prosperity during the Guomindang rule, especially the coastal city of Shanghai, which had been a centre of Western presence already during the last decades of the Qing dynasty. Its population, although looked down on and discriminated against by Westerners, had also familiarized itself with foreign ways of life and now embraced their modernized culture and relative freedom with eagerness. This increased the demand on popular culture, from journals and literature to light music, theatre, and film. Cultural industries experienced a boom, especially in demand were works that represented 'new youth', liberal-minded, and independent people with Western values.

Especially notable was the effect on the situation of women. Already Kang Youwei and Liang Qichao had written about the need of women's liberation during the last decades of the Qing dynasty, and Chinese feminism had found itself an early voice in the work of **He-yin Zhen** (1884?–1920?), who emigrated to Tokyo with her scholarly husband in 1904. Both of them contributed to anarchist press. He-yin Zhen articulated her views in several manifesto-like articles, claiming that the liberation of society is impossible without the establishment of a true equality also for women, and that would imply the abolition of the standard of monogamous marriage. She was also rather critical of liberal male advocates of female liberation. Their position, she argued, was motivated by entirely selfish reasons – first, they wanted to imitate the West, where women enjoyed a better position than in China, second, in times of hardship 'liberated' women could be expected to contribute more efficiently to the family economy, and, finally, 'liberated' women would be more efficient in managing households and raising new citizens. In her view, all of this had nothing to do with real liberation, which would pose no demands and limits to how the women were to conduct themselves. As opposed to such male-defined 'liberation', anarchistic feminists claimed their right to free love and the abandonment of traditional gender roles – in both theory and practice – a process which liberal male feminists started to view with increasing unease.

The dispute between anarchistic and liberal male feminism was never resolved, especially as the Guomindang started to espouse traditional family values and suppress even those freedoms women had won for themselves during the early years of the republic. The communists were not really interested in female agency and, although they acknowledged them as equal 'comrades', in practice this meant the freedom to support the cause on par with men.

Nationalism and the state ideology. Most of the Chinese political thinkers of the twentieth century were men of action rather than systematic theorists, even if some of them are now remembered as the latter. Although **Sun Yat-sen** or Yixian

(1866–1925, also known by his sobriquet Zhongshan) is claimed to be the founding father of the modern Chinese state both on the mainland and in Taiwan, he had very little to do with the actual overturning of the monarchy. Still, movements and societies that he had organized certainly played a pivotal role. He was not a capable administrator and his failures in this field may even have contributed somewhat to the decline of the new regime into a failed state where warlords held control and battled each other. Raised in Hawaii, educated in Hong Kong, living most of his life abroad according to a Western lifestyle, and being a Christian on top of all that, Sun was certainly not the figure to impersonate the new Chinese nation. However, his merits are undeniable in putting the new China on the world map as well as in the development of revolutionary organizations that finally evolved into Guomindang, or the Party of the Nation.

Sun was also not a systematic political thinker, although the Three Principles of the People, or the fundamental ideas according to which the new China should develop, have been formulated by him. The word translated as 'principle' in this phrase actually consists of the characters normally rendered as '-ism', so 'ideologies' would perhaps be a better equivalent. The three principles are nationalism, democracy, and welfare. Sun never wrote about them explicitly, but preferred to expound them in lectures, and therefore was able to change their actual meaning according to current political need. Before the overthrow of the Qing, nationalism primarily meant an anti-Manchu sentiment, but after the establishment of the republic, Sun adopted a more inclusive and political idea of the nation, in the style that had been advocated by Liang Qichao. Democracy meant everything from a Western-style political system to democratic centralism that put the interests of the state first, and welfare, or 'people's livelihood' signified mainly governmental concern for the living standard of the people, which could be attained in theory by both liberalized capitalist economic practices and the state planning proposed by communists.

Sun's efforts to recruit support for China and his search for allies within it indeed motivated him to promote both the nationalist and traditionalist sentiments and to form a pact with communists, even inviting Soviet advisors to help him restructure the Guomindang into a more efficient and centrally controlled structure. **Chiang Kai-Shek** (Jiang Jieshi, 1887–1975), his heir, rejected the communist connection and interpreted Sun's three principles as an ideology compatible with traditional Ru ethics. Chiang's own personal concessions to Westernization were mainly formal and served other purposes. His wife was Christian, so he also converted, as, given the inclination of the US government to support Christian politicians overseas, this was also convenient to ensure his regime of US protection. In practice, however, Chiang was a conservative traditionalist and nationalist, and the remedy he always preferred for solving social problems was more ideological control to ensure proper morality. This may have cost him the rule of China, as his 'new life' movement, launched in the areas of rural China where communist sympathies ruled large, only alienated him further from the people, who expected real relief in their miserable economic situation. In Taiwan Chiang strictly persisted in his belief that a moral renewal is the only thing needed for the arrival of prosperity. He was also convinced that the interests of the state should prevail over all individual interests, a principle he shared with his sworn enemies, the communists.

Chinese communism. Various currents of radical political thought, including anarchism, Marxism, and its Leninist variety, were imported into China during the May Fourth movement and found eager recipients in university professors and their idealistic students. Indeed, many of the active participants of the student demonstrations were either already professed Marxists or joined the communist movement at a later date. The initial reception of Marxism was thus constructing it as an alternative to the Chinese tradition and an allegedly scientific discourse able to explain the shortcomings of the current political situation. The victory of the Bolsheviks in the Russian civil war and their subsequent takeover of the international communist movement pushed the orientation of Chinese communism in the direction of Leninism and Stalinism, and other currents of left-wing thought quickly died out. Both Marx and Lenin had mentioned an 'Asiatic mode of production' in their writings, and this helped the Chinese Marxists to explain away the apparent incompatibility of much in the communist ideology with the actual situation they were facing.

However, the complexities of dialectical and historical materialism did not offer much by which to mobilize the broader masses of the often-illiterate population to the communist cause. When the communist movement was consolidated into a powerful political and military force under capable organizers such as Mao Zedong, it also developed a simple and more accessible ideology, in which the ideas of Marx, Lenin, and Stalin had been integrated with elements inherited from traditional Chinese thought. As a result, communism gradually changed from the radical views of a small intellectual group into an ideology for the broad masses. Outwardly, however, it rigorously maintained the form of Stalinist orthodoxy and denied such traditional components, which ensured Chinese communists the support of the Soviet Union and the international communist movement.

Mao Zedong (1893–1976). Born in a wealthy peasant family in the Hunan province and raised in Buddhist faith, Mao grew up as a free-thinking young man interested in history and political theory, in which he was largely self-taught. In his twenties, he was an individualist, whose views were shaped by mainly Western thought, including Nietzsche, Rousseau, and social Darwinism, and though he later criticized his attitudes of those times, a strong inclination towards philosophical voluntarism, or the idea that the revolutionary will of the people can triumph over actual reality, continued to characterize him throughout his life. Aspiring to become a teacher, he enrolled in a pedagogical school, where one of the professors recommended a radical communist newspaper to him. Mao became an enthusiastic reader and contributor, and in 1918 moved to Beijing in search of new challenges. He worked at the library and informally attended the lectures of his intellectual heroes, some of whom had now openly endorsed Marxism and promoted the Russian revolution as a model for China.

In the aftermath of the May Fourth movement, Mao drifted increasingly towards the communist left. He briefly edited a radical journal in his home province, which was soon prohibited by the authorities, but had already attracted the attention of leading intellectuals in the capital, including Hu Shi. After the foundation of the Communist Party, which was initially only a study group of leftist literature, Mao became active in the movement and helped to transform it into an institution for political activism.

After an initial anti-imperialist alliance with the Guomindang was broken when Chiang assumed the leadership of the Party of the Nation, warlords and nationalists launched a vicious attack against communists, and thousands of them were killed. As a reaction, peasant militias were formed and then united into a Red Army. Mao, who had proved himself as a capable organizer, was appointed as its commander. In 1927 he faced his first battles, but lost because of the defection of a part of the forces under his command. As a result, he was expelled from the leadership of the party, so he set himself up as a minor independent warlord of a mountain territory governed in the spirit of the communist ideology. Battles with the Guomindang and clashes with the party leadership went on for quite a few years, during which communist factions loyal to Moscow and groups of independent communists also competed with each other for the leading role in China's revolution. In 1930, Mao established the Soviet Republic of China in the area under his control. Though the Guomindang continued to attack it and its administration was plagued by internal conflicts between competing factions as well as the central leadership of the party, this semi-state held up until 1934, when the technologically and numerically superior forces of Chiang were finally ready to crash it.

The Long March and Mao's rise to leadership. The events that followed have historically contributed to the legend of Mao as the supreme leader. In 1934, he led about 90 000 people – the soldiers of his army as well as his administration and other people fearful of nationalist reprisals – out of the circle of siege and took them on a year-long exodus of about 6000 km known as the Long March. Many of those who started out died in battles with the Guomindang and of hardship on the way or dispersed. But the core of Mao's loyalists reached north-western China, where they had a position from which to regroup their forces and to recover.

From that point onward, nobody questioned the status of Mao as the leader of Chinese communists. During the next several years, he spent much of his time studying, as he realized that for his authority to hold, he also needs a better command of communist theory than he actually had. Most of his philosophical endeavours come from this Yan'an period, named after the provincial city where his headquarters were.

The undisputed position of leadership also enabled him to take the surprising decision to offer an anti-Japanese alliance pact to Chiang and the Guomindang in 1937 – a move recommended by Stalin, which indeed greatly contributed to the successful defeat of the Japanese invasion. After the war, hostilities between Mao and Chiang resumed with Chiang's defeat and retreat to Taiwan as a result.

As the leader of the People's Republic of China, proclaimed on 1 October 1949, Mao was both unchallenged and unpredictable. He led the country in short impulsive campaigns and could also reverse his course momentarily, if he was unsatisfied with the results. Thus, in 1956, he announced the so-called 'hundred flowers' approach, meaning that all kinds of thought was to be tolerated, including criticism of the communist regime, but when such criticism actually started to appear, he cracked down on it without mercy, as if such a purge of dissenters would have been his initial goal. Some campaigns, such as the eradication of the widespread opium habit among the people and the promotion of literacy and the simplification of the Chinese script, were quite successful, others had devastating results. Hundreds of thousands of peasants were given land, millions killed as counter-revolutionary saboteurs or bourgeois sympathizers, tens of millions persecuted. This did not concern only the simple people. When Mao's policies caused dissatisfaction, his opponents were blamed and purged, and those sometimes included even his close allies from the days of the Long March. This happened after the 'great leap forward' and during the 'cultural revolution', which only increased mismanagement and the intensity of ideological control. In the meantime, Mao himself assumed the features of an almost religious figure, his words acquired scriptural authority and, during the 'cultural revolution', Red Guards regularly carried little red books of Mao's most important quotations with them, so that they could recite something important-sounding at any occasion.

Ideas: a Sinicized Marxism. Mao's intellectual endeavours were eclectic and most of the time completely subjugated to his practical goals. There was nothing wrong with his classical education – in fact, his poetic achievement in traditional genres is well above average – nor was it without precedent for someone with scholarly credentials to voice concerns over the plight of the common people. If anything, the communist ideals of Mao ranked a distant second to the much more radical vision of 'great unity', expressed by Kang Youwei only a few decades before. However, as a representative of the May

Fourth generation, Mao's primary impulse was to reject, at least in name, all of his classical heritage, so what he retained from it were just things that appeared to be commonsensical. Nonetheless the classical lens has shaped his understanding of imported ideas to a significant extent, and quite a few elements of the theory were indeed similar to tenets of the classical Chinese thought system.

Thus, materialist dialectics was easily understandable to someone who had been accustomed to view the world as a totality of primordial stuff that evolved according to patterns of binary forces. The unity of opposites held a much more prominent place in Mao's view than, for example, in the theory of Stalin. The internal logic of history replaced the Way as the cosmic regulatory principle of the human world, and the creative potential of consciousness – a key element in Mao's thought – took the place of Wang Yangming's active mind. As quite a proportion of such traditional philosophical and cosmological views were understood by the Chinese as common sense, their integration with an ideology that proclaimed its innovative and scientific character may have strongly contributed to its appeal. It also enabled to do on the theoretical level what Mao repeatedly stressed in his own theoretical statements: Marxism in practice has to be particular and localized, never abstract, but always adjusted to context. This is not something Western or Russian Marxists would necessarily have agreed with, and this view eventually contributed to the split between Mao and the post-Stalinist Soviet Union. Mao's stress of the Chinese character of his thought indeed became more prominent after that, and he even started to quote foundational passages from Engels as incorrect.

Of course, the Chinese elements of Mao's thought were still articulated with Marxist terminology and integrated with the central positions of Marx and Lenin: economic determinism of consciousness, class struggle as the dynamic that moves history forward, and revolutionary dictatorship as the means to social emancipation. However, Mao also made a crucial innovative change without which the theory could not have been adopted in China. Instead of the class-conscious revolutionary proletariat, which was envisaged to be the leading revolutionary class in traditional Marxism, Mao allocated this role to peasants, who were considered reactionary by his theoretical predecessors. Indeed, in China there was almost no working class to begin with, so constructing a revolutionary force out of the peasantry was simply a matter of necessity. In fact, Mao argued that the poverty and backwardness of peasants were not a weakness, but a strength, as they were ready to absorb the new ideology, while the workers of more advanced capitalist societies were prone to seduction and the loss of their revolutionary potential as a result.

Mao's views on knowledge and action. The other main contribution of Mao to Marxist philosophy is his theory of consciousness and practice. It remains a matter of debate whether Mao was an orthodox materialist in his epistemology or reintroduced an idealist element to his thought through the back door by admitting that consciousness, or human will, might be able to reshape reality. Mao's revolutionary practice clearly seemed to follow this latter view, when he decided to change China into an industrial nation just over the span of five years, with the catastrophic 'Great Leap Forward'. Also, in his theory, Mao endows the human mind with a creative potential that can, however, only be realized in material and social practice, and in the best case leads to knowledge, but not necessarily along the most direct route.

The classical Marxist view of consciousness is captured in the so-called 'reflection theory', which was developed by Engels and Lenin from the premises articulated by John Locke, namely that the ideas of the external world in our consciousness amount to 'reflections' of how things objectively are. This enabled Marxist theory to envisage consciousness as a high-level pattern of organization of matter in the human brain, capable of producing and processing these reflections. Such a position resembled the received Chinese view of human intelligence as the purest way on how the primordial stuff of *qi* could condensate. The Neo-Confucians had started their deliberations on knowledge and action from this position, and so did Mao. Knowledge, for him, was not the result of something akin to a sudden realization, or a spontaneous product of how consciousness works, but the gradually emergent state of mind of someone actively engaged with the world. Neither the mind nor reality could remain the same after cognition/practice had taken place. In other words, knowledge and action were inseparable in principle. It is in this sense that Mao has identified the processes of production, class struggle, and scientific experiments as types of social practice that can produce objective knowledge.

After the People's Republic of China was established in 1949, communism became the ideology of the state, and by that time the educational system had made sure its connections with traditional Chinese thought were more or less forgotten. Chinese history was completely rewritten along the lines of class struggle, and the this was also actively practised in the persecution of dissidents. During the cultural revolution, the population was simply divided into 'people', who were loyal to the communist cause, and 'enemies', who were not, and it was often a group of hysterical teenagers who had the authority to decide who belonged to which category.

Post-Maoism. Mao's personality cult was enforced by a strictly controlled educational system and a powerful repressive apparatus, and grew to grotesque dimensions until his death in 1976. It had also precluded the system from preparing anyone to the role of the new leader, as such a person would have been perceived as a threat to the great leader during Mao's lifetime. The 'Gang of Four', a group including Mao's last wife, made a desperate effort to keep things the way they were, but failed quickly. Power fell into the much more capable hands of **Deng Xiaoping** (1904–1997), who ruled through proxies and steered the country through a series of liberalizing reforms towards a market economy and prepared the way for the Chinese boom that has led China into its present state. Deng maintained a careful balance between old-school conservatives, of whom there were quite many in the upper echelons of the party, and social reformers, who would have gladly supplemented economic freedoms with civic and democratic ones.

In this situation, mainland Chinese philosophy professionals were faced with the task of explaining how Deng's reforms are a continuation of the communist ideology and not its rejection. Some unsuccessfully called for the restoration of orthodoxy, others turned towards the traditional values and engaged them in support of Deng's reforms. Yet others left the constraints of the Marxist paradigm far behind in their speculations, even though they might have paid it lip service. The party line has been balancing between all these, sometimes tending towards more, sometimes less liberal views. Although China's current leader, **Xi Jingping** (b.1953), who also styles himself as a theorist for the new century, programmatically speaks about 'carrying on the enduring spirit of Mao Zedong thought', he refers nearly as often to the *Analects* and Mengzi as to Mao in his speeches. It seems therefore that traditional thought has once again been restored to the status of a source of inspiration for the ruling ideologues. The ideas of past thinkers are engaged selectively, however, and only to legitimize the statist politics, which continue to be based on social control rather than those democratic elements that are also inherent in the tradition.

Modernity and religion. The People's Republic of China as a state committed itself not only to secularism, but also to atheism, and was strongly opposed to religion as outdated superstitions, a leftover from the past, as well as deeply suspicious of all kinds of religious professionals. The landholdings of temples were nationalized, so they lost their source of income and could rely only on donations. Nonetheless, established religions were not attacked immediately, but were granted a certain degree of protection that also involved state control. This, however, did not concern the practices of popular religion, as they did not form a controllable institution. The situation changed considerably during the 'cultural revolution', when religion was declared to be one of the 'four olds' to be eradicated from Chinese society: temples were being actively destroyed or closed and manifestations of religious behaviour forbidden or strongly discouraged. The situation improved only in 1978, when religious freedom was restored, many temples were rebuilt and people gradually returned to practising in the open what they were forced to do in secret during the years of ideological repressions. Presently, the official policy of the People's Republic of China declares freedom of religion to be respected so that believers and non-believers can live together in a harmonious society. As said, certain central principles of the Chinese traditional worldview have also been co-opted into the current form of Chinese state ideology.

In practice, things are much more complicated. The freedom granted to religion does not involve popular religious movements, for example. This is not a specifically modern or communist problem: the Chinese state has traditionally been suspicious of charismatic leaders and their spiritual movements, as these have often attracted dissenters and repeatedly become the carriers of violent revolts in history. While traditionally such movements have been local, however, contemporary movements of the sort are able to spread more quickly and when they are repressed, this occurs on a larger scale.

A case in point is a new religion called **Falun Dafa** ('The great teaching of the Dharma wheel') or Falun Gong ('Dharma wheel practice'). It originated in the 1990s, during the nationwide spread of a diverse spiritual and health movement called *qigong*, '*qi*-energy practice', which combines the principles of Chinese medicine with Dao discourses of 'internal alchemy' and is practised as a set of physical and psychotechnical exercises. After the cultural revolution, which had viewed all traditional Chinese practices with a strong suspicion, *qigong*, in a de-mystified form, was actively promoted as a health routine and acquired hundreds of millions of practitioners throughout China. Falun Dafa capitalized on this success by reintegrating *qigong* exercises with a set of spiritual beliefs and teachings. Initially, it was tolerated by the authorities, but as the movement grew in size, reaching an estimated 70 million practitioners, and became increasingly uncontrollable, the government started to view it as a danger to society. After a massive demonstration of Falun Dafa practitioners in 1999 requiring official recognition for their movement, it was prohibited, declared a threat, its internet sites were blocked and vocal supporters arrested, reportedly tortured and abused. Currently, Falun Dafa remains prohibited in China, but its representatives abroad claim that it continues to be widely practised in secret.

Islam. Among the established religions that appeared to enjoy the protection of the Chinese state, Islam has also recently become a target of repressions, especially in the north-western Xinjiang area. The sizeable Muslim population of China is rather diverse and can be divided into two large groups. The Hui are ethnically and linguistically Chinese, but descendants of Muslim ancestors, who arrived in China centuries ago, intermarried with locals, but kept their faith, and their descendants were not accepted as fully authentic Chinese for that reason. They differ culturally from mainstream Chinese, for example, by keeping the Muslim ban of eating pork, as well as clothing styles. Conflicts between the Hui and mainstream Chinese occasionally arise, especially when other disputes take on a religious character, but they have not been targeted by the government as a group.

The situation is different for Turkic-speaking north-western Chinese Muslims, however, who make up about half of the country's Muslim population. Most of them are Uyghurs, who have a proud political and cultural history – the Uyghur khans have been both allied to and in conflict with Chinese rulers in the past, with fortunes swaying both ways. The Uyghur capital city of Kashgar was, in the Middle Ages, one of the most important centres of Turkic Islamic culture, a flourishing hub of commerce and learning, and some of the first and finest examples of Turkic classical literature have been composed in the Uyghur language.

The Xinjiang ('New Frontier') region was annexed by China relatively late in its history, as the result of a long process of both political and military operations by the Qing emperors. After the declaration of the republic, its fate was still not clear and wars involving local armies, Chinese warlords, and Soviet invaders continued there throughout the 1930s, with parts of the region declaring allegiance to Moscow. Chinese control was restored only in the 1950s. Due to the relative poverty of the region and its distance from the political centres, it was not very central to Chinese politics until the death of Mao, but ethnic tensions sparked when more and more ethnic Chinese started to migrate to the region during the economic reforms. Violent conflict resulted, with Uyghur separatist feelings rising. The government has responded with a brutal crackdown, giving the ethnic tensions an ideological hue. So-called 'vocational education and training centres' for people suspected of 'Islamic extremism', are in fact internment camps that have been set up to indoctrinate Uyghurs and other non-Chinese ethnic minorities with the official ideology. Reportedly, these camps contain hundreds of thousands, perhaps even a million Turkic Muslims – a policy compared by observers to the atrocities of the 'cultural revolution'.

Contemporary folk religion. In spite of the spurning by the authorities, the folk religion turned out to be remarkably resilient in mainland China, as it survived the rule of Mao and the 'cultural revolution', and returned into the open as soon as the circumstances allowed. For most Chinese, the observation of some traditional religious customs in some form is not necessarily perceived to be religious practice, but something like Christmas celebrations for secular people in the West. Moreover, most of the deities of the folk religion have evolved from actual or presumable historical persons. It is believed that the spirits of the dead stay in touch with the living and serve as intermediaries between them and the higher powers of the spiritual abodes. This is one of the reasons for ancestor worship and sacrificial ceremonies, ranging from small daily offerings to large-scale ceremonies, usually conducted in the context of important days such as rites of passage of their family members. People without children – or those forgotten by their descendants – may end up as ghosts and start to cause mischief, because no one cares about them. Ghosts may adopt actual people as their descendants posthumously, which turns them into their legitimate 'ancestors', and occasionally they may also start protecting a certain group of people, thereby earning the status of their tutelary deity.

The most important annual festival of the ancestor cult is called *qingming*, 'clean and bright', known in English also as 'tomb-sweeping day'. This festival is celebrated on the 15th day after the spring equinox and involves the cleaning of the burial sites of one's ancestors, as well as bringing sacrifices to their graves. One particular type of sacrifice practised on that day is the burning of specially prepared paper money, which is believed to reach the ancestors and give them the possibility to acquire what they need in afterlife, or even to bribe celestial officials. The custom has evolved in contemporary times to the burning of paper effigies not only of luxury goods – villas, sports cars, and the like – but even of papier mâché dolls modelled after the winners of China's beauty pageants, to serve as concubines of the ancestors in their afterlife. Although the customs of folk religion are no longer frowned upon by the state, this particular practice has elicited the criticism of state officials, who in 2006 even issued a cautionary decree advising people to refrain from it.

In addition to ancestors, respect is also paid to tutelary deities of the local community or professional group (which may coincide). Shrines to these gods stand in a hierarchical relationship to each other, as the inauguration of a shrine normally presumes the presence of incense ash from a previously established one, of which it becomes a filial. Another presence in a village is usually the shrine of the earth-god, who is not really a separate deity, but a sort of celestial supervisor of the village's affairs and different deities can fulfil the office at different times. Earth-gods are expected to bring the problems of the community to the attention of the higher spheres, much as village headmen act as spokespersons for the people they represent, and also look after the following of the rules decreed from above. A stove-god, whose picture hangs in the kitchen of the house, fulfils the same purpose for a single household, and is expected to deliver a report on the household's behaviour at the end of every year – thus they are ceremonially seen off and then welcomed back, and a new picture has replaced the old one in their place of dwelling.

Philosophical developments: 'New Confucianism'. While in mainland China the traditional cultural heritage was officially reduced to nothing but an interpretive bias to which the ideas of Marx, Lenin, and Stalin should be subjected, it continued to thrive in the Chinese-speaking world outside its borders. A movement usually called **New Confucianism** was inaugurated in 1958 by the publication of an article entitled 'A Manifesto for a Re-appraisal of Sinology and Reconstruction of Chinese Culture', which strongly criticized the suppression of the tradition in Mao's China and called for its re-evaluation and development in a modern context. The text was a collective work of four authors. All of them had been students of a relatively unknown philosophy professor of the Beijing University, Xiong Shili, and subsequently escaped to Taiwan and Hong Kong, while their teacher remained in Beijing.

The main thesis of the article was that the Ru tradition was not an embodiment of reactionary conservatism, but the core of a specifically Chinese outlook of the world, which was capable of evolution and adaptation and not incompatible with scientific rationalism or democratic political theory. The authors were critical of Western appraisals of Chinese culture as backward and exotic, and of the mainland efforts to reconstruct Chinese society according to a communist blueprint. Confident that Marxism as a theory with no strong ties to the Chinese tradition will eventually be abandoned, the authors proposed a creative development of the tradition that would incorporate the best aspects of world civilization. They were also convinced that the Chinese tradition had much to give to the world and while China needed to learn from the West, the West should also learn from China. The Ru tradition should, accordingly, not remain a purely Chinese affair, but develop a global dimension.

These ideas became the shared basis of the 'New Confucian' movement. Some scholars prefer to call it 'contemporary Neo-Confucianism', as an extension or retake of the revival of the tradition during the Song and Ming dynasties. It continues to be the most influential and productive current of contemporary Chinese philosophy and has indeed attracted an international following, albeit a relatively modest one, in the guise of 'Boston Confucianism', a group of American thinkers who have begun to formulate their own ideas in a New Confucian framework.

Xiong Shili (1885–1968). By the merits of his thought, **Xiong Shili** should stand among the most important philosophers of the twentieth century, alongside such figures as Wittgenstein, Whitehead, Heidegger, and Nishida. By historical chance, he is known only to a small, albeit slowly broadening, circle of scholars of modern Chinese thought. The striking originality of his philosophy and the polemics following the publication of his main work, 'A New Theory of Consciousness-Only' (or 'A New Philosophy of Yogācāra') in 1932 attracted several bright disciples during the 1930s, but his decision to remain in mainland China severely reduced his influence, although he was permitted a certain degree of intellectual freedom under Mao's regime. That, too, was revoked during the 'cultural revolution' and the last years of Xiong were spent in misery.

Xiong's intellectual quest began with the study of Buddhist philosophy, which he soon started to analyse critically and creatively. He was invited to Beijing University to lecture on Yogācāra thought, but when he published his development of it, this was met with a critical rejection in Buddhist circles. Xiong answered their critique with a rebuttal, and the debate attracted larger attention. Xiong became a model for those who wanted to engage the Chinese tradition creatively. Although his disciples were more inclined towards the Ru heritage, Xiong approached all thought of the past with a similar attitude, developing what he considered important and criticizing what he thought was leading to dead ends. From the Ru tradition, he valued the *Yijing* most highly. This book was indeed a Ru classic, as it had been incorporated into the tradition early on and also served as the source of inspiration for many Neo-Confucians of the Song and Ming eras. However, the ideas of the *Yijing* had very little to do with the social and ethical concerns of the Ru and lived on in other Chinese thought traditions as well. It is therefore slightly unjust to cast Xiong only as a 'new Confucian', as his ideas transcend the boundaries of the Ru tradition and engage the tradition as a whole.

During Mao's rule, Xiong had to make certain efforts to reconcile his ideas with the tenets of Marxism, but he showed considerable intellectual courage by not abdicating from his central ideas. Strangely enough, this was tolerated, perhaps because his work was too complicated to cause any trouble for the regime. Xiong nonetheless developed a theory of dialectics that was compatible with both Marxism and ancient Chinese cosmology and also articulated his sociopolitical views, drawing on the idea of 'great unity' in *The Book of Rites* and Kang Youwei's utopian work. He also produced some textual scholarship of dubious quality, claiming, again similarly to Kang, that Kongzi had been a social reformer with democratic ambitions, whose teaching had been later distorted and adjusted to the needs of imperial authoritarianism. A bit like the Teutonic musings of Heidegger, these aspects of Xiong's later thought have largely been ignored and his philological fantasies were rejected by most of his disciples.

Ideas: the unity of substance and function. Xiong formulated his ideas in an idiom of traditional Ru and Buddhist terms, which often do not have precise Western equivalents, and that adds a further layer of complexity to his thought.

In a nutshell, the vision he defends is a monist ontology that seeks to transcend the opposition between matter and mind. This is expressed in his thesis of the unity of 'substance' and 'function', two terms with a long history in Chinese thought, introduced by Wang Bi and again brought to the limelight by Zhu Xi. Xiong, however, conceptualizes them more in the tradition of Huayan Buddhist philosophy, and even borrows a metaphor from it, seeing substance as the ocean and function as the waves, which cannot be meaningfully separated from one another.

Substance, for Xiong, is neither material nor mental, but constitutive of both. Unlike Western notions of substance, which tacitly imply its static nature, Xiong's substance is inherently dynamic and cannot exist without being cast into one or another 'function'. Substance is absolute, eternal, complete and real, and everything that happens is reducible to it. Accordingly, it also contains all possible principles of ordering, and also all virtues. It is creative and vital, and therefore in constant transformation.

The particular forms that this transformation takes are its functions. Xiong has borrowed two terms from the *Yijing* to account for the changes, 'closing' and 'opening' – the first reflects the tendency of substance to stabilize itself into concrete forms, the second reflects the tendency to open up towards any other form, which brings with itself the disintegration of a previous form and the production of something new. These two tendencies are constantly present and do not mutually exclude or reject each other. Together, they produce the diversity of the world and its change.

---

substance   in Xiong Shili's philosophy, the unitary ontological ground of being, which is inherently dynamic and contains all possible transformations of itself

function   a particular pattern or form that substance is manifested in

closing and opening   the two tendencies by which substance either reifies itself into particulars or opens these particulars up to each other and their own internal potential of change

testimony   the experience by which the human mind has access to the substance as itself

---

Two truths revisited. Since the substance is absolute and all-encompassing, and its dynamic character is ultimately also the ground in which resides the cognitive potential of the human mind, Xiong claims that the substance is accessible to each individual from within their own particular experience. The 'metaphysical truth' of such an experience cannot be adequately expressed in language, which relies on the 'closing' functions for its operation. However, even though Xiong occasionally employs the term 'enlightenment' for the cognition of this truth, it seems that the 'internal testimony' by which it can be attained is nonetheless available at the core of the human psychic process and does not have to be reached through a mystical, supranatural experience. This metaphysical truth corresponds to the ontological position of substance, while functions are captured by 'scientific truth', which is predicated on the postulation of a physical universe of objects. Xiong's position is not that on some deeper level, this universe does not 'really' exist, but that the language necessary for producing shareable descriptions of it cannot capture its essential unity. Scientific truths indeed have to be intersubjectively available and also relatively stable, but only relatively, as it is also in their nature to be debated and changed if necessary. They are always formulated through concepts that are created by an observing mind, but only work if they achieve correspondence with what they describe.

This reformulation of the two truths theory is also reflected in Xiong's views on knowledge. He distinguishes between instrumental and essential, or 'testimonial', knowledge – the first of these is based on measurements and objectivized characterizations of reality in its particular form, while the other is directly grounded in the metaphysical truth. Similarly, Xiong distinguishes between the 'original mind' that is a derivate of the creative potential of substance and also carries with it a moral-ethical charge, and the 'habitual mind', which operates on the daily basis with a contingent and necessarily reifying conceptual apparatus. However, although the discourse he employs clearly has its roots in Buddhist views, he does not advocate a retreat from daily life as an avenue of approach to the 'original mind' – on the contrary, he is closer to Wang Yangming here in that testimonial knowledge can be both acquired and realized only in the course of an active engagement with one's world.

The second generation. Xiong's creative interpretation of traditional Ru and Buddhist ideas and their synthesis into an original system inspired many students who, unlike him, left China when the People's Republic was established, and taught in the universities of Hong Kong and Taiwan. This second generation of 'New Confucians' includes the authors of the 1958 manifesto and a few others who shared its sentiments. Two of the most prominent among them were Tang Junyi (1909–1978), who developed the theory of the moral self and later expanded his system into a complicated edifice of nine horizons or aspects of the spirit, and **Mou Zongsan** (1909–1995), one of the most influential Chinese philosophers of the twentieth century. Mou's spectrum of interests was exceptionally wide: he was well versed in the different traditions of Western philosophy and wrote extensively on logic and particularly on the philosophy of Kant, but also on the traditions of Chinese thought, all of which he considered to be valuable.

Unlike some other Chinese philosophers, Mou did not consider either the Western or the Chinese way of thinking to be superior, but envisaged a synthesis, in which the Western foundations of science and political theory could be linked with the ethical core of Chinese thought. He considered Kant to be the epitome of Western thought and set himself the task of bringing Kant and the Ru tradition together. The need for this, according to Mou, was the apparent inability of Kant to ground his ethical theory in his ontology and metaphysics. Mou reasoned that when Kant distinguished between 'things for us', as perceived by cognition, and 'things in themselves', as the entities which our mind cannot reach, he denied the human mind the capacity, 'intellectual intuition', to reach the essential nature of things in the world – this was an ability that only a (philosophical) god could possibly have. At the same time, Kant had posited ethical behaviour as an extension of free will, or 'moral autonomy', that would choose to follow the categorical imperative, or a moral law also attributable to the same philosophical god. For Mou, this resulted in a contradiction – a 'moral metaphysics' –, which would be able to establish a connection between the ontological ground and its ethical articulation is only possible, in his view, if the ability of intellectual intuition is also granted to the human mind. But such a human mind is not the particular intellect of a single person – it is the shared and transcendent 'original mind' that Xiong Shili had extracted from previous Ru and Buddhist philosophy. This mind Mou now identified with Kant's philosophical god, but with the crucial difference that this god resides in each human being – as the infinite wisdom of humaneness (*ren*) or the 'perfect wisdom' (*prajñā*) in Buddhism.

Mou was a prolific writer and his positions evolved considerably over the years, but he kept returning to the issues that concerned him most. Of all the second-generation New Confucians, he was perhaps closest to Xiong Shili in his metaphysical thinking, and notable also for his contributions to the historical study of Chinese thought.

The third generation: New Confucianism as a world philosophy. The most prominent representative of the third generation of New Confucianism is undoubtedly **Tu (Du) Weiming** (b.1940), who was born in China, but grew up in Taiwan and studied with Mou Zongsan, Tang Junyi, and others as an undergraduate. He earned his doctoral degree at Harvard, and has been working at various US universities (Princeton, Berkeley, Hawaii, Harvard) ever since. Tu has been active internationally, he has been elected to the Academia Sinica in Taiwan and also appointed to a professorship in Beijing University, in addition to numerous visiting professorships, honorary doctorates, and other academic awards from institutions around the world.

With Tu, New Confucianism went global. The group of 'Boston Confucians', largely inspired by Tu's presence, has theorized about the 'portable' character of the Ru tradition, which can transcend its Chinese cultural roots just as Buddhism or Christianity have done in the past. The Boston Confucian group has also fostered a dialogue of Ru thought with Christian theology and the American philosophical tradition of pragmatism. The latter indeed has long-standing Chinese connections, starting with the influence of John Dewey on Hu Shi and his own visit to China.

The third generation of New Confucian thinkers has also achieved a re-entry of their thought to mainland China. Some Chinese academics, who are committed to the communist pretences of the official ideology view the movement with suspicion, because of the outspoken anti-communist stance of second-generation thinkers such as Mou, while other mainland scholars have explicitly identified themselves with this group. New Confucians are also criticized on non-ideological grounds because of their adherence to the tradition as the source of inspiration. In a world which is no longer the same as where the core ideas of the tradition were formulated, this attitude is seen as self-defeating. Nonetheless, the dialogue goes on and the Ru tradition has become an increasingly relevant voice in global debates, especially in the domains of ethics and philosophy of mind.

3

Japan

Introductory remarks. Although Japan does not compare in originality to India and China, it merits more attention than most other smaller Asian cultures for several reasons. Historically, Japan was one of the very few Asian countries that remained independent and almost untouched by the effects of Western colonial expansion. Then, from the last decades of the nineteenth century, Japan has emerged as the first country not only in Asia, but outside the range of the traditional 'West' in general, to modernize itself and to develop into a great power during the twentieth century. Japan has thus demonstrated that non-Western cultures are able to successfully function in the modern paradigm without forsaking their roots.

On the darker side, Japan has experienced a period of military totalitarianism, claimed leadership over the entire region, and threatened the whole Pacific basin. The construction of a new and contemporary social model after World War II, again relying on both traditional and new ideas, can with justification be seen as a second wave of modernization. Moreover, Japan has been and, in many places, continues to be the model of modernization for other Asian countries. A heterogeneous and syncretic tradition that has successfully contributed to the ideological base of a twenty-first-century technological giant should certainly interest us both for its present and its past. And so it does: post-war Japan has for long been one of the Asian countries to elicit most interest among both the academics and the general public in the West.

Syncretic character of Japanese worldviews. The paradigm of Japanese worldviews differs in several aspects from continental East Asian religiosity. First of all, the spiritual beliefs have been consolidated at a rather early stage into a semi-institutional form called Shintō that has been integrated into the political system. Shintō has never reached the degree of coherence or organization that characterizes Christianity, for example (even with its constant splits and internal disagreements), but has been a more distinct presence in Japanese political life

Asian Worldviews: Religions, Philosophies, Political Theories, First Edition. Rein Raud.
© 2021 John Wiley & Sons Ltd. Published 2021 by John Wiley & Sons Ltd.

than, for example, the spectre of folk religions in China has achieved. The Japanese imperial house, in particular, has been for most part of its history primarily a symbolic and spiritual centre of authority that has articulated its claims in Shintō terms. Only a few Japanese emperors have wielded any real political power over the centuries, but in spite of the many ups and downs the imperial house has remained essential to the maintenance of the political system to this day. Second, for most of the time, various teachings of continental origin have not only coexisted, but been thoroughly intertwined with this domestic institution, to the point where an effort to separate them at the end of the nineteenth century proved to be a rather difficult task. Hostilities such as the persecution of Buddhists in China by an emperor supporting the Dao creed would have been completely unimaginable before the advent of modernity and its requirement for clear borders between distinct worldviews – there had never been any in the Japanese past.

Buddhism has, throughout centuries, been the primary basis for most intellectual endeavours that reach beyond the everyday. Officially introduced from Korea in the sixth century, Buddhism soon became the dominating ideology of the Japanese imperial court and even started to threaten its authority. Sponsored by aristocratic clans, Buddhist institutions erected temples that became economically powerful hubs of both spiritual and intellectual activity as well as centres of learning networks, which operated schools throughout the provinces. Buddhism thus provided a channel of social mobility for talented commoners. Moreover, through monks travelling back and forth it upheld a channel of the traffic of ideas with the continent at times when official contacts were infrequent. Initially a mostly elite affair, Buddhism acquired a massive popular following in the thirteenth century and in the fifteenth to sixteenth centuries provided the backbone for a rebellious peasant republic that rejected warrior domination. After a backlash at the beginning of the modern era, Japanese Buddhism re-established itself in the twentieth century both in the form of ubiquitous temple networks catering to the spiritual needs of the people and as an influence on the intellectual scene not only of Japan, but of the whole world.

A third presence on the landscape of Japanese worldviews is Ru/Neo-Confucianism. There are just a couple of Confucian shrines in Japan and virtually nobody would have a strong personal preference for Kongzi's thoughts among the available worldview choices. Neo-Confucian values are nonetheless deeply entrenched in the corporate ideology as well as family values, and a strong feeling of hierarchy as well as responsibility is a characteristic of the network of Japanese social relations. The group mentality of the Japanese has also been influenced by the Neo-Confucian principles that were at the basis of the social organization of Japan in the Edo period. The ideas of Kongzi, and what has been made of them, have been a constant presence in Japan over the centuries and have shaped the outlook of the Japanese society and ethos in many ways.

Such syncretism has characterized both the 'low' religious and spiritual practices of the people and has also been quite influential on the 'high' intellectual undertakings. A certain division of labour exists between traditions: birth rites are normally the domain of Shintō priests who introduce the newborn into society, but the Shintō obsession with pollution caused by death, combined with the more optimistic Buddhist outlook on afterlife have relegated burials to the Buddhist temples. Thus it is sometimes said that the Japanese are born in Shintō but die as Buddhists. Nowadays, one could add that they marry as Christians, presumably not least because of the appeal of the white wedding dresses, so many buildings with crosses are actually wedding parlours complete with restaurants and even small hotels where the guests from out of town can stay. This is not the only place where the borders between consciously religious practice and mere social ritualism have been blurred. Similarly to many Westerners, who celebrate Christmas and Easter without religious motivation, many Japanese also engage in shrine rites and celebrate Buddhist holidays without any actual religious feelings. It can thus be said that the ideas and practices of Buddhist or Shintō origin have firmly established themselves in the Japanese social and cultural environments, to the point where it is no longer pertinent to question whether a rite is religious or simply an enactment of sociocultural norms.

Periods of cultural history. Unlike China or Korea, where ruling houses have replaced each other quite frequently over the centuries, Japan has officially always been governed by the same dynasty, which was believed to have descended from the sun goddess Amaterasu until the emperor himself denied his divine ancestry at the end of World War II. Therefore, the names used to designate most periods of cultural history derive from the seats of the factual political power, which the court almost never held.

For the present purposes, Japanese cultural history can be divided into three main periods. The first includes the prehistory and comprises the processes that led to the establishment of a Chinese-type state with Buddhism as its official worldview, which later became dominated by aristocratic clans. During that time, Japan came into intensive contact with the mainland of Asia (Korea and China), started to import various texts and ritual practices, and also remodelled its own social and intellectual environment as a result. Buddhist, Ru, and Lao-Zhuang theories influenced the development of the Japanese worldview, as did fengshui and *Yijing*-based divination. After the establishment of the first permanent capital in Nara, Buddhist leaders gained more and more influence over the economy and politics, which led to clashes with the aristocracy and finally the imperial house itself. This led to the emperor's break with the powerful Buddhist institutions and the removal of the capital to Heian (Kyōto), and the import of new forms of Buddhism as a counterweight to the old temples of Nara. This was a period of quick development resulting in the rise of many indigenous Japanese cultural forms, which were heavily influenced by Buddhist learning, since the aristocracy and the temples were now enjoying a more friendly symbiosis.

A second period was introduced by the civil wars of the twelfth century that led to the establishment of a military 'field government' that took control of the practical affairs of the whole country. The shōguns, as the military dictators were called, were keen on promoting yet new cultural forms and in the thirteenth–fifteenth centuries also sponsored many new schools of Buddhism, which had transformed itself from a mainly aristocratic pursuit to a worldview of the broad masses by the end of the thirteenth century. Another civil war ripped the country apart in the fourteenth century, when there were, for a time, even two competing emperors – a fact that promoted the development of different political theories, among them, a theoretical grounding of the divine authority of the imperial line. The shōgun's government had started to weaken during the fifteenth century, however, and by the sixteenth century the country was split into small independent political units. The struggle for the reunification of the country coincided with the first contacts with Europeans, who brought both firearms and Christianity, and warlords coveting the former quite often also accommodated the latter.

This political chaos was brought to an end by the victory of the Tokugawa clan with their capital in Edo (now Tōkyō), who in 1600 subdued all his enemies and established a strong regime, closing the country to all foreigners except for one little outlet of trade with the Dutch. The import of Western books was allowed some time later, and there was even a school of learning based on them. Neo-Confucianism became the official ideology of the Tokugawa, and both Buddhist and Shintō institutions and activities were carefully controlled. Nonetheless the Edo period produced remarkable advancements for both, especially the latter – the school of 'native learning', calling for the revival of indigenous ideas and practices as a counterweight to the dominant Chinese learning developed an interest in the Shintō traditions, producing both commentaries on Shintō texts and political programmes articulated in Shintō terms.

The **Meiji Restoration**, the starting point of the third period, that of Japanese modernity, was initially led by xenophobic pro-imperial clans who sought to restore the power to the emperor as the descendant of the gods. The subsequent decades were again a time of intense and hectic cultural imports, where new technologies, Western learning, Enlightenment ideas, Christianity, ideologies of nationalism and imperialism, as well as anarchism and communism entered the country and started to compete, sometimes forming unlikely alliances with each other and the local tradition. This was also the time when Japanese philosophers, well versed both in Western philosophy and traditional Japanese thought, first created a remarkable blend of the two known as the Kyōto school.

Intoxicated with its success at modernization, Japan began to see itself as the leader of the Asian nations in their struggle against the colonial regime, while in fact the leaders of Japan were devising a colonial regime of their own as a substitute for Western domination. This also affected the Kyōto school, some of whose representatives were carried away with Japan's planned new leading role in the world order and started to indulge in the narratives justifying Japan's aggression. A turning point arrived after the war, when Allied occupation launched Japan on the course of economic recovery and technological advancement reflected in a postmodern blend of old and new traditions. One characteristic feature of the most recent times has been the increase in number and importance of new religious movements, both offspring of the old traditions and entirely new creations, which attract followers in the new urban society, capitalizing on the downfall of traditional social networks while quite a few people still yearn for closely knit communities. Some of them have become rich, others branched off into politics, yet others, such as the notorious Aum Shinrikyō, into terrorism. In the meantime, traditional institutions have gone nowhere and Western thought is a constant presence in the intellectual world. As a result, the map of Japanese worldviews is more colourful today than ever before.

Prehistory and the Aristocratic Period

Background. The Japanese islands were first populated more than 15 000 years ago and its forager inhabitants had reached a remarkably sophisticated level of culture by the standards of that time, but it was only during the first centuries CE that a politically more organized society emerged. This process was caused by the invasion from the continent, in around 300 BCE or possibly earlier, of tribes that brought with them new and superior technologies, such as wet rice farming as well as the use of metals and horses. Soon the invaders had chased the original population to the fringes of the archipelago. Their society of farmers stratified and clans started to vie for domination, using supernatural discourses for legitimation. Thus Chinese records inform us of a shamaness called Himiko (Sun Queen) reigning over the people with witchcraft at the turn of the second to third centuries CE. Large tombs testify to the existence of multiple centres of power. Contacts with the continent brought knowledge of Chinese statecraft to the Japanese clan chieftains, and in the sixth century an organized state emerged.

A significant role in this process was played by the introduction of Buddhism around that time, which served, among other things, as a neutral, clan-independent ideology that helped the ruling house to consolidate its power. In the eighth century, the first permanent capital was established in Nara, but when the

Buddhist monasteries started to meddle in politics too strongly, the capital was transferred to what is now Kyōto (called Heian at the time). The emperors also started to support new forms of Buddhism as a counterweight to the old institutions in Nara.

The aristocratic age of the Nara and Heian periods was a time of intense cultural import. Japan's progress had been incredible: from a barely civilized society of militant clans it had emerged as one of the centres of East Asian civilization, proudly boasting the uncovering of a giant statue of the Buddha in the biggest temple in the world in 752 and abandoning its regular embassies of formal tribute to China in 894. This was the golden age of Japanese culture, its literature and arts, cultivated by a court that placed aesthetic sensitivity above all other human qualities, although learning was also cultivated in the scholarly and monastic circles.

This period was brought to an end by the rise of the warrior estate and its claims to political power, which resulted in a series of civil wars in the twelfth century. The initially successful Taira warrior clan that had started to emulate the ways of the court and tried to put the existent power patterns to work for its own use had to yield to the Minamoto clan, which devised parallel power structures and established its base in eastern Japan, far from the culturally tempting, but corrupting influences of the court. The political model that they created – a military dictator ruling on behalf of a helpless emperor – remained in place for the next seven centuries.

Chinese and Japanese cultural elements. During the entire aristocratic period, the role of Chinese (and to a lesser extent, Korean) cultural imports was a dominating presence, and even after the formal embassies were abandoned, commercial and cultural traffic still continued back and forth. Classical Chinese was the official language used in court documents as well as for scholarly purposes and most Buddhist writing. Initially, Japanese, although structurally very different, was also written with Chinese characters, some of which were adopted for their approximate phonetic values and later organized into two syllabaries based on the pattern of the Indian devanāgarī script. Simultaneously, a method was devised for the Japanese to read texts in Chinese aloud: small signs were inserted into the text indicating how to change the order of characters so that the pattern would fit the Japanese word order, and grammatical markers were added where the sense of the text would otherwise be obscure. This way of preparing texts is still in use in many editions of Chinese texts today.

The continental influence was not restricted to just written material, however, but extended to virtually every sphere of life, from fashions and incense to the forming of government structures and legal codes. Nonetheless the Japanese were quick to make adjustments wherever necessary. For example, the logic of clan society did not go well with the Chinese idea of individual achievement and meritocracy. Therefore, although the Japanese state adopted the ranking of officials according to merit, ranks were bestowed on aristocratic children at birth, so that they would qualify for high office on reaching maturity. Such selective adaptation of foreign cultural material has been a hallmark of Japanese cultural logic ever since.

The indigenous Japanese worldview. The indigenous Japanese worldview is usually called **Shintō**, which is actually an umbrella term that unites a broad range of practices and beliefs from local forms of folk religion or spirituality to the nationalist imperialist ideology that the Japanese state strongly supported before and during World War II. The term itself is first met in an early historical chronicle, but before the advent of modern times it was used by very few Japanese, and chiefly by zealous professionals. Shintō partisans claim it to be the indigenous and 'pure' Japanese worldview, although it has been influenced by mainland imports from very early on. Thus the initial organization of spirit practices was structured in Japan according to the model of the Dao creed (for example, *tennō*, the title of the Japanese emperor, is borrowed from some Chinese rulers with Dao sympathies), while a large part of the later development of Shintō took place in symbiosis with Buddhism. However, Shintō is more than just a Japanese local version of the general Asian spirit beliefs. Even though some scholars have argued that Shintō is, in fact, one of the 'new religions' of Japan that only came into being at the end of the nineteenth century as a result of the restructuring of the Japanese mental landscape, it has wielded considerable political influence throughout history and some of its current practices have truly old roots. The first systematically organized government in the seventh century placed the council of 'divine affairs' over its counterpart dealing with earthly matters, and during the civil wars of the fourteenth century, Shintō lore was used to construct the narrative of the unbroken imperial line that reaches up to the sun goddess Amaterasu. Certain imperial rituals, such as thanking the deities for the harvest, have been performed by the Japanese emperors since the beginnings of recorded history, as the chronicles of the Nara period testify. All in all, the system of power and the system of spirit beliefs have lived in a mutually beneficial symbiosis in Japan for the better part of reliable history.

The idea of the sacred in theory and practice. One of the primary characteristics of Shintō is the absence of distinct borders between the sacred and the profane. It has frequently been described as an 'animist' worldview, which is correct only if we do not separate the 'spirit' from what it is supposedly the spirit of: Shintō does not assert that, for example, certain awe-inspiring natural phenomena are inhabited by deities, but that they are, as such, 'divine'.

Written with different characters, the Japanese word for deity, *kami*, signifies 'upper' or 'superior' and also 'hair' as the highest point on the human body. Quite a few kami are known by individual names and stories about them, but the majority of them are not independent personal actors. The whole universe is alive, filled with spiritual energy. Some places have a higher concentration of that energy than others, and this elicits respect and admiration from the people. Kami are nothing else than sometimes more, sometimes less explicitly personified heuristic objects of that admiration. Even though the mythology tells us stories, for example, about Amaterasu, the sun goddess, it is nonsensical to ask whether Amaterasu exists, since she is not distinct from the Sun shining in the sky.

According to Shintō beliefs, everything is alive on a certain level, and it is possible for humans to interact with it. Most Westerners only talk, usually aggressively, to their computers and cars when they do not function. The Japanese, however, often thank their working tools or apologize to plants that they have forgotten to water. The attitude of Shintō towards the sacred and the deities is not one of submission to a transcendent power, but that of respect, not quite between equals, yet for beings who are a part of the same paradigm. Initially this took place privately, then collectively in open air at specific locations, and finally, during the last decades of the seventh century, in shrines that were built in places of high spiritual energy concentration as part of an effort to bring these spontaneously organized practices under political control.

As the concentration of spiritual power is seen to be unequal in different places, everyone is constantly in a state of betweenness. In the most sacred of accessible spaces, there is still something more sacred a few steps away from us, and in the most defiled place it is still possible to get even dirtier. The imperial family is at the top of the spiritual hierarchy, but its members, too, have clearly designated places inside the most important Shintō shrine at Ise determining how far any of them, the emperor included, is allowed to step. Today, non-Japanese visitors to shrines often wonder why they have to take such a long path to a building that is so unimpressive, but the movement towards the sacred is precisely the point of the visit. One continuously moves from less sacred spaces towards a higher concentration of spiritual energy, with entries to the next level marked by double-beamed *torii* gates, of which there are typically quite a few along the way. The shrine itself is not entered by the casual visitor, who can summon the attention of the deity by pulling a chord with a bell, and then cast a coin as a token of respect into a large box, bow and clap their hands twice while addressing the deity in their thoughts. For most Japanese, this is the main form of Shintō practice. Inside the shrine, there are no figures of divine personages, but usually just a mirror as contact point with the kami – thus even in the final instance, the actual sacred is one step removed.

Other Shintō rituals include local festivals, where able-bodied young men carry the local kami around the territory under its guardianship in a heavy palanquin kept for the purpose. Customs vary from place to place, but usually such festivals involve a local fair and lots of merrymaking. Shintō deities are not strict and solemn, and celebrating them is a matter of celebrating life and being together.

---

kami   Shintō deities, personified, but frequently anonymous instances of the spiritual energy that fills the entire universe

---

An independent tradition of spirit possession has survived the effort of institutionalization of spirit beliefs, and continues to this day. Japanese mediums are typically young girls. Virginity is believed to enhance the ability to communicate with the otherworld, and therefore dangerous to women who wish to lead a normal life, however, certain shrines have had female priestesses and, according to Chinese chronicles, the first rulers of Japan were also shamanist priestesses. The *miko*, or spirit mediums, are usually controlled by a male guide, who is there to facilitate the communication between her and her audience or clients. The same word – a cognate of 'prince(ss)' – is now also used for shrine dancers and female servants, who are not expected to perform spiritual acts, but outside of the shrine system, the practices go on.

Categories of deities. These local festivals are held in the honour of tutelary deities. On the whole, kami are divided into three spheres according to the social division of space typical of Japanese culture. First, there is the inner circle, one's family and closest friends, which corresponds to 'the kami of the clan', derived from ancestor worship, personifications of the collective pool of mental energy to which the spirit of the individual returns after death. Second, there is the public domain, where people from various inner circles interact. In traditional rural society, this area was where 'the kami of the fields' made their appearance, deities whose collaboration ensured a good harvest and the success of other jointly undertaken enterprises. A third category, 'the kami of the forests and mountains' comprises those spiritual beings who inhabit the areas outside the village and relations with them are scarce and unstable – something like between total strangers in a neutral social space, people to whom one owes nothing. Contact with such beings is sometimes unavoidable, when one has to leave one's usual space, and it is therefore better to maintain a relationship of mutual respect with them.

Obsession with purity and ethical neutrality. In close connection with the Shintō idea of the sacred is its preoccupation with purity and pollution. The Shintō deities represent a primordial purity, which is why humans who wish to be in harmony with them should also keep themselves pure. The Japanese people have therefore kept strict hygienic standards from the earliest times onwards and also distinguish the spaces that they inhabit according to degrees of purity. For example, it is not permissible to wear the same slippers in the living room and in the toilet, which is a more polluted area. As death is one of the most active sources of pollution and the death of the emperor pollutes more than that of an ordinary individual, the ancient Japanese moved their capital to a new site every time an emperor died, and only established a permanent site of power in the eighth century when Buddhism had become the chief worldview of the court. Keeping purity is also the reason why many Shintō shrines, including the one at Ise, are being dismantled after a period of time and then rebuilt according to the same blueprint from new and pure materials. People also have to be periodically purified. A visit to a shrine necessarily entails rinsing one's hands and mouth at a well, and more complicated purification rituals enable people to relieve themselves of the mental dirt that unavoidably accumulates in their minds. But pollution can also stick. As a result, the groups of people who are in constant contact with polluted things because of their profession – for example, those who work with leather and by proxy with dead animals – have in the past been excluded from the mainstream society and labelled 'non-people' (*hinin*) or 'heaps of filth' (*eta*), even though they do not differ from other Japanese in any way. Contact with those people was considered polluting by proxy. Although after the Meiji Restoration their discrimination was officially forbidden, it persists to this day and one of the tasks of the private investigators whom both sides often hire before a marriage is concluded, is to find out whether the other side has any outcast blood.

Being born an outcast is almost the only irreparable misfortune that one can encounter in the Shintō world. Shintō deities are themselves morally neutral and they do not punish people for not doing as they are told. The word used in contemporary language for 'sin' may have originally derived from 'piling up' (written with a different character), which indicates that feelings of guilt and traces of wrongdoing are a kind of pollution that gathers in the mind and can be conveniently taken care of by purification rituals. Gathering mental dirt is unavoidable in the world that is itself impure, but almost none of it is irredeemable.

'The spirit of words'. Shintō followers also entertained a belief in the magical power of words. In Japanese there was initially no distinction between the words 'thing' and 'word' (even though this word – *koto* – referred only to a particular, processual, embedded kind of thingness). Only after the introduction of Chinese script were these words distinguished by different characters used for writing them down – before (and also after) that, if necessary, words could be called 'edges of things' (*koto-no-ha*), later poetically transcribed as 'leaves of words'. Sometimes the two characters for 'word' and 'thing' were even used interchangeably, for example, in the name of a deity (Kotoshironushi). This internal relationship between words and the things they denote manifests itself in the magic power, or 'spirit' of the words, called *kotodama*, which is mentioned in early poetic anthologies. It is unclear, however, how systematic the belief in this power was and how far it might have reached beyond the typical belief in spells and incantations, but, regardless, it seems to have been most strongly associated with poetry or song.

Shintō narratives. Much of Shintō lore has been preserved in narrative form. The most important of such texts, though technically not a 'scripture', is the **Kojiki**, a chronicle compiled in 712 soon after the permanent capital of Nara was established, written down by a scholar well versed in Chinese from the words of a memorist (a court official whose duty was to preserve oral knowledge). *Kojiki* is written in Japanese, but with Chinese characters used for their pronunciation, which makes it very difficult to decipher. The work was not widely known until the eighteenth century, when **Motoori Norinaga** (1730–1801), one of the scholars of 'native learning', produced a 50-volume comment on it and made it available to interested readers.

The *Kojiki* tells the story of how the earliest kami emanated from chaos, how the divine couple Izanagi and Izanami created the Japanese islands, of Izanami burning herself to death when she gave birth to fire, and Izanagi's trip to the Land of Darkness to rescue his wife and his narrow escape from there. Next, we hear about Izanagi's purification rites which resulted in the birth of Amaterasu from his eye and the thundergod Susanoo from his nose.

What follows clearly indicates the nature of the *Kojiki* as a political project. Uniting the Japanese clans under the rule of the imperial house entailed also the adjustment of particular mythological narratives into a general whole. Susanoo, whose main shrine is in Izumo, had been the main deity of the Izumo clan, another powerful contender to overlordship. The *Kojiki* bears traces of that, showing Susanoo as a short-tempered and occasionally dangerous figure, whose descendants finally recognize the superiority of the imperial clan. Susanoo is expelled from the Fields of Heaven, after defecating in his sister's palace and destroying the irrigation systems of her rice fields, and settles down in Izumo. Only a few generations later will Amaterasu send her grandson to reclaim the earth, to plant rice, and eventually to become the forefather of the imperial house.

Kojiki a historical chronicle compiled in 712, containing the most important narratives of Shintō lore

---

The spread of Buddhism. Officially, Buddhism was introduced to Japan in 538 CE, although individual monks had appeared on the islands before that. Hoping for Japanese help in his war against his neighbours, the king of one of the Korean states, Baekje, sent gifts to the Japanese court, which included statues of Buddha and Buddhist manuscripts. After a heated debate, one of the influential clans was granted permission to worship these objects privately, but officially Buddhism had no status. This changed rather soon. When that particular clan rose to prominence and gained increased influence over the imperial house, Buddhism started to occupy a central place. After a coup in 645, Buddhism retained its high status as a clan-independent worldview that helped the rulers consolidate the state into one whole. Initially, Buddhism was considered by the Japanese to be just another cult of certain overseas deities. However, soon enough the court discovered that the new religion was something qualitatively different from the indigenous worldview. Temples, monks, meditation, and scriptures were something Japan had not seen before and left a strong impression on many aristocrats, convincing them of Buddhism's cultural superiority.

Nara Buddhism. During the Nara period devoted emperors built a capital full of temples, including Tōdaiji, still the largest wooden building in the world, which established Japan's cultural credibility all over Asia at the time of its construction. Japanese Buddhism was then divided into six schools, each of them based on a certain text or group of texts (such as the works of Nāgārjuna) that the monks studied. Members of the different schools frequently lived together in the same temple. Their understanding of the teaching differed greatly from the views of the general population, for whom Buddhism continued to be just a superior version of spirit belief and magic, with figures such as the 'Medicine King' among the most popular, someone to take care of your illnesses, to whom two separate temples at Nara were dedicated.

The Buddhist temples of Nara wielded significant political power. Although the state controlled the number of monks who could enrol in various schools, it also provided temples with land revenue grants and leading aristocratic families sponsored Buddhist activities. Shintō shrines established alliances with Buddhist temples, based on political and economic interests, which also led to collaboration in the sphere of ideas. Local deities were enlisted as protectors of temples and small shrines set up for them on temple grounds to ensure their benevolence. In later times, this developed into a still tighter relationship: approximately from the beginning of the eleventh century Shintō deities came to be envisaged as Japanese manifestations of Buddhist personages. This resulted in a symbiotic coexistence of the two worldviews that irreversibly cemented the syncretism of the Japanese worldview.

Soon, however, the might of the Buddhist institutions started to cause problems for the aristocratic clans, until the incident of Dōkyō upset the balance completely. Dōkyō (700–772) was a monk who gained the confidence and favours of the mentally unstable ex-empress Kōken and was rewarded with consecutive titles including Reverend Prime Minister, but Dōkyō was even more ambitious and desired to become emperor. Instead, however, he was stripped of his titles and exiled. The imperial house took precautions against the power of the temples and finally moved the capital away from them.

Buddhist independents. In spite of the immense influence of Nara temples on the court, they were not allowed to accept more than a specified quota of monastics annually. Those not admitted often chose to practise Buddhism on their own. Some monastics, having received initial instruction, also left the temples for various reasons and either lived as hermits in the mountains or wandered around the country. Records show that the ruling powers viewed them with suspicion and, when possible, tried to co-opt them back into the system as popular holy men. Comforting the people in their economic hardship assured some of them of large followings. Others were less interested in popularity and more inclined to study esoteric texts in small groups or simply in wandering around in the mountains as a form of spiritual discipline, which included the practice of austerities, for example, standing in waterfalls for prolonged periods. The teachings they spread creatively combined Buddhist elements with bits taken from the Dao creed as well as local and Shintō lore, with mystical additions by its teachers themselves. Such wandering mountain ascetics, or *yamabushi*, were credited with healing powers by the populace. Fairly soon the movement evolved into a separate teaching called **Shugendō**, 'The Path of Discipline and Trial', which traces itself back to the half-legendary figure of En no Gyōja, a mystic and herbalist of the seventh century. En no Gyōja had been exiled by the court on the charge of sorcery, but then became the hero of many miraculous tales. Shugendō was forbidden after the Meiji Restoration, but restored after World War II and is practised to this day.

Tendai. During the next century, two new schools were imported to Japan, both with the pretention to be all-embracing substitutes for the Nara institution. The first of them was **Tendai**, the Japanese version of Chinese Tiantai. **Saichō** (767–822), a discontented monk who had left Nara and taken up a solitary hermitage on Mt Hiei not far from the new capital, attracted the attention of the emperor and was dispatched to China on a mission in search of new knowledge. On his return, he brought the teachings of Tendai with him. Mt Hiei now developed into the headquarters of the school with several large temples, and other temples also sprang up elsewhere.

The original Tiantai had a complicated metaphysics, positing multiple overlapping 'worlds' or perspectives on reality, and then reducing all these to one thought moment, which could capture the entire multitude in itself. The attainment of this thought moment was the goal of the Tendai meditation technique called *shikan*, 'standstill and contemplation', a development of Indian meditation techniques focusing on one single object in order to achieve maximum concentration and then projecting that concentration onto the non-essentiality of the follower's own selfhood. Tendai meditation proved to be hugely influential on Japanese intellectuals, for example, innovative court poets, who adopted it as a technique for writing in order to reach cosmic emotional heights through in-depth realization of a single particular image. The attitude remained characteristic of Japanese traditional aesthetics.

Tendai also taught a rather bold version of the 'original enlightenment' doctrine, or the idea that each sentient being is already enlightened, but the entanglement in worldly affairs does not let most of us see it. Japanese Tendai thinkers supported the even stronger claim that absolutely everything, plants and stones included, shared in the universal Buddha-nature.

> As all sentient beings with bodies that distinguish their selves from their others are ultimately suchness, they are also the Buddha. Therefore, since grasses and trees as well as stone rubble, mountains and rivers, the great earth, the great ocean and emptiness, too, are all suchness, there is no thing that would not be the Buddha. ... Therefore, in the mere single particle of 'dust' in front of my eyes, all the buddhas and bodhisattvas of ten directions are summarily contained.
>
> (Genshin, *A View of Suchness*)

Japanese transformations. The original Chinese Tiantai underwent serious changes on Japanese soil. Saichō was a good enough politician to understand what the court wanted from him: an umbrella teaching that would impress the aristocrats and provide the spiritual support that they needed. Thus Tendai contains a lot of material from other sources – for example, it imported and developed an esoteric strain of its own and also allowed certain other doctrines, such as the Pure Land teachings, to evolve within its fold. The new leaders of the reform movements that appeared after the civil wars of the twelfth century had all received their primary Buddhist education on Mt Hiei.

Tendai headquarters was not only an intellectual centre, but also a political influence and military might. Court politicians often interfered with nominations of Tendai leaders to ensure that the monasteries close to the capital would be friendly, and with good reason. Because of inter-temple skirmishes in disputes of leadership, temples started to accept among the ranks of monks 'rough' men who had probably escaped justice for violent crimes and now served as 'soldier monks', defending their temple from outside interference. Or attacking others, on command of their leader. During the twelfth century's civil wars the monks of Mt Hiei could be a formidable ally (or enemy), and even during the unification process of the sixteenth century warlords frequently had to cross swords with them.

> Three things I cannot control: the waters of the Kamo river, the cast of dice, and the monks of Mt Hiei.
>
> (Emperor Shirakawa)

Kūkai. The other school that became prominent during that period was the esoteric teaching of Shingon, imported to Japan by **Kūkai** (774–835) who was born in the provinces and grew up as the heir to his father's family tradition of Chinese learning and the shamanic bloodline of his mother.

He was a scholar and one of the best experts on Chinese language and literature of the time, writing treatises on poetry. Reportedly, he was once even asked by Chinese fellow students to write a letter for them because of his superior command of style. It is notable that unlike most educated Japanese, he studied actual Chinese, not a Japanized form of vocalizing written Chinese texts, and was therefore sensitive to the tonal variations of it, which may have influenced his theory of language and the idea that parts of conveyed meaning are hidden in the sound patterns of the words used. Kūkai also became proficient in Sanskrit, which he learned in the cosmopolitan Chinese capital Changan, studying together with a Christian missionary. But Kūkai was also a religious seeker, who dropped his university studies to join an illegal group of mountain ascetics experimenting with meditation techniques outside the Nara orthodoxy. After a time, he managed to be sent on a mission to China with a plan to stay there for 20 years. He returned after only 30 months though, having been chosen as one of the six new leaders of the Shingon school at the deathbed of his teacher. The other five lineages became extinct fairly soon, however, and the school quickly declined in China. Esoteric Buddhism therefore survives to this day as an ongoing practice only in Tibet and Japan.

Shingon: esoteric Buddhism. Even though Tendai, as said, also developed esotericism, the primary site of such activities in Japan was the Shingon school. The basis of its teaching is the theory of the three bodies of the Buddha, which had matured in Indian texts. Some of the early Pāli texts mention the 'teaching-body' (called later in Sanskrit *dharmakāya*) of the Buddha as an aspect of him that linked his physical presence to the ideas that he represented. Mahāyāna *sūtras* elaborated on this and constructed a model that separated the physical, phenomenal body of the Buddha first from the imagined body that one could get in touch with during deep meditation (and which legitimated the composition of new teachings, allegedly received from such manifestations of his), and, finally, the ultimately real cosmic 'teaching-body', which was the basis of all reality, neither essentially spiritual or material, but both equally. This *dharmakāya* Buddha was identified in the Shingon school with **Mahāvairocana**, whose name was conveniently translated into Chinese and Japanese as the Great Buddha of the Sun, something easily to be identified with Amaterasu, the Shintō sun goddess and progenitor of the imperial house. The whole cosmos was the body of the Buddha, and every single movement within it a meaningful act of his will, although the meaning remains hidden to all but the initiated. This move was based on an ingenious reversal of the Buddhist theory of the no-self, or *anātman*. If our selfhoods are illusory in that they do not have a permanent basis in reality, coming instead into being as temporary and contingent relations between independent elements, then why should we not treat the ever-moving and impermanent cosmos, a totality of contingent relationships, also as a person? Notably, the illusory nature of that personality gets lost in this reversal and the Buddha not only embodies the total order, but also directs it according to his will. Mahāvairocana also had a special quality of 'attraction', a spiritual power which he extended to sentient beings and made them susceptible to salvation through esoteric techniques.

---

dharmakāya the cosmic body of the Buddha, the basis of all reality, which embodies the teaching and continues to expound it secretly in everything that happens

---

An esoteric theory of language. Kūkai was also the first Japanese thinker to present a philosophical theory of language. He was unique among his countrymen in that he had studied both Sanskrit and Chinese to perfection and was also well educated in the literatures of both languages. Accordingly, his views on language were influenced by both. From the Indian tradition he inherited the belief in the secret and powerful meanings inherent in the phonetic form of words, from the Chinese 'dark learning' the idea that the natural world could and should be

Prehistory and the Aristocratic Period

read as a text. Integrating this idea with both esoteric Buddhist theory and native Japanese cosmological ideas, Kūkai came up with a proto-semiotics of the world which is both systematic and rather original.

As it is customary with esoteric teachings, he distinguishes between two layers of meaning in the text: the exoteric, or publicly available semantic meaning, and the esoteric, which is a hidden meaning that opens itself only to the initiated. Kūkai is thus sceptical about language in its everyday sense as our natural way of exchanging meanings, but at the same time attributes to it enormous powers on a higher, cosmic level, because in his view not only words, but also single syllables or letters have profound esoteric meanings. And it is not only text that has such hidden depths: each of the five elements that make up the universe also possesses a hidden meaning, which is unknown to the uninitiated, and therefore all the things that consist of them are secretly meaningful as well. Actual sacred texts in verbal form are just places of concentration of this significance, just as holy sites are places where the concentration of divinity is at its strongest. Since the universe is in constant flux, it also constantly produces new meaning. Accordingly, all things as such are signs, reducible to essences that are organized themselves into a primordial linguistic system. The source of all these enunciations is none other than Buddha Mahāvairocana himself. One of the tasks of the follower is thus to open up to this cosmic speech, to receive the messages from the Buddha of whom the entire universe is a manifestation.

This is why Kūkai needs a rather detailed proto-semiotic theory, to which he dedicates a separate treatise. He distinguishes three main elements in the signifying system, that is the sound, the sign, and the referent. But each of these terms has a much broader, cosmic essence. 'Sound' is the form of any tension or vibration that takes place when the great elements combine to form reality, and 'sign', or 'letter', is a fixed instance of this sound, a pattern that can be repeated and put into correlation with the world. Outwardly, this pattern takes the form of a body, or a sense-object, the referent of the sign. So cosmic sound is anterior to words, and signs are anterior to the objects they denote. The things we consider to be of the material world thus actually arise only as a result of distinction, which is the work of these patterns in action. Not surprisingly Kūkai considers A, the first letter of the devanāgarī script and simultaneously the negative prefix in Sanskrit, to be the symbolic basis of signification by distinction – only by being able to say what something is not can we conceive of it in its identity.

It is difficult to say how much influence Kūkai's theories have actually had on later Japanese linguistic philosophy, especially since most of it has been developed on quite different premises and from a more sceptical point of view as to the capacities of language. Even so, there are elements in the theories of later authors, such as Dōgen, to be discussed below, which remind the reader of his grand vision of the universe as constant linguistic play. Another influence of Kūkai may have been the radical reading of the *Lotus Sūtra* by Nichiren (1222–1282), who saw this text as the embodiment of the historical Buddha, who thus remained constantly in this world and was concentrated in the title of the scripture, so that chanting this title was a way to uphold cosmic order and to simultaneously pay one's respects to the founder of the teaching.

Technologies of spiritual progress. Another claim of Japanese esotericists, and one that guaranteed them a lot of popularity with the aristocrats, was to be able to bypass the rigorous and long training process of the Buddhist practitioners, which might not even bring rewards after this immediate lifetime. To emphasize this thought, *Attaining Enlightenment in this Very Existence* is the title of one of Kūkai's best-known works. Instead of a long and difficult progress, the Shingon school proposed a shortcut, a combination of secret and effective technologies that could bring about the desired result without too much effort. The name of the school means 'words of truth' and refers to *mantras*, or specific formulas derived from Sanskrit that supposedly had a direct effect on the psyche of the practitioner, creating a state of mind in harmony with the undulations of the universe. *Mūdras*, or specific gestures presented a way of adopting the practitioner's body to cosmic shapes. Another technology was mediation on *mandalas*, mental maps of the cosmos, which was depicted as an assembly of spiritual figures, Buddhas and bodhisattvas, with Mahāvairocana at the centre. By concentrating on how they were specifically situated in relation to each other and the particular principles each of these figures embodied, the initiated practitioner was allegedly able to penetrate the fabric of reality and assimilate aspects of the hidden order behind it. In due course, Shingon also developed colourful ceremonies that sometimes involved the use of fire and intricate movements with swords – acts of defence against malevolent forces. These had much more entertainment value than monotonous recitals of scripture and were therefore much more attractive for the lay participant and potential sponsor. Although the headquarters of Shingon were further away from the capital, the school gained quite a lot of popularity among aristocrats, which occasionally caused strain in its relations with Tendai and also

Both Tendai and Shingon were aristocratic in nature. The imperial court and the influential clans surrounding it were their main target audience and source of income. Lucidity of teachings and an appeal to the broader masses was, for neither, a primary concern, and even though Kūkai reached out to the general public by establishing a school in the capital in 828 to accept students regardless of their descent, this was mainly to recruit talented students and not to bring learning to the people. A broader appeal was something Buddhism only acquired after the bloody civil wars of the twelfth century.

put some pressure on the latter to develop esoteric teachings of its own. Slightly later, Shingon produced a few offshoots, one of them, for example, seeking a closer synthesis with Shintō, another promoting tantric sex practices and glorifying courtiers famous for their amorous pursuits as bringers of salvation to many women.

The Age of the Warriors: From Kamakura to Edo

Background. The Minamoto clan, which emerged victorious from the civil wars of the twelfth century, established its power base in the small town of Kamakura in Eastern Japan from which the first period of military rule (1192–1333) derives its name. The Kamakura rulers were quick to realize that too much of an integration with the court may cause the warriors to lose their cultural identity and therefore used various tactics to rule through parallel systems, simultaneously undermining the power mechanisms of the court. They also soon started to patronize the new Buddhist school of **Zen**, which, in addition to its separation from court-sponsored schools and channels of access to more recent Chinese sociopolitical thought, also provided answers to existential questions that warriors had, such as how to combine a profession that involves taking lives with the ethical ideals of respect for all living beings.

By the fourteenth century, however, the Kamakura establishment had gone into decline. Towards the end of the thirteenth century it had to withstand two Mongol invasions, which took its toll economically, and there were no strong military leaders able to regain control of the country. In the capital, however, a capable emperor emerged who tried to take advantage of the situation in order to return the power to the imperial court. He failed in that, but the Kamakura establishment was overthrown in the process, and a new dynasty of shōguns took control, after a period of division, during which samurai clans supporting the emperor continued to fight them. The Muromachi period (1338–1573) derives its name from an area in the capital where the new shōgun established his residence. From the prosperity and stability that followed the end of hostilities in 1392, the Muromachi establishment, too, declined under poor leadership and the country was divided into a large number of de facto independent provinces.

This was accompanied by the first contacts with Europeans, who brought Christianity and firearms to the islands. Samurai lords coveting the latter often saw the conversion to the former as a means to obtain what they wanted. This changed the character of warfare and led to a period of turmoil, which again resulted in the victory of one clan, the Tokugawa, who chose the town of Edo, a bit to the north of Kamakura, as their residence. A new era started, known either as the Edo or the Tokugawa period (1600–1868).

The first Tokugawa shōguns were true administrative geniuses. They adopted Neo-Confucianism as their official ideology and divided the society into four estates according to a doctrine that developed certain Chinese attitudes, but abandoned its meritocratic spirit that made social mobility possible, at least in principle. The new system placed the samurai at the top, followed by peasants, who provided the food, craftsmen, who provided other needed things, and merchants at the bottom, because they only lived out of speculative profit. Erstwhile enemies were dispersed to coastal areas, so that they could not form a united base for rebellion. All clans had to maintain a residence in Edo and spend a part of the year there, and provide hostages for the remaining time. It is easy to see how the purchasing power and need for services that this policy produced quickly changed the small town of Edo into a bustling metropolis with around a million inhabitants.

Seeing the potential threat of Westerners interfering with Japanese politics, the Tokugawa also closed the entire country to foreign traffic. Foreigners were not allowed to arrive in Japan, and the Japanese were forbidden to leave at the penalty of death. Even castaways rescued by foreign ships could only return home via the one opening that remained the exception during that period: a little Dutch trading mission on the island of Deshima near Nagasaki. The Dutch had earned this position because of their assistance to the shōgun during a conflict with rebellious Christians and their Spanish Jesuit instigators.

The Buddhist reform movements of the Kamakura period. During the civil wars, the Buddhist idea of impermanence gained a lot more credibility, because nobody, regardless of wealth or rank, could be sure of the future. The powerful temples of Tendai participated in these conflicts as well, and the losing sides provided an influx of warrior monks to any accepting monastery. This caused dissatisfaction among those who had initially taken vows in order to actually study Buddhism, but found themselves in institutions more concerned with worldly matters. That, in turn, led to the development of the theory of *mappō*, or 'latter-day law', according to which the state of the Buddhist teaching deteriorated in time, from the actual presence of the Buddha, then just his disciples, and so on, until no one had direct memory of the blessed times and everything started to go wrong. The idea itself was imported from the continent, where it had been elaborated previously in troubled times to indicate that the world is in crisis, but the Japanese produced their own detailed chronological calculations to make it fit their own situation. These showed the people what was manifest anyway: that the time of decline had arrived, and measures needed to be taken. This inspired several reform movements that changed the shape of Japanese Buddhism for good.

mappō ('latter-day law')   a period of decline that was supposed to arrive after a long time had passed since the lifetime of the Buddha

Classification of Kamakura schools. The movements of the Kamakura period, possibly the most active time of Buddhist thought in Japanese history, divide into two mainstreams and an anomaly. The mainstreams differ in one basic question: whether it is at all possible for individuals, by their own efforts, to exit the predicament that the times have imposed. One group among the reformers, relying on the Tendai version of the doctrine of 'original enlightenment', claimed that this was indeed possible and everything one needs to emancipate can be found within oneself. For the purpose they introduced a set of meditation techniques and a philosophy to go with them, which is known as Zen. Another group was not convinced. The effects of *mappō*, they believed, were so devastating that it is more useful to call for outside help, namely to the Buddha Amitābha, or Amida in Japanese, who had vowed to save all sentient beings and established for the purpose a Pure Land, a celestial abode to which anyone who so wishes can be reborn and practise Buddhism in more favourable circumstances. For that one need not do anything else than call out to Amida, chant the 'name of Buddha' or *nembutsu* formula ('Namu-Amida-Butsu'), and this will happen. And, finally, there was one religious leader who claimed that everybody else was wrong and he alone was right. Why that was so he did not explain in much detail. The historical circumstances combined with his own self-confidence were such, however, that he, too, attracted quite a large following.

nembutsu   a formula, the chanting of which would attract the attention of Buddha Amitābha, who would ensure the rebirth of the practitioner in the Pure Land, a celestial abode where nothing prevents practising Buddhism

Pure Land schools: the beginnings. Although outside Japan Zen is the best-known of all these currents, in Japan itself the Pure Land schools have proved to be the most successful. Most of their leaders, just as those of other reform movements, received their Buddhist education in the Tendai temples of Mt Hiei, where forms of devotion to Amida had been practised for quite some time. The doctrine relies on several Indian *sūtra* texts and comments by a few Chinese enthusiasts, although in China the practice never developed into a prominent school. In Japan, however, there eventually emerged four separate schools of this kind. The first influential figure to promote the idea was **Hōnen** (1113–1212), who advocated the abandonment of other practices in favour of the *nembutsu*. In spite of criticism by Tendai authorities, he gathered a remarkable following including some leading aristocratic politicians and even members of the imperial family. This was put to an end after a scandal, when some handsome disciples of Hōnen were discovered to have spent the night in the quarters of the ladies in the retired emperor's palace, apparently chanting *nembutsu* together. The perpetrators were executed and the aged Hōnen himself exiled with his most important disciples, being allowed back only a few years later, just before his death.

Shin Buddhism. Hōnen's school survives to this day, although it was soon overshadowed by one of his main disciples, **Shinran** (1173–1263), who developed the Pure Land tradition into the leading form of Buddhism it still is today. He, too, started at Mt Hiei, and only left his monastery after a vision, in which the bodhisattva Kannon allegedly promised to incarnate and marry him, if he so wishes. He indeed married, possibly twice, and created a new form of Buddhist school where the leadership is passed on in the family. Shortly after leaving Mt Hiei he joined Hōnen and in 1207 was exiled to the eastern provinces, where he spent almost 30 years, having found a receptive audience to his teachings there. Shinran's school of Shin ('True Pure Land') Buddhism initially operated as a network of groups rather than temples: people gathered in someone's household to recite the *nembutsu* together, and afterwards shared a meal. His adversaries soon started to claim that this was not legitimate Buddhist practice, especially because Shinran taught that seeking of personal merit was pointless. This was so because 'good' people tried to be good themselves, that is, they had some confidence in their own capacity to be good, rather than the benevolence of the Buddha, which was a grievous mistake. Some of Shinran's followers evidently interpreted this as an encouragement to abandon the precepts, enjoy meat and alcohol, and bring loose women to those Buddhist gatherings, which caused concern in the Kamakura field government. In fact, Shinran never taught such things. On the contrary: he believed that evil was the result of seeking one's own pleasures, which necessarily hindered the workings of Amida. Shinran did not credit the individual with the capability of calling out for Amida's help by oneself, and thus even *nembutsu* practice was not a conscious effort, but a reflection of Amida's goodness. By abandoning all selfish pursuits the individual opened up to the Buddha and thus their acts became those of Amida's, that is, ultimately ethical.

The structure of Shinran's communities fostered a spirit of solidarity and thus in the fifteenth to sixteenth centuries the followers of his Shin Buddhist school established a Buddhist republic, which lasted over 100 years, by driving away all warlords and governing quite a large territory by elected peasant representatives, ultimately surrendering only to one of the warlords who unified Japan.

> If even a good person can attain rebirth in the Pure Land, how much more so an evil person!
>
> (*Tan'ishō*, a primer of Shin Buddhist thought)

Zen: Buddhism for the samurai estate. The second branch of the reform movements was Zen, which soon came to be favoured by samurai leaders, not the least because Zen monks often travelled to China and brought with them also other kinds of high culture, from styles of painting to Neo-Confucian statecraft. The individualistic attitude of Zen and the philosophy of 'no-self', which made it possible for the samurai to mentally disassociate themselves from the killing that their profession entailed, also had strong appeal. Zen texts and teachings had been known in Japan since at least the eighth century, and one of Saichō's teachers had been versed in Zen, which was partly incorporated in the Japanese eclectic Tendai. However, it became more popular during the twelfth century, when various monks claimed to have received a direct transmission from the Chinese masters. **Eisai** (1141–1215), in particular, enjoyed popularity with the Kamakura warriors and is thus credited to be the official importer of Zen to Japan. What these masters taught was mostly an eclectic mix of Zen, tantrism and other teachings, even though they tried to organize their temples according to Chinese patterns. In fact, the Kamakura authorities had to wait until the mid-thirteenth century, when Chinese monks started to come to Japan and brought with them a purer version direct from the source. Sponsored by the military government, Zen became the leading form of Buddhism for the warrior estate.

Dōgen (1200–1253). One Zen transmission was an exception to that movement. A young aristocratic monk named **Dōgen**, disappointed with the intellectual atmosphere on Mt Hiei, was advised by one of Eisai's disciples to seek instruction in China and returned from there with a transmission of the 'silent' Zen tradition. After a period of failed attempts to attract attention in the capital, he accepted the invitation of a warlord and built his main temple in north-central Japan. Dōgen was one of the greatest philosophical minds that Japan has ever produced and now deservedly famous for a collection of essays called *The Core Transmission* (borrowing the title from the founding myth of Chan/Zen) and written in classical Japanese. Soon after his death, this book was more or less forgotten, undoubtedly because of its complicated nature. Dōgen's language is notorious. He takes quotations from scriptures or Chinese masters and reinterprets them, ascribing them meanings which are most of the time possible grammatically, but not semantically, and then derives from them his own philosophy of time, being, subject, language, and many other topics.

The motif that has attracted most attention among Dōgen's philosophical statements is undeniably his view of time. Earlier researchers have read his essay on time as a statement of identity between time and being, having him claim that the very nature of being and time are essentially the same. More recently, it has been suggested that Dōgen's view does not presuppose durational time, and therefore can be read as an elaboration on the Indian Sautrāntika view that existence is momentary. The emptiness of things consists in their being nothing but configurations of dharmas, or minimal carriers of being, and though they occur in causal chains with traces of their past affecting how they are configured and possible future trajectories predictable on that basis, these configurations really exist only for a dimensionless moment.

Another central tenet in Dōgen's views is that there is no gap between practice and enlightenment. In other words, since all sentient beings are originally enlightened, they need not pursue enlightenment as a goal in the future, but simply practise it in sitting meditation. For a seasoned follower, even sitting meditation was no longer necessary. The same attitude towards reality could be transferred to any kind of activity and thus daily tasks such as cooking food or cleaning the room became the most advanced forms of Buddhist practice.

It is difficult to summarize Dōgen's thought briefly and do it justice, and most of his successors did not even try to digest it. The eventual success of his school was not due to the depths of his thought, but to the quite different style of one of his followers who captured the rural audiences with boldly imaginative tales about his own previous lives and miraculous birth. This ensured a steady following of Dōgen's school that also preserved his works, and monks with a more scholarly frame of mind started to read them again in the Edo period, until they caught the attention of academics in the twentieth century.

Firewood becomes ashes and it cannot become firewood again. Although this is so, we should not see ashes as 'after' and firewood as 'before'. You should know that firewood abides in the dharma-configuration of firewood, for which there is a 'before' and 'after'. But although there is a difference between 'before' and 'after', it is within the limits of this dharma-configuration. Ashes abide in the dharma-configuration of ashes, and there is a 'before', and there is an 'after'. Just like this firewood, which will not become firewood again after it has become ashes, a human being will not return to life again after death. ... Life is a momentary configuration, death is a momentary configuration. This is like winter and spring. One does not say that what was 'winter' has now become 'spring', one does not say that what was 'spring' has now become 'summer'.

(Dōgen)

Nichiren (1222–1282). The last but not least of the persons who restructured the mental landscape of Buddhism during the Kamakura period was **Nichiren**, a charismatic leader of humble origins, who studied in several centres of learning, but was satisfied with none of them. His time on Mt Hiei left him with the conviction that the *Lotus Sūtra*, the chief scripture of Tendai, was undeservedly buried under an eclectic amalgam of different teachings and practices, while this text itself represented the historical Buddha in the 'latter-day' world and had to be restored to its deserved glory. The essence of that text was condensed in its title, and so Nichiren offered to his followers a simple practice resemblant of the *nembutsu* – chanting the *daimoku*, a mantra hallowing the title of the *sūtra*. Neglect of this scripture and the proliferation of dangerous other forms of Buddhism had, according to Nichiren, caused the native gods of Shintō to flee Japan and leave it at the mercy of foreign invaders who would soon arrive and destroy the whole country if the spiritual power over Japan were not immediately transferred to him. As chance would have it, the Mongol conquerors of China were planning to move further to Japan just at this historical moment. The first invasion of 1274 was repelled at great costs and with the help of a storm considered to be divine involvement on the Japanese side. Nonetheless the fulfilled prophecy rendered credibility to Nichiren's claims, ensuring him of a certain following. The vehemency of his rhetoric and acts of violence against all other forms of worship undermined his reputation, however, to the extent that he finally decided to build a place for himself and his followers on a mountain to which he then retreated. Nichiren's followers remained militant and conducted attacks against other Buddhist denominations, notably the Shin school, over the following centuries. Thus this development is perhaps the only one in Japan that might rather be called a 'sect', not a 'school'.

---

daimoku in the Nichiren school, a formula glorifying the title of the *Lotus Sūtra*, which was thought to encompass its whole teaching

---

Development of Zen practice. During the Muromachi period the form of Buddhism favoured by the power centres continued to be Zen. This was a mixed blessing: quite a few skilful temple administrators managed to secure the patronage of the 'field government', who valued their services more for their Chinese learning and cultural background. Apart from these activities, monks in the temples engaged, of course, in meditation exercises, particularly the concentration on certain extracts from mostly Chinese Zen stories, called 'public cases' or *kōan*, which presented the follower with logic-transcending or sometimes openly absurd situations, in order to open up their mind to an unconceptualized universe. For example, an extract of a dialogue of the Chinese master Zhaozhou with a monk consisted of the question 'does a dog have Buddha-nature?' – something the doc-trine of original enlightenment would surely require to be answered with a 'yes' – and Zhaozhou shouting 'No!' In Japanese translation, this 'No' was even pronounced differently than a simple 'no' would be. The task of the student was to acquire meditative insight into such an unsolvable problem – in the case of the example, the deep idea of 'No' – and then to look for appropriate 'solutions' in anthologies of Zen verse. These were then presented to the master and debated in dialogues that included also non-verbal communication, including shouting and hitting, until the master approved one of their proposals.

Institutional developments. The powerful sponsors of Zen were hardly ever engaged in such activities, although they enjoyed writing poetry and discussing philosophy with their Zen instructors. However, wary of their growing influence, the samurai leaders also held them in check. Temples under official protection were organized into a system called 'five mountains', patterned on the leading five temples in China, though in Japan the number signified ranks of importance and reached down to less important provincial temples, thus containing them in a nationwide network. Quite a few temples preferred to stay out of this net, how-ever, and kept their independence by securing support from the merchant cities or provincial samurai, or occasionally the court. In fact, the lineages most vigorous to this day are those that continued at these independent temples, some of which also developed into cultural centres where painting, poetry, and tea ceremony were practised and developed.

Various ways to attract support were used. Some provincials were eager to invite a 'five mountains' network monk to their local temple for the cultural prestige as well as a direct communication line to the authoritative centres of the capital. The monks of Dōgen's lineage, however, opted for a more popular strategy of mixing their teaching with local beliefs and conducting ceremonies for ensuring a good harvest or necessary precipitation. They also introduced Buddhist burials for lay-people, which granted them a nationwide success. Buddhist ceremonial codes had only regulated the burial of monks or nuns, but this obstacle was overcome by ordaining the dead posthumously. Other schools quickly caught up on this, but not before this Zen lineage had established itself in most parts of the country, converting old abandoned temples to their network with the blessing of local powerholders. This, however, did not mean that the lineage would become less strict in their internal discipline and practice of spiritual exercises, although one can certainly say that the philosophical thought of their founding master was not studied with the attention it deserved.

Zen personalities. Just as Chinese Chan, Zen was organized according to lineages of direct personal transmission. This made the figures of individual masters more important than in other schools – it mattered greatly whose Zen one had inherited, and it was actually possible to speak about the Zen of someone particular. This is one reason why Zen continued to produce influential figures while most other schools preferred to venerate their founding figures. Some of these famous Zen masters owed their reputation to their character and cultural achievement. **Ikkyū** (1394–1481), for example, was both an accomplished poet in classical Chinese and a cultural hero, famous for his drinking and visits to brothels, which his poetry documented. Many openly erotic and passionate verses written to the mistress of his later days, a blind musician, are rather uncharacteristic of a Buddhist monk and ensure us that the legends about him, most of which were written down much later, are not quite without foundation. Another popular poet-monk, **Ryōkan** (1758–1831), led a quieter life as a hermit and light-hearted eccentric.

To the head monk, on leaving the monastery
Ten days I was here, but my mind is not yet free.
From times of old, the red thread of passion has tied up my feet.
If at some point you want to see me, perhaps talk to me,
Find me in the fish market, in the pub, find me in the brothels.

(Ikkyū)

Position of Buddhism in the Edo period. During the Edo period the leadership of Japan favoured Neo-Confucianism over all other worldviews. Viewed with a certain suspicion, all Buddhist temples were subject to more rigorous rules and also a new function, which turned them into an instrument of governmental control of the population. All Buddhist activity had to be organized on a temple basis, with itinerant monks discouraged, and each household also had to be registered at a certain temple, which helped to keep track of their movements and numbers. Following the example of Shin Buddhism, which allowed its priests to marry, other schools also gradually abandoned the requirement of celibacy and many temples became family affairs, passed from fathers to technically illegitimate sons by 'temple caretakers'. This practice has continued to this day.

Quite a few of the more interesting Buddhist thinkers of the time were people with a careless attitude towards official restrictions, who preferred to live as hermits or move around, depending on the support they could individually solicit. Only occasionally could Buddhist monks achieve a position of direct political influence, for example, when one Tokugawa leader issued in 1690s 'edicts of care for living beings', especially dogs, the killing of whom was equated to murder – something which in the city of Edo where stray dogs were numerous did not earn him much of a reputation.

Bankei (1622–1693). But there were also monks who made serious philosophical contributions. **Bankei**, officially registered to the temple in his home village, spent the better part of his career travelling between various monasteries and patrons and preaching his Zen, which he envisaged as a return to the uncorrupted classical times, where no superfluous learning had been imposed on it and its main goal was to elicit a spontaneous response, an affirmation of reality, from any follower. He was convinced, a bit like Wittgenstein about philosophy, that Zen was actually easy, only made complicated by our own messed-up conceptualizations of the world. Bankei's most famous concept is the Unborn – his version of the original enlightenment, received by all at birth from their parents and something that can simply be embraced, without any recourse to rigorous training or intellectual reasoning. Bankei was extremely democratic and rejected all prejudices, for example, when a female listener asked him about her chances of being enlightened – which some Buddhist teachers denied, asserting that she would have to be reborn as a man first – Bankei simply asked her since when she has become a 'woman'. All such conceptual categories are just obstacles in our communication with the Unborn within us.

Hakuin (1686–1769). The most influential Zen thinker of the Edo period, however, was a much more institutionally inclined man. **Hakuin** almost single-handedly raised his own Zen lineage to prominence by reforming meditation practice and *kōan* study in particular. Although Zen had traditionally taught sudden enlightenment, Hakuin insisted that there is a correct path towards it and arranged the *kōan* texts according to the understanding of the practitioner, one solved puzzle leading to the next level. Hakuin also made up quite a few *kōans* himself. In addition, he imposed more rigorous standards on the testing of his disciples' understanding, since need for patronage had made the practice rather lax over the centuries. Hakuin also made up exercises for those who had already achieved enlightenment. All in all, he provided Zen with a higher level of systematicity that ensured its sustainability – but, at the same time, depraved it irreversibly of the spontaneity and antinomianism that had inspired the movement in its early stages in China and surfaced occasionally also on Japanese soil.

What is the sound of one hand clapping?

(Hakuin)

The Ru tradition and Neo-Confucianism. In the Edo period, Song-style Neo-Confucianism became the official worldview of the state. However, the tradition had been a minority presence in Japan for a long time. First Ru scholars are reported to have arrived in Japan in the fifth century, bringing texts with them, and the interest in the teaching grew when Japan embarked on the building of a mainland-type state apparatus. The 17-article constitution allegedly promulgated by Prince Shōtoku in 604, although it admonishes the subjects of the empire to cherish and respect the Three Jewels of Buddhism, is otherwise formulated in Ru rhetoric. The same is true of later historical chronicles. Ru centres of learning participated in domestic political struggles to some extent, notably at the end of the ninth century, when one emperor tried to check the power of the aristocrats by promoting the career of scholars such as Sugawara no Michizane (845–903), who was later exiled, but soon after his death, as his political enemies had started to suffer from various calamities, restored in honours and even proclaimed a Shintō deity of learning. The official class also had strong influence in the affairs of the military 'field governments'. Some shōguns, such as Ashikaga Yoshimitsu (1358–1408), who united the two fighting imperial lines under his control in 1392, had a keen interest in the new Neo-Confucian theory as a practical statecraft. However, the most important period of Neo-Confucian influence in Japan was the Tokugawa government, which raised it to the status of its official ideology and promoted Chinese learning among its samurai officials.

Japanese modifications. The main characteristic feature of Japanese Confucianism is the shift from the importance of genetic bloodlines to personal loyalty. In the Ru tradition, loyalty had always been a two-way street: those on the lower steps of the hierarchy have to obey their superiors, but the superiors have to deserve that loyalty by being responsible for those under their care. Filial piety, one of the chief Ru principles, was always taken rather literally in China, while in Japan the interpretation was much less rigid. Obviously, this meant no disrespect for one's mother and father, but this was not limited to one's biological parents. The Japanese practice of adoption of a son into someone else's family to learn a trade, for example, also meant the transfer of one's filial obligations. Relatives who were distant by bloodline but lived in the family – up to totally unrelated servants – deserved a more important place in one's world than those with whom the connection was only formal. But most importantly, if forced to choose, it was justified to prefer one's lord over one's rebellious family, because by forsaking their loyalty to their superior they no longer deserved a similar respect themselves. Obviously, this was something very much to the liking of a ruling samurai clan like the Tokugawa, always wary of plots and conspiracies. How this principle worked in practice sometimes still became an object of debate for Japanese Neo-Confucian scholars.

In a famous incident of 1703, 47 retainers of a provincial lord, who had been ordered to commit suicide 2 years earlier, avenged him by beheading the man who had caused his death, brought the head of their enemy to the grave of their lord, and then surrendered to the authorities. This divided the leading Neo-Confucian scholars of the time in two camps: those who saw the 47 retainers as the inheritors of true samurai values, remaining loyal to their lord beyond the grave, and those who saw this as a rebellious act directed against the state authorities, who had not endorsed such a vendetta. The popular feeling was undoubtedly on the side of the former, and the 47 samurai have remained popular cultural heroes to this day.

The question of loyalty also emerged as one of the chief issues for the thought of the Mito school, a Neo-Confucian centre of learning established by the head of one of the lesser branches of the Tokugawa clan. The compilation of a huge history of Japan led the scholars of that school to conclude that the main unifying line throughout it was the imperial dynasty, and the usurpation of power by the military rulers, which was well-nigh absolute in their times, accordingly disloyal. It was the Mito scholars who first coined the expression 'revere the emperor, expel the barbarians' that led to rebellions against the Tokugawa after the opening of Japan to foreign ships in 1854 and thus provided a Neo-Confucian rationale to the overthrow of the military government. In a way, the ideology embraced by the samurai rulers thus also contributed to their demise.

Ogyū Sorai (1666–1728). If anyone among the Japanese Confucian thinkers deserves special mention for the originality of their thought, it is **Ogyū Sorai**. As a son of the physician in service of the shōgun, Sorai received training in medicine and in philosophy, but it was the latter that he chose for his calling. Having studied the teachings of Zhu Xi, he opened his own school and started lecturing about them, and his approach soon caught the attention of one of the shōgun's councillors, who retained him as an advisor. With the changes in power, Sorai's fortunes alternated back and forth, and his views also received some criticism from powerful adversaries, but he was careful not to make his more radical views public in order to escape direct repercussions, thus some of his works now considered most important were published only after his death.

At a certain point in his career, Sorai turned against the legacy of Zhu Xi, so to say, because of following his advice to the letter: just as Zhu Xi had advocated a return to the texts themselves and the rejection of traditional interpretations that had been crystallized by the tradition, Sorai also rejected Zhu Xi's and his followers' views in order to develop his own on the basis of the classics. Moreover, he abandoned the traditional way of reading Chinese texts adjusted to the Japanese way, which, in his view, only obscured them, and started to teach the classics on the basis of living, contemporary Chinese. His reflections on the nature of meaning and its linguistic articulation led him to develop a philosophy of language. Following the Ru doctrine of 'rectification of names', according to which meanings are secondary to realities and should be brought into accordance with them, and at the same time insisting that categories of moral virtue are not simply terms, but normative prescriptions how people should behave, he came to the conclusion that virtuous behaviour must have arisen as an inaugural event that made civilized society possible, similar perhaps to the appearance of life on earth. This event he found in the mythical history of China, in the appearance of the sage kings whose acts were described in the *Book of Documents*. Kongzi, in his view, was not the beginning, but the endpoint of the development of the teaching, and after him the appearance of further sages was neither possible nor to be desired.

This, however, did not mean that the teaching was ready and all posterity had to do was to follow it. In Sorai's view, the world was in constant change and the duty of the leaders of any particular age consisted precisely in realizing how the teaching had to be adopted for the needs of the present. The Way, so to say, was not an unchangeable, constant entity, but something always reconstructed for the purpose of the historical context. The responsibility for this lay on the shoulders of the people who were uniquely qualified to lead. Sorai did not think that people were equal by their moral capacities. In contrast to some of his colleagues, who insisted that the responsibilities of the samurai arose from their privileged status, Sorai thought that this status was theirs by their essential superiority to all other social groups, an ethical backbone that a samurai had inherited by birth, and that others simply did not have the talent for maintaining a stable society for the common good.

Bushidō. The influence of Neo-Confucian thought on the samurai-centred social system was very strong, but in fact the code of conduct known as **bushidō**, 'the way of the warrior', was a syncretic construct that also contained traces of other streams of thought. In particular, the fusion of certain Lao-Zhuang ideas and Tendai Buddhism with court culture had created, in the late twelfth and early thirteenth century, an ideology known generally as *michi*, 'way', which claimed that spiritual progress can be attained also as a result of professional development. The book of Zhuangzi contained extracts with just such a message, for example, the tale of the cook who did not need to sharpen his knife, because years of training had let him fuse with the meat he was cutting to the extent that his knife only moved along the empty spaces between fibres of flesh. Initially these may have been just a critique of status-conscious scholars, but, accommodated by the Japanese courtiers, they came to mean much more. Combined with the Tiantai/ Tendai idea that the entire multiverse can be accessible through any single thing on which one concentrates with particular strength, and possibly influenced also by Dōgen's view that correctly exercised daily tasks equate advanced practice, this view yielded a particular consciousness for practitioners of specialized skills, such as fine arts or sports. The newly self-conscious warrior estate naturally broadened the concept to also include military exercises and their way of life in general, creating a ground for their autonomous value system, juxtaposed and not inferior to the high culture of the court. The Zen ideas of 'no-self' and action beyond the limits of one's mind, were soon added to the mix. Quite a few Edo period Zen masters, themselves former samurai or eager to win the patronage of the military rulers, used images related to the world of war in their writings, for example, explaining the cultivation of the self in terms of swordsmanship or overcoming the fear of death. Soon these ideas left the domain of Zen proper and became a part of a distinctly samurai worldview, to which the label of *bushidō* applies.

---

michi ('way') the idea that any way of life, properly practised, can lead to spiritual progress, including traditional arts as well as the 'way of the warrior'

Bushidō texts. The term itself was intermittently used in earlier writings as well, but gained larger currency with the publication, in 1899, of *Bushidō: The Soul of Japan* by **Nitobe Inazō** (1862–1933). Nitobe, a Christian and a Westernizer, wrote the book in English while on research leave in the United States in order to explain Japan to Westerners, but a Japanese translation of the work proved to be enormously successful as well, its appearance coinciding with a point in the Japanese modernization process where sufficient self-confidence had appeared to reclaim a part of the cultural tradition on new terms. An earlier and equally influential exposition of the *bushidō* ideology was the **Hagakure** (Covered by leaves), a collection of sayings by Yamamoto Tsunetomo (1659–1719), a former warrior prohibited from accompanying his late master in death. Written well into the peaceful Edo period, the *Hagakure* outlines the principles of the samurai code of conduct regardless of what is happening in the world, be it peace or war – the samurai still has to think of his life as death, and, being dead, to be ready to die at any moment, should the interests of his lord so require. The book was revitalized in the 1930s as a propagandistic text requiring the readiness of every Japanese to die for the emperor. After World War II, *bushidō* ideology has had a strong influence on the Japanese work ethic, transferring the loyalty from the lord or the emperor to the company and requiring every worker to do their utmost to achieve its goals.

Nativism. During the Edo period, a scholarly faction called *kokugaku*, or 'native learning', turned its attention to the Japanese indigenous heritage and later started to develop philosophical and political theories that included (or claimed to include) Shintō beliefs in its foundations. Opposed both to 'Chinese learning', or the Neo-Confucian official ideology, and 'Dutch learning', or efforts to integrate Western science (available only through Dutch books) into the Japanese intellectual field, 'native learning' combined literary criticism and historical textual scholarship with a search for an ideology that would be free from foreign imports. Nativist scholars made an important contribution to the study of Nara and Heian period historical and literary works, but also developed the discourses of Japanese nationalism. They admired the early and often naive expressions of awe and admiration of Japanese nature and glorified the simple patriotism expressed in the 'songs of the border guards', to be found in an eighth-century poetic anthology, as the 'true Japanese spirit'.

The *kotodama* ideology was also resurrected by the nativist scholars of the eighteenth and nineteenth centuries, who were constantly searching to find evidence in earlier texts for the belief in the magic powers of language, which some of them, enthusiastic Shintō practitioners, actually shared. This sentiment inspired the invention of various 'sacred scripts' at some Shintō shrines that pretended to be old autochthonous writing systems independent of any Chinese influence, but were actually patterned on the model of the Korean *hanggeul* alphabet that became known in Japan after the attempts to invade Korea in 1592 and 1597.

Nativist scholars also formulated the claims of Japan to have a unique status in the world. So, for example, Motoori Norinaga argued that although the sun goddess is responsible for providing daylight to the entire world, she is still an essentially Japanese deity, which means that Japan has a special place in the world. This was countered by another nativist scholar and writer of famous ghost stories, Ueda Akinari (1734–1809), who argued that all nations and cultures are equal and each has the right to their own stories and legends. Japan, therefore, is not special, but one culture among many.

In the end, however, it was the tendency represented by Motoori that prevailed, and in an even more radical form. **Hirata Atsutane** (1776–1843) developed nativist scholarship into a radical and potentially violent political ideology, claiming the entire Shintō tradition as its basis. Like Herder, of whom he was unaware, Hirata believed that it was the simple people who preserved the national spirit in its purest form. He combined bits and pieces of folkloric material into a systematic teaching for Shintō, complete with visions of afterlife and an ethical doctrine that determined individual posthumous destinies. According to his views, death in the service of the divine emperor would be rewarded with a rebirth in paradise. Hirata's doctrine, in fact, is not 'purely Japanese' at all, but contains unmistakable Christian influences that had become a part of folk beliefs during Japan's short encounter with the West in the sixteenth to seventeenth centuries. Nonetheless, his ideas inspired popular patriotic uprisings and were also used during World War II to bolster nationalist hysteria.

Christianity. Japan's first encounters with Christianity occurred during the century of Western influence from the arrival of the first Europeans in 1543 to the closing of the country in 1639. During the civil wars of the unification period, Japanese warlords were eager to procure firearms and thus some of them looked favourably on Western settlers, who soon began proselytizing. Francisco Xavier (1506–1552), one of the founders of the Jesuit order, heard about Japan from an escaped murderer while on a trip to Malacca, baptized the man and enlisted him as his interpreter. Their mission to Japan proved to be successful and soon the number of Christians started to grow there, eventually reaching about 300 000. Conflicts arose, however, when it became apparent that converts to the newly imported faith were no longer permitted to practise other worldviews. It seems that most converts, many of them introduced to the new faith by mass baptisms following the conversion of their lord, appreciated Christianity just as a set of powerful spiritual technologies (such as sacraments) and instruments (such as amulets) for enhancing their situation in life, and were rather ignorant about its doctrines. Matters were further complicated by the first translators' use of the Japanese name Dainichi (Mahāvairocana) as the equivalent for God, which, for the uninitiated, approximated the teaching to Shingon Buddhism, and even elicited enthusiastic response from Shingon monks. The massive apostasies that occurred at the time of later persecutions and the relatively modest appeal of martyrdom, at the time propagated by the Jesuits, was only to be expected under the circumstances.

Tokugawa persecutions and 'hidden Christians'. After a rebellion inspired by Jesuits, the Tokugawa authorities took a negative attitude to Christianity, which they considered subversive, and finally ended in banning it altogether. Christians were forced to forsake their religion and random checks were performed around the country, for example, at checkpoints by bridges and provincial borders, where travellers had to trample on clay tablets with the image of Christ, and those refusing were arrested. Quite a few Christians nonetheless kept their faith and formed underground communities. Over generations and with no contact to Christians elsewhere, the teaching they professed started to mix with Shintō beliefs and practices. For example, some communities even identified the Virgin Mary with the daughter of the sea god, who appears in the *Kojiki*. After the Meiji Restoration, when the ban on Christianity was lifted, some 'hidden Christians' re-entered the Catholic Church, others, however, kept to their own syncretic faith, which is now on the border of extinction.

Japanese Modernity: From Meiji to the Present

Background. In the middle of the nineteenth century, the shōgun's grip on Japan gradually started to loosen. Western powers, having established their outposts in China in the wake of the first Opium War (1839–1842), started to turn their attention to Japan. While the shōgun's administration tried to push back their advances, it also realized that it is no match for the Westerners militarily, and finally in 1854 agreed to open several ports for foreign trade. Oppositional clans, which governed many coastal areas, took the unsteady position of Edo for a weakness and started to require political reform on a xenophobic and nationalist basis, calling for a return of the political power to the emperor and the expulsion of foreigners. The final years of military power saw the emergence of a plurality of new political forces, which, in concert, forced the last shōgun to stand down, accomplished the transfer of the imperial capital from Kyōto to Edo, now renamed Tōkyō, and started a wholesale reform of the political and social system. These events are collectively called the **Meiji Restoration** of 1868, after the new era name declared by the emperor now nominally holding all power. The primary aim of the Meiji reformers was to attain a level of development which would make Japan the West's equal. This involved the promotion of Western science both through the establishment of new schools and universities at home and the sending of talented young Japanese to Europe and the United States to study. Many former institutions were dismantled and new ones, based on Western blueprints, established in their place.

This led to a quick transformation of the society and also incited calls for more radical democratic reform, which the leaders of the emerging elites were just as unwilling to hear as their former opponents had been. Modernization, not Westernization was the reformers' goal, captured in the slogan of 'Japanese spirit, Western abilities'. Very rapid cultural change therefore provoked strong conservative counter-critique. The nationalist sentiment that had driven the opposition in the first place finally took over the entire political system in the 1930s. Japan moved towards a military regime which led the country to war, both on the continent, where China and South East Asia were attacked, and the Pacific basin, where the interests of Japan clashed with those of the United States. The war ended with Japan's surrender, after immeasurable damage had been done by the first-ever use of nuclear bombs, dropped by the United States on Hiroshima and Nagasaki on 6 and 9 August 1945, respectively.

After the war, Japan was occupied by the Allied powers, mainly by the United States. The country was quickly transformed from a former adversary into an ally against the rise of Asian communism. Economic aid and political reforms, largely wrought by enthusiastic American liberals, created the framework of a society that, on paper, was even more democratic and liberal than the United States themselves. In practice, it took about a decade of effort for the Japanese to restore their economy to pre-war levels. But it did not stop there: the economic miracle, while no longer fuelled by US military procurements, had started to turn the tables and Japanese exports to the West soon overgrew Japanese imports by a wide margin. Even though several economic crises have hit Japan since that time and the country has suffered major damage as a result of a devastating earthquake in Kōbe in 1995 and a series of disasters in the north-eastern area in 2011 (an earthquake followed by a tsunami and the meltdown of a nuclear reactor), it has stayed among the leading industrial nations of the world, while also becoming a global cultural presence.

A new paradigm. Japan was the first society in Asia that had to overcome the contradiction between the Western ways to speak about people's beliefs and views and its own mixed syncretic reality. This was a part of a much larger task to fit Western discourses to its own sociocultural reality. As it happens, it was in Japanese that many neologisms were coined that later successfully migrated into Chinese and beyond, words for new concepts derived from available linguistic material. The words for religion (*shūkyō*) and philosophy (*tetsugaku*) were among them. Their etymology indicates the nature of the problem clearly. *Shūkyō* literally means 'the teachings of schools' and indicated, first, that the Japanese perceived the focal point of Western-type religiosity not to be so much in its practice, but in things that people were supposed to believe, and second, that these teachings had a distinctly separate, sectarian character – they could not be true at the same time as other similar teachings. The encounters with Christianity indeed left that impression – even today, the Japanese Christians are among the few Japanese not to visit Shintō shrines to pay respects to the local deities, something that even fervently practising Buddhists have normally done. This also explains why many high-ranking Shintō priests argued that Shintō was not a religion, not a *shūkyō*, because it had no imposed teaching nor did it oppose what other worldviews had to say.

The case of philosophy was similar. The word means 'the science of clarity' and it was coined not as an equivalent, but the exact opposite of the 'pursuit of wisdom', declared to be the goal of a sage in the works of the Neo-Confucian Zhou Dunyi. The first proponents of philosophy only meant by it the Western rational discourses that should be used for the discussion of social and political problems instead of tradition-based ones. Later, when original Japanese philosophers appeared and united the Western way to philosophize with attitudes and concepts from the Buddhist tradition, clarity was not always preserved, but the discipline kept its name. So in the Japanese context, the question of whether philosophy is exclusively Western by nature has an additional overtone: not at all in denial of the intellectual character of the Japanese heritage, present-day Japanese still would not call it *tetsugaku*, because Western-type rationality was not among its concerns, moreover, the term was invented for Western thought and its emanations, so that is what it should be used for.

Import of Western ideas. The Meiji Restoration of 1868 introduced an era of transfiguration of all spheres of life, with worldviews most prominently in the foreground. In just a couple of decades, the Japanese society passed through processes that had taken several centuries in the West, but simply had to be completed in order for Japan to become a modern nation, able to stand alongside the Western powers as an equal. The nature of this process brought along important consequences. First, it could not possibly be organic: many new practices and principles were adopted automatically, without necessarily understanding their underlying logic. Just as in the case of Christian conversions a few centuries before, this made possible relapses easy and painless. Second, this process could not proceed as a spontaneous polylogue between interest groups equal in power. It was controlled by the state, and even though multiple ways of reasoning and development scripts were laid on the table, it was the authorities that decided which course to take. Thus, the objective of the proponents of every discourse was not so much to convince opponents, but the powers that be. Rallying popular support could contribute to that end, but also cause suspicion as to whether the discourse would serve the interests of the powerholders in the long run, or perhaps contribute to mass discontent.

Apart from particular new discourses promoted by Shintō and Christianity discussed above there were three main directions of sociopolitical thought active at the time. One was the movement for greater freedom, which combined different Western theories, not necessarily always aligning with anyone in particular. The second tendency was that of nationalist conservatism and cultural particularism. The third was the ruling discourse of the authorities, a combination of selected modern and Western elements carefully adjusted to the needs of the oligarchy in power. The common denominator of all these three trends was the building of a new Japan, and therefore an interest in and promotion of Western learning was shared by almost all. Due to the efforts of **Fukuzawa Yukichi** (1835–1901), an active propagandist of Western ideas and a scientific approach to solving the problems facing Japanese society, an official translation committee was organized that produced translations of many crucial Western works. For most Japanese, Fukuzawa is associated with his 'Encouragement to Learning' series, promoting education and self-cultivation. As a result of such activities, second-generation Meiji intellectuals, such as **Ueki Emori** (1857–1892), already had a pretty good grasp of Western ideas even without studying foreign languages or travelling abroad.

Ueki and **Nakae Chōmin** (1847–1901) were leaders of the People's Rights movement, which based its vision of society on the ideals of the French Revolution.

Nakae, in particular, spoke out for the equality of all people, including the poor and also national and cultural minorities such as the outcasts. During the debates about the future constitution, Ueki even drew up his own version in which the state sovereignty was supposed to be with the people, and the emperor would serve the state as a civil servant, not lead it as a sovereign.

Christianity and modernization. The Meiji Restoration introduced new interest in Christianity, which many Japanese modernizers saw as the reason behind Western technological superiority. Many students who were dispatched to the West converted, and quite a few did the same at home as well. Thus Japan had, for a time, a fairly large proportion of Christians among its influential intellectuals. Soon the atmosphere changed, however, and Christianity also lost its appeal as it was discovered that Western science had developed in opposition to rather than because of Christianity. The political atmosphere also grew less and less liberal. **Uchimura Kanzō** (1861–1930), probably the most original Christian thinker of Japan and the founder of the 'no-church' Christian movement, was even accused of *lèse-majesté* and harassed in the press because of his refusal to bow to the imperial seal attached to a framed document. With the advance of other modern ideologies the importance of Christianity as a religion gradually dwindled and many Christian churches currently operate only or primarily as marriage parlours.

Conservative reaction. Such developments were not quite what the Meiji leaders had in mind. In 1879 an imperial rescript on education was published that announced a conservative turn in the Japanese intellectual climate. The document was critical of Western ideas of freedom and proclaimed their incompatibility with the Japanese tradition. 'Ancestral teachings', including the promotion of Confucian values, were henceforth to be the ground on which Japanese thought rests.

This development was welcomed by many. Towards the end of the century the initial enthusiasm about Western ideas was gradually replaced with disappointment in the effect that these ideas were having on the society; superficial imports were threatening traditional practices where the latter could have continued to function quite well. After the war with China in 1894–1895, Japan recovered and with renewed confidence started to fashion itself as a regional power and potential leader to be respected by Western powers, not to be seen as their immature student anymore. In 1903, the artist-scholar **Okakura Kakuzō** (Tenshin, 1862–1913) published a book in English entitled *The Ideals of the East* where he claimed that there exists only one single Asian civilization of which Japan is currently the highest point of development. Other such declarations of cultural particularism also gained prominence around the turn of the century, notably the so-called *nihonjinron*, 'theory of Japanese-ness', or studies of how and why the

Japanese culture is unique among the cultures of the world, which has left a deep imprint on the Japanese identity discourses to this day.

---

nihonjinron   theories about the alleged uniqueness of the Japanese race and culture, frequently used to justify aggressive ideologies

---

Imperial Shintō. As an embodiment of Japanese specificity, the state adopted and transformed the creed of Shintō for its own purposes. The divine ancestry of the imperial house has been, for centuries, the cornerstone of the political dimension of Shintō. Indeed, the emperor had been the high priest of Shintō for a long time and to this day has to perform the ceremonial opening of the sowing and the harvesting seasons. This is a cult that also emerged as a result of the political project of the imperial clan to control the country and to instil the folk spiritual practices with an ideological element supporting these claims, for which a network of permanent shrines was created in the seventh century with ranked priests to disseminate these views. However, the argument of divinity as a support for political claims was first systematically presented only relatively late in a historical work written by one of the imperial generals in the fourteenth century. More prominently the topic started to feature in the discussions of the scholars of the eighteenth and nineteenth centuries, especially in the last decades of the Edo period. After the military government had opened several ports to alien ships and foreigners started to enter the country, one of the slogans of the opposition was to 'revere the emperor, expel the barbarians', and even though the latter part never happened, the former was the foundation on which the new regime was built. However, many Japanese at the time did not even know Japan had an emperor and considered the shōgun to be the only ruler of the country. This is why during the first years of the Meiji period the new emperor travelled widely around the country and was made visible in every possible way. Ambitious Shintō leaders sensed their chance. In the following years, the heterogeneous belief system and the local cults joined by a family resemblance were forged into a state ideology with rites of its own. One of the basic claims of State Shintō, as this ideology is commonly known, was that it was not, in fact, a religion, and therefore practitioners of other religions were not exempt from Shintō rituals. This was a problem for many newly converted Christians, for whom the idea of the emperor's divinity was preposterous and who accordingly refused to bow to his image.

Opposition to Buddhism. Throughout the centuries, Japanese Buddhism and Shintō had coexisted in a peaceful manner; an entanglement that affected both of them to the core. Alliances between temples and shrines had existed since the Nara period and successfully continued throughout history, and both worldviews complemented each other in a number of ways: without a doctrine, Shintō was incapable of responding to metaphysical questions, which Buddhism was comfortable with, while Buddhism in its pessimistic outlook was unable to provide a framework for joyous celebrations in the manner that Shintō did. Thus, for example, the rites of passage had been shared accordingly, Shintō taking care of births and weddings, while Buddhism was responsible for funerals.

In the early Meiji years, however, the nationalist spirit emboldened by the imperial restoration started to look for a 'pure' Shintō untainted by an association with Buddhism. A government decree requiring the 'separation of gods and Buddhas' provoked a massive anti-Buddhist movement that resulted in the tearing down or closing of thousands of temples, the destruction of their property, including artwork and books, and the forced return of priests to lay life, or their re-ordination into Shintō. The policy was abandoned soon enough as counterproductive to social order, but it damaged many Buddhist institutions, and caused them an immense loss of prestige. Shintō, in the meantime, was now perceived in the public eye as something different and independent from Buddhism, which had hitherto dominated the spiritual sphere.

The emperor and society. One specific theory imposed on the Japanese at the time was that of *kokutai*, or 'body politic', a term borrowed from old Chinese texts by Neo-Confucian scholars in the Edo period, and used to signify a specific Japanese relationship between the ruler and society. Combining ideas of different origin, it envisaged the whole society or, more precisely, the entirety of all properly Japanese people, to be embodied in the emperor, whose divine lineage linked them to the cosmic order and thereby granted him sovereignty to rule over them. The Japanese state was thus basically an extension of the emperor. This made it possible to require unquestioned loyalty from every Japanese citizen and, for example, during the war, turned self-sacrifice on behalf of him into a supreme form of self-realization. It is notable that the emperor most affected by this construct, Hirohito, made no secret of his preference for a constitutional monarchy, similar to the British system, and even interfered several times in the efforts of radicals to rebel against democratic institutions, although these were eventually also taken over by militarists. After World War II the ideology of State Shintō was discredited and has now survived only in marginal extreme right groups, although remnants of such thought still persist in institutions such as the Yasukuni Shrine. This large shrine next to the imperial palace in Tōkyō is a site for honouring the war dead (including war criminals), and visits by Japanese politicians to the shrine cause deserved outrage abroad, especially in the countries that suffered most under Japanese occupation.

kokutai **('body politic')**   a term used to signify an allegedly specifically Japanese relationship between the ruler and society

Political reactionism and leftist advances. The ideological emphasis on the divine character of the monarchy signified a gradual move away from Enlightenment values, which came to be reflected in political thought more widely. One of the most influential Japanese extreme right thinkers, **Kita Ikki** (1883–1937) actually started out as a socialist, but soon became disillusioned in that movement, which was not sufficiently 'pure of heart' for him. His social ideal still continued to reflect the comfort of a communal existence, with commonly owned property, the unity of the society manifested in the emperor. Kita's work was a source of inspiration for many right-wing young officers, who organized a series of coups in the late 1920s and 1930s. All of these failed, but nonetheless led to an increasing influence of the military in politics. But that was in accord with the Japanese political thinking of the time: for example, popular sentiment was against political parties having too much say in where the country should head, because it was felt that each of the parties only represented a segment of the society. The army, on the other hand, would defend everyone in spite of their social status or wealth, and therefore could also make the right political decisions. The idea of a society that defined its course after discussions between interest groups and not as a manifestation of a united collective will was still alien to many Japanese.

At the same time, there was also a strong leftist undercurrent in social thought. Japanese was the first language into which the collected works of Marx and Engels were translated, and many historians, in particular, were taken in by Marxist ideas, because these provided a comprehensive and universal logic for understanding the historical process. Thus the atmosphere at the end of the Meiji era is well summarized in two incidents: in 1911, 24 Marxists and anarchists were condemned to death on spurious evidence and some of them executed, allegedly because of a plot to assassinate the emperor. In 1912, when the emperor did die, General Nogi, a war hero, and his wife committed suicide in order to accompany their lord in death in the traditional manner.

The birth of Japanese feminism. The introduction of Western social and cultural practices quickly led to the questioning of the strictly hierarchical value system inherited from the Edo period. While the older generation may have considered modernization to be a set of technological and organizational elements that could be superimposed on the Japanese ethos without transforming it, the younger generation saw its liberating potential and started to emulate Western social practices, preferring it to 'backward' traditionalism.

Starting with the 1910s, the streets of Japanese cities became populated with people who identified themselves as *moga* and *mobo*, abbreviations for 'modan gaaru' (modern girl) and 'modan boi' (modern boy). Especially in the case of women, the difference with the previous generations was striking – *mogas* took jobs and earned money, and spent it as they pleased, they clothed in Western styles and spent time in cafés, smoking and drinking in public. In short, they behaved in a way that was considered shocking from the traditional point of view.

These steps towards the liberation of women were accompanied by the emergence of female voices in the intellectual arena. One of the first journals of Japanese feminist thought, *The Bluestocking* began to appear in 1910 under the editorship of **Hiratsuka Raichō** (1886–1971), a writer and activist, whose father had been a ranking member of the Meiji bureaucracy. Soon, a number of independent women authors gathered around the journal to attack the residual order and to demand the freedom for women to make their own life decisions. One issue of the journal was dedicated to the discussion of Ibsen's 'Doll House', for example, and another one – eventually banned by the authorities – discussed a married women's adulterous relationship. *The Bluestocking* also became a centre for social activities. It organized lectures, social gatherings, and, once, a collective excursion to the red-light district of Tōkyō for its authors. This caused a scandal and the journal was perceived as a threat by the authorities and was forced to close in 1915. But the movement already had a good start, and many other journals, including well-established literary journals without feminist sympathies, carried on the debate.

The evolution of Buddhist thought. When the initial hostility of Japanese modernizers towards Buddhism had subsided, Buddhists carefully started to reposition themselves, re-interpreting their teaching to bear on the problems important for the transforming society, as well as to integrate it into a broader worldview that would be compatible with Western science and philosophy. Another direction was to make Buddhism understandable to Westerners. Many of the most remarkable figures involved in such activities worked at the fringes of the Buddhist institution, not necessarily as ordained temple priests, but they often founded study groups, movements, and societies. Such people include Kiyozawa Manshi (1863–1903), a practitioner of Shin Buddhism, who studied philosophy at the University of Tōkyō under Ernest Fenollosa and wrote about the absolute Other power of Amida in the context of Hegel's philosophy. Another highly influential figure was **Inoue Enryō** (1858–1919), whose role in the emergence of modern Buddhist thought is second to none. Inoue had been ordained as a Shin Buddhist priest and was destined to inherit his father's temple, but was first sent to Tōkyō to study. He became interested in philosophy and started promoting a world philosophy that would integrate all varieties of philosophical thought into one whole. He considered the 'four sages', Buddha, Kongzi, Socrates, and Kant as the pillars of this system, and in his view their teachings complemented each other. In 1887, Inoue founded a small school for teaching philosophy that has now become Tōyō University (where philosophy is still a mandatory course for all students of all subjects). Inoue also established a publishing house and a journal for popularizing philosophy, and, beginning in 1904, he started the Philosophy Park, a public philosophically themed park to promote mental cultivation, over 52 000 square metres in size, with paths and various spots dedicated to philosophers and philosophical topics.

Other promoters of Buddhism were less inclined to take it merely as the base for the construction of a new, cosmopolitan worldview. **Suzuki Daisetsu** (1870–1966), a scholar and practitioner of Zen, became one of the foremost mediators of Japanese cultural traditions to the West. During his studies in Waseda and Tōkyō Universities he acquired a working knowledge of classical Chinese, Sanskrit, Pāli, and English, which he perfected later during an 11-year stay in the United States. Beside lecturing at universities in Japan and the United States, Suzuki collaborated with some Western authors and also on his own wrote a large number of essays and books, mostly about Rinzai Zen, and translated scriptural texts from classical Asian languages into Japanese and English. For many early Western enthusiasts of Zen, Suzuki's books were the primary gateway into the tradition. In more recent times, his work has been criticized by scholars of younger generations for their outdated approach, but his merit in making Zen better known in the West is unquestionable.

Nishida Kitarō and the Kyōto school. Although a neologism was coined for 'philosophy' soon after the Meiji Restoration, the word continued to refer only to Western thought until the emergence of **Nishida Kitarō** (1870–1945), the founder of what we now know as the Kyōto school of Japanese philosophy. Nishida's first work, *An Inquiry into the Good*, was published in 1910, and secured him a position at Kyōto University. He published regularly until his death just a few months before the end of World War II while leading a rather uneventful life, dedicated to thinking, reading, and writing, but with several personal tragedies – the death of his first wife and four of his eight children. The route of his daily walk in Kyōto is still known as 'the way of philosophy'.

Nishida was the first Japanese thinker to be well versed in both Western philosophy and the tradition of Japanese and Chinese thought, having studied Kant and Hegel at Tōkyō University and undergone Zen training in a temple in Kyōto. Nishida was also a lifelong friend of Suzuki Daisetsu, with whom he often discussed various aspects of the Zen teaching.

Ideas: from 'pure experience' to 'place'. Nishida's philosophy can be characterized as an attempt to express some fundamental insights and positions of the East Asian tradition in the idiom and according to the conventions of European continental thought. Following Hegel, Nishida spoke about a fundamental 'logic' that goes much deeper than rules for forming correct propositions, but unlike Hegel he based it on predicates, not subjects, because subjects would create an illusion of substantiality to things, which is not actually there. This he considered to be a crucial difference between East Asian and Western thinking. In a similar move, he adopted other Western concepts for his own use: for example, 'pure experience', a central concept in his first book, was borrowed from William James, but Nishida's description of it is more reminiscent of verbal accounts of Buddhist enlightenment, for example, the Unborn mind of Bankei or the enlightenment inherent and potentially actualized in everything one does, taught by Dōgen. The latter bears more than just a casual resemblance to him also in other respects. For example, a central concept of Nishida's philosophy is 'place' (*basho*), the unescapable site of existence where each particular is constantly redefined by all of the others it encounters. This is indeed reflected by his and his disciples' constant use of the word 'standpoint', indicating the impossibility of a neutral, unsituated gaze on reality. The idea of 'place' itself, however, seems to bear traces of Dōgen's idea of enlightenment – the true grasp of how reality works – as 'authentication by all things', which, for Dōgen, was the ongoing process of realizing one's self without essentializing it. This concept occupies a central place in Nishida's work from 'Place' (1927) until his last finished essay, 'The Logic of Place and the Religious Worldview'.

It would be wrong, however, to treat Nishida just as a translator of early Japanese philosophy into a Westernized idiom. In his thought, the two traditions are intertwined as equals and produce original results. Thus Nishida's concept of 'absolutely contradictory self-identity', something that characterizes each particular that is interacting with others in 'place', is a way to preserve both the Western need for absolutes and selfhood and the Asian ideas of impermanence and processuality of things. Another crucial synthesis of this kind is his 'absolute nothingness', the meeting point of Western absolute and Buddhist emptiness or the Zen 'No'. This is what Nishida considered the foundation of his thought, and the reason why he thought of it as religious. 'Religion' is indeed a central concept for all Kyōto school philosophers. However, this does not make their philosophy 'religious' in the sense that this word is usually understood. What we should not forget is that the Western idea of religion was itself relatively new in Japan during that time and, in attempting to erect a philosophical edifice conforming to Western standards but incorporating their own tradition, they were actually reinventing the 'religious', a central element in the Western tradition, for their own purposes.

Thus, for example, their speaking about morality having a religious foundation does not mean much more than saying it is not based in established conventions, but in principles outside the immediate social practice, a belief that an atheist might quite possibly share.

---

basho ('place')   a central term of Nishida's mature philosophy, the unescapable site of existence where each particular being is constantly redefined in interaction with all others

---

Nishida's disciples. The implications of the concept of 'absolute nothingness' led **Nishitani Keiji** (1900–1990), one of Nishida's leading disciples, to elaborate the differences between Kyōto school philosophy and Western nihilism, which he found incompatible with each other. The Kyōto school idea of nothingness, paradoxical as it may sound to Western minds, is positive and creative (as is the Buddhist idea of emptiness in its function of conceiving reality). As Nishitani writes, 'the being of things in emptiness is more truly real than what the reality of real being of things is usually taken to be (for instance, their substance)' – because it is independent of attributes, qualifications, and processed experience grafted on it by the observer, but simply real as it is, in its 'suchness'.

Another disciple of Nishida and his successor as a professor of philosophy in Kyōto, **Tanabe Hajime** (1885–1962), developed his own position concerning the relation of the individual and the totality of reality, prioritizing the intermediate level of 'species'. For Tanabe, the identity of any particular being was not a manifestation of its ineffable essence, but rather its distinction from all of its others, a self-affirmation through negation. Such a relation to others was, in his view, never direct, but always mediated through other relations. In his interpretation, absolute nothingness meant precisely the absence of absoluteness in being as such, not to speak of any particular being. Moreover, these particulars were not permanent or self-identical, but always in the process of becoming, and not in an abstract space, but in a concrete sociocultural setting. If philosophy was to help the individual to overcome the unescapable irrationality of this site of existence, it had to clear its relationship to what held it together and made that individual a part of it. This led Tanabe to develop a 'logic of species' or of 'the specific', which for him was not just a logical category, but an ontological reality. In his own sociocultural setting of an increasingly militarist Japan striving to redefine itself for a new international existence, he came to assign to the nation the role of this link that made a connection between an individual and the universal possible, thereby giving his philosophy up to those who wished to harness it to the war effort.

Quite a few scholars are of the opinion that the Kyōto school thinkers compromised themselves before and during the war by supporting the imperialist government. Nishida had written a popular treatise on 'The Problems of Japanese Culture', Nishitani had written an essay for and participated in a round table on 'Overcoming Modernity' in 1942, in which he endorsed the Japanese war effort as that of liberating colonized Asia from Western imperialism, following the official rhetoric of the times. During the war, these texts were actually criticized as only half-heartedly patriotic, but after the war they were denounced as collaboration with the militarist regime. Most likely, however, Nishida and Nishitani tried to support the moderate wing of the authorities against the radical militarists, while Tanabe was in fact sympathetic to aggressive nationalism. After the war, this led him to make a sharp turn in his philosophical thinking to develop a new system called 'metanoetics', a philosophy of repentance.

Watsuji Tetsurō (1889–1960). Watsuji Tetsurō was possibly the most important pre-war Japanese philosopher not directly associated with the Kyōto school, even though he lived and worked in Kyōto at the time when the school developed. He shared many of its concerns, such as the need to reinterpret the Japanese thought tradition in dialogue with Western philosophy. And yet he developed a distinct idiom of his own. Watsuji's groundbreaking work, *Climate and Culture* (1935), was written under the influence of Heidegger after his return from travels to Europe. In that book, he argued for a cultural determinism and particularism brought about by an environment comprising geographical, but also social and cultural, factors, thus sympathizing with *nihonjinron* theories. Watsuji had had a deep interest in the Japanese heritage all along: for years he had been writing *A Study of the History of the Japanese Spirit* (1925–1935) a part of which was dedicated to Dōgen's thought, introduced to a broader non-religious audience for the first time. In his later work, Watsuji turned to ethics and published a large three-volume study on the topic, again trying to develop a specifically Japanese version of the discipline based on the primacy of interpersonal relations to any form of individuality.

From post-war to postmodern. After World War II Japan faced the difficult task of coming to terms with its immediate past and the need to construct a viable intellectual framework for rebuilding the country from new but understandable premises. The administration of the Allied Powers had employed many democratically minded young and enthusiastic people who used their chance to contribute to a democratic society by influencing the Japanese legal system so that it became, in places, more democratic than that of the United States at the time, for example, concerning women's rights. This atmosphere created a prolific climate for different currents of thought, but, alarmed by the rise of communism both in Japan and elsewhere in Asia, the occupational government soon embarked on a 'reverse course', among other things, absolving some prominent wartime politicians and suppressing left-wing activities lest Japan became another North Korea. As a result, Japanese politics took on a stable and corporative character and the national identity of the Japanese people came to be bolstered by the powerful economic performance of the country. That, in turn, was credited in great part with traditional values and the specific character of Japanese society. For quite some time, a veritable ideological industry existed both in Japan and the United States that discussed the reasons why Japan was able to achieve so much so quickly and whether the development was sustainable in the long run. Such theory mixed anthropology, history of ideas, political science, and economics and some of it is still essential reading for anyone who intends to do business with the Japanese, even though the post-war economic system has at present evolved into something quite different.

Post-war Shintō. Although more than 90% of the Japanese now agree that Shintō is a part of their life, only very few, again mainly professionals, are committed to it with any ardour. Most people who practise Shintō share a certain vague set of ideas associated with it, but despite the efforts of some Shintō ideologues, such as Ueda Kenji (1927–2003), a professor at the Shintō university, Kokugakuin, these have not evolved into a systematic and detailed teaching known to and embraced by its adherents. Neither does it have a centralized institution: the Association of Shintō shrines, established in 1945, unites perhaps three quarters of all of them and even then it does not control their activities in a way that a Christian church would. Some separate shrines have developed and cultivated their own practices with teachings that are not necessarily derived from folk beliefs, but reflect the eclectic views of their scholarly priests, accumulated and transformed over generations, quite often within one family. In history, such teachings occasionally competed with each other, vying for political influence, but had virtually no meaning for the general populace. Some other local traditions and practices, however, have emerged as the result of a broader creative process.

In today's world, Shintō has maintained a role in celebratory rites of passage, while Buddhism is used in funerals. Children are introduced to their local Shintō shrine for the first time soon after birth, as well as around their third, fifth, and seventh birthdays, and some couples also prefer to be wed in the traditional Shintō manner, although the more spectacular Christian churches-cum-marriage-parlours are becoming more popular. Another sphere where Shintō is doing quite well is by providing spiritual assistance to the corporate sphere: new endeavours are often blessed by Shintō priests and collective releases from piled-up mental dirt are also offered. Some of the rituals take the form of a spectacle, with girls performing slow-movement dances to Japanese classical music. But most of the traffic in Shintō shrines still amounts to casual visits, which involve a token sacrifice of money, a greeting to the deity, and perhaps a silent formulation of one's hopes and wishes. Sales of amulets and protective tablets make up another source of revenue.

New religions. Japanese new religions are too many to be investigated in detail here, but their continuing success is an important trait of contemporary Japanese society. The first among them emerged in the nineteenth century as offshoots of Shintō, crystallizing around charismatic individuals, often women, who brought a salvific message to their immediate surroundings. These new religions combine Shintō lore and modified practices with teachings of their founders and sometimes also material adopted from other sources. Some of them have been economically successful: for example, the **Tenri** community has evolved into a complete municipality, with numerous believers outside its borders and even abroad. Other groups have sprouted from Buddhism. **Sōka Gakkai**, for instance, has grown out of a society of lay believers in Nichiren, and has also done remarkably well both at home and abroad. Sōka Gakkai also has had strong ties to the Kōmeitō party. Neither of these have, however, retained the aggressive militant stance of the original movement.

Usually, however, these religions combine material from the Japanese traditions and also Western sources to present an eclectic mix, most often centring on their founder or leader. Quite a few proselytize through weird postmodern entertainment, and others, such as the notorious doomsday cult **Aum Shinrikyō**, shelter their followers in closely knit communities, where they can be brainwashed not only into donating all their belongings to the cult, but also into committing aggressive and outright terrorist acts against the rest of society.

The usual reason given to the success of these movements in a rational, successful, and highly modernized society is the dissolution of traditional social structures, such as the extended family, and the growing numbers of singles living in urban environments, often engaged in work to which they feel no internal commitment. As opposed to traditional religious movements, which are mentally related to the past, the new religions offer spiritual experiences without such connotations, as well as a group with which one can solidarize. Sometimes the reasons for new followers to enrol in a community may be rather accidental, for example, finding a temple that can be reached on the person's subway line without transfer. It is therefore no wonder that some of these religions prove, on closer imagination, to be cynical commercial ventures rather than embodiments of honest spiritual quests.

Contemporary thought. As to the intellectual scene, the domination of the Kyōto school has been replaced by other, new authors, many of them explicitly left-wing, others influenced by such ideas by proxy, for example, through French theory, which has been popular since Japanese encounters with Sartre and Barthes to the introduction of postmodern thinkers and beyond. Most of this thought is less concerned with the Japanese and other Asian traditions than the Kyōto school, even in spite of common topics, and have often arrived at philosophical topics through other fields of intellectual inquiry. Thus, for example, Ōmori Shōzō (1921–1997) had a first degree in physics, and took up phenomenology and analytical philosophy afterwards, while Kimura Bin (b.1932) started as a psychiatrist. Both Ōmori and Kimura have theorized much about personhood and time, both important topics for the Japanese philosophical thought.

The Japanese themselves now make a sharp distinction between the field of 'philosophy', which means academic philosophy and is found only at universities, and the much more vague sphere of 'thought', which embraces some literary and some political theory, some cultural studies and some psychology, organized around a core of ideas that resemble Western critical theory, but are not limited to it. Some prominent authors of 'thought' are actually also academic philosophers, while others write for weekly magazines and can be seen on TV talk shows. Only some such authors, notably **Karatani Kōjin** (b.1941), a literary critic turned cultural and political theorist, have made it to the international scene, although quite a few would merit a much closer acquaintance not just as Japanese, but as world-class thinkers for our time.

4

Korea, Tibet, and South East Asia

This final chapter will present brief overviews of the other Asian civilizations that have been influenced by India, China, or both, during the course of their development. The summaries of their intellectual histories will be more cursory not because they would have less intellectual merit, but because empirically they have, up to now, been globally less influential and interest in them has been restricted mostly to the academic sphere and circles of enthusiasts. Some of these regions are still closed or not readily accessible for foreigners, but other countries have been developing at enormous speed and, in the case of South Korea, have already joined the ranks of global economic powers. It can only be hoped that the rich cultural traditions of all these countries will in due course also acquire a broader range of recognition than they presently have.

Korea

Periods of cultural history. Recorded beginnings of Korean history start with a foundation myth, according to which the son of the god of heaven descended to the Earth, married a she-bear and had a son, who founded the state of Korea towards the end of the third millennium BCE. A more reliable history of the country begins in the fourth century CE. At this time, the peninsula was divided between three more or less equally developed states, Goguryeo, Baekje, and Silla, and a number of smaller ones, which were quickly absorbed by the three dominant centres of power. The three states developed separately, and towards the end of the period started to battle each other for supremacy, until Silla, allied with Tang China, subdued its competitors and established itself as the sole ruler of the peninsula in 676. But when China wanted Silla to acknowledge its suzerainty, ties to the Tang court were loosened, even though cultural traffic remained intense

Asian Worldviews: Religions, Philosophies, Political Theories, First Edition. Rein Raud.
© 2021 John Wiley & Sons Ltd. Published 2021 by John Wiley & Sons Ltd.

both in the direction of China as well as to and from Japan, which depended heavily on Korean cultural imports during the initial period of its own state-building.

The Silla period was the first golden age of Korean culture. Buddhism became the dominant worldview, arts flourished, and literature and history-writing took root. The cultural apex of Silla in the eighth century was followed by a period of decline and disintegration, and during the last part of Silla rule the country was divided between different contenders and warlords. The next unification was accomplished in 935 by the state of Goryeo, which envisaged itself both as the heir of the ancient Goguryeo kingdom and the legitimate successor of Silla. Government was centralized and reorganized on a meritocratic basis, which included the introduction of civil service examinations following the Chinese model. Buddhism, however, was the main official worldview that enjoyed the support of the court – one of the most notable testimonies to this was the royal commission of printing woodblocks of the Buddhist canon, now known as the Tripitaka Koreana, the oldest comprehensive edition of the scriptures, containing more than 52 million characters of text in total. Korean 'high' culture of the time reflected significant influences from China in both form and spirit, which were superimposed on elements preserved from the native vernacular heritage. This was also a time of technological development – for example, movable printing type was developed and implemented for the printing of books already in 1234.

Nominally, the Goryeo period lasted until 1392. But, in the twelfth century, Goryeo kings had to relinquish real political power to military leaders. The dynasty was finally overturned by the Mongol invasion in the thirteenth century, which Korea was unable to repel in spite of vigorous resistance. Korean rulers became vassals of the Yuan empire until 1356. But as soon as the Yuan dynasty started to lose control of China, a rebellion against the Mongols also erupted in Korea. When the new Chinese dynasty of Ming again sought to establish its power over the peninsula, a Korean general from the house of Yi took matters into his own hands and finally ascended the throne as the first king of a new dynasty ruling over a country that he now called Joseon.

The Joseon period was the longest in Korean history and lasted from 1392 until 1910. The first centuries of this era were characterized by a cultural renaissance, on the one hand – this included the invention of the Korean script and the consequent rise of national culture – and the imposition of a strict hierarchical order on Korean society, on the other. The Neo-Confucian doctrines of the Zhu Xi school were established as the state-sponsored orthodox worldview, and criticism of these was discouraged, to the extent that even the reading of the works of Chinese Neo-Confucians not strictly in line with Zhu Xi was condemned. Nonetheless, within the boundaries of the orthodoxy, quite vigorous philosophical debates went on. Buddhism, however, lost its official support altogether, although it continued to be practised by the people and also sponsored by some individual members of the elite.

A Japanese effort to conquer Korea at the end of the sixteenth century was successfully repelled with the help of Ming China, but from the mid-seventeenth century, Joseon kings had to pay tribute to the Manchu rulers of the Qing dynasty, with which Korea maintained carefully controlled cultural contacts. Scholars often travelled to Beijing, and these trips served as the main conduit of information from the outside world. Otherwise, Korea was content not to participate in much international traffic until the end of the nineteenth century, when it became evident that the political system of East Asia is going to change, and Korea would not remain untouched by the process. Another drive for change originated in the political factionalism and ongoing competition for domination in the Joseon court.

The last Joseon king undertook some efforts to open the country and modernize it after the Japanese model without relinquishing its cultural heritage. These attempts were not very efficient, but nevertheless elicited the wrath of conservatives. Korea was soon in turmoil, and targeted by other regional players, that is, China, Russia, and Japan, as well as Western powers that were asserting their presence in East Asia. In 1905, Korea became a protectorate of Japan and officially annexed as a colony in 1910. After the defeat of Japan in World War II, the victorious allies soon turned against each other and their visions for the future of Korea had nothing in common. The division of Korea into the Soviet-occupied North and US-occupied South resulted in the emergence of two entirely different countries. These sought to subdue each other, with the help of their former occupiers, during the Korean war of 1950–1953, which was, in fact, a proxy war between the Soviet Union (USSR) and the United States, which ended with a stalemate that has continued to this day. There is hardly any other place on Earth were societies of people who speak the same language and share the same cultural heritage differ from each other so completely as in the totalitarian regime of North Korea and the capitalist South Korea.

Folk religion and shamanism. The tradition of shamanism continues to be alive and well in contemporary South Korea, and its roots go back to the times of the emergence of Korean statehood. However, unlike the Dao creed in China or Shintō in Japan, it never organized itself into a recognized institution, and holders of power also preferred to support the imported ideologies of Ru and Buddhism. The only attempts to organize shamanism were undertaken by the state in order to control and supervise it, not to help it to proliferate. Even though representatives of the elites may have consulted shamans on occasion (there was even a royal shaman at the beginning of the Joseon period), in the course of the rise of the Neo-Confucian orthodoxy they were considered increasingly suspicious and potentially subversive, while commoners blended their faith in shamanistic practices seamlessly with whatever other worldview they claimed to profess.

The core assumptions of Korean shamanism were reminiscent of most other Asian spirit beliefs (as well as shamanistic creeds elsewhere): the world is inhabited by spirits of various origin, such as local and ancestral ones, and communion with them is possible through the mediation of spiritual professionals. In the Korean tradition, again similarly to other East Asian shamanisms, these were often women. Evidence from the Joseon period suggests that in regular households, responsibility for rituals was differentiated by gender. Men were responsible for rituals acknowledged by the Neo-Confucian orthodoxy, such as ancestor worship, while women had to take care of domestic spirits, which lived in every house. The most important of these spirits was supposed to live behind the house and receive offerings of food on a regular basis, while lesser spirits, each with their own proper name, dwelled in the kitchen, beams, and rooms and there was even a separate guardian, a young girl, for the toilet. Korean folk religion also has a broader view of spiritual space extending beyond the household, but sacred sites are only demarcated by poles or piles of stones and not specific architectural structures.

The services of shamans as healers and diviners were often sought by the common people. Most shamans were, as said, women, and their status did not preclude them from having a regular life and a family. Shamans can perform different roles: the best known are those who invite spirits to descend into them during a ceremony and can then speak on their behalf, but there are also fortune tellers who use a combination of divination techniques to communicate with spirits and those who can perform spirit-appeasing techniques on behalf of their community without going into a trance.

At present, Korean shamanism has acquired a strong commercial dimension, and trances are more often staged for ticket-buying customers than for clients in need of spiritual consultation or consolation. The market is vibrant and also includes sales of lucky charms and magic objects with different purposes. It should be stressed, however, that commercial shamanism is not the only surviving form of the creed in urban settings, and shamans also participate in ceremonies dedicated to the spirits of those who have died in national tragedies or suffered unjustly.

Korean Buddhism. Buddhism arrived in Korea soon after its introduction to China, and became the dominant state-sponsored worldview first in Baekje and Goguryeo, and was later also adopted by Silla, eclipsing the Ru tradition, which continued to control the educational system. The Buddhist institution, complete with architectural structures, hierarchically ordered priesthood and a scriptural tradition, made a strong impression on Korean aristocrats, strengthened further by reports of miraculous healing performed by Buddhist monks. At the time, Buddhism was most likely interpreted as a superior form of spirit-appeasing techniques, and its own doctrines were largely ignored by most of the people, including those who endorsed it. The situation changed in the seventh century. Monks began to travel to

China in search of a more authentic teaching, and several efforts were undertaken to unite the multiplicity of doctrines into one whole. **Uisang** (625–702) studied in China (together with Fazang) the teachings of the Huayan school, which he brought back to Korea as Hwaeom and considered a suitable base for uniting all other schools of thought. His scholarly approach was countered by his close friend **Wonhyo** (617–686), who was also a prolific writer and the author of commentaries on many *sūtras*, but at the same time a popularizer of Buddhist teachings for broader audiences. Wonhyo never left Korea, because he is supposed to have experienced enlightenment on his way to China. After discovering on a morning that he had drunk water during the night from a human skull, he realized that enjoyment and adversity to things are merely the product of our mind, and there is no need to look outside it for an understanding of how it works. He, too, was looking for a unified doctrine, but did not associate it with any of the existing Chinese (or Indian) schools.

These early efforts to systematize Buddhism were soon superseded by the school of **Seon**, which is the Korean equivalent of Chan/Zen. It was first introduced to Korea in the seventh century, but gained more currency sometime later, especially due to the efforts of **Jinul** (1158–1210), one of the most influential Korean Buddhist personalities in history.

Jinul is notable not only as an institutional figure, but also for his original philosophical contribution to Seon thought. In Jinul's view, concentration, or achieving a calm state of mind through the practice of meditation, and wisdom, or a penetrating insight into the nature of things, which is accompanied by a mental alertness to the world, are not two complementary aspects of the mind to be pursued separately. For him, they are identical, and together form the Mind as such, which is again not simply shared between sentient beings and the Buddha – as the doctrine of Buddha-nature would lead us believe – but directly identical with the Buddha, so that there is no Buddha separate from this Mind nor any mind outside the Buddha. The difference between the Buddha and the individual mind of a sentient being is not objective, but only arises due to the contamination of the latter in perception.

For the explication of this scheme, Jinul borrows the binary unity expressed by two terms often discussed in Chinese thought and introduced to Korean Buddhist thought by Wonhyo. These are 'substance' and 'function'. Jinul casts the concentration of the calm Mind as the substance of both empirical and mental reality, while wisdom represents how the alert Mind is 'functionally' aware of all things. Through establishing the presence of this Mind at the core of the psyche, the follower is expected to realize enlightenment as the result of 'practice without practice', or 'cutting off [delusions] without cutting off' – the radical monism of Jinul rejects any reification of 'practice', or 'delusions' as the object of one's striving.

As a result of Jinul's activities, the Seon school became the leading form of Buddhism in Korea, and other forms of practice, such as Pure Land style invocations of the name of the Buddha, were incorporated into it. At the same time, however, the fortunes of Buddhism gradually went into decline. Little by little, Neo-Confucian Joseon state ideologues came to picture Buddhism as a quietist nihilism indifferent to the plight of the populace and blamed it for the decline of society. This was soon followed by administrative discrimination, for example, Buddhist monks and nuns were prohibited from entering the capital city. Buddhism had to retreat to the margins of society. While monasteries continued to exist, they were restricted to remote, mountainous areas and lost contact with the people. This situation continued until the advent of modernity.

Neo-Confucian orthodoxy. Up until modern times, Koreans have taken great pride in their role as the upholders of the Ru tradition in the form of Neo-Confucian orthodoxy. During the early periods, arguments taken from Ru sources were used for elaborating administrative policies, but the teaching as a whole remained in the background. With the rise of the Joseon state, however, Neo-Confucian thought became the orthodoxy and the whole society was gradually remodelled according to its norms. Some of the traditional folk religious practices, such as the veneration of ancestral spirits, were recast in a Neo-Confucian mould, others marginalized.

When the new teaching had confidently established itself, it started to impose strict hierarchical structures on the social fabric which resulted, among other things, in a drastic deterioration of the position of women. In order to fit into their preordained roles of obedient daughters and wives, women were gradually deprived of their rights to do many things, from horseback riding to inheriting property. They had no right to initiate divorce proceedings, while men were able to leave them for seven reasons, such as display of jealousy, excessive talking, disobedience to the husband's parents, or the inability to produce a male heir. Widows did not have the right to remarry.

Philosophically, the orthodoxy included only the teaching of Zhu Xi and his heirs, whose ideas could not be criticized and reading Wang Yangming, for example, was possible only in private. Suggestions that Zhu Xi's work could be elaborated upon or developed in some way would be severely censored. However, the need to maintain this strict orthodoxy invited a fairly lively debate on issues that were considered open to discussion. The sixteenth century produced two of the most important Korean Neo-Confucian thinkers, **Toegye** (Yi Hwang, 1501–1570) and **Yulgok** (Yi I, 1536–1584). Their debate concerned the primacy of *li* and *qi*, 'principle' and 'basic stuff' – Toegye ascribed primacy to the former, Yulgok to the latter. They also disagreed about the status of human nature, even though they both followed, as orthodox Neo-Confucians, Mengzi's thesis that it is essentially good. The problem was rather in how the 'seven feelings' (an enumeration taken from *The Book of Rites*) were related to the 'four sprouts' that Mengzi had defined as the source of virtuous behaviour. Feelings were not always positive, as the list also included hate, fear, and anger, but the sprouts had to be good – but how did they then relate to each other? Toegye's answer was that the sprouts were the manifestations of *li*, while the feelings arose from the way *qi* was organized. Yulgok, in contrast, argued that they could not have a different origin, because this would imply that good and evil had separate objectively existing foundations, which was not permissible.

During the Joseon rule, it was this kind of debate that occupied the minds of most scholars in the Neo-Confucian tradition, who always had to walk the line lest they appear to be in contradiction with the orthodoxy.

Silhak. The final centuries of Joseon rule saw the emergence of another school within the Neo-Confucian tradition that is called **Silhak**, or 'practical learning'. This label comprises a broad range of writings on various topics, from the administration of agriculture to education, finance, and military affairs. The emergence of Silhak is sometimes related to the appearance of a large number of private academies, which were associated with various political factions and served as think-tanks and centres of learning. There were reportedly hundreds of such institutions in Korea in the eighteenth century, and the factional competition of their sponsors encouraged the scholars of these academies to speak up on social issues.

Silhak writers did not break with the orthodoxy, but raised concerns about its current application to social affairs. Some scholars consider them to be the first harbingers of modernity, although they endorsed the basic foundations of traditional Korean society, such as the naturality of hierarchies and the corresponding essential inequality of people. They did have more pronounced characteristics of nationalism, however, concentrating on Korean society as their only relevant topic of investigation and object of criticism.

Silhak authors had broad interests and the visions they expressed were systematic. Establishing social justice was one of their primary concerns, even though solutions that they proposed to current problems were often presented as the return to long-forgotten practices of ancient times (such as the model of land distribution of the Tang dynasty, for example). Some of them, in particular **Dasan** (Jeong Yakyong, 1762–1836), went as far as to suggest that the world was changing to the extent that ways to deal with the problems of the present were not always to be found in the past. Dasan was interested in Western science and medicine as well as Japanese scholarship, which he considered methodologically superior in its habit of reading ancient sources critically. He had also studied Christian texts and it has even been claimed that he converted to Christianity together with his two brothers.

Korean Christianity. Korea is one of the few countries in Asia in which Christianity has had a considerable degree of success. But this did not happen quickly – after first contacts with Christianity, Koreans were not impressed and considered the faith to represent a significantly lower level of civilization, as it had selfish values and insisted that its followers accept nonsensical superstitions and miracle stories on faith. The first real success of Christianity came when it attracted scholarly interest in conjunction with Western science, and Korean intellectuals who travelled to China on fact-finding trips started to make it a habit to visit the Jesuit missionary stations there as well. Initially, it was believed that Christianity and Neo-Confucianism were compatible with each other and that Christian doctrines could even invigorate the Neo-Confucian teachings and introduce new methods of achieving sagehood. Some Korean scholars converted to Catholicism on the basis of the texts they read, and even baptized themselves, as there were no priests available in Korea. The Korean rulers did not take this well and in 1785 Christianity, or 'Western learning' (Seohak), as it was now known, became outlawed as a heresy. Persecutions followed suit, with many converts killed. For quite some time, Christianity lost its position.

The second wave of Christianity started in the late nineteenth century with the arrival of mainly anglophone Protestant missionaries. Unlike the Catholics, they were not met with hostility, as they offered their services to the government in the fields of medicine and education. The first Western-type hospital of Korea was opened in 1885, two schools, one for boys, one for girls, were established soon after. Initially, this did not result in many actual conversions, but after the Japanese conquest the situation changed. Protestants supported Korean nationalism and many leaders of the anti-Japanese movement were practising Protestants. They also organized the translation of Christian scriptures into Korean and their services were conducted in Korean as well, which brought their faith closer to the population. The tendency continued after World War II, and the growth of the Protestant community in South Korea has been such that various Protestant denominations currently make up around 20% of the entire population.

Donghak. One of the most significant events in the early modern intellectual history of Korea occurred in 1860, when a poor scholar called Choe Je-u (1824–1864) had a religious vision in which he was visited by a god who told him that he should embark on a mission to save humanity. The vision inspired him to establish a new religious movement called **Donghak** ('Eastern learning'). This step subsequently led first to the biggest peasant rebellion in Korean history and later on contributed to the establishment of a large number of new religions, many of which occupy a prominent position in Korean spirituality to this day.

Donghak borrowed freely from the Ru tradition as well as Christianity, the shamanistic folk beliefs as well as Buddhism. It was monotheistic (and the use of the Catholic word for 'god' eventually led Choe into trouble with the authorities), but advocated traditional Ru virtues, and also taught a doctrine of divinity residing in every human heart not unlike the idea of the Buddha-nature. In its practical form, Donghak employed practices similar to the folk religion, such as collective singing and dancing and initiation rituals on sacred mountaintops. The government, which had been suspicious of the movement from the beginning, finally decided that it was heterodox, and Choe was apprehended and executed in 1864. However, this did not crush the movement, which continued under his successors and, if anything, the martyrdom of its founder only strengthened its appeal.

Attracting more and more peasants who were dissatisfied with their lot and opposed to the rampant corruption of the government, Donghak also developed a political teaching of 'great transformation', an event to occur in the foreseeable, yet indeterminate future, which would usher in a new era of happiness and prosperity. This gradually led to the maturation of revolutionary moods. Donghak was organized as a hierarchy of groups: small local cells had a leader, several local leaders formed a next-level cell, which elected its own leader and finally there were assemblies to overview larger territories. One of these assemblies, defying the other, decided to lead the faithful into an armed struggle against the government. The Donghak rebellion erupted in 1894 and soon overturned the local authorities in most of south-west Korea. At the same time, Japanese troops occupied Seoul and started to suppress the rebellion. Discord arose also in the ranks of Donghak followers. The northern assembly correctly feared that the rebellious activities would result in the suppression of the entire movement, so they also attacked the army of the rebels in order to demonstrate their loyalty to the powers. The rebellion was crushed in 1895, its leaders were executed, and the third head of the Donghak had to flee to Japan. When the Japanese protectorate was established, some of the previous Donghak leaders supported it, which gave them room for operation, but diminished their authority in the eyes of most Koreans. The exiled leader of Donghak was also dissatisfied with the situation, and reorganized the movement into a modern religious community of **Cheondogyo**, 'The Teaching of the Heavenly Way', which severed its ties with the folk religion and presented itself as a Korean alternative to Christianity, that is, a teaching compatible with modernization and nation-building according to Western models.

The proliferation of new religious movements. Another inheritor of the millenarian ideas of Donghak was Gang Ilsun (1871–1909), also known by his religious name of Jeungsan, the leader of another, more peaceful spiritual movement that has spawned a multitude of new religions in contemporary Korea. Born and raised very near the epicentre of the Donghak rebellion, Jeungsan reportedly had scholarly inclinations since childhood and studied different disciplines,[1] and was at the same time also concerned with the deepening social chaos. He anticipated the defeat of the Donghak, however, and formed a group of his own which did not join the rebellion. Some time after the defeat of Donghak, Jeungsan revealed to his followers that he was, in fact, the incarnation of the supreme god that had presented himself in the vision of Choe Je-u, who was now cast in the role of his predecessor. Jeungsan was able to attract a large number of previous Donghak followers and also made new converts. He continued to be politically careful under Japanese rule and advocated reconciliation with it to his followers, which did not dissuade the authorities from arresting him on suspicion of subversive activities.

The many contemporary claimants of Jeungsan's heritage stress different aspects of his teaching. Some stress the eschatological predictions of the 'great transformation', which he inherited from Donghak, others rely mainly on the ethical core, which is almost indistinguishable from old Ru virtues. Some Jeungsanist movements are also active overseas, but there they are overshadowed by the **Unification Church**, another aggressive new religion founded by Sun Myong Moon (1920–2012). Moon came from a Christian family in north-west Korea and supposedly had a vision in his teens, when Jesus appeared to him and explained that the good work on Earth is still unfinished and must be completed by Moon. At first Moon declined, and in 1939 went to study engineering instead. He continued to be religiously active as well as to participate in the Korean independence movement. After the Japanese defeat he was first active in North Korea, but was arrested and tortured, and sent to a labour camp, from which he was liberated during the Korean war. He then moved to South Korea and in 1954 officially launched his movement, based on his own conservative and idiosyncratic interpretations of the Bible and a strong promotion of his idea of family values. In 1971, Moon moved to the United States, where he had gathered a large following. Moon also engaged in various businesses and had been convicted of tax fraud, which his supporters claim to be religious persecution. His movement has now spread to more than 100 countries and is perhaps best known to the public by his mass weddings called 'blessings', where hundreds if not thousands of couples are joined together in marriage by a priest of the Unification Church. According to its doctrines, marriage conducted in this way is eternal and only couples who have been 'blessed' will be able to enter paradise after resurrection.

The religious revival in post-war South Korea has also affected Buddhism, and new forms of it have emerged. In particular, **Won** Buddhism, founded in the early twentieth century by Pak Chungbin (1891–1943), has gathered support as a

Buddhist response to the challenges of modernity. Won Buddhism's doctrines are intellectual and do not stress the authority of Buddhas as transcendent entities with capacities to affect the followers' lives (in the Mahāyāna tradition of 'skilful means'), but advocate a simplified version of philosophical Buddhism, without complex rituals and imagery, directed to maintain a balanced and mindful relationship with one's (presumably modern) living environment. Won followers are not supposed to engage in long sessions of meditation practice, but encouraged to maintain an alert state of mind, coupled with an awareness of the 'fourfold debt' (to one's parents, to other people, to nature, and to society), at all times. Meditation exercises are only recommended as a helpful technique for those who have trouble with these 'debts'. Another method to support one's alertness is to chant the name of the Buddha, but followers are advised that they are indeed only calling out to their own Buddha-nature and not to an external authority, who would take them to a Pure Land.

North Korea: juche. Quite a different picture is presented by the society of North Korea. Initially, the communist regime of **Kim Il-sung** (1912–1994), a former guerrilla fighter picked by the Soviet Union to be their stooge, was committed to the ideological foundations of his two supporters, China and the Soviet Union. Gradually, however, his views diverged from both Leninism-Stalinism and Maoism. Under the leadership of his son **Kim Jong-il** (1941–2011) a very particular ideology called **juche** (literally 'subject', used in the sense of self-reliance) has been installed as the state orthodoxy. Juche still emphasizes revolutionary ideals, but it officially severed its connections to Marxism-Leninism in 1992, when a reference to these was deleted from the North Korean constitution. An earlier version of juche was also called 'Kimilsungism' in reference to the ideas of the founding father of the regime.

Juche has thus changed quite a lot over the years. It started out as a local version of communist ideology, complemented with the principles of independence in politics, self-reliance in economics, and self-defence in the military sphere. Independence meant, among other things, that when the split between China and the USSR occurred, North Korea kept amicable relations with both of them. One further principle was added after the death of Mao and the ascension of the faction of Deng to power in China, and that was the right of the leader to choose his successor. This was meant to avoid both the dangers posed by an internal power struggle and the 'lapse' of the country from its revolutionary course. In practice, this has made the supreme power of North Korea a hereditary affair.

Kim Jong-il has further developed the juche theory into a doctrine that sees the North Korean state as a sociopolitical organism consisting of three concentric circles forming a sharp conus: the leader, who represents the inner core and the highest top, is surrounded by the party, which is in turn surrounded by 'masses'.

None of the three can function without the others. Juche does not posit the privileged position of a working class, which is simply a part of the 'masses', and the party assumes the role of the proletariat in the Korean version of the Leninist scheme of proletarian dictatorship. Juche also stresses its particular 'humanism', placing human beings in the centre of the universal edifice (much as traditional Chinese philosophy has done most of the time) and crediting them with the three attributes of independence, creativity, and consciousness. 'Independence', in this case, means the capacity to do without support from others, which animals are supposed to lack. 'Creativity' is interpreted in line with Mao's theory of voluntarism and the ability to change the world according to one's wishes. 'Consciousness', however, is not the mind of the individual, but something like a revolutionary Buddha-nature, or the capacity to develop an internal attitude that is fully concordant with the official ideology. This was to be achieved through education and training, in other words, brainwashing.

The ideology of contemporary North Korea has thus very little in common with its Marxist roots. It is nationalist, isolationist, and unabashedly totalitarian, and has managed to create the only dynasty of supreme rulers of a communist country in history. In practice, it has inflicted suffering on several generations of the people of North Korea, and most importantly deprived their society of the capacity to renovate itself, should history even provide the chance.

Tibet

The beginnings of statehood. The kingdom of Tibet emerged in the seventh century when various territories, primarily in south-central Tibet, were united under the rule of a chieftain who claimed divine descent. Under the strong rule of king **Songtsen Gampo** (d.649?), Tibet developed and evolved into an empire that threatened China and controlled Nepal and the small city-states on the Silk Road. The moving centres of power were replaced by more permanent ones among which Lhasa gradually grew into prominence as a thriving cultural centre. Gradually, the lifestyle of Tibetan aristocratic clans started to imitate that of their Chinese and Indian peers. Songtsen Gampo also sponsored the creation of a writing system, credited to the legendary figure of **Thonmi Sambhota**, who supposedly travelled to India and mastered a number of writing systems on which the Tibetan script was based. This elevated the classical Tibetan language to the status of lingua franca used between peoples of various origins. Songtsen Gampo is also supposed to have issued a code of laws, which further contributed to the development of his empire into a centrally administrated polity. At the same time, as the result of hosting exiled kings and forging alliances through royal marriages, the first Buddhist temples were built in Lhasa, but any interest in the new faith was still limited to the court, so the attribution of the adoption of Buddhism to Songtsen Gampo is an exaggeration.

Bön. The Tibetan native religion is called **Bön** (Bon), as it came to be known after the introduction of Buddhism and its restructuration under its influence. The source of Bön was a system of beliefs that resembled other Asian folk religions and combined shamanism, spirit worship, and divination practices, and was the predominant worldview of most Tibetans until the arrival of Buddhism. Later Bön started to claim that it was also a long-standing spiritual tradition, not unlike Buddhism in its teachings and goals, and, moreover, that it had been imported to Tibet earlier from the north-west. In reality, the scriptures on which such claims are based come from a much later time and have been compiled under the influence of an overwhelmingly Buddhist scholarly culture.

The term Bön also applied to Tibetan religious professionals, while initially the creed itself was just a part of common knowledge and did not need a specific designation. The responsibilities of the Bön included elaborate funeral practices and the erection of impressive burial mounds for the aristocrats, complete with anything their inhabitant would need in their afterlife. Traditionally, when a leader would die, his loyal servants would have to accompany him in death, but at some point this custom was changed into transforming the status of those people into living dead, who dwelled in the tombs, accepted the offerings brought to the dead on their behalf, and subsisted on these offerings as well as on what they could gather or kill in the cemetery area. Over the next centuries, Bön would retreat before Buddhism, but survive as a folk religion, adopt a number of institutional features and teachings from Buddhist models, and develop its own scriptures and monasteries. It still exists as a minority faith in present-day Tibet.

The introduction of Buddhism. In the eighth century, the empire of Tibet continued to be a major political player in inner Asia, which attracted the interest of Buddhist missionaries. This period saw the first large-scale conversion efforts. The first, carried out under the sponsorship of a Chinese princess married to the Tibetan king, was initially successful and gathered a significant Buddhist community in Lhasa, but failed when a plague decimated the population, including the queen herself, and the remaining Buddhists were expelled. **Padmasambhava**, an Indian monk, is credited with more success by the tradition, even though little is reliably known about his life. He is nonetheless revered as the 'precious teacher' of the Tibetan people and also considered to be the person to have introduced Indian esoteric Buddhism to Tibet.

Initially, however, it was unclear whether Tibet would adopt an Indian or a Chinese form of Buddhism. Cultural traffic was strong with both countries and adherents of the Indian, gradual way towards enlightenment competed with the supporters of the Chinese, sudden teaching of Chan. Towards the end of the eighth century, the first Buddhist king of Tibet, Tri Songdetsen, decided to settle the matter and in or around 793, a public dispute was organized between the representatives of the two parties, known as the **Samye debate**. During this event, Kamalashīla, an Indian scholar of the Madhyamaka school from Nālandā, debated Moheyan, a Chinese Chan monk, and, as later sources claim, ultimately Kamalashīla's arguments seemed more convincing to the Tibetan king, so that the Indian version of Buddhism became dominant in Tibet after this event.

To ensure the correctness of the Tibetan translations of Buddhist texts from Sanskrit, an extraordinary linguistic reform was undertaken in Tibet in the early ninth century, which established one-to-one correspondence between Tibetan and Sanskrit vocabulary, and also adopted some grammatical conventions to reflect Sanskrit usage. As a result of this reform, Tibetan translations of Sanskrit texts are amazingly precise and offer valuable information on the history of Buddhist thought. A large number of texts, which did not survive the decline of Buddhism in India, are available today as a result of these Tibetan translations as well as original Indian manuscripts preserved in the libraries of Tibetan monasteries.

The character of Tibetan Buddhism. Tibetan Buddhist traditions view spiritual advancement of an individual being as a long path that is supposed to take multiple lifetimes and to proceed according to certain stages, which allows the teaching to take multiple forms appropriate to the level of advancement of the people who practise them. On the lower end, Buddhism blends seamlessly with spirit beliefs in a this-worldly mix and emphasizes virtuous behaviour and the cultivation of compassion as the means to advance to a higher level. The opposite pole of this axis consists in esoteric practices for a select and initiated few, on the one hand, and sophisticated philosophical discussions, on the other hand. In the Western world, general interest in Tibetan Buddhism has been directed towards the esoteric teachings, which indeed have an important position in all monastic lineages, however, the practice of the majority of Tibetan monastics is much more conventional. Regular Buddhist training includes mostly initial techniques of meditation, elementary knowledge of scriptures, as well as a few other subjects necessary for the observation of ritual duties and, if necessary, for the administration of spiritual services and guidance to the lay population. Only a small number of monks advance from the lower ranks to centres of learning where doctrinal debate and the study of scriptures continue on a higher level, and fewer still go through the initiation procedures necessary for accessing the esoteric teachings.

One specific characteristic of Tibetan Buddhist meditation (from its earlier stages on) is its use of visualization exercises. Followers are expected to train their minds to such levels of concentration that they would ideally be able to produce in their inner vision images of deities that are comparable in their intensity to natural perception. Elementary visualization exercises include, for example, the imagining of each inhalation as black smoke containing the grief and suffering of all sentient beings, while each exhalation is a radiantly shining extension of one's love and compassion for all the sentient beings of the universe. Much more complicated techniques are involved with tantric practice, during which the followers visualize themselves as deities and thereby accumulate the mental energy and powers traditionally attributed to these.

Tantric practices also rely on another distinctive feature of Tibetan Buddhism, the extremely strong bond between teacher (lama) and disciple. The teacher needs to be given absolute trust and loyalty, and a transgression against one's teacher is among the biggest offences a person can commit. This accounts for the social role and status of Tibetan lamas, who collectively form the most efficient network of authority in Tibetan society.

Further developments. During the eighth and ninth centuries, Tibet had attained the status of a regional power comparable to that of China, and even briefly forced the Chinese to recognize their superiority. However, this situation changed quickly after a Tibetan king had reportedly initiated a persecution of Buddhism and was killed by a monk. According to the tradition, this was done as an act of mercy, in order to prevent the ruler from accumulating more bad karma. The Tibetan kingdom nonetheless soon disintegrated into independent areas, some of them forging alliances with external powers to maintain their distance from the rulers of Lhasa. A new centralized government strong enough to control the country appeared only when Mongols started to conquer Tibet in the thirteenth century. Several monastic lineages attempted to use this occasion for establishing themselves as the rulers of Tibet with Mongol help. One of the leading monasteries succeeded in this effort: the monk they sent to negotiate with the Mongol khan in fact managed to impress him so that the khan converted to Buddhism and accepted the monk as his spiritual teacher. This initiated the model of 'priest–patron-relationships', which proved to be an efficient model of government – an outside political entity guaranteed the status of a lineage as the supreme authority in Tibet in return for religious legitimation. Although the Buddhist lineage was nominally just representing the patron, in practice its power of decision-making was independent. Tibet was thus de facto ruled by influential monasteries, which often competed for the leading position, and secular aristocratic clans maintained their status through their ties to a particular monastery or lineage.

The lineages based on teacher–disciple relationships were particularly strong because they constituted the pattern of transmission of knowledge and authority. Sometimes political and religious arguments interfered with each other, when a faction in power questioned the legitimacy of the doctrine of another lineage that was perceived as a threat. But the plurality of lineages also ensured that scholarly debate continued and this occasionally also led to the establishment of new schools.

Possible the best-known religious figure of this period is the renowned ascetic and poet **Milarepa** (1040?–1123?). According to his semi-legendary biography, Milarepa had been born into a prosperous family, but after his father died, his uncle and aunt seized their wealth and Milarepa's family was reduced to poverty. At the instigation of his mother, Milarepa started to study black magic in order to avenge their lot, learned to control the weather, and eventually murdered an entire wedding party that had gathered in his uncle's house as well as destroyed the crops of the whole village with a hailstorm. However, he then regretted the crimes that he had committed and sought out a teacher with whom he would study and rid himself of his guilt. The teacher assigned to him a number of arduous tasks, in particular, the construction of several stone towers, so that he could destroy his bad karma. Milarepa complied, and then proceeded to rigorous ascetic training. Having received a number of tantric transmissions, Milarepa became an accomplished teacher himself. He is famous throughout Tibet not only because of this ability to advance from the status of a common criminal to a highly advanced Buddhist teacher, but also for his spirited religious poetry.

The reform of Tsongkhapa (1357–1419). The most successful new school of Tibetan Buddhism, and one that does not trace itself back to a single direct transmission from India, was initiated through the monastic reforms of **Tsongkhapa**. Concerned with the decline in religious discipline and the excessive political ambitions of the competing lineages, he combined tantric teachings of several schools, classic meditation techniques, and a rigorously argued philosophical grounding to form his own system. This became the foundation of a new monastic lineage that eventually came to be called **Geluk-pa** ('the virtuous'), which paradoxically soon evolved into the Tibetan school with most political power. Members of Geluk-pa are colloquially also known as 'yellow hats', because of their distinctive headgear.

Tsongkhapa was a prolific scholar as well as an ardent practitioner of meditation. With time he had acquired a popular reputation of a superior religious personality, which also caused a certain suspicion towards his activities from the side of the then-dominant lineages. According to Tsongkhapa, the spiritual progress of a devotee has to follow a strict outline of progress, specifying which teachings can be accessed at which level of development. Hierarchies of teachings were not a new invention, but previous schools had allowed for a certain degree of pluralism within themselves, and meditation exercises were given to followers at the discretion of the teachers, according to their character and abilities. Tsongkhapa's followers adopted a highly structured pedagogy, which, for example, does not permit them to start tantric training before a very high level of competence has been achieved in other domains. This has elicited criticism from other lineages, which sometimes erroneously claim that Geluk-pa neglects the esoteric tantric core of Tibetan Buddhism. However, tantric practices are just as much a part of Geluk-pa teachings as they are of the other schools.

The institution of Dalai Lama. In 1578, the Geluk-pa asserted their authority on a completely new level. A rebellious Mongol khan was looking for an alliance with Tibetan monasteries in order to raise his legitimacy and invited the leader of the school to a meeting. The two men concluded a new priest–patron relationship in which the khan gave the monk the title of **Dalai Lama** ('dalai' meaning 'ocean' in Mongolian and 'lama' is Tibetan for 'spiritual teacher'), while the monk declared the khan to be an incarnation of the great Khubilai, the founder of the Yuan dynasty in China. He also assumed for himself the status of only the third Dalai Lama, conferring the title in retrospect also to his two predecessors at the head of the Geluk-pa school. This greatly contributed to the conversion of Mongols to Tibetan Buddhism in its Geluk-pa form.

The institution of Dalai Lama gradually gained authority among Tibetans, especially after the fifth Dalai Lama managed to expel all contenders to power from Tibet and to consolidate the power into his own hands, even if he ruled with the support of a Mongol army. He also initiated the construction of the Potala palace in Lhasa in 1645 and, in 1653, travelled to Beijing on an invitation from the Manchu emperor of the newly installed Qing dynasty in China. However, his successor, the sixth Dalai Lama, proved to be a disappointment to the religious establishment. He was less interested in religious life than in women and poetry, wrote scandalously erotic verse himself, and finally abdicated from his position. This led to an increased intervention of the Qing dynasty in Tibetan affairs up to the establishment of a protectorate in 1720.

An unpredictable leader such as the sixth Dalai Lama could only attain the position of highest spiritual authority because of the system of succession of high-ranking Tibetan clerics, which is legitimized by claims of reincarnation. It is supposed that someone with sufficient accomplishment can freely decide the place and form of their next rebirth. There are approximately 3000 lineages in Tibet, in which a particular teacher has allegedly decided to dedicate his future rebirths to the cause of Tibet and to be constantly reborn there. Some time after the passing of such a teacher a commission is sent out to find the incarnation in the predicted area. In the case of the Dalai Lama, the procedure is especially strict, the child has to recognize objects that had belonged to the previous incarnation and to answer questions about him. In practice, a child is always found and claimed to be the correct one. During the time when the new Dalai Lama was a minor, the country used to be governed on behalf of him by a regent.

Tibet in modern times. Tibetan religious leaders managed, with intermittent success, to keep their power by accommodating foreign 'protectors' to the extent that it seemed necessary, but not more. This especially applied to China, which was increasingly trying to involve itself with Tibetan affairs. At the beginning of the twentieth century Tibet also started to attract the interest of both Britain and Russia, whose colonies bordered it.

After the fall of the Qing dynasty Tibet declared independence. However, the territory it controlled was much reduced, and the warlords, then the nationalists, and then the communists of China made efforts to regain it and to integrate it more permanently into their political systems – and there were also authoritative Tibetans who thought that together with the Chinese they would be able to modernize their country more efficiently, some among them even entertaining the hope that Mao's version of communism and the Tibetan traditional way of life could peacefully coexist.

But this was not to be. The communist invasion of Tibet in 1950, carried out under the slogan of liberating the Tibetan people from a medieval theocracy, was followed by bloody repressions and the dismantling of many traditional Tibetan institutions, which are currently serving primarily in the role of tourist attractions, if at all. At the same time, numerous ethnic Chinese have been resettled to Tibet so that the indigenous population is becoming a minority in some areas.

In 1959, when it was feared that the Dalai Lama would be abducted by the Chinese powers and removed from Tibet, he decided to flee, and numerous clerics and well-to-do families followed him. The exiled government of Tibet has since operated in India, in the city of Dharamsala in the hills of Himachal Pradesh, one of the Indian states bordering Tibet. Dharamsala also houses numerous monasteries and centres of learning. The Dalai Lama has ever since tried to find a peaceful solution that would enable Tibet to maintain its cultural identity, but without success.

Indic South East Asia

Introductory remarks. 'South East Asia' is originally a military term and refers to the group of countries to the east of India and to the south of China, both on the continent and on the adjacent islands. This is the home to many ancient 'high' cultures, some of them extinct, others thriving in their present form, but also to cultural groups who continue to live without a wholesale acceptance of modern civilization. Traditionally, both India and China have had a strong influence in this region, and India, in particular, has been successful in exporting its cultural norms and texts. Variants of the Rāmāyaṇa epic, for example, have been developed throughout the region, and its narratives have been integrated into local mythologies. Hinduism and versions of Buddhism have been officially endorsed by different rulers, while local spirit beliefs have also persisted and found various ways of symbiosis with the imported worldviews. Over the last several centuries, Islam has gradually advanced into a strong position mainly in maritime South East Asia, spreading first among merchants, then gradually to local elites and the general population.

The bigger part of the region is culturally more indebted to India, but Vietnam and Singapore are exceptional in having a stronger Chinese influence. Therefore, in this section the term 'South East Asia' as a generalization will be used in reference to all other countries of the region (Myanmar, Thailand, Cambodia, Laos, Malaysia, Indonesia, and a number of small states on the Malay peninsula), while Vietnam will be treated separately.

The main characteristic of South East Asian worldviews is pragmatic syncretism. Concerns of cultural or ethnic purity and religious orthodoxy have historically not been strong and their presence in the societies of today is mostly the product of colonial times and imported Western (including Islamic) conceptual language. Historically, there have been many strong political centres competing with each other, but never have these reigned over linguistically and culturally homogeneous populations or even clearly demarcated territories, nor have they seen themselves as centralized administrative systems until modern times. A prestigious foreign language such as Sanskrit or Pāli has often been preferred as a vehicle of communication to the spoken languages of the elites. Therefore, a Western-type division of the region into nation-states with distinct ethnocultural identities, especially in a historical perspective, is rather misleading.

Kingdoms and empires. The first strong cultural and political centres of continental South East Asia started to emerge in the ninth century. The Khmer kingdom of Angkor (a deformation of Sanskrit *nagara*, 'city'), established in 802, controlled at its apex a large area comprising what is now Cambodia and Thailand, and struggled for supremacy with another Indic centre, now culturally extinct, called Champa, with its centre near Danang in Central Vietnam. The first kings of Angkor were Brahmanist/Hindu and adopted the Indian doctrine of *devarājā* or 'divine rulers', whose very person was sacred as the guarantee of the cosmic order prevailing on Earth. They erected magnificent temples, which were architectural embodiments of cosmic and historical narratives just as they were sites of power and worship, and the ruins of the city of Angkor remain one of the most impressive sights in the whole of Asia to this day. A large part of this heritage testifies to an ideological change that took place in the empire of Angkor in the twelfth century, when an ambitious monarch called Jayavarman VII vanquished the Champa threat, converted to Mahāyāna Buddhism and embarked on a programme of public works, constructing roads, hospitals, and water reservoirs – as well as numerous temples, often featuring his portraits. Jayavarman VII envisaged himself in the Buddhist tradition of a *dharmarājā*, or 'ruler by teaching', who earned his legitimacy by deeds that serve the common good. Two generations later, however, Khmer kings again reverted to the Hindu view. By this time, their power was already declining, the Champa were again asserting themselves and a new Thai kingdom had emerged that started to carve their empire up, until it finally gained control of it in the fourteenth century. After a mutiny against the Thai, the capital of Angkor was devastated by the Thai army and subsequently abandoned.

The other major early political centre of continental South East Asia was the north Burmese kingdom of Pagan, established in 849. In the centuries that followed, Pagan kings subdued the neighbouring areas and gradually consolidated their power, until king Anawrahta came to power in 1044 and turned his little fief into a veritable empire. Burmese chronicles assert that even Khmer rulers of Angkor and the island of Java had to acknowledge his superiority, but no independent evidence confirms this; nonetheless, under Anawrahta's rule the Pagan empire had quickly become a major regional power, and also a champion of Buddhism in the region. The capital was filled with newly constructed temples, the number of monks and scholars grew exponentially and soon enough Pagan was also promoting Buddhism outside its borders, helping to restore it to its previous position in Sri Lanka, where it had suffered because of the invasions of Hindu Tamil kings.

At the height of its power, the Pagan empire ruled directly over more or less all of the area of modern Myanmar and also claimed tribute from a number of adjacent states. During the thirteenth century, however, the kingdom went into decline. One reason for this was the excessive tax-free granting of agricultural land to temples, which emptied the royal treasury and caused wide dissatisfaction. When the Mongol armies of the Yuan dynasty defeated Pagan and established an outpost in upper Burma, the empire disintegrated shortly afterwards.

The island of Java was the political centre of most imperial projects in maritime South East Asia. The earliest kingdom of Medang was established on the island in the eighth century and soon grew into a regional power, but internal differences, in particular a struggle between the supporters of Hinduism and Buddhism, caused its downfall. The greatest glory was achieved by Javanese rulers during the rule of the Majapahit empire from the end of the thirteenth century to around 1500, when it controlled the whole of present-day Indonesia and Malaysia as well as other neighbouring territories. In the sixteenth century, however, the Majapahit empire disintegrated into small states, some Hindu, some Muslim, and despite the occasional emergence of able and ambitious rulers, nobody managed to bring the whole of maritime South East Asia under their control for a long time. This period coincided with the appearance of European missionaries and traders, who soon became a major political presence in the area. As a result, small states fell one by one to superior Western invaders and were converted into colonies and dominions.

The youngest, but ultimately most successful, South East Asian kingdom was Thailand, which emerged in the thirteenth century, replaced the Khmer and Burmese empires as the major regional power soon afterwards and in the sixteenth century developed diplomatic and trade relationships with countries even as remote as France. Despite many political ups and downs, replacements of dynasties, and moving of capitals, Thailand persisted as a local power and finally became the only country in the entire South East Asia (Chinese-influenced areas included), which managed to modernize itself in the late nineteenth century and escape colonialization by Western powers.

Traditional beliefs and practices. The original beliefs and practices of most ethnic and cultural groups of South East Asia have proved to be remarkably resilient and have survived the official conversions of their holders to all imported religions. Researchers report that even Islam has produced local versions, so that the followers themselves consider certain of their practices to be Islamic, while scholars of religious studies judge them to be animistic.

The traditional beliefs still influencing daily practice include, for example, the cosmological hierarchy of high and low, and the corresponding axis of purity–impurity. For example, in a Thai temple, visitors need to be careful not to sit so that their feet (low, impure) are pointing towards the image of the Buddha, because this indicates disrespect. In Bali, people of lower caste are not supposed to sit on seats that are higher than those for persons of higher caste. Menstruating women are not allowed to enter temple grounds. Offerings to benign spirits are placed on higher surfaces, offerings to placate malign ones on the ground.

Spirit beliefs are also taken into account in the cultural formation of space in other ways. Thus, for example, a Bali living compound, which adopts the structure of a temple, has a separate standalone wall built opposite the entrance with the sole function of stopping malign spirits from entering – namely, those spirits can allegedly only move in straight lines, while everybody else is able to make the two quick turns around the wall and enter. It is also customary to leave small boxes with food offerings for the spirits at the corners of buildings, and in some places, Thailand and Cambodia in particular, special small houses are built for otherworldly entities, where offerings are left for them. These include both the spirits of ancestors and other supernatural beings, such as the spirits of place. Certain rituals for the spirits are also performed in front of the houses, for example, after funeral ceremonies, spirits of the dead persons are directed back home and shown where a spirit house is prepared for them to inhabit.

Another widespread phenomenon related to spirit beliefs is spirit possession. Professional mediums, more often women than men, perform these possessions during important occasions. Reports of these practices go back as far as the first descriptions of South East Asian customs by Christian missionaries in the sixteenth century and the tradition continues to this day largely in the same form. The mediums have a highly appreciated status in the community, which often provides an avenue to social respectability for the economically disadvantaged or members of marginalized groups (such as homosexual or transgender men, for example). In the Burmese tradition, they are called 'spouses of spirits' (*nat kadaw*, the same term is used also when the envisaged relationship is that of a child to a parent, or a sibling), while in some Thai traditions they are referred to as teachers, as the spirits that the mediums succumb to are the ancestors of the family or the larger group. Scholars report that mediums are first 'approached' by spirits during an exceptional experience, such as illness or a strong emotional shock, and then need to undergo professional training under a master for many years before being allowed to manage a possession on their own. Sometimes, as in the Burmese tradition, the mediums are also ranked in a hierarchy according to their accumulated skill.

Transformations of Indian worldviews. According to historical sources, when the Burmese empire-builder Anawrahta was converted to Theravāda Buddhism by a monk who advocated the reform and purification of the religious establishment from corrupt practices, Anawrahta supposedly said that the people at large should not be subjected to a similar campaign as the monasteries and left alone to practise according to their syncretic beliefs. In actual truth, Anawrahta might have adhered to a more syncretic worldview himself as well, while the 'purification' campaign with the focus shift to Theravāda probably occurred somewhat later, and even then it was not as complete as the Buddhist institution would like it to have been in retrospect. The approach of South East Asian elites seems to have been to adopt and support whatever works, either separately or in combination. Thus, a phallus dedicated to Shiva might be installed in a Cambodian temple together with Buddhist paraphernalia, and the cults of Vishnu and Shiva were practised side by side, and Theravāda and Mahāyāna Buddhist doctrines could merge as well. Royal interest in the purity of religion arose often in conjunction with the need to fill the treasury, which meant that some lands needed to be confiscated from (allegedly) corrupt monasteries. If critical contemporary accounts are to be believed, such corruption was indeed rampant at times. For example, the Ari sect of Buddhism in Burma had allegedly installed a 'right of the first night' for tantric monks to have sex with women about to be married.

Islam and Christianity. In the sixteenth century, the religious landscape of South East Asia began to change as both Islam and Christianity started to gain a foothold, especially in the maritime area of the region. One reason for the spread of Islam may have been its impartiality to local feuds. Small royal houses continued to compete with each other after the decline of the Majapahit empire, which made it difficult for traders allied with one of these houses to trade in areas under the control of others, but Muslim traders had none of these problems. Indeed, the only area to remain more or less untouched by the advent of Islam was the kingdom of Bali (with holdings on adjacent islands), which was a strong centre of power at the time of the quick spread of Islam in the neighbouring areas.

A major milestone was the conversion of the Malay ruler of Melacca to Islam around 1400 and his subsequent sponsorship of Muslim scholars. When the Portuguese conquered the port in 1511 and closed it to Muslim traders, they began to seek for a similar sponsor in other islands. Several rulers saw the opportunity and converted. In due course, Islam spread to most of the major islands of South East Asia that have urban and trade-intensive cultures, and it continues to be the dominant religion in the area.

Christianity was less successful, but also made some quite substantial gains. Among the factors impeding the spread of Christianity was its disdain of local culture, which often manifested in cruelty and violence, and the internal conflicts between Catholic and Protestant conquerors. It is even speculated that the Christian presence might have contributed to the spread of Islam, as Christianity was the more brutal and violent from the two newly arrived religions, whereas Islam promoted economic prosperity and scholarship.

Modernity: nationalism, royalism, and communism. While institutional religions usually enjoyed the support of the modernizing governments of the late nineteenth and twentieth centuries, spirit-related practices were opposed by them, or at most given an air of respectability by integrating them as 'customs' into established worldviews. The first actively modernizing monarch of Asia, king Mongkut of Thailand (1804–1868), had been a Buddhist monk at the time when he was forced to return from his monastery and ascend the throne because of a succession dispute. Earlier in his life, he had established a movement to integrate Buddhism with Western science and to transform Theravāda into an ideology suitable for nation-building. His son Chulalongkorn (1853–1910) went even further and reorganized the Buddhist community under a centralized structure, as he did with all institutions of authority. This was motivated by a need either to incorporate or to marginalize the local charismatic holy people, who often enjoyed broad authority on account of their spiritual exploits. Elsewhere, religious motivation often contributed to anti-colonial struggles. Islam, in particular, assumed more militant and fundamentalist modes in some places where local aristocrats, who had maintained their positions under colonial rule, were being attacked for their collaboration with non-believers.

However, the opposition to colonial regimes was more effectively mobilized by nationalism, even though the South East Asian demographic and cultural situation is extremely unsuitable for the construction of nation-states on an ethnic or even linguistic basis. Thus, for example, Indonesia has adopted as its official language a variant of Malay, which was used as the lingua franca among tradespeople all over the region. The language is now called 'Indonesian' and some of its features have been distanced from standard Malay, and several generations have grown up with it as their main vehicle of communication, but at the moment of birth of the Indonesian state the language was an acquired skill to nearly all of the people who used it. Religion has also been mobilized to govern such diversity. Islam holds the predominant position in Indonesia, but the government is officially semi-secular, in that it provides for freedom of conscience, but you have to choose a religion from among the traditionally established ones in order to have the rights of a citizen.

In Thailand, nationalism has taken the form of royalism for a large number of people. The Chakri dynasty has seen more energetic and more passive rulers, but it has connected itself firmly to the success of Thailand in maintaining political sovereignty and of modernizing the country more efficiently than any of its neighbours had managed. Conveniently associated with the historical discourses of kingship, modern royalism has provided a stable discourse of statehood, which has been accepted by the population at large – but also enforced with strict *lèse-majesté* laws, so that offending the king, or any previous king, or a family member of the king, or even the pet of the king is a criminal offence that could bring with it a prison sentence of a maximum of 15 years. In practice, this paragraph has occasionally also been used to silence dissident intellectuals. Most of the population is nonetheless happy with the king and his portrait is regularly seen in Thai (and even Lao) homes. Other South East Asian ruling houses have been less lucky and royalism has not proved to be a sustainable political discourse in Laos, Cambodia, or Malaysia, although it works in some smaller states such as Brunei.

Communism as a political ideology has in South East Asia resulted in some of the bloodiest crimes carried out in its name. In particular, this applies to the regime of the Khmer Rouge in Cambodia, which governed the country between 1975 and 1979. The movement had a longer history, however. Its leadership consisted of people who had been sent to study in France during the heyday of the colonial era, which happened to coincide with the ascent of communism in the French academia. One of the future leaders of the Khmer Rouge, Khieu Samphan, indeed defended a doctoral dissertation in Sorbonne in 1959 on the topic of how Cambodian economy and politics should be reorganized. Among other things, he indicated the 'non-productive' nature of the labour of certain social classes in this work, thus foreshadowing the genocide that the Khmer Rouge effectively organized during the years of their rule.

The leaders of communist movements were often highly educated members of the elite, and the founder of the Pathet Lao, or the communist party of Laos, was even a prince of the royal dynasty. However, in practical activity they often relied on the least educated and anti-establishment groups of their respective countries. The Khmer Rouge mobilized teenagers to its cause, similarly as Mao had done during the 'cultural revolution' in China, and led them to participate in mass killings of 'parasitic elements' – which included, for example, everyone with eyeglasses, as these were indicative of excessive reading. The rank-and-file members of communist movements often had little or no grasp of the ideology for which they were supposedly fighting, apart from a few jargonistic slogans, which could comfortably co-exist with traditional spirit beliefs. Thus, a veteran of the Lao communist movement writes in her memoirs about a comrade who had talismans that rendered him bulletproof and invisible as well as granted him the ability to move through walls, and in some Lao villages shrines have been erected for worshipping communist leaders.

All in all, South East Asian worldviews cannot be comprehended on the basis of a strict categorization of sects and teachings, and the pragmatic syncretism of the early ages has survived to this day. At present, the situation has become even more complicated because of the commercialization of religion both for tourists eager to see 'authentic' local culture and for the domestic middle-class, who has retained their affinity to traditional practices in the midst of a secular society.

Vietnam

Periods of cultural history. The ancestors of the contemporary Vietnamese are the people who inhabited the northern part of the country in its current shape, and their early state was subdued by the Chinese in the last centuries BCE. While they accepted the fruits of Chinese civilization, they did not assimilate, however, and made frequent attempts to rid themselves of foreign domination, until the Vietnamese state finally achieved independence in 938. A succession of dynasties, with those of Ly (1009–1225) and Tran (1225–1400) being more stable than others, ruled over northern Vietnam during the following centuries, repelled the attacks of Mongols from the north and Champa from the south and finally had to battle against the expansion of China under the Ming rule. Under the Le dynasty (1428–1789), which came to power after expelling the Chinese, Vietnam expanded southward and occupied the territories formerly ruled by Champa as well as a part of the disintegrating Khmer empire. The Le period was characterized by political upheavals and a golden age of culture. A period of mutinies and civil wars brought Le rule to an end in the eighteenth century, and after a period of turmoil the throne was seized by an ambitious general who founded the Nguyen dynasty in

1802. This, in turn, fell to the French in 1858, although Nguyen kings remained officially on the throne as figureheads until 1945, when the last of them handed his power over to the communists.

The French rule was harsh and unpopular. The example of Japan's modernization inspired them to promote new technologies and education as a form of resistance, and many young Vietnamese went to Japan to study. The French administration also provided stipends for talented youth to study in France. As the French administration had been loyal to the Vichy government during World War II and collaborated with the Japanese, while the resistance movement led by Ho Chi Minh worked together with the United States, the Vietnamese expected to regain their independence after the war, but the United States supported the reinstalment of French colonial rule instead. This led to decades of warfare. When the French were defeated in 1954, the country was divided into North and South Vietnam and hostilities soon resumed. The North was backed by China and the Soviet Union, the South by the United States. The North defeated the largely unpopular and corrupt regime of the South in 1975 and unified Vietnam under communist rule. The government now relied a lot on Soviet support, which came to an end during the weakening of communist ideology under Gorbachev. The Vietnamese government reacted by announcing a policy of 'renovation' in 1986 and has since been developing quickly, although the damages done by the long war and earlier communist policies have not been easy to repair.

Traditional beliefs. The Vietnamese worldview is structurally similar to that of its South East Asian neighbours by being eclectic and unsystematic, but its components differ significantly from Thailand, Laos, and Cambodia in that a Sinic element takes the place of the Indic in it. Its basis, however, is a similar system of spirit beliefs and shamanistic practices. While religious professionals make distinctions between their denominations and doctrines on the higher level, the popular worldview integrates all of them, including the sages of Ru, the deities of the Dao creed, and even the original anti-symbolic ethos of Thien (Chan) Buddhism, not to speak of Pure Land doctrines, into an amalgam of beliefs and practices that range from spirit veneration to magic and is oriented very much to the solution of this-worldly problems rather than spiritual emancipation.

The Vietnamese are reported to believe that human beings have a large number of souls of different types, and women have more than men. A pregnancy thus results not only from the union of parents, but may need a soul to enter the body of the mother-to-be from bathwater or touching an object in which a soul resides. Some of these souls may be maliciously inclined, other peaceful, and this accounts for the range of feelings and dispositions in a person's character. After death, some of the souls remain in the vicinity of the deathplace, others depart. Human souls may also join the ranks of the celestial pantheon, which is organized according to the pattern of a bureaucratic state. It is presided over by the Celestial Jade Emperor, and individual deities are organized in a strict hierarchy. They may be promoted for doing something good, or demoted and punished when they act out of step with the natural order. Accordingly, it is only natural that outstanding figures of Vietnamese history have also been promoted to the status of celestial beings after their death and their cults are widespread.

Spirits can also reside in objects, in particular trees and stones, which can help people in distress, and some animals also have spirits that command respect. For example, it has been reported that tigers are believed to be just and never to attack anyone whose actions have not merited punishment – and in the rare case when a tiger has killed an innocent, it will make good for its mistake and its spirit will help the relatives of the victim.

The Vietnamese also have shamanistic rituals and a long-standing tradition of spiritism. For example, it has been customary to invite the spirit of a recently deceased person after a certain number (usually 50) of days after their death to possess a medium and to communicate with remaining relatives. Certain spiritist practices have also been adopted by new religious movements to confirm their authority to the believers.

Vietnamese Buddhism. The early stages of the Vietnamese state were much indebted to Buddhism, which had a long-standing presence: ports in the delta of the Red River in North Vietnam had been stations on the southern route between China and India, and thus often visited by Buddhist monks. This led to the establishment of temples and provoked local interest. Flourishing centres of Buddhism were established there as early as the second century CE, if not earlier. The traffic of ideas included theories of statecraft and the Ly emperors in particular often relied on the counsel of Buddhist monks in their organization of state affairs. From early on Vietnamese Buddhism assumed an eclectic character, blending freely with local forms of religious practice, and not organizing itself into clearly demarcated schools. Most Chinese schools have had some influence on Vietnamese Buddhist thought. Among them, Thien (Chan) has been most widespread, even though it has accommodated many beliefs and practices from other schools, such as the Pure Land, over the centuries. In popular practice, the intellectual finesses are mostly ignored, and images of Buddhist personages are worshipped in the manner of traditional beliefs.

An effort to develop a distinctly Vietnamese Buddhism is the 'Bamboo Grove' school established by Tran Nhan Tong (1258–1308), an emperor of the Tran dynasty who became a monk and tried to integrate various philosophical currents, including Neo-Confucianism and the Dao creed, into a Thien Buddhist basis. This school has gone through a revival in the twentieth century. Another major contemporary Thien Buddhist current is the Plum Village tradition, established by **Thich Nhat Hanh** (b.1926), the author of many popular books, most of them in English, who has combined traditional Buddhist learning with Western ideas and taught in Princeton and Columbia universities as well as Vietnamese Buddhist institutions. The ideas of Thich Nhat Hanh have thus had a strong influence world-wide, including the promotion of 'engaged Buddhism' (a term introduced by him) and the mobilization of Buddhist ideas for resisting social and political injustice as well as environmental problems. In 1967, Martin Luther King nominated Thich Nhat Hanh for the Nobel peace prize.

The Neo-Confucian tradition in Vietnam. Ru ideas also arrived in Vietnam at an early stage and were selectively employed in the development of its statecraft, and one of the surviving landmarks of Hanoi is indeed a temple for Confucius, built as early as 1070 by an emperor of the Ly dynasty. The Tran emperors established a civil service complete with an examination system following the Chinese model in the 1230s, and Ru classics were a major part of the curriculum while Buddhism held the dominant position. This led to the emergence of a learned aristocracy, which soon came to see itself as the carrier of political continuity. During the Mongol invasion, which the Tran empire successfully repelled, a Vietnamese theory of the Mandate of Heaven was developed, claiming that there is a separate mandate for the territories under Tran rule, and that the Vietnamese emperor is therefore equal to his Chinese colleague. Tran rulers did accept the nominal overlordship of the Yuan, however, in order to avoid further conflict, but the theory continued to resurface in difficult political situations after that.

The Ming efforts to colonize and assimilate the Vietnamese had curiously dissociated themselves from Neo-Confucian philosophy – perhaps because they were incompatible with its core virtues – which enabled the Vietnamese opposition to adopt Neo-Confucian rhetoric for a call to resistance. The scholar, poet, and military strategist Nguyen Trai (1380–1442), whose efforts were seminal in securing the Vietnamese victory over the Chinese, and who subsequently became the tutor to the crown prince, exemplified the turn that Vietnamese culture had taken: the learned aristocracy, whose status as a political force was bolstered by Neo-Confucian ideas, was collectively claiming Vietnamese statehood as its own. Simultaneously, however, this signified the opening up of a constantly widening gap between the aristocrats and the common people, to whom the Neo-Confucian establishment remained culturally alien.

During the centuries that followed, a bureaucratic Neo-Confucian state was the model adopted by all monarchs, up until the dismal failure of this ideology when faced with the French advance in the nineteenth century, when emperor Tu Duc was too busy trying to be a loyal son to his ailing mother and could not be bothered with organizing any resistance. And yet, in the twentieth century some

Vietnamese ideologues, such as Tran Trong Kim (1883–1953), have hailed Neo-Confucianism as an ideology that could potentially be enlisted for battling French colonial rule. But Neo-Confucianism did not measure up to this task, and the position was taken by communism.

Vietnamese communism. The character of Vietnamese communism is exceptional among other branches of Marxism in Asia in that it is predominantly an outgrowth of nationalism. The unchallenged first leader of Vietnamese communists, **Ho Chi Minh** (1890–1969), had a Neo-Confucian background. As the son of a patriotic Ru scholar he came from fiercely independence-minded, but culturally conservative circles. Ho left Vietnam in 1911 for France after receiving a French education in an elite school for the training of local administrators. During his studies, he had already started to participate in independence demonstrations and later adopted the pseudonym of Nguyen Ai Quoc (Nguyen the Patriot). In France, however, he realized that the only global political force sympathetic to his struggle against the colonial regime were communists, which is why he joined their ranks. In 1919 he was a member of the Vietnamese nationalist group who tried to persuade the participants of the Versailles peace treaty negotiations to extend the right of national self-determination to Vietnam, and the failure of this attempt only strengthened his conviction that communists were his only allies in the West. During the 1920s and 1930s he was active in the Comintern, serving the cause of Stalin.

In 1941, he adopted the name of Ho Chi Minh and became the leader of the anti-Japanese and anti-French guerrilla movement in Vietnam, collaborating with the Americans to liberate his country, but when he appealed to this connection and wrote to president Truman asking for help and recognition after the war, he was ignored. Again, only communist support was available. After the Sino-Soviet split he opted for the Soviet side, a move prompted by the long-standing historical hostility between Vietnam and China and by the consideration that the relative distance to Moscow granted him more independence, which was always his primary concern. However, his long-standing involvement in the Comintern, as well as the conditions that his supporters set him, contributed to his active promotion of communist-style authoritarian and centralized methods of government. Although Vietnam never became such a drastic dictatorship as Cambodia under the Khmer Rouge – whom Vietnamese troops ultimately helped to depose – or had to go through such cataclysms as China endured under the 'cultural revolution' of Mao, communist policies were nonetheless harsh and authoritarian in Vietnam as well, including the suppression of dissident voices, the marginalization of religion, and the centralization of economic control.

New religions: Caodai. The twentieth century in Vietnam has also seen the development of quite a few new religious movements, some of them efforts to revive Buddhism in a mode uncontaminated by amalgamating with folk religion, others efforts to organize and systematize the folk religion into new and more modern forms. However, the most successful and possibly most original Vietnamese religious innovation was neither. This is the religion called **Caodai**, established in 1926 in south-western Vietnam, with its centre not far from Saigon, near the Cambodian border.

The Caodai creed presents an effort to unite the entire positive heritage of humankind into one comprehensive tradition dominated by its Vietnamese founders. It proclaims faith in the 'Supreme Being' (Cao Dai), also known as Celestial Jade Emperor, Brahmā, Buddha Amitābha, as well as by a large number of Western designations. This being revealed itself to a group of people on Christmas Eve, 1925, during a spiritist seance and urged them to inaugurate a new faith. According to Caodai teachings, the same being had also manifested itself to the Buddha, Kongzi, Jesus, and other religious leaders in the past, and the Caodai faith indeed venerates as holy people the representatives of many nations and cultures, including Moses and Muhammad, Jeanne d'Arc, William Shakespeare, Louis Pasteur, Lenin, and Thomas Alva Edison. Its most highly revered saints are Victor Hugo, Sun Yat-sen, and a Vietnamese poet-scholar called Nguyen Binh Kiem (1491–1585), who is famous for an obscure prophetic poem with nationalist sentiments. The three are often depicted together in veneration of the Caodai.

During the Vietnam war, Caodai commanded its own armed forces which managed to hold all sides at bay and secured a relative stability in the region where the faith was widespread. It was also critical of communism and therefore banned after the reunification of Vietnam, but its rights were restored in 1997. Today, approximately 4.5 million people profess the Caodai faith. For outsiders, this religion is characterized primarily by its colourful and bizarre architecture and design, which is resemblant of postmodern contemporary art rather than anything in the Asian sacred traditions. This is why Caodai has done very well not only as a religion, but also as a tourist attraction.

Further Reading

It is impossible to present a cursory overview of all the literature to which anyone interested in Asian worldviews could turn. It is clear that any bibliography on Asian worldviews gets outdated very quickly as new excellent work is being published constantly. The works listed here are meant only as next steps, more detailed introductions to specific areas of Asian intellectual history, and should be mostly understandable to anyone who has read this book.

My general recommendation to a beginner in the field would be to always check the academic credentials of the authors and publishers of books with promising titles, as Asian worldviews have generated a lot of provocative, but not necessarily accurate accounts and misreadings. Usually, books published by academic presses can be trusted for their quality, but there are also minor and non-academic publishers that have put out important volumes, including translations of source texts. However, minor and non-academic publishers often indulge in commercially promising, but academically dubious ventures. Newer translations are usually to be preferred to older ones, as they have had the opportunity to make use of more recent scholarship. Books on religion published by religious organizations should always be handled with care, which does not mean they are always suspect.

A good resource for all regions is the *Companion Encyclopedia of Asian Philosophy*, edited by Brian Carr and Indira Mahalingam (Routledge, 1997), which is not actually an encyclopedia, but a collection of essays, mostly by best specialists in particular areas, although the quality varies somewhat. Routledge has also started to publish a series of histories of world philosophies by country, and volumes on China (edited by Bo Mou, 2009) and on India (edited by Purushottama Bilmoria, 2018) are available to date. The Blackwell Companions to Philosophy Series with *A Companion to Buddhist Philosophy* (edited by Steven M. Emmanuel, 2013), *The Blackwell Companion to Hinduism* (edited by Gavin Flood, 2003), *The Wiley-Blackwell Companion to Chinese Religions* (edited by Randall L. Nadeau, 2012), and *A Companion to World Philosophies*

Asian Worldviews: Religions, Philosophies, Political Theories, First Edition. Rein Raud.
© 2021 John Wiley & Sons Ltd. Published 2021 by John Wiley & Sons Ltd.

(edited by Eliot Deutsch and Rob Bontekoe, 1999) are authoritative collections of excellent essays both with a more general range and more specific topics. A similar series of Continuum Companions features a volume on Hindu Studies (edited by Jessica Frazier, 2011). The Dimensions of Asian Spirituality Series, published by Hawai'i University Press, contains useful and trustworthy, but accessible volumes on specific concepts (such as karma), religious denominations (such as the Sikh faith and Chan Buddhism), and other issues (such as socially engaged Buddhism).

There are also useful reference works available. The *Oxford Dictionary of World Religions* (edited by John Bowker, Oxford University Press, 1997) and its concise version (2000) are authoritative reference tools with large coverage of Asian material. The same goes for the *Oxford Dictionary of World Mythology* (edited by Arthur Cotterell, Oxford University Press, 1990). For Buddhist thought of all regions and times, *The Princeton Dictionary of Buddhism* (edited by Donald S. Lopez and Robert E. Buswell, Jr, Princeton University Press, 2014) remains unsurpassed both by range and by quality of research. Edinburgh University Press has published small reference volumes in the Philosophy A–Z Series – there is one on Indian philosophy by Christopher Bartley (2005) and one on Chinese Philosophy by Bo Mou (2009).

Among many excellent introductions to Indian thought, I would single out *An Introduction to Indian Philosophy* by Christopher Bartley (Continuum, 2011), which contains expositions of all major schools together with translated extracts from main works. Richard King's *Indian Philosophy* (Georgetown University Press, 1999) similarly provides an overview of both Brahmanist/Hindu and Buddhist schools, with a comparative perspective. A more detailed overview of Hindu thought, yet still accessible for the non-specialist is *Perspectives of Reality* by Jeaneane Fowler (Sussex Academic Press, 2002). For the more advanced student, *Classical Indian Philosophy* by J.N. Mohanty (Rowman & Littlefield, 2000) can be of much interest, a problem-based comparative overview of Indian philosophical schools, addressing texts from the earliest times until after the classical age. Similarly, anyone with a background in philosophy would find Jonardon Ganeri's excellent study, *Philosophy in Classical India* (Routledge, 2001), to be very insightful.

A good introductory volume that overviews all significant religious traditions of India is Fred Clothey's *Religion in India: A Historical Introduction* (Routledge, 2006). More usually the traditions are treated separately, as in Gavin Flood's *An Introduction to Hinduism* (Cambridge University Press, 1996), Peter Harvey's *An Introduction to Buddhism: Teachings, History and Practices* (Cambridge University Press, 2013), Paul Dundas's *The Jains* (Routledge, 1992), and Arvind-Pal Singh Mandair's *Sikhism* (Bloomsbury, 2013) – all excellent books.

Compared to the classical traditions, modern Indian thought has been much less studied, but *Modern Indian Political Thought: Text and Context* by Bidyut Chakrabarty and Rajendra Kumar Pandey (Sage, 2009) provides an extensive introduction.

Many translations of Indian thought are available, although no comprehensive anthology has appeared in recent decades to replace *A Source Book in Indian Philosophy* by Sarvepalli Radhakrishnan and Charles A. Moore (Princeton University Press, 1957). The early period in particular is well represented, from complete translation of the *Rigveda* by Stephanie W. Jamison and Joel P. Brereton (Oxford University Press, 2014) to the many excellent translations by Patrick Olivelle (*The Early Upanisads*, Oxford University Press, 1998; *Dharmasūtras*, Oxford University Press, 1999; *Manu's Code of Law*, Oxford University Press, 2005), and many others. The *Bhagavad-Gītā* has also been translated many times, and a verse rendering by Gavin Flood and Charles Martin (W. W. Norton, 2013) as well as a well-commented rendering-cum-study by Ithamar Theodor (Ashgate, 2010) recommend themselves among the most recent ones. Indian Buddhist texts are also covered, with *Buddhist Philosophy: Essential Readings*, edited by William Edelglass and Jay Garfield (Oxford University Press, 2009) as a good starting point (the coverage of the volume extends to China, Korea and Japan). The situation is a bit less rosy with other philosophical systems, although Advaita Vedānta is well represented by *The Essential Vedanta* (edited by Eliot Deutsch and Rohit Dalvi, World Wisdom, 2004) and a good scholarly translation of the Yogasūtra is provided in the appendix to Daniel Raveh's *Exploring the Yogasutra* (Continuum, 2012).

While Islam is only treated as a cultural import in this book, here are a few suggestions for those readers who would like to be better informed about its history and teachings. *Islam: A New Historical Introduction* by Carole Hillenbrand (Thames and Hudson, 2015) and *Islam: A Brief History* by Tamara Sonn (Wiley Blackwell, 2010) provide solid overviews of the history and practices of the Muslim faith, and *An Introduction to Classical Islamic Philosophy* by Oliver Leaman (Cambridge University Press, 2001) is still one of the most useful introductory overviews of Muslim thought, while *A History of Islamic Philosophy* (Columbia University Press, 2004) by Majid Fakhry provides more detailed coverage of single authors and schools.

There are several excellent introductions to Chinese thought, such as Bryan van Norden's *Introduction to Classical Chinese Philosophy* (Hackett, 2011), *An Introduction to Chinese Philosophy* by Karyn Lai (Cambridge University Press, 2008) and *An Introduction to Chinese Philosophy* by JeeLoo Liu (Blackwell, 2006). Of these, Van Norden's is the most accessible and Liu's the most detailed. Unfortunately, all of them only cover the early period of Chinese philosophy (Liu also has a good section on Chinese Buddhism), but none of them deals with Neo-Confucianism. Fortunately, there is also *Neo-Confucianism: A Philosophical*

Introduction by Stephen C. Angle and Justin Tiwald (Polity, 2017), an accessible and up-to-date volume that fills this gap. On a slightly more advanced level, *A Daoist Theory of Chinese Thought: A Philosophical Interpretation* by Chad Hansen (Oxford University Press, 1992) is an excellent, albeit provocative book. *Contemporary Chinese Philosophy*, edited by Nicholas Bunnin and Chung-ying Cheng (Blackwell, 2002) brings the story of Chinese thought up to date.

On the side of religions, Mario Poceski's *Introducing Chinese Religions* (Routledge, 2009) is considered to be the best book available, and *Religions of China in Practice* (edited by Donald S. Lopez Jr, Princeton University , 1996) provides a lot of interesting supporting material. Authoritative introductions to the indigenous Chinese thought traditions from a range of perspectives are *An Introduction to Confucianism* by Xinzhong Yao (Cambridge University Press, 2000), *A Reader's Companion to the Confucian Analects* by Henry Rosemont, Jr (Palgrave MacMillan, 2013), *Taoism: The Enduring Tradition* by Russell Kirkland (Routledge, 2004), and *The Daoist Tradition: An Introduction* by Louis Komjathy (Bloomsbury, 2013).

As to modern Chinese political thought, a useful introduction is *The Intellectual Foundations of Chinese Modernity* by Edmund S. Fung (Cambridge University Press, 2010). *Marxism in the Making of China: A Doctrinal History* by A. James Gregor (Palgrave MacMillan, 2014) overviews the development of communist thought from its beginnings to the post-Mao era. Stuart Schram's work, in particular *The Thought of Mao Tse-Tung* (Cambridge University Press, 1989), provides a thorough analysis of Mao's views and the emergence of communist thought in China.

Bryan van Norden has edited a two-volume set of translations from Chinese philosophy (*Readings in Classical Chinese Philosophy*, with Philip J. Ivanhoe, Seven Bridges Press, 2001; and *Readings in Later Chinese Philosophy*, with Justin Tiwald, Hackett Publishing, 2014), which has partially replaced the now outdated *Sourcebook in Chinese Philosophy* by Wing-Tsit Chan (Princeton University Press, 1963). Many Chinese thinkers represented in Chan's book are regrettably not accessible in newer translations. The massive two-volume set of *Sources in Chinese Tradition*, edited by William T. de Bary, Irene Bloom and Richard Lufrano (Columbia University Press, 1999–2000) and *Chinese Civilization: A Sourcebook*, edited by Patricia Buckley Ebrey (Free Press, 1993) should also be mentioned for their well-introduced translations of important texts. The *Encyclopedia of Chinese Philosophy* (edited by Anthonio S. Cua, Routledge, 2003) is a trustworthy and detailed reference work for Chinese thinkers of all ages. A series published by Springer, Dao Companions to Chinese Philosophy, with volumes not only on many schools of thought and individual thinkers, but also on Chinese-influenced philosophies of Korea and Japan, is an excellent resource for the more interested student.

An essential resource for Japanese thought of all ages is *Japanese Philosophy: A Sourcebook*, edited by James Heisig, John Maraldo, and Thomas Kasulis (University of Hawai'i Press, 2011), which contains translated extracts of most major works, with brief introductory essays, from the earliest times to the twentieth century. *Engaging Japanese Philosophy* by Thomas Kasulis (University of Hawai'i Press, 2018) can be considered a companion volume to this book and is likely to remain the most authoritative comprehensive treatment of Japanese philosophical thought for a long time. Richard Bowring's *The Religious Traditions of Japan, 500–1600* (Cambridge University Press, 2005) is in turn probably the most authoritative source for early religious thought, as *Modern Japanese Thought*, edited by Bob T. Wakabayashi (Cambridge University Press, 1998), is for the social and critical thought from the Meiji period to post-war Japan, and *Philosophers of Nothingness* by James Heisig (University of Hawai'i Press, 2001) for the Kyōto school in particular. *Religions of Japan in Practice*, edited by George J. Tanabe Jr (Princeton University Press, 1999) offers a selection of translations from various sources dealing with religion in social and cultural context.

Thomas Kasulis's *Shintō: The Way Home* (University of Hawai'i Press, 2004) and *A New History of Shintō* (Wiley Blackwell, 2010) by John Breen and Mark Teeuwen complement each other as short introductions to the indigenous Japanese worldview, approaching the subject from very different viewpoints, the first as a lived spirituality, the second from a more analytical point of view. Helen Hardacre's monumental *Shinto: A History* (Oxford University Press, 2017) is the book for the more interested student. *A Cultural History of Japanese Buddhism* by William E. Neal and Brian Ruppert (Wiley Blackwell, 2015) provides the most up-to-date introduction to the institutional history of Buddhism in Japan, with less coverage of the teachings. The two volumes of *The Foundation of Japanese Buddhism* by Alicia and Daigan Matsunaga (Buddhist Books International, 1976) present a slightly outdated approach, but provide a lot of useful detail on doctrine. A monograph by Kiri Paramore entitled *Japanese Confucianism: A Cultural History* (Cambridge University Press, 2016) is a good historical introduction to Confucian schools in Japan.

A concise introduction to Korean religions is available by Don Baker as *Korean Spirituality* (University of Hawaii Press, 2008), and *Religions of Korea in Practice* (edited by Robert Buswell, Jr, Princeton University Press, 2007) is an anthology of sources covering the rich multiplicity of Korean religious history. Possibly the best well-balanced introduction to the intellectual history of Tibet is *Tibetan Buddhism: A Very Short Introduction* by Matthew Kapstein (Oxford University Press, 2014), and *Religions of Tibet in Practice* (edited by Donald S. Lopez, Jr, Princeton University Press, 1997) can also be recommended. As far as I know, similarly trustworthy introductions to South East Asian thought remain to be written.

Glossary of Names and Terms

abhidharma Buddhist metaphysics, developed in the last centuries BCE on the basis of the earlier tradition, but not universally accepted by all Buddhist communities

Abhinavagupta (tenth–eleventh century) a tantric Shaivist philosopher from Kashmir, who defended a philosophy of extreme idealism, rejecting the reality of material objects as well as the unmoving absolute of Advaita Vedānta and the Buddhist view of the impermanence of being

adhyāsa the 'superimposition' of an ignorance-based illusion on the absolute reality, which results in the production of our phenomenal world according to Advaita Vedānta philosophy

Ādi Granth 'First book', the scripture of the Sikh faith, a collection of around 6000 hymns

Advaita Vedānta a form of Vedānta philosophy developed by Shankara in the eighth century that posits pure, contentless, eternal, unconditioned consciousness as the absolute

ahimsā the originally Jain principle of complete abstention from any kind of violence towards other living beings, later adopted by Mahātma Gandhi as a principle prescribing non-violence also in political resistance

Akbar (1542–1605) the most famous Mughal emperor of India, known for his tolerant religious politics and support for learning

Ambedkar, Bhimrao (1891–1956) the first minister of law and justice of the Republic of India, a member of the 'untouchable' *dalit* group by birth and an advocate against caste-based discrimination; his conversion to Buddhism was followed by large numbers of members of the discriminated group

Amitābha (Jp. Amida) a mythical Buddha who has vowed that he will accept anyone in his Pure Land who appeals to him in earnest, venerated in Pure Land Buddhist schools

Asian Worldviews: Religions, Philosophies, Political Theories, First Edition. Rein Raud.
© 2021 John Wiley & Sons Ltd. Published 2021 by John Wiley & Sons Ltd.

anātman the Buddhist idea that the view of selfhood as self-reliant, independent, and enduring is false; empirical selfhood is grounded only in the temporary co-occurrence of various factors, such as body and consciousness, themselves also transient

arhat a disciple of the historical Buddha; the alleged ideal of traditional Buddhism striving only for one's own liberation

Arthashāstra 'The Science of Wealth', an Indian treatise on political and economic theory presumably from the fourth to third century BCE

Ashoka (c. 268–c. 232 BCE) the third and most successful ruler of the Maurya dynasty, a patron of Buddhism

ātman in the doctrine of the *upanishads* and later orthodox Indian philosophy the core individual self, which survives after the death of the person and transmigrates to another body; it is the form in which the absolute is present in each individual

Aum Shinrikyō a Japanese new religion, known for brainwashing its followers and instructing them to commit terrorist acts

Avatamsaka Sūtra 'Flower Garland Sūtra', a Mahāyāna scripture on which the Chinese Huayan school of Buddhism is based

avatar the form an Indian deity takes to appear and act on Earth

Bankei (1622–1693) an itinerant Japanese Zen monk who developed an uncompromising and simple form of popular philosophy

Bhagavad-gītā a Hindu sacred text, a section of the *Mahābhārata* epic, a dialogue between the warrior Arjuna and the god Krishna

bhakti devotionalist Indian religious practices (including chanting, dancing, etc.) seeking communion with the absolute, which is personified in a particular deity

Bhartrihari (c. fifth century CE) a linguistic philosopher who introduced the concept of universals as the carriers of meaning into Indian philosophy

Bengali renaissance a nineteenth-century movement of mainly Bengali intellectuals to restore the status of Indian culture under British rule

Besant, Annie (1847–1933) a radical feminist of Irish origin, joined the Theosophical Society and became its president, as well as stepmother to Jiddu Krishnamurti

Blavatsky, Helena (1831–1891) the founder of the Theosophical Society, who sought to increase the legitimacy of her system of thought by incorporating elements of Indian worldviews as 'ancient wisdom' into it

Bodhidharma (sixth century) an Indian monk, the semi-legendary founder of the Chan school of Chinese Buddhism

bodhisattva the Mahāyāna Buddhist ideal of a being who has attained enlightenment, but forsaken entry to nirvāna in order to help other beings still entrapped in the cycle of rebirths

Bön (Bon) the Tibetan native religion, later redesigned on the basis of the Buddhist model

Brahmā a personalized creator god, appears in the last layers of Vedic texts and later writings

Brahman according to the *upanishads*, the all-pervasive world soul, the absolute, a philosophical derivate of an omnipotent and ubiquitous divinity

Brahmanism a term designating the earlier forms of veda-based Indian religion, of which the main form of practice is sacrificial rituals

Brahmo Samaj a society founded in 1828 to promote a reformed culture that would be Indian in spirit, but cleansed of the socially oppressive traditions such as the self-immolation of widows (*sati*) and caste prejudice

Buddha (Siddhārtha Gautama Shākyamuni, fifth to fourth centuries BCE?) the historical founder of Buddhism; in later times, any being who had attained the final stage of spiritual development and achieved enlightenment

Buddha-nature the capacity of all sentient beings to attain Buddhist enlightenment

bushidō 'the way of the warrior', a set of ethical ideas meant to regulate the conduct of the Japanese samurai, a syncretic construct based on Neo-Confucian theory, but also contains elements of other streams of thought

Caodai a Vietnamese new religion established in 1925 as an effort to unite the entire positive heritage of humankind into one comprehensive tradition dominated by its Vietnamese founders

Cārvāka a materialist and hedonist heterodox philosophical system in early India

caste the four hierarchical social groups of Indian society, into which one can be born (priests, warriors, self-employed, and hired worker); the three higher castes are called 'twice-born', because their members are initiated into the knowledge of vedas, while below the castes are the 'untouchables', with whom no one of the castes is allowed to associate

Chan a school of Chinese Buddhism, which emphasized direct transmission from teacher to disciple without reliance on scripture and sudden enlightenment achieved through transcending ordinary logic

Cheng brothers Cheng Hao (1032–1085) and Cheng Yi (1033–1107), early Neo-Confucian thinkers, who elaborated a theory of the dichotomy of 'principle' (*li*) and its manifestations

Cheondogyo 'The Teaching of the Heavenly Way', a new form of Donghak established after its defeat in Korea, which severed its ties with the folk religion and presented itself as a Korean alternative to Christianity, a teaching compatible with modernization and nation-building according to Western models

Chiang Kai-Shek (Jiang Jieshi, 1887–1975) leader of the Republic of China in the warlord era and beyond, a nominally converted Christian, conservative traditionalist, and nationalist

Dai Zhen (1724–1777) a late Neo-Confucian theorist, who developed a hermeneutic theory of meaning and a naturalistic theory of mind

daimoku in the Nichiren school of Japanese Buddhism, a formula glorifying the title of the *Lotus Sūtra*, which was thought to encompass its whole teaching

Dalai Lama a title first conferred on the spiritual leader of the Tibetan Geluk-pa monastic lineage in 1578 by a Mongol khan, a status claimed to be transmitted through rebirth

dalit 'broken', the designation of untouchable social groups by reformers who spoke out against their oppression

dao 'way', a central term in Chinese philosophical discourses, generally signifying the objectively proper way for the world-process to evolve; in the Ru school the natural order, which is the basis of ritual propriety and moral excellence, the prerequisites of a harmonious society; in the Lao-Zhuang school an ineffable cosmic principle, which cannot be enforced by conscious action

Dao creed often called religious Daoism, a variety of religious, mystical, and alchemic practices loosely associated with Lao-Zhuang thought and aiming at the achievement of immortality

Daodejing a Chinese philosophical text from approximately the third century BCE, a collective work containing aphoristic statements on metaphysics, ethics, and politics that embody the worldview of the Lao-Zhuang school

Dark learning a school of Chinese thought of the third–fourth centuries, which advocated the idea that the world is in itself semiotically significant and decodable

darshana 'way of seeing', the six orthodox Indian philosophical systems

Dasan (Jeong Yakyong, 1762–1836) a Korean thinker of the Silhak school, who argued for an integration of the Neo-Confucian tradition with Japanese and Western learning

Deng Xiaoping (1904–1997) the ideologue of post-Mao China, proponent of efficient economic liberalization and slow social reforms

dharma (i) legal coding of social order; (ii) 'carrier' of existence, the minimal momentary instance of being in Mahāyāna doctrine; (iii) teaching (usually Buddhism)

dharmakāya according to esoteric Buddhism, the cosmic body of the Buddha, the basis of all reality, which embodies the teaching and continues to expound it secretly in everything that happens

Dharmakirti (sixth–seventh century) Buddhist logician, who developed Dignāga's system

Dignāga (480?–540?) one of the founders of Buddhist logic, who claimed negations of negations can be used to make positive statements about reality

Dōgen (1200–1253) a sophisticated Zen thinker and the importer of the Caodong (Sōtō) lineage of Zen to Japan, the author of the first philosophical treatises in the Japanese language, known for his idiosyncratic style of writing and his theories of time and Buddha-nature

Donghak 'Eastern learning', a Korean millenarian religious movement established by Choe Je-u (1824–1864), which led to the biggest peasant rebellion in Korean history and was later developed into a multitude of new religions

Dvaita Vedānta a version of Vedānta philosophy, according to which the absolute is not an active, pre-existent cause or creator of the phenomenal world, but only a necessary condition for the existence of the universe, which is constantly sustained by it

Eisai (1141–1215) the founder of the Zen Buddhist institution in Japan

Falun Dafa (Falun Gong) a Chinese new religion reintegrating *qigong* exercises with a spiritual teaching, which acquired a large following in China and was then outrooted by the government in the 2000s

Fazang (643–712) the leading thinker of the Huayan school of Chinese Buddhism, known for his theory of non-interference and interpenetration of all things

Four Noble Truths the foundational teaching of Buddhism: (i) everything leads to pain, nothing in life provides satisfaction; (ii) everything we perceive is caused by desires causally grounded in ignorance; (iii) it is possible to exit from the causal nexus and the ensuing cycle of rebirths, to cease to be determined by it, to be liberated (*nirvāna*); (iv) in order to achieve this liberation, one should refrain from the two extremes of worldly pleasures and radical austerities, and follow the eight prescribed forms of behaviour

Fukuzawa Yukichi (1835–1901) an active propagandist of Western ideas and a scientific approach to solving the problems facing Japanese society in the Meiji period

Gandhi, Mohandas Karamchand (Mahātma, 1869–1948) the leader of the struggle for Indian independence, known for his tactics of *satyagraha* (civil disobedience)

Gautama a name adopted by the historical Buddha during his years of wandering

Geluk-pa 'the virtuous', also known as 'yellow hats', a Tibetan monastic lineage established by Tsongkhapa in the fifteenth century, which later assumed the political leadership of the country

Ghose, Aurobindo (1872–1950) a spiritual teacher bent on the reformulation of traditional Hindu views in terms suitable for the modern age

Gongsun Long (320?–250? BCE) a Chinese philosopher from the 'school of names', who contested the referential adequacy of compound terms

Great Peace a Chinese millenarian movement of the third century, loosely associated with the Dao creed

Hagakure 'Covered by leaves', a collection of sayings by Yamamoto Tsunetomo (1659–1719), a former warrior prohibited from accompanying his late master in death, outlines the principles of the samurai code of conduct

Hakuin (1686–1769) a reformer of Japanese Zen, who devised rigorous standards for the transmission of the teaching

Han Feizi (280?–233 BCE) the chief proponent of the Chinese legalist school of political thought, which advocated a strong government and the enforcing of the law by a system of rewards and punishments

Hu Shi (1891–1962) philosopher, diplomat and educator, a professor of Beijing University and an influential figure in the movement for cultural innovation during the early years of the Republic of China

He-yin Zhen (1884?–1920?) one of the first Chinese feminists, an anarchist criticizing the moderate agenda of women's liberation put forth by male liberal social theorists

hīnayāna 'small vehicle', a derogatory term used by Mahāyāna adherents for Theravāda

Hinduism a later development of Brahmanism less concerned with sacrificial ritual and placing more importance on *bhakti* practice

Hindutva 'Hindu-hood', a nationalist ideology claiming India for Hindus, often compared to fascism

Hirata Atsutane (1776–1843) a Japanese scholar, developed nativist scholarship into a radical and potentially violent political ideology, claiming the entire Shintō tradition as its basis

Hiratsuka Raichō (1886–1971) one of the founders of the feminist movement in Japan, the editor of the 'Bluestocking' magazine

Ho Chi Minh (1890–1969) a patriotic Neo-Confucian scholar who evolved into the leader of Vietnamese communists

Hōnen (1113–1212) the first Japanese proponent of Pure Land Buddhism with lasting influence

Hridaya-sūtra 'Heart Sūtra', a short *prajñapāramitā* ('perfection of wisdom') sūtra often used in liturgy, most likely a Chinese compilation based on other translated texts

Huainanzi an eclectic collection of essays by Chinese scholars gathered around Liu An (179?–122? BCE), attempting to base philosophical and political reasoning in a cosmological framework

Huang-Lao an eclectic current of Chinese thought from the Han dynasty, a practical teaching combining the *Daodejing*'s political ideas with practices of individual self-cultivation, bearing traces of legalist and Ru influence

Huayan a school of Chinese Buddhism based on the *Avatamsaka Sūtra* and the philosophical ideas of Fazang, stressing the mutual connectedness of all particular existents

Hui Shi (370?–310? BCE) a Chinese philosopher, an early proponent of the paradoxical 'school of names', possibly a friend of Zhuangzi

Huineng (638–713) the sixth head of the Chan school of Chinese Buddhism, known for the *Platform Scripture*, an autobiography and exposition of the teaching attributed to him

Ikkyū (1394–1481) an idiosyncratic and unconventional Japanese Zen monk and cultural hero, known for his erotic poetry

Indra the most important among Vedic gods, the slayer of the dragon Vritra, the god of thunder, often depicted as a warrior

Inoue Enryō (1858–1919) a modern Japanese philosopher and the proponent of a Buddhism-based system of world philosophy

Iqbal, Muhammad (1877–1938) poet and mystic, an advocate of pan-Islamism in the 1920s and the first proponent of the idea of separating India into Hindu and Muslim territories

Īshvara 'the Lord', a philosophical deity posited by Indian orthodox philosophical systems such as Yoga and Advaita Vedānta

Jain one of the early reform movements against Brahmanist orthodoxy that evolved into a separate religion and has continued to the present

jātaka instructional tale about the meritorious deeds of the Buddha in his previous lives, both in human and animal form

Jinnah, Muhammad Ali (1876–1948) a Muslim lawyer and politician who became the first leader of Pakistan after the partition of India

Jinul (1158–1210) a Korean proponent and developer of Seon Buddhist thought

juche the North Korean state ideology elaborated by Kim Jong-il, relying on the principles of independence in politics, self-reliance in economics, and self-defence in the military sphere; officially severed its connections to Marxism-Leninism in 1992

junzi 'superior man', the ethical ideal of the Chinese Ru school, people capable of studying, self-cultivation, and the development of their virtues and therefore entitled to lead others

Kabīr (fourteenth–fifteenth century) 'The Great', poet and religious visionary, who urged his followers to transcend the limitations that organized religions such as Hinduism and Islam impose on them

Kālī the Hindu goddess in her frightening aspect, the destructive feminine power

kami deities in the Japanese indigenous worldview (Shintō), personified, but frequently anonymous instances of the spiritual energy that fills the entire universe

Kang Youwei (1858–1927) a Neo-Confucian scholar, who proposed radical reforms of the Chinese society and envisaged a utopia of worldwide harmony

Karatani Kōjin (b.1941) a contemporary Japanese literary critic turned philosopher and social thinker, known for his views on the philosophy of history

karma in Indian thought the consequences of one's actions, which influence one's destiny in future existences

karunā compassion towards all other sentients, one of the two primary qualities of an enlightened being

Kim Il-sung (1912–1994) a former guerrilla in North Korea, picked by Soviet and Chinese sponsors to act as their stooge, who gradually emerged as the 'supreme leader' of his country

Kim Jong-il (1941–2011) son of Kim Il-sung, the second 'supreme leader' of North Korea and the theorist of *juche*, or the specifically North Korean state ideology

Kita Ikki (1883–1937) an ultra-right social thinker, whose work inspired the nationalist tendencies growing among the officers of the Japanese army

Kojiki an eighth century Japanese chronicle of mythical history, contains a systematic exposition of Shintō lore

kokutai 'body politic', a term used to signify an allegedly specifically Japanese relationship between the ruler and society

Kongzi (Confucius, 551–479 BCE) the central authority in the tradition of Ru, the ethico-political thought system maintained by scholar-officials that has, in various forms, ideologically characterized the political system of China for most periods throughout written history

Krishnamurti, Jiddu (1895–1986) a thinker who was raised by Annie Besant as the incarnation of the Buddha, but rejected any ideas of supernatural descent and became an influential author synthesizing many insights derived from Asian worldviews

Kūkai (774–835) the Japanese monk responsible for the introduction of esoteric Buddhism to Japan, known for his original contributions to it, such as his esoteric theory of semiotics

Kumarajīva (344–413) the best-known translator of Indian Buddhist texts into Chinese

Kundakunda (second–third centuries CE?) a Jain mystic who reinterpreted the doctrine of omniscience as the full cognition of one's own soul

Lao-Zhuang the school of Chinese thought based on the ideas expressed in the *Daodejing* and Zhuangzi's work

Laozi the mythical sage to whom the authorship of the *Daodejing* is credited, allegedly an older contemporary of Kongzi

li two concepts of Chinese thought, written with different characters: (i) 'propriety', initially the essence of rituals, which gradually came to mean proper, conventional, socially acceptable, and morally commendable behaviour that is in accordance with the cosmic order; (ii) 'principle', an early term picked up by Buddhist schools (notably Huayan), which was elevated into a central metaphysical category by Neo-Confucians, signifying the single-rootedness of all things in their various manifestations

Liang Qichao (1873–1929) one of the most vocal proponents of the 'Chinese Enlightenment', promoting Western thought in order to improve the state of the Chinese society

Lotus Sūtra a Mahāyāna scripture popular especially in East Asia, where many of the new doctrines are expounded in detail

Lu Jiuyuan (Xiangshan, 1139–1193) a Chinese Neo-Confucian thinker and early critic of Zhu Xi, known for his emphasis on practice and his view of a unitary, mindful reality that is manifested in the individual human being by their own consciousness

Lunyu *The Analects*, one of the classics of the Ru school, a collection of sayings and aphorisms by Kongzi

Mahābhārata an Indian epic depicting a civil war between two clans; the *Bhagavad-gītā*, usually read independently, is a part of this text

Mahāvairocana a mythical Buddha venerated especially in esoteric Buddhist schools

Mahāyāna 'great vehicle', a form of Buddhism that arose during the first century BCE, claiming one need not become a monastic in order to attain liberation; became dominant in East Asia

Mānava-dharmashāstra 'Laws of Manu', also known as *Manusmriti*, an Indian legal treatise from around the second century CE, which takes the caste system as the basis of legal practice and stipulates in extreme detail what the desirable conduct of particular people should look like

mandala symbolic map of the universe, depicted with religious imagery

mantra powerful words or phrases encapsulating the sacred that could be used by practitioners for harmonizing their consciousness with the universe

Mao Zedong (1893–1976) the strategist and ideologue who led the communists to their victory in China, known for his campaign-based politics and idiosyncratic interpretation of Marxism, mixed with traditional Chinese ideas

mappō 'latter-day law', a concept particularly influential in Japan in the thirteenth century as a motive for reforming Buddhism, a period of decline that was supposed to arrive after a long time had passed since the lifetime of the Buddha

May Fourth movement initially a nationalist protest against the territorial concessions of the Chinese government in the treaty of Versailles (4 May 1919), which evolved into a movement for cultural innovation of China

Meiji Restoration the nominal restoration of imperial rule in Japan in 1868, the starting point of quick modernizing reforms

Mengzi (372–289 BCE) a Ru thinker, second only to Kongzi in authority, known for his thesis that human nature is essentially good

michi 'way', the Japanese idea, popular from the twelfth century onwards, that any way of life, properly practised, can lead to spiritual progress, including traditional arts as well as the 'way of the warrior'

Milarepa (1040?–1123?) one of the most famous personages in Tibetan Buddhism, a legendary ascetic and poet, who reportedly managed to free himself of bad karma caused by his crimes through rigorous ascetic training

Milindapañhā 'The Questions of Menander', a Buddhist treatise from between 100 BCE and 200 CE, takes the form of conversations between a Greek king ruling over a successor state of Alexander's empire in north-western India, and a Buddhist monk

Mīmāṃsā also known as Pūrva Mīmāṃsā, or 'first philosophy', one of the six orthodox Indian philosophical systems (*darshanas*), elaborating a theory of an eternal and sacred order that governs constant change

Motoori Norinaga (1730–1801) a scholar in the Japanese 'native learning' tradition, known for his comments on the *Kojiki* and theorizations on the special status of the Japanese nation and its culture

Mou Zongsan (1909–1995) a 'New Confucian' philosopher, envisaged a synthesis, in which the Western foundations of science and political theory, and the thought of Kant in particular, could be linked with the ethical core of Chinese thought

Mozi (470?–391? BCE) a Chinese thinker and founder of the Mo school, known for his argumentative style, utilitarian outlook and advocacy of 'impartial concern', the view that we are morally obliged to everyone in the same degree

mūdra in Indian religions, specific significant gestures or poses that convey spiritual meaning and can be used by followers to manipulate the psychophysical processes believed to take place in their bodies

Nāgārjuna (ca 150–250) Indian Buddhist philosopher, exponent of the Mahāyāna doctrine of emptiness as well as the two truths theory of Buddhism

Nakae Chōmin (1847–1901) one of the leaders of the radically democratic People's Rights movement in Meiji Japan

Nānak (1469–1539) a spiritual leader and the founder of the Sikh faith

Nehru, Jawāharlāl (1889–1964) a close collaborator of Gandhi and the first leader of the Republic of India, known for his rational and progress-oriented politics combining a version of state socialism and ancient Indian political theory

nembutsu in Japanese Buddhism, a formula, the chanting of which would attract the attention of Buddha Amitabha, who would ensure the rebirth of the practitioner in the Pure Land

Neo-Confucianism a Western umbrella term for the various Chinese philosophical schools, based on the Ru tradition, that emerged as the result of incorporating Dao and Buddhist concepts into its fold

New Confucianism a philosophical school developed in the twentieth century by thinkers active in Hong Kong, Taiwan and elsewhere outside mainland China, advocating a synthesis of Chinese thought with Western philosophy and science

Nichiren (1222–1282) the founder of a militant form of Japanese Buddhism

nihonjinron theories about the alleged uniqueness of the Japanese race and culture, frequently used to justify aggressive ideologies

nirvāna 'extinction', the early Buddhist version of individual liberation, cessation of existence, exit from the cycle of rebirths, described both as a state of bliss and as a state empty of all cognitions, including blissful ones

Nishida Kitarō (1870–1945) the founder of the Kyōto school of Japanese philosophy, known for his theory of 'place' as the unescapable site of existence where each particular being is constantly redefined in interaction with all others

Nishitani Keiji (1900–1990) a Japanese philosopher, one of Nishida's leading disciples, elaborated the idea of nothingness as opposed to Western nihilism

Nitobe Inazō (1862–1933) a Japanese Christian Westernizer, known for his treatise on the bushidō, written in English

Nyāya one of the six orthodox Indian philosophical systems (*darshanas*), known for its elaboration of logical argumentation techniques

Ogyū Sorai (1666–1728) a leading Japanese Neo-Confucian thinker, who developed his own view of the sociopolitical ideal as something that has to be constantly redefined according to the historical circumstances

Okakura Kakuzō (Tenshin, 1862–1913) a Japanese artist-scholar, who argued for the exceptional nature of the Japanese culture in his books, written in English

Padmasambhava (eighth century?) a semi-legendary Indian monk, revered as the 'precious teacher' of the Tibetan people and credited with the introduction of Indian esoteric Buddhism to Tibet, even though little is reliably known about his life

Pānini (around 400 BCE) the linguist who systematized the grammatical norms of the Sanskrit language according to structural principles

Phule, Jotirao (Jyotirao, Jotiba, 1827–1890) an early activist fighting against caste-based discrimination in India

Phule, Savitribai (1831–1897) the first teacher of the first Indian-run school for girls, the wife of Jotirao Phule

prajñā 'perfect wisdom', the in-depth comprehension of the empty nature of all reality, one of the two primary qualities of an enlightened being

prajñāpāramitā 'perfection of wisdom', a group of Mahāyāna *sūtras* expounding the Buddhist doctrine of emptiness

Pure Land a concept originating in Indian Buddhism, developing in China and reaching vast popularity in Japan; 'Pure Land' is a celestial abode where nothing prevents practising Buddhism, a paradise-like place created by Buddha Amitābha, where everyone is accepted if they sincerely and humbly appeal to the Buddha, recognizing their own powerlessness to improve their situation

qi the energetic force field that, according to early Chinese thought, makes up the whole universe; condensations of *qi* form matter in various states

qigong '*qi*-practice', a doctrine of healing that combines principles of Chinese medicine with Dao discourses of 'internal alchemy' and is practised as a set of physical and psychotechnical exercises

Qin Shi Huang-di (259–210 BCE) the first emperor of China, who unified the large number of independent states into one whole and ruled it briefly with an iron fist

Radhakrishnan, Sarvepalli (1888–1975) a philosopher synthesizing Indian and Western traditions, the second president of the Republic of India

Ramabai, Pandita (1858–1922) one of the first Indian activists for the equality of women

Rāmāyana an Indian epic relating the adventures of the righteous prince Rāma, an avatar of the god Vishnu, the preserver of the cosmic order

ren 'humaneness', the primary virtue of the Ru school, the principle that ought to be at work in ideal interpersonal relationships, the attitude towards one's peers that entails wishing them well, understanding their situation and problems, and taking them into account, which may entail constructive criticism

Rigveda one of the four vedas, the oldest and most important collection of Indian Brahmanist hymns; divided into 10 books and contains 1017 hymns used for summoning gods to participate in the ritual

Roy, Ram Mohan (1772–1833) one of the leaders of the 'Bengali renaissance' and the founder of the Brahmo Samaj

Ru 'scholar, educated person', the shared worldview and textual tradition of the Chinese literati class, synthesized by Kongzi

Ryōkan (1758–1831) a popular Japanese Zen poet-monk, a light-hearted eccentric hermit

Sai Baba (1926–2011) a charismatic religious leader whose organization has attracted thousands of members from across the world

Saichō (767–822) the Japanese monk responsible for introducing the Tiantai (Tendai) school of Buddhism to Japan

samsāra in Indian thought the cycle of rebirths, the conditions of which are determined by one's karma and liberation from which is considered to be the target of one's earthly striving

Samye debate a debate, organized around 793, by the first Buddhist Tibetan king Tri Songdetsen, between the Indian scholar Kamalashīla and the Chinese monk Moheyan, in which the views of the first are reported to have prevailed and thus ensured the domination of Indian forms of Buddhism in Tibet

sangha a term denoting the early Indian republics, later used for the Buddhist community

Sānkhya one of the six orthodox Indian philosophical systems (*darshanas*), developed the idea that entanglement with matter cannot corrupt the soul

sati the self-immolation of widows during the cremation ceremony of their deceased husbands, advocated by conservative Hindu ideologues as proper and noble behaviour

satyagraha 'insistence on truth', a form of civil disobedience advocated by Mahātma Gandhi, combined with the principle of non-violence, inducing protesters to peacefully suffer the punishments inflicted because of their refusal to bend to oppressive laws and regulations

Seon the Korean name for the Chan school of Buddhism

Shaivism a sectarian form of Hinduism, which venerates Shiva as the supreme deity

Shakti literally 'power' or 'energy', a supreme female sacred figure, the name mostly used for female divinity in devotional practice

Shākyamuni 'the sage of the Shākya clan', a title of the historical Buddha

Shankara (eighth century) a central proponent of the Advaita Vedānta philosophical system

Shinran (1173–1263) the founder of the True Pure Land school of Japanese Buddhism, which has become the most widespread form of Buddhism in Japan

Shintō the indigenous Japanese worldview, based on respect for the kami-deities and communal rituals, in later times espoused by the imperial house as its legitimizing ideology

Shiva one of the central deities of Hinduism, the destroyer of evil

Shugendō 'The Path of Discipline and Trial', an eclectic Japanese teaching and discipline that combines elements of Buddhism, the Dao creed, Japanese lore and is practised by mountain ascetics

shūnyatā emptiness, in Mahāyāna doctrine, the absence of an internal self-nature, the characteristic of all existence

Siddhārtha the birth name of the historical Buddha

Silhak 'practical learning', a school that emerged within the Neo-Confucian orthodoxy in Korea in the eighteenth century and comprises a broad range of writings on various topics, from the administration of agriculture to education, finance, and military affairs

Sōka Gakkai a Japanese new religion, which evolved out of a lay society of practitioners of Nichiren Buddhism

Songtsen Gampo (d.649?) the architect and ruler of the centralized Tibetan kingdom

stūpa a term of Buddhist architecture, a pillar initially built for containing relics, but later used as an architectural element

Sun Yat-sen (Yixian, Zhongshan 1866–1925) the main ideologue of the republican order in China, which was to rely on the three principles of nationalism, democracy, and welfare

Sunzi (544?–496? BCE) a Chinese general to whom a treatise on military strategy is attributed

sūtra a discourse of, or attributed to the Buddha; an instructive text of any nature

Suzuki Daisetsu (1870–1966) a scholar and practitioner of Zen, one of the foremost early mediators of Japanese cultural traditions and Zen thought to the West

swadeshi '[produce] of own country', a shorthand for the boycott of imported goods as a means of political protest

swaraj 'own rule', a political slogan demanding the government of India by Indians elected by Indians

Taiping a millenarian movement led by Hong Xiuquan (1814–1864), a self-proclaimed brother of Jesus Christ; the movement evolved into a rebellion, seized and held a large territory around the city of Nanjing for more than 10 years

Tanabe Hajime (1885–1962) a Japanese philosopher, one of Nishida's leading disciples, whose work in ontology and logic as embedded in historical settings led him to embrace the Japanese war effort

tantra a category of Hindu, Buddhist and Jain scriptures, esoteric teachings, which claim to provide the follower with technologies for mobilizing the energies of the body for the pursuit of perfect knowledge

Tao Hongjing (456–536) a Chinese scholar, artist, and polymath, responsible for the systematization of Dao creed teachings into the 'Way of Supreme Clarity'

Tendai the Japanese name for the Tiantai school of Buddhism

Tenri a Japanese new religion based on rethinking Shintō lore, now evolved into a complete municipality inhabited by believers

Theravāda the form of Buddhism that claimed to uphold the initial teaching of the historical Buddha after the introduction of Mahāyāna innovations

Thich Nhat Hanh (b.1926) a prominent Vietnamese thinker in the Thien (Chan) tradition

Thonmi Sambhota (seventh century?) a probably legendary scholar credited with the invention of the Tibetan script

Tian 'Heaven', in early Chinese view an anthropomorphic, personalized deity who supervises the present world from high above and has an arbitrary will, later evolved into a term designating the natural order of things, a combination of physical and moral laws, which had the same degree of validity

Tiantai a school of Chinese Buddhism based on the *Lotus Sutra* and Zhiyi's philosophical thought, known for its sophisticated metaphysics of multiple worlds

Toegye (Yi Hwang, 1501–1570) a leading Korean theorist of Neo-Confucian thought

Trimurti the Hindu trinity of Brahmā, Vishnu, and Shiva, embodying the three divine powers of creation, preservation, and destruction

Tripitaka (Sanskrit) or Tipitaka (Pāli) the early canon of Buddhist scripture, consisting of *sūtras* (sutta), or the Buddha's talks, *vināya*, or rules for monastic life, and *abhidharma* (abhidhamma), Buddhist metaphysics

Tsongkhapa (1357–1419) the most famous scholar and reformer of Tibetan Buddhism, the founder of the Geluk-pa monastic lineage

Tu (Du) Weiming (b.1940) a New Confucianist philosopher of the third generation, responsible for the global spread of this school

Uchimura Kanzō (1861–1930) an original Christian thinker of Japan in the modern era, the founder of the 'no-church' Christian movement

Ueki Emori (1857–1892) one of the leaders of the radically democratic People's Rights movement in Meiji Japan

Uisang (625–702) a Korean Buddhist monk, who studied Huayan with Fazang and transmitted the school to Korea

Unification Church a Korean new religion founded by Sun Myong Moon (1920–2012), known for its conservative social ideology, aggressive proselytizing, and mass collective weddings

upanishads the last layer of Vedic literature, philosophical texts that have been composed mostly in the eighth–fourth centuries BCE and significantly differ in content from earlier Vedic scriptures

upāya 'skilful means', teachings and practices which, in reality, were untrue or empty of meaning, but were adopted as beneficial for people who were unable to grasp the truth of Mahāyāna Buddhism without preparation

Vaisheshika one of the six orthodox Indian philosophical systems (*darshanas*), known for its atomist metaphysics

Vaishnavism a sectarian form of Hinduism, which venerates Vishnu as the supreme deity

Vajracchedika-sūtra 'Diamond-cutting *sūtra*' or '*Sūtra* that cuts like a thunderbolt', one of the best-known short *sūtras* of the *prajñāpāramitā* ('perfection of wisdom') group

Vārānasi a holy city in central India revered by Hindu, Buddhists, and Jains alike

Vardhamāna Mahāvīra (d.425 BCE?) the historical founder of the Jain faith

Vasubandhu (fourth–fifth century CE) an Indian Mahāyāna thinker, author of a systematic critique of the earlier *abhidharma* philosophy and an exponent of the Yogācāra school

veda 'knowledge', the scriptural tradition of Brahmanism/Hinduism, collections of ancient, initially orally transmitted hymns and comments to them

Vedānta 'end of the vedas', also known as Uttara Mīmānsā, or 'final philosophy' one of the six orthodox Indian philosophical systems (*darshanas*), exists in the three forms of non-dual (*advaita*), unity in complexity (*vishishtādvaita*) and dual (*dvaita*) Vedānta

Vimalakīrti Sūtra a Mahāyāna text famous for posing a layman as its principal figure

vināya rules of Buddhist monastic life, theory of morality

Vishnu one of the central deities of Hinduism, the keeper of order

Vishishtādvaita Vedānta a version of Vedānta philosophy, according to which empirical reality is real, dependent on the absolute, yet distinct from it

Vivekananda, Swami (1863–1902) proponent of an innovated Hindu faith and a modernized version of its philosophy, loosely based on the Vedānta, meant to be compatible with Western thought

Wang Anshi (1021–1086) a reformist politician, who advocated 'New Policies', a technocratic rationalization of Chinese statecraft

Wang Yangming (1472–1529) a Chinese Neo-Confucian thinker of the Ming dynasty, who argued that 'things' come into being in the interaction of mind and reality and is also known for his thesis of the unity of knowledge and action

Watsuji Tetsurō (1889–1960) a Japanese philosopher, a theorist of cultural determinism and interpersonal ethics

Way of the Celestial Masters a Chinese millenarian movement of the third century, associated with the Dao creed

wen 'patterns', a Chinese term designating practices that on the social level fulfil the same role that *dao* accomplishes in the cosmic totality

Won a simplified and purely intellectual form of Korean Buddhism founded by Pak Chungbin (1891–1943), without rituals and imagery, directed to maintain a balanced and mindful relationship with a modern living environment

Wonhyo (617–686) a Korean Buddhist monk, both a scholar and a popularizer of the teaching for broader audiences

wuwei 'non-striving', a Chinese ethical ideal; in the Ru school, the ideal sociopolitical situation, where all the rules have been internalized by all political agents to the extent that no conscious effort is needed on the part of the ruler to keep the state running smoothly; in the Lao-Zhuang school, refraining from deliberate efforts and strict criteria of efficiency, especially in managing state affairs

Xi Jingping (b.1953) ideologue and leader of China, advocating a synthesis of Mao-style sinified communism with the conservative Chinese tradition

xiao 'filial piety', a Ru virtue, obedience to and caring for one's parents

Xiong Shili (1885–1968) a Chinese philosopher and the teacher of many 'New Confucianists', formulated a sophisticated metaphysical system on the basis of Ru and Buddhist thought

Xuanzang (602?–664) a Chinese Buddhist monk who undertook a pilgrimage to India, studied in the Nālandā monastery and brought a huge collection of texts to China, also known as a translator and the transmitter of the Yogācāra school

Xunzi (310?–235? BCE) a Ru thinker and critic of Mengzi, known for his thesis that human nature is bad, inclined towards self-gratification

Yang Zhu (440?–360? BCE) a hedonistic Chinese philosopher, criticized by the Ru school

yi 'integrity', a Ru virtue, the quality that ensures that the actions of the superior man are just and unbiased

Yihetuan 'Righteous Fist', a martial arts society with an eclectic, semi-mystical conservative ideology, which rose to rebel against Western influence on China in 1899–1901 and was defeated by an alliance of foreign military forces

Yijing 'The Book of Changes', a manual used by Chinese divination professionals, expounding a theory that each particular situation in reality can be reduced to a hexagram, a schematic representation in six lines representing the two world-defining principles of yin and yang

yin and yang two characteristics of *qi* that, in Chinese thought, represent the female and the male, darkness and light, flexibility and rigidity, rest and activity respectively, and all existents are characterized by constantly changing patterns of their mutual entanglement

yoga (i) any practical discipline aimed at harnessing the psychophysical resources of an individual for attaining spiritual progress; (ii) written with a capital letter: one of the six orthodox Indian philosophical systems (*darshanas*), a theistic version of Sānkhya

Yogācāra 'yoga practice', one of the two dominant philosophical schools of Mahāyāna Buddhism, which negates the reality of stable, continuous, self-same material objects and insists these take shape only in contact with a perceiving mind

Yulgok (Yi I, 1536–1584) a leading Korean theorist of Neo-Confucian thought

Zen the Japanese name for the Chan school of Buddhism

Zhang Zai (1020–1077) an early Neo-Confucian thinker, who stressed the connection of the cosmological with the sociopolitical

zhi 'wisdom', a Ru virtue, the capacity to discern the particular needs of a situation and to assess the character of other people

Zhiyi (538–597) the founder of the Tiantai Chinese Buddhist school, known for his three truths theory and the idea that a multiverse is contained in every thought-moment

Zhou Dunyi (1017–1073) one of the initiators of Neo-Confucian reforms, known for his attempt to integrate Dao creed cosmology into the Ru conceptual framework

Zhu Xi (1130–1200) the central figure of the Neo-Confucian revival of Chinese thought in the Song dynasty, who elaborated its metaphysical system on the basis of a close reading of the classics

Zhuangzi (369?–286? BCE) a thinker of the Lao-Zhuang school, known for his parables on perspectivism and theory of non-action as non-effort, the mental removal of oneself from one's actions, which allows them to blend with the natural flow of the world process

Chronological Table

Time	India	South East Asia	Tibet	China	Korea	Japan
Second millennium BCE	Until 1300 BCE: The development of the advanced Indus Valley civilization in Harappa and other city-states. 1500–1300 BCE: Arrival of Aryan tribes from the North-West. Development of the caste system, with the caste of Brâhmans (priests) at the top; the Indian variant of the Indo-European mythology-based worldview crystallizes into Brahmanism legitimizing this social change			Shang dynasty: an advanced civilization relying on agriculture, with several large urban centres, highly developed rituals and strong political and cultural institutions.		
1000 BCE				1041 BCE: Zhou dynasty overthrows the Shang. The theory of the 'Mandate of Heaven' is proclaimed by the Zhou as the reason for their victory		

500 BCE	
Around 600 BCE: Consolidation of small settlements into a number of states, some with republican, some with monarchic governments, and the rise of the warrior caste to the top of the society; reform movements such as Jains and Buddhism challenge the position of Brahmanism, while new trends in the Brahmanism provide it with new vigour; legal and political thought starts to develop.	475–221 BCE: The 'Warring States' period and development of the 'Hundred schools' of philosophy
322–180 BCE: Unification of India by the Maurya dynasty; cultural and economic growth.	221 BCE – The state of Qin briefly unifies China into an empire.
265 BCE: Buddhism receives the support of the Maurya king Ashoka and spreads quickly over the entire subcontinent.	206 BCE–220 CE: Han dynasty – a period of relative stability and prosperity. The Ru school, integrated with cosmological beliefs, becomes the officially supported Chinese worldview; the Dao creed starts to emerge and becomes the ideological basis of several rebellious millenarian movements

(Continued)

(Continued)

Time	India	South East Asia	Tibet	China	Korea	Japan
0	Buddhism splits into two main branches, Theravāda, which is carried on only by the monastic community, and Mahāyāna, which teaches that enlightenment is attainable also by laypeople; great monasteries arise and Buddhism spreads to the neighbouring countries.					
500	240–590: The Gupta empire rules over India, another period of cultural and economic boom.			222–589: 'Six dynasties', a period of disunity, during which northern China is ruled by non-Chinese tribal chieftains, in southern China the imperial dynasties replace each other with short intervals. Buddhism becomes a strong intellectual and cultural presence; the Dao creed is systematized.	Fourth–seventh centuries: 'Three kingdoms', the peninsula is dominated by three states, Goguryeo, Baekje, and Silla	Sixth century: Contacts with the continent lead to the formation of more stable political structures

India/Southeast Asia	Tibet	China	Korea	Japan
c. 650–1200: India is divided between several competing empires; urban culture continues to flourish; Hinduism evolves as a religion and classical philosophical systems take shape.	c. 650: A strong, centralized Tibetan kingdom emerges, quick cultural development follows and Tibet develops into a regional power comparable to China; Buddhism is introduced and gradually becomes a major cultural influence.	618–907: Tang dynasty, a period of economic and cultural bloom. 755–763: The An Lushan rebellion and the ensuing civil wars deliver a blow to Tang power. 845: Buddhist schools are persecuted as the result of a rise of nationalist sentiment.	676: Silla becomes the sole political power in the peninsula, initiating a period of economic prosperity and cultural bloom.	645: State structures are reformed according to Chinese models
Early ninth century: Kingdoms of Angkor (Khmer), Champa (Central Vietnam), Pagan (North Burma), and Medang (Java) emerge under strong Indian cultural influence.	c. 850: The 'era of fragmentation' begins; different regions of Tibet ally themselves with foreign powers to maintain their independence from the centre.			710–794: Nara period – strong influence of Buddhist institutions on state power.
1009–1400: Ly and Tran dynasties rule the kingdom of Vietnam, promoting Buddhism and Neo-Confucian thought.		960–1279: Song dynasty, the development of cities and urban culture; scholars engaged in textual study initiate the Neo-Confucian revival of the tradition, which integrates Dao and Buddhist elements and becomes the new orthodoxy.	935: The Goryeo state reorganizes the political institutions according to the Chinese model.	794–1192: Heian period: golden age of aristocratic culture; new schools of Buddhism are imported from China.

1000

(Continued)

(Continued)

Time	India	South East Asia	Tibet	China	Korea	Japan
	1206–1526: Delhi Sultanate, the first Muslim state in India. Massive introduction of Islam brings down the Buddhist network of temples, but does not subdue Hinduism, with which it establishes a precariously balanced coexistence. 1526–1857: Mughal empire. 1556–1605: The rule of Akbar, characterized by prosperity and religious tolerance.	Decline of Pagan and Angkor, rise of the Thai kingdoms of Sukhothai and Ayutthaya. Majapahit empire of Java controls maritime South-East Asia. 1428–1789: Le dynasty rules Vietnam.	Thirteenth century: A centralized administration is restored by priest–patron alliances, monastic lineages supported by mostly Mongol khans.	1205: Genghis Khan mounts his first expedition into China, which ultimately leads to the conquest of the whole country. 1271–1368: Yuan (Mongolian) dynasty. 1368–1644: Ming dynasty. Competing schools of Neo-Confucian thought engage in debate with each other.	Thirteenth century: Mongols dominate over Goryeo state, which nominally holds the power until 1392, after which Korea becomes a vassal of the Yuan. 1392–1910: Joseon period – a cultural renaissance and an imposition of a strict, Neo-Confucian-based order on the Korean society.	1192–1333: Kamakura period – a military government takes the power into its hands; reformist schools of Buddhism achieve popular appeal. 1338–1573: Muromachi period – a civil war ends with the establishment of another military government, which patronizes Zen Buddhism in particular. 1543: First contacts with Europeans, who introduce Christianity and firearms.
1500	1600: The British East Indian Company is established, and gradually starts to extend its control over Indian territories.	Islam spreads in maritime South East Asia.	1578: The title of Dalai Lama is conveyed to the leader of a monastic lineage by a Mongol khan; the lineage of Dalai Lamas becomes the supreme authority in Tibet.	1644–1912: Qing (Manchu) dynasty. Neo-Confucian thought is gradually becoming stale, until radical scholars try to invigorate it in order to engage with social problems in the nineteenth century.	The Joseon court has to pay tribute to the Qing empire.	1603–1868: Edo period – the Tokugawa clan emerges victorious from another period of civil wars; Neo-Confucianism is adopted as the state ideology; Christianity is forbidden, the country is closed to the outside world (1639).

			Silhak, or the 'practical learning' school gains popularity in Korea.
			1868: The Meiji Restoration starts the modernization of Japan.
	1720: Tibet becomes a protectorate of Qing China.		
1767: Ayutthaya is destroyed by the Burmese, the Thai capital moves to present Bangkok.			
1782: Chakri dynasty starts to rule Thailand.			
1789: The fall of Le dynasty in Vietnam.			
1802: Nguyen dynasty seizes power in Vietnam.			
1850: Thai kings start a careful modernization process.	1850–1864: The Taiping rebellion – a millenarian movement holds power in the region around Nanjing		
1858: Vietnam becomes a French colony, although the king remains nominally in power.			
1886: Burma becomes a British colony.			1894–1895: The Donghak ('Eastern learning') millenarian movement inspires a massive peasant rebellion and spawns numerous new religions.

1800

1857: The British East Indian Company is dissolved and India is placed under the jurisdiction of the British empire as a colony.

1920s: Non-violent independence movement of civil disobedience gains massive support among Indians.

1930: The idea of dividing India into Hindu- and Muslim-ruled territories is articulated for the first time.

(Continued)

(Continued)

Time	India	South East Asia	Tibet	China	Korea	Japan
1900	1947: Republic of India and Republic of Pakistan are established. 1971: Indo-Pakistani war results in the independence of East Pakistan, now called Bangladesh.	1942: Japan invades Burma and Indonesia. 1945: Indonesia proclaimed independent. 1948: Burma becomes independent. 1954: The French, who have attempted to retake control of Vietnam after World War II, are defeated. 1954–1975: Vietnam is split into two countries, communist North and US-supported South, which reunite after a long war. 1962: A military junta takes over the Burmese government.	1912: Tibet declares independence. 1951: China invades Tibet and annexes it. 1959: The Dalai Lama escapes from Tibet and establishes an exile government in India.	1912: – The Republic of China is proclaimed. 1916–1928: – During this 'Warlord Era' different strongmen are vying for control of the country. 1927–1949: The Chinese Civil War rages between nationalist and communist troops. 1949: The communists proclaim the People's Republic of China, nationalists withdraw to Taiwan. 1966–1969: The 'cultural revolution' shatters the Chinese society. 1976: The death of Mao Zedong ushers in a more relaxed era of economic, but not political liberalization.	1910–1945: Korea is a Japanese colony. 1945: Korea is divided into the North, controlled by the Soviet Union, and South, controlled by the US; the parts become sovereign states. 1950–1953: North Korea tries to gain control of the whole peninsula, but is defeated by the US-assisted South.	1930s: – Japan is increasingly militarized, attacks China and conquers large areas in maritime and continental Asia. 1945: Japan surrenders unconditionally at the end of World War II and is occupied by Allied forces. 1952: Japan re-established as an independent country, ally of the US, and embarks on a road of quick economic development.

Index

Asian Worldviews: Religions, Philosophies, Political Theories, First Edition. Rein Raud.
© 2021 John Wiley & Sons Ltd. Published 2021 by John Wiley & Sons Ltd.